W9-BIU-723

The Robert Lehman Collection

XI

The Robert Lehman Collection

XI

Glass

DWIGHT P. LANMON
WITH DAVID B. WHITEHOUSE

The Metropolitan Museum of Art, New York
in association with
Princeton University Press, Princeton

Egbert Haverkamp-Begemann, Coordinator

Published by The Metropolitan Museum of Art

John P. O'Neill, Editor in Chief
Sue Potter, Editor
Bruce Campbell, Designer
Susan Chun, Production Supervisor
Jean Wagner, Bibliographer

All photographs of objects in the Robert Lehman Collection were taken
especially for this volume. Radiographs of Nos. 88–98 were taken in the Sherman Fairchild Center for
Objects Conservation, The Metropolitan Museum of Art. Photographs of Nos. 1 (top view), 15, 16,
22, 50, 52, 53, 63 (detail of stem), 73 (overall), 98, 103, 104, and 106 (detail of side panels)
were taken by Schecter Lee, New York. All other photographs of objects in the Robert
Lehman Collection were taken by Sheldan Collins, Weehawken, New Jersey

Type set by U.S. Lithograph, typographers, New York
Printed and bound by Jean Genoud, S.A., Lausanne, Switzerland

LIBRARY OF CONGRESS CATALOGING-IN-PUBLICATION DATA

Lanmon, Dwight P.
Glass / Dwight P. Lanmon, David B. Whitehouse.
p. cm. – (The Robert Lehman Collection; 11)
ISBN 0-87099-678-9 – ISBN 0-691-03405-2 (Princeton)
1. Glass – Catalogs. 2. Glass, Italian – Catalogs.
3. Lehman, Robert, 1892–1969 – Art collections – Catalogs.
4. Glass – Private collections – New York (N.Y.) – Catalogs.
5. Glass – (New York, N.Y.) – Catalogs.
6. Metropolitan Museum of Art (New York, N.Y.) – Catalogs.
I. Whitehouse, David B.   II. Title.   III. Series.
N611.L43M46   1993   708.147'1   86-12519

Contents

Preface

Even though glass seems to have been but one of many collecting interests for Robert Lehman, his glass collection contains several spectacular objects, and it spans two thousand years of glassmaking history. The objects range from iridescent first-century Roman blown glass to an early twentieth-century Art Nouveau vase by Louis Comfort Tiffany (which coincidentally imitates the brilliant iridescent colors of the Roman glass). In between are significant collections of Renaissance Venetian and *façon de Venise* glass (acquired in a single purchase from the dealer Leopold Blumka) and eighteenth-century French lampworked glass figurines (acquired at the sale of the King collection at Sotheby's in 1958).

This is an idiosyncratic collection and does not aim at comprehensiveness. Neither does it reach for the same levels of quality throughout. The most outstanding objects are undoubtedly the Venetian pieces. They demonstrate the superlative Venetian techniques of forming and decorating and help explain why Venetian glass was so coveted throughout Europe in the fifteenth, sixteenth, and seventeenth centuries. Robert Lehman also acquired Renaissance glass made in the Venetian style in northern Europe, but it is generally not as remarkable as the Venetian glass. The two exceptions are a magnificent reverse-painted dish (No. 25) and a richly enameled armorial goblet (No. 21) that may both have been made at the court glasshouse in Innsbruck in the Tyrol. These are extraordinary works and, indeed, I count them among the most important and beautiful European glass objects in any American collection.

Also emanating from northern Europe is the group of glass figurines attributed to eighteenth-century Nevers, France. These miniature works were created by a process called lampworking. The figurines, some of them installed in elaborate tableaux, may have been relatively inexpensive when they were new, but they are rare today because of their fragility. The Robert Lehman Collection is one of the richest in this category in American museums and includes particularly beautiful figurines of Mercury and Diana (Nos. 88 and 89).

Robert Lehman's collection of reverse-painted panels and objects is also included in this catalogue. Six of the eleven reverse-painted objects and all but one of the panels were made using rock crystal, not glass. They are included here because most reverse paintings were produced using glass as the substrate for the decoration. The reverse paintings in the Robert Lehman Collection are consistently of very high quality; they are mainly of sixteenth-century North Italian origin, where the art was perfected.

The ancient Roman and early Islamic glass in the collection is less interesting from the technical and historical points of view. It is limited to fairly simple blown forms and lacks examples of luxury glass. Blown Roman glass is not, in fact, uncommon; many pieces have survived because so much was made and because of the practice of burying funerary offerings, which were often made of glass. It is likely that most of these pieces were acquired for their colorful iridescence. Under just the right conditions of temperature, soil moistness, and acidity, some buried glass deteriorates in a way that forms microscopically thin surface layers that reflect and refract light to produce brilliant, iridescent colors.

My introduction provides a cursory review of glassmaking history so that readers might better understand how the various segments of the collection relate historically to each other. Because there are several comprehensive histories of glassmaking in print, and because the Lehman glass collection is not comprehensive, the approach I have taken in this catalogue is not primarily historical. Instead, I have taken advantage of the large number of Renaissance Venetian vessels and *verre de Nevers* glass figurines to focus my comments on the objects themselves, and particularly on features that help us understand how they were made and decorated. Such objects are often impossible to attribute to a particular area, let alone to a specific glasshouse or glassmaker. Failing absolute documentation (such as a signature) for establishing the authorship of an object – and that is almost never present on glass made before the nineteenth century – we are forced to use every clue at hand. For too long, the telltale clues left behind by the artisan's tools and habits have been overlooked. Comparisons of the technical "fingerprints" on these objects with those found on documented pieces in other collections, many of which we have illustrated here, may ultimately help scholars identify related groups and refine attributions.

Chemical analysis of the glass and enamels may also enable us to replace the catchall attributions of "Venice" or "*façon de Venise*" now given to much Renaissance glass. Although good quantitative analysis requires sacrificing tiny pieces of the material, there are nondestructive surface analytical techniques that yield some information about the chemical composition of glasses. Elemental analysis by energy dispersive X-ray spectrometry (EDS), for example, was used to examine the glass of three of the *verre de Nevers* figurines in the Robert Lehman Collection (Nos. 95, 96, 98). Identifying chemical differences between Venetian and Venetian-style glasses has begun, but until a library of analyses is assembled to establish Venetian norms and similar work is done on documented Venetian-style glass produced elsewhere, attributing and dating objects will remain difficult.

In the meantime, there is a simple, inexpensive, nondestructive tool that can be used to examine glass: an ultraviolet lamp. I have examined all the glass objects in the Robert Lehman Collection except the Roman and Islamic glass under ultraviolet light. My observations are noted in each entry of the catalogue and are summarized in the Appendix.

I have no doubt that some of the attributions presented in this catalogue will eventually be changed. It is my hope that the technical details noted here will provide the basis for such changes, and that other students will find these methods of interest and test them further.

Dwight P. Lanmon

Acknowledgments

We wish to thank Egbert Haverkamp-Begemann, who guided this project thoughtfully and carefully and provided endless courtesies and helpful comments with grace and charm. In addition, we would like to thank particularly The Metropolitan Museum of Art staff who saw us through the catalogue project: Laurence B. Kanter, Curator of the Robert Lehman Collection; Susan Romanelli, formerly of the Robert Lehman Collection; Patrick Coman, Watson Library; Jessie McNab, European Sculpture and Decorative Arts; Lisa Pilosi, Mark Wypyski, and Robert Koestler, Objects Conservation; and Sue Potter, Editorial Department.

We are grateful to Elizabeth Wahle for supplying the drawings of the ancient Roman and early Islamic objects and to Helmut Nickel for his invaluable help with the heraldic descriptions. Dwight Lanmon also wishes to thank William Gudenrath for so generously sharing his knowledge of Renaissance Venetian glassmaking techniques. This catalogue would have been diminished without his interest and help.

We wish to thank the following:

Daniel Alcouffe, Musée du Louvre, Paris
Michael Archer, Victoria and Albert Museum, London
Gail P. Bardhan, Corning Museum of Glass
Sigrid Barten, Museum Bellerive, Zurich
Rosa Barovier Mentasti, Venice
Margrit Bauer, Museum für Kunsthandwerk, Frankfurt am Main
Wolfgang Beeh, Hessisches Landesmuseum Darmstadt
Fritz Biemann, Zurich
Ian M. Burgoyne, Pilkington Glass Museum, Saint Helens
John Carswell, Sotheby's, London
Ann Chevalier, Musée du Verre, Liège
Günther Dankl, Tiroler Landesmuseum Ferdinandeum, Innsbruck
Moira Day, Sotheby's, London
Rudolf Distelberger, Kunsthistorisches Museum, Vienna
Attilia Dorigato, Museo Correr, Venice
Dr. Dräger, Verwaltung der Staatlichen Schlösser und Gärten, Bad Homburg vor der Höhe
Olga Drahotová, Uměleckoprůmyslové Muzeum, Prague
P. C. Ritsema van Eck, Rijksmuseum, Amsterdam
Luc Engen, Musée du Verre, Liège
Pierre Ennès, Musée du Louvre, Paris
Raymond F. Errett, Corning Museum of Glass
Wendy Evans, Museum of London
Henri Fettweis, Musées Royaux d'Art et d'Histoire, Brussels
R. A. Foster, National Museums and Galleries on Merseyside, Liverpool
Peter Fusco, J. Paul Getty Museum, Malibu
Paolo Galluzzi, Museo di Storia della Scienza, Florence

Mary Suzor, National Gallery of Art, Washington, D.C.
G. Hugh Tait, British Museum, London
Anna-Elizabeth Theuerkauff-Liederwald, Berlin
Jill Thomas-Clark, Corning Museum of Glass
Giuliana Tucci, Venini S.p.A., Venice
Ian Wardropper, Art Institute of Chicago
Oliver Watson, Victoria and Albert Museum, London
Patricia J. Whitesides, Toledo Museum of Art
Nicholas L. Williams, Corning Museum of Glass
Clementine Schack von Wittenau, Kunstsammlungen der Veste Coburg
Ernesto Wolf, Paris
Virginia L. Wright, Corning Museum of Glass
Rainer Zietz, London

These colleagues, and others we may have forgotten to name, helped us in countless ways.

Dwight P. Lanmon, *Director, Winterthur Museum*
David B. Whitehouse, *Director, The Corning Museum of Glass*

I would like to acknowledge especially the generous help and support of Laurence B. Kanter, Curator of the Robert Lehman Collection, and his staff, especially Monique van Dorp, Veda Crewe, Evelyn Donatelli, and Pia Palladino. I wish to thank as well Sue Potter and those who assisted her, in particular Jean Wagner, for their intelligent and painstaking preparation of the manuscript for the press. We are grateful to Jill Thomas-Clark and Virginia L. Wright of the Corning Museum of Glass, who never failed to answer queries with great patience and alacrity. We thank Bruce Campbell for his elegant design and Susan Chun for overseeing the production of the volume. And, as has been the case with previous volumes in this series, we owe a debt of gratitude to Paul C. Guth, Secretary of the Robert Lehman Foundation, for his continuing assistance with the scholarly catalogue project.

Egbert Haverkamp-Begemann
John Langeloth Loeb Professor of the History of Art, Institute of Fine Arts, New York University; Coordinator of the Robert Lehman Collection Catalogue Project

NOTE TO THE READER

All objects have been remeasured for this catalogue. In the provenance sections, names and locations of dealers are enclosed in brackets. References to books and articles have been abbreviated to the author's name and the date of publication, and references to exhibitions have been abbreviated to city and year. The key to these abbreviations is found on pages 319–32. References in the text to the *Bulletin de l'Association Internationale pour l'Histoire du Verre* and the *Journal of Glass Studies* have been abbreviated to *Bulletin AIHV* and *JGS*.

Introduction

Glass is an easy compound to make: heating a mixture of ordinary sand and plant ash until it melts is all that is necessary. It can be produced in simple mud-brick furnaces fired with wood. The origin of glassmaking is obscure. It probably grew out of ceramics technology. The earliest surviving glass objects, tiny beads, were made before the middle of the second millennium B.C. in Mesopotamia and Egypt. The earliest surviving glass vessels, most of them made by covering a friable ceramiclike core (probably made of animal dung and clay) with molten glass, also date from the middle of the second millennium B.C. Dark and light blue, yellow, and opaque white were the most common colors of this early glass. The surfaces of vessels were usually decorated by trailing and combing threads of contrasting color, and handles and rims were added to complete them. After the glass was cooled slowly (annealed) to reduce internal strains that might cause it to crack, the core was removed by picking and scraping. Other ancient methods of making glass vessels included fusing, mold slumping and pressing, and carving (treating the material as if it were stone). These techniques were laborious and tended to limit the size of the objects produced. During the first fifteen hundred years of glassmaking history, glass objects were rare luxuries.

Blowing, the most important breakthrough in the history of glassmaking, was first used about 50 B.C., perhaps in the eastern Mediterranean. This discovery, along with the slightly later development of full-size molds, caused glassmaking production to explode. Glass vessels were adapted to many uses: storing, serving, and consuming foods, and even as burial urns to hold cremated remains. Glass was as inexpensive for the ancient Romans as it is today, but the Romans also made lavish glass objects that must have been among the most costly ever produced. For example, carved cameo glasses, the most famous surviving example of which is the Portland Vase in the British Museum, were made with scenes of one color glass superimposed on one or more contrasting colors. Roman glassmakers also created enameled and gilt vessels and objects made of colorful twisted cables, *millefiori*, and mosaic elements.

Roman craftsmen carried glassmaking technology throughout Europe and into North Africa and the Near East. When the Roman Empire shrank, glassmaking in the empire declined. It continued and prospered in the Middle East in the Sasanian and Islamic empires and in East Asia. In the Middle East, glass carving reached new heights of artistic refinement, and enameling and gilding were perfected in the thirteenth century.

The Dark Ages in Europe were anything but dark as far as glassmaking was concerned. Carved cameo and other luxurious works in glass perfected by Roman artisans were no longer being made, but it is not true that glassmakers in the north were able to make only Coke-bottle-green glass. Quantities of green glass were made using unpurified river sands contaminated with iron and ash from burned wood and plants, but brightly colored blue and amethyst glass vessels were also produced in Europe as early as the eighth century. In fact, intentionally colored glass may have been made more or less continuously from Roman times.

Knowledge of how to make colored and colorless glass was widespread in Europe by the twelfth century. The stained-glass windows decorating European Gothic cathedrals like those at Chartres and Canterbury and the glass mosaics in churches in Italy, Greece, and Turkey are the most impressive and visible evidence. The windows were made of thousands of pieces of blue, green, red, and colorless glass held together with strips of lead channeling. They were also decorated with metallic stains to produce amber-colored designs, and details were added with fired black enamel.

As European city-states grew in power and wealth during the Middle Ages, trade with the Islamic Near East increased. Raw materials and technical information for glassmakers eventually flowed west in the Levantine trade along with precious silks and spices. Venice controlled the trade, so it is not surprising that the first luxuriously decorated table glass made in Europe after the fall of Rome was produced in Venice about the middle of the fifteenth century. Venetian glassmakers had been organized into guilds early in the thirteenth century, and the entire industry (except the beadmakers) was moved to Murano, in the lagoon, in 1291. The stated reason for the move was to protect Venice from fire, but the export market had become extremely profitable, and moving the glass industry to an isolated island also helped prevent glassmakers from escaping with their precious secrets. By the end of the fifteenth century colorless and brilliantly colored enameled and gilt Venetian glass was being shipped throughout Europe and to the Near East. Despite legal restrictions that threatened those who were captured with fines, imprisonment, and bodily harm, some glassmakers did emigrate. Venetian craftsmen produced Venetian-style glass in many European centers. Unfortunately, because we are rarely able to identify stylistic characteristics of Venetian-style glass made elsewhere, much of this glass is simply classified as *façon de Venise*.

The long-guarded secret glass formulas of Venice became available throughout Europe when Antonio Neri published *L'arte vetraria* in Florence in 1612. Venice was not, however, the only place in Italy where fine glass was made during the 1400s and 1500s. Many other cities in Italy with important glass industries were less paranoid about losing their manufacturing secrets. Glassmakers from Altare, near Genoa, for example, were encouraged to emigrate to Catalonia and France.

Venetians exported enameled glass to Germany in the fifteenth and sixteenth centuries. By the middle of the sixteenth century German glassmakers were producing their own enameled glass. Especially popular were large cylindrical beer glasses called *Humpen* with armorial, political, or mythological decoration. The distinctly non-Venetian form of *Humpen* and the style of the enameling often make it possible to identify where they were made. Enameling was also practiced in France and Spain, and those products are recognizably different from German glasses, more closely allied to Italian models.

Throughout history glassmakers have produced imitation precious and semiprecious stones. In the early sixteenth century Venetian glassmakers were making vessels that looked as if they were made of chalcedony. Colorless glass, perfected in the fifteenth century, may not have been considered to be an imitation stone per se, but it was often compared to rock crystal. That the word for colorless glass is "crystal" in English, *cristallo* in Italian, and *Kristall* in German is no accident. Toward the end of the sixteenth century European stone carvers and engravers began turning to colorless glass as a substitute for rock crystal. The colorless glass of Venice was the best available, but it usually had a slightly yellowish tint, so thick-walled vessels could not be made of it.

Glass chemists in the German states (including Bohemia) and England began to search for ways to produce a glass free of tint so that it could be used to make thick forms that could be carved like chunks of rock crystal. Success was achieved almost simultaneously in several areas. In England, lead oxide was the critical ingredient for producing a lustrous "white" glass, while chalk was one of the key additives to the formula perfected in Brandenburg and Bohemia.

Venetian glassmakers attempted to keep up with the shift in the seventeenth century from the refined and delicate Renaissance style to the bolder and more massive Baroque by making ever more contorted and elaborate forms. By the end of the century, however, the finicky glass of Venice had given way to the more massive "crystal" glasses of northern Europe. These glasses were typically decorated by carving, engraving, and gilding. Carving was used to create facets to refract and reflect candlelight, and engraving produced intricate surface designs. These methods quickly replaced enameling and diamond-point (scratched) engraving on fashionable glass, although they had brief periods of popularity afterwards.

The artistic revivalism of the nineteenth century also found expression in glass. Early nineteenth-century neoclassical interiors were enhanced by brilliantly faceted colored and colorless glasses that were sometimes decorated with minutely engraved, enameled, and gilt scenes. Later, Gothic, Renaissance, Rococo, Moorish, and other styles were resurrected. Most of these objects were no more than vague imitations of old pieces, but some were certainly made with the intent to deceive the unwary buyer. Some of these clever copies are difficult to identify with certainty today.

At the turn of the nineteenth century artists in Europe and America reacted against what they considered the sterility of revivalism. Some looked to the Orient and to nature as design sources. The Art Nouveau style emerged and flourished briefly in glass and other materials in the hands of artists like Émile Gallé and Louis Comfort Tiffany. Others stripped away all ornament, to develop a movement culminating in what is considered "modern" today.

Dwight P. Lanmon

LITERATURE: Tait 1979, Charleston 1980a, Tait 1991, Corning 1992.

BLOWN GLASS VESSELS

Sixteenth to Twentieth Century

Venetian and Façon de Venise Blown Glass and Its Decoration

The basic glassblowing techniques used in sixteenth-century Italy, and still used today, were developed in Roman times. The essential tools are a long iron tube (blowpipe), a spring-form tool with pointed jaws (pucellas), an iron or stone slab (marver), shears, and an iron rod (pontil). The process begins with molten glass in a pot in a furnace. Openings in the side of the furnace permit the glassmaker to dip the blowpipe into the pot to gather molten glass onto the end of the blowpipe. The gather is rolled on the marver to center it on the blowpipe and give it a regular shape. The glassmaker inflates the gather with his breath and shapes it with the pucellas.

If the vessel is to become a stemmed and footed goblet, molten glass is added at the base of the bubble and a stem is formed using the pucellas. Another bubble of glass can be attached to the stem and opened and flared to form the foot. The pontil is then attached to the center of the foot using a wad of molten glass. The bubble forming the bowl is separated from the blowpipe and the glass is reheated at the furnace mouth. The bowl is then shaped into its final form. When the glassmaker is satisfied with the shape, the pontil is cracked off the foot and the vessel is placed in a chamber above the furnace, where it is cooled gradually, or annealed, to relieve the stress that developed in the glass while it was being worked. The jagged scar where the pontil was broken off was usually left untouched by Renaissance glassmakers. (On some eighteenth-century vessels it has been ground away.) Indentations in the bottoms of bowls and high feet kept the pontil scars from scratching table tops.

Today, enameled and gilt decoration is applied to a finished glass object, which is then fired in a kiln to fuse the enameling and gilding to the glass. In the late fifteenth and early sixteenth centuries, glassmakers in Italy, and probably elsewhere in Europe as well, would usually process an object only to an intermediate form before applying the enameling and gilding.[1] When the enameling and gilding were applied to a tazza like No. 1, for example, the flared bowl was probably straight-sided and cylindrical, and the foot might not have been flared to its ultimate diameter and shape.

Before the glass was decorated, it was annealed and the area to be gilded was coated with a thin, smooth layer of gum arabic or other adhesive. Gold leaf was applied in linear stripes, lozenges, and panels. Because the overlaps between adjacent sheets of gold leaf formed distracting stripes of brighter gold color, the gilder was careful to minimize them, although a certain amount of overlap was unavoidable. The gilder scraped away any excess leaf before he began scribing patterns into the stripes and panels. Most often, the pattern was stylized scales formed of staggered rows of scribed arcs (see Nos. 9–13) and flanked by narrow linear bands, most likely made by using a decorating table like those potters use. Lozenges or rounded pelmets (see No. 2), linked rings (Nos. 7, 14, 18, 21), and formal floral devices, occasionally elaborate wreaths (see Nos. 7, 9), were also scribed into the gilt bands, presumably freehand.

Painted gilding (as opposed to leaf gilding) is generally readily identifiable by its thin, watery, brassy appearance, by the lack of overlapping bands, and by the fact that because it was applied after the enameling, it does not extend beneath it. On sixteenth-century Venetian objects painted gilding is limited to minute details within elaborate motifs. Fine armorial details, for example, which would have been difficult to achieve using leaf, were produced with precipitated gold or finely powdered gold leaf that was mixed with a binder, painted on, and then fired (see Nos. 21, 59). Where gilding is used on sixteenth-century glasses to form scale bands or finishes on rims (see No. 59), it is always leaf gilding. Vessels decorated with painted gilding only (sometimes with vertical stripes or bands painted in to re-create the effect of overlapping strips of gold leaf) were probably made in the nineteenth century.

The proportion of scribed gilt decoration on Renaissance glass was carefully designed for the scale of the object. For example, small ribbed bowls such as Nos. 15 and 16 were typically decorated with narrow bands of small scales. Larger objects like Nos. 10–13 were given wider bands containing more rows of larger scales. The individual scales in the narrower bands usually received

Fig. A. William Gudenrath demonstrates the finishing of a tazza blank to an intermediate form. After annealing, the gold leaf and enamel decoration are applied.

Fig. B. After the enamels have dried, the tazza is placed in a cool oven and gradually heated to below the softening point of the glass. A pontil is then attached to the tazza.

Fig. C. The vessel is then exposed to the heat of the furnace. This softens the rim, melts the enamels, and fuses them and the gold leaf to the glass.

Fig. D. The tazza is withdrawn from the furnace mouth and rotated rapidly. Centrifugal force causes the softened sides and rim to expand and curve outward. Photographs, taken by Steven Barall at the New York Experimental Glass Workshop, courtesy of William Gudenrath

no further scraped decoration. Larger scales were usually highlighted with multiple scratches, which lighten them and give them a three-dimensional quality, so that they look almost as if they were curving outward. The scratches seem to have been created by scribing the surface of each scale two or three times (usually vertically) with a five- or six-toothed comblike tool.[2] The top row of large scales was usually left plain, without any scraped highlights. Scale bands were also typically decorated with enamel dots, which were applied after the "combed" arcs. In narrow bands the small scales might each have a single dot; in wider bands each scale might have three bicolored dots, or three dots of three different colors (red, green, and light blue). Or each large scale might be embellished with a single large enamel dot (see No. 13), the dots sometimes arranged within the gilt band in diagonal rows of matching color. Scribed arcs are usually outlined with rows of pinkish white dots or curves.

In the late fifteenth and early sixteenth centuries enameled details were always applied to vessels after the gilding, and both the enameling and the gilding were fired in one operation. An object with leaf gilding applied after the enameling might be suspected of being a later product (although in the nineteenth century some glassmakers did apply the gilding first). Enamels are made of colored glass that is ground to a powder and mixed with a binding agent until it has the consistency of paint. Some colors require higher temperatures to fuse: yellow enamels, for example, require a much higher temperature than do white, blue, and green. After the enamels had dried, the vessel was heated slowly, probably by placing it in the annealing chamber above the furnace. A fifteenth-century manuscript in the Convent of San Salvatore in Bologna describes the process:

> Then put the glass upon the rim of the chamber in which glasses are cooled, on the side from which the glasses are taken out cold, and gradually introduce it into the chamber towards the fire which comes out of the furnace, and take care you do not push too fast lest the heat should split it, and when you see that it is thoroughly heated, take it up on the pontello and fix it to the pontello and put it in the mouth of the furnace.[3]

The pontil, typically an iron rod, was attached to the vessel with a tiny wad of molten glass. Although it was occasionally attached inside the bowl of a goblet or tazza (see No. 1), most often the pontil was attached to the bottom, where the object had been held after it was separated from the blowpipe. The double pontil scar can only rarely be clearly discerned (see Nos. 9, 12).

The vessel, attached to the pontil, was subjected to the full blast of heat. As the glass softened, the adhesive holding the gold leaf and the binding medium in the enamels burned off, the enamel melted and glistened, and the gilding fused to the glass. Considerable skill was necessary to fuse all the enamels fully without burning some (since they melted at different temperatures) and to avoid softening the glass so much that it melted and became deformed.

Nearly all enameled and gilt decoration on Venetian Renaissance glass was applied to objects that were partially formed. While the glass was heated to the point of softening, the final shaping was done. By spinning it rapidly, the glassmaker flared the bowl on a tazza like No. 1 (no tool was necessary). Similarly, a straight-sided goblet bowl like that on No. 18 could be flared to a gentle cyma curve like that on No. 2. The shaping the glass was subjected to after the gold leaf and enamels were applied is recorded permanently in the decoration. Gold leaf does not stretch but shatters into fine slivers that spread farther and farther apart as the glass is enlarged (see No. 1). Enamels, on the other hand, flow with the glass when they are molten. As the glass stretches, circular enamel dots become more and more oval, the ovals all aligned in the same direction (see No. 14). On objects that received little or no further shaping during the firing of the decoration (see No. 21), the gilding remains uniform and bright and not shattered, and the enamel dots keep their shape.

Intentionally changing the form of an object at the last stage of its manufacture, after the decoration was applied, may seem strange today, but there were technical reasons for doing so in the late fifteenth and sixteenth centuries (and probably before). Glass furnaces were fired with burning wood, and the heat loss from the working ports (where the glass was gathered from melting pots and objects were reheated for forming and for firing enamels and gilding) was considerable. These openings had to be kept as small as possible. Otherwise, too much heat would escape, lowering the temperature of the furnace, possibly enough to make the glass in the melting pots difficult to work or even to endanger the fabric of the furnace, which could crack if temperature gradients were too great. It was simpler, therefore, for the glassmaker to apply the enamel and gold-leaf decoration to a smaller form, then heat it in the glory hole until the enamels melted and fused to the red-hot glass. Final shaping followed immediately, without additional reheating, using centrifugal force to open and flare straight-sided cylindrical bowls. Also while the vessels were attached to pontils for firing the decoration, the glassmakers applied handles and spouts, and even trailed rims, sometimes on top of the enameling and gilding (see No. 3).

Firing the gilding and enameling while an object was attached to a pontil was also a liability, however. Because the iron rod was a good thermal conductor and carried heat away from the glass, the coolest part of the object while it was being reheated was the part nearest the pontil attachment. The enameled decoration inside footed bowls like Nos. 6–8 and 14 therefore often tends to be inadequately fired; the enamels are frequently granular in appearance and are sometimes flaking noticeably. The additional wear on gilding on the feet of some vessels is also a result of the pontil-firing technique. When an object such as No. 21 was attached to a pontil under the foot and exposed to the heat of the furnace, the rim of the bowl got far hotter than the foot rim. As would be expected, the gilding on the foot did not fuse as completely as that on the bowl and was therefore more prone to wear. (Incompletely fired gilding is sometimes mistakenly identified as "cold gilding," which implies that the gold was never fired.)

The authenticity of the crude and badly fired decoration on some Renaissance glass objects has sometimes been questioned. It has been suggested that the decoration was applied much later, in the late nineteenth century, to enhance the objects' value and salability. But the poor quality of the enameling can usually be ascribed to the pontil-firing process, wherein parts of the glass do not get as hot as others. There are other objections to the re-enameling theory. Heating a piece of five-hundred-year-old glass until it is red hot is, of course, fraught with danger. A tiny crack in the glass (and Venetian Renaissance glass often has tiny cracks) would cause the piece to shatter during heating. That the original pontil-firing technique would be attempted is extremely unlikely. The objects would probably be fired in a kiln, where the temperature could be controlled exactly and increased gradually, but then the enamels would not be either granular or underfired or overfired—the imperfections one usually finds in enameling on Renaissance glass. The object could slump in the kiln, or the expansion characteristics of the enamels may not match those of the glass, leading to internal stress and cracking of the glass around the decoration or the enamels popping off. That an object had been refired would be fairly easy to detect, as any sharp edges on the glass (such as those on the pontil mark) would tend to soften in the heat. Enameling and refiring five-century-old glasses is therefore unlikely to have been attempted very frequently, if at all.

The opportunity to examine so many examples of Renaissance blown glass simultaneously in the Robert Lehman Collection has made it possible to look for characteristics that may prove useful to scholars attempting to attribute related objects. Lacking documentary evidence to the contrary, such objects are usually attributed to Venice, even though it is supposed that many may not have been made there. Documented products of the several glasshouses that were in operation elsewhere in Italy and in Europe in the sixteenth century are extremely rare, and we have few benchmarks for attributions.

A few indelible features of such objects may eventually help us to separate and identify the products of particular areas or factories. On the simplest level, molded patterns should be checked for specific idiosyncrasies, and objects with similar patterns should be checked to see if those details are repeated. Many Renaissance bowls, for example, were decorated with radial ribbing. The most common have 12, 16, or 40 ribs. Close examination of the bowls with 40 ribs in the Robert Lehman Collection (Nos. 1, 15, 16) reveals that the gaps between the ribs are not uniform. Measuring and comparing rib patterns on a large number of objects would probably help determine whether objects like the Lehman tazza with the arms of Louis XII of France and Anne of Brittany (No. 1) were made in a northern European or a Venetian factory.[4]

Enameled glasses dating from the late fifteenth century and the first half of the sixteenth century have customarily been grouped by comparing forms and enameling styles. Until recently no one had noted, much less published, observations on how the pieces were made and how the gilding and enameling were applied and fired.[5] The explanations for many of the similarities and differences observed in this study of objects in the Robert Lehman Collection are not obvious. We are not yet able to determine, for instance, whether two objects share details of craftsmanship because they were made in the same studio or area or because they were made by artisans who learned similar habits from a single master. Although differences in methods of applying and firing the decoration did in some cases provide valuable negative evidence (see, in particular, Nos. 20, 24), it has not been possible to prove that any of the objects with technically related gilt and enameled decoration in the Robert Lehman Collection were made in the same factory. In future, with a bank of comparable technical data on objects in collections throughout the world to draw upon, we may have a basis for a more refined and definitive interpretation.

NOTES:

1. For a comprehensive account of gilding and enameling from antiquity to the eighteenth century, see Charleston 1972, pp. 18–32. An article on the same subject by William Gudenruth is planned for a future issue of the *Journal of Glass Studies*.
2. A rare exception is a bowl in the Louvre (Fig. 10.1), where the scratched highlights run horizontally.
3. Quoted in Charleston 1972, p. 19.
4. Such a project may be complicated, however, by the possibility that molds were used in more than one factory. In the nineteenth century iron pattern molds were so valuable that they were often sold to other glasshouses, and the same may have been true centuries earlier.
5. William Gudenrath of the New York Experimental Glass Workshop has demonstrated the usefulness of noting these details. He examined all the glass objects in the Robert Lehman Collection with me and generously shared his extensive knowledge of the techniques of Renaissance glassmakers. For his excellent survey of those techniques in words and photographs, see Tait 1991, pp. 213–41.

Probably Venice, possibly *façon de Venise*, France,
1499–1514

1. Armorial tazza

1975.1.1194
H. 22.1 cm, diam. of rim 27.6 cm. Colorless (slightly gray)
nonlead glass. Blown, pattern molded, enameled, gilt.

The everted, underfolded rim of the bowl is decorated on the
exterior with a band of scribed gilt scales, each with a pale
blue enamel dot, flanked by rows of enamel dots, white above
and blue and white arranged in triangles below; at the inner
edge of the rim is a trailed thread embellished with white
enamel dashes. The bowl's rounded sides have forty molded
radial ribs with gilding at the upper ends. The stem, attached
to the bowl with a flattened merese, is composed of a short,
solid, columnar section with plain gilt bands around the lower
half and the flared ends; a hollow ovoid knop covered by a
wide scribed gilt scale band flanked by two rows of pinkish
white enamel dots; and a large gilt disk with a row of pinkish
white enamel dots on the underside. The trumpet-shaped foot
has a gilt, trailed, ridged band at the rim and a gilt band at the
top (flanked by two rows of pinkish white enamel dots) and
bottom (with white enamel dots below and blue and white
dots arranged in triangles above). On the front and back of the
foot are the arms of Louis XII of France and Anne of Brittany:
azure, three fleurs-de-lys or (France), impaling ermine (Brittany).
Above each shield is a crown highlighted with red, white, and
blue enamel dots and suspended from red and white enamel
ribbons. One rough pontil mark inside the bowl and another
under the foot.

Slight traces of crizzling, with several small spalls missing from
the bowl and under the foot; a section of the trailed thread on
the bowl missing; wear on the gilding at the top of the foot.

Longwave fluorescence. Glass: strong yellow-green. Enamels:
white and pinkish white = strong pink, blue = inky blue, red =
dark red. *Shortwave fluorescence.* Glass: faint greenish
tan. Enamels: white and pinkish white = brilliant bluish
white, blue = dark blue, red = black. Gilding: generally no
fluorescence, although the gilding on the ribs and foot fluoresces
slightly pink.

PROVENANCE: Frederic Neuburg, Vienna; Otto Hopfinger, New
York; [Blumka Gallery, New York].

EXHIBITED: Corning 1958, pp. 48–49, no. 28, ill.; Cincinnati
1959, p. 42, no. 543.

No. 1, *detail of rim*

No. 1, *top view*

No. 1, *detail of foot*

No. 1

LITERATURE: Schmidt 1931, pp. 3–4, 20, no. 1, pl. 1; Szabo 1975, p. 45, fig. 167; Charleston 1977, p. 17; Rochester (N.Y.) (and other cities) 1981–82, fig. 12; Hayward 1982, p. 16, fig. 11.

When the enamels and gilding were applied to this tazza the bowl was probably nearly straight-sided and may have looked much like a footed bowl in the Cleveland Museum of Art (Fig. 1.1).[1] The markedly oval enamel dots and the granulated gilding on the rim indicate that it was flared considerably during the firing process. The foot, however, was substantially in its present shape when the enamels were applied; the dots near the rim are nearly

Fig. 1.1 Footed bowl. Cleveland Museum of Art,
Purchase from the J. H. Wade Fund

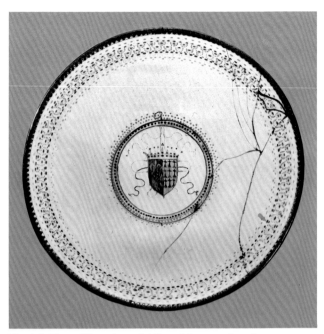

Fig. 1.3 Plate. Victoria and Albert Museum, London.
By courtesy of the Board of Trustees of the Victoria and
Albert Museum

Fig. 1.2 Tazza. Musée National de la Renaissance, Château
d'Écouen. Photograph: Réunion des Musées Nationaux

Fig. 1.4 Tazza. Toledo Museum of Art, Toledo, Ohio,
Museum Purchase

circular, and the gilt band is not granulated. The gilt of the fleurs-de-lys and the black enamel of the ermine were applied over the enamel grounds. The wear on the gilding at the top of the foot is probably due to inadequate firing, which makes the gilding less stable. This may indicate that the tazza was held only by a pontil on the foot to fire the enameling and gilding. The pontil may have been attached inside the bowl only while the foot was being flared to its present form (before enameling). The similar tazza in the Rijksmuseum, Amsterdam (Fig. 1.6), which can be attributed to the same glasshouse, has a large white enamel dot over the pontil mark inside the bowl, indicating that it was not held there while the enamels and gilding were being fused. See also Nos. 15 and 16. The trailed rim on the foot of No. 1 is related in form to those on the necks of Nos. 3 and 59.

Louis XII of France (1462–1515, r. 1498–1515) and Anne, duchess of Brittany (1477–1514), were married in 1499 at the Château de Nantes. This tazza bearing their arms may have been part of a service made to celebrate their marriage. No documentary evidence that such a service existed has as yet been found, although it is said that two tazzas are depicted in a now-lost painting or tapestry made at the time of the wedding. A matching tazza in the Musée National de la Renaissance, Château d'Écouen (Fig. 1.2),[2] a large plate in the Victoria and Albert Museum, London (Fig. 1.3),[3] and a diamond-molded tazza in the Toledo Museum of Art (Fig. 1.4),[4] all with the same arms, probably belong to the same service.

The details of construction of the Lehman and Écouen tazzas are sufficiently close to permit the attribution of both to the same glasshouse, and probably to the same glassblower. There is nothing to indicate that one of them is a later copy of the other. Whether they are of Venetian or French manufacture is not certain. Enameled glass was probably being made in France at the end of the fifteenth century by Venetian glassmakers. The crizzling on the Lehman tazza would suggest French manufacture. Crizzling, a slow deterioration of the glass caused by the glassmaker using too little lime in the batch, is unusual in any early sixteenth-century glass, but it is rarely found in Venetian glass of the period. The use of a forty-rib mold is typically Venetian (see Nos. 15 and 16), but Venetian workers in France would have been able to produce such a mold relatively easily.

A tazza in Kynžvart Castle, Czech Republic (Fig. 1.5),[5] and one in the Rijksmuseum, Amsterdam (Fig. 1.6),[6] are similar enough to the two tazzas bearing the French royal arms to support an attribution of all four to the same

Fig. 1.5 Tazza. Kynžvart Castle, Czech Republic

Fig. 1.6 Tazza. Rijksmuseum, Amsterdam

source. The bowls of all four tazzas have forty ribs with gilt tops and rims decorated with a gilt scale pattern above a trailed thread picked out with enamel dashes. All four have a similarly ridged foot rim.[7] The tazzas in the Rijksmuseum and the Kynžvart Castle differ only slightly in form and decoration. On the Rijksmuseum tazza the scales on the bowl rim are arranged horizontally, rather than vertically, and the scales are outlined with white enamel arcs and embellished with red, blue, or green enamel dots arranged in diagonal rows of matching color. There is a large white enamel dot inside the bowl at the center, over the rough pontil mark, and the foot is decorated with stylized foliage in polychrome enamel. On the Kynžvart Castle tazza an unidentified coat of arms is repeated three times inside the bowl, and the tops of the ribs on the bowl's sides are enameled as well as gilded. The foot is ribbed, with a stylized foliate band at the rim. The gilt knops on the stems of both these tazzas are melon-ribbed (with twenty ribs), rather than smooth, and have no scale decoration.

Another enameled glass service made for the French royal family bears the arms of Catherine de Médicis (1519–1589) and presumably dates from the middle of the sixteenth century. A footed bowl from that service is at the Château d'Écouen (see Fig. 12.1).[8] The arms of Catherine de Médicis and Henry II of France (1519–1559, r. 1547–59) appear on a large plate, unrelated to the Lehman and Écouen tazzas, the rim of which is covered with an elaborate gilt foliate pattern; it may have been made to commemorate their marriage in 1533.[9] A tazza with the enameled arms of France is in the New Orleans Museum of Art.[10]

NOTES:

1. Cleveland Museum of Art, 49.176 (ex coll. Nathaniel de Rothschild, Alphonse de Rothschild); Comstock 1950; Foote 1950; Cleveland 1956, p. 44, no. 88; Cleveland Museum of Art 1958, p. 227. The bowl is attributed to Venice and dated to the late fifteenth or early sixteenth century.

2. Musée National de la Renaissance, 4921; Gerspach 1885, p. 197, fig. 90; Honey 1946, p. 67; Charleston 1952, pp. 156, 157, fig. 1; Barrelet 1953, pl. 36, p. 198; Ennès 1982, cover ill.; Erlande-Brandenburg 1987, p. 177, fig. 51; Bellanger 1988, p. 391.

3. Victoria and Albert Museum, C.132-1914; Honey 1946, p. 67. Honey suggests that the tazza may have been made in France.

4. Toledo Museum of Art, 32.1 (ex coll. Frédéric Spitzer); Garnier 1891, p. 101, no. 58; d'Hondt [1893?], p. 108; Spitzer sale 1893, lot 2037, pl. 49; Hutton 1963, p. [3]; Toledo Museum of Art 1969, p. 47.

5. Kynžvart Castle, 4619; Bulletin AIHV, no. 4 (1965–66), p. 81; Prague 1973, no. 4, fig. 2b; Venice 1982, p. 105, no. 117.

6. Rijksmuseum, RBK1978-20 (ex coll. Rothschild); Galerie Fischer sale 1937, lot 483; pl. 32; Bulletin van het Rijksmuseum 26, no. 1 (1978), pp. 72, 78, fig. 3; JGS 24 (1982), p. 92, fig. 16.

7. The ridge is also present on the large twelve-ribbed footed bowl in the Cleveland Museum of Art (Fig. 1.1) and on a goblet in the Hermitage, Saint Petersburg (see Fig. 18.1). It also appears to be present on a large ribbed compote that was formerly in the Frédéric Spitzer collection, Paris (Spitzer sale 1893, lot 1983, pl. 51).

8. See No. 12, note 2.

9. See Laméris and Laméris 1991, pp. 82, 83, no. 58.

10. Ex coll. Melvin Billups; Corning 1958, p. 27, fig. 37.

Venice, ca. 1500

2. Goblet

1975.1.1161

H. 26.7 cm, diam. of rim 15.6 cm. Colorless (slightly grayish) nonlead glass. Blown, pattern molded, trailed, enameled, gilt.

Below the rim of the large bell-shaped bowl is a wide band of scribed gilt scales, each with a tiny blue enamel dot, flanked by two rows of red dots on gilt framing lines and two rows of white dots, with a band of gilt pelmets below. The lower two-thirds of the bowl is vertically ribbed, the tops of the twelve angular ribs with traces of gilding, the lower halves highlighted with white enamel stripes, and the spaces between the ribs decorated with alternating red and blue enameled serpentine rays with black centers; at the flat base of the bowl is a trailed, pincered band with traces of gilding. The tall, trumpet-shaped foot has nineteen vertical ribs and a trailed foot rim. Rough pontil mark under the foot. Painted in bright red-orange under the foot: L.56.31.63 (a Metropolitan Museum loan number).[1]

No. 2

No. 2, *detail of rim*

Slight wear on the bowl rim and the side of the foot; heavy wear on the foot rim; the gilding worn throughout.

Longwave fluorescence. Glass: strong yellow-green. Enamels: white = pink, red = dark red, blue = dark blue. Gilding: none. *Shortwave fluorescence.* Glass: faint, creamy. Enamels: white = strong bluish white, red flames = gray, red dots = inky blue, blue = dark blue. Gilding: bluish white.

PROVENANCE: J. Pierpont Morgan, Jr., London and New York (Morgan sale 1944, lot 250); Otto Hopfinger, New York; [Blumka Gallery, New York].

EXHIBITED: Corning 1958, pp. 44–45, no. 22, ill.; Cincinnati 1959, p. 42, no. 538, ill.

The bowl of the goblet was probably cylindrical and straight-sided (like No. 18) when the enameling and gilding were applied. The enamel dots below the rim are markedly oval, and the gilt band is granulated.

The size and form of this goblet make it imposing, but it is the decoration of red and blue serpentine rays that makes it so striking. The rays, or so-called flame decoration, perhaps derived from the radiance typically depicted behind the Virgin and Child, appear often on Venetian and Spanish (Barcelona) glass. They were used, for instance, on the cover of a goblet dated 1511 that was in the collection of Georg von Kopidlnansky von Kopidlna, Dresden;[2] on the cover of the Deblin goblet in the British Museum, London;[3] at the base of the neck of a ewer in the J. Paul Getty Museum, Malibu, that has been dated

to the late fifteenth or early sixteenth century;[4] and on other Venetian glasses in the Museo Civico Cristiano, Brescia;[5] the Corning Museum of Glass;[6] the Cecil Higgins Museums and Art Gallery, Bedford, England;[7] the Uměleckoprůmyslové Muzeum, Prague;[8] the British Museum;[9] the Hermitage, Saint Petersburg;[10] the Victoria and Albert Museum, London;[11] and a private collection in the Netherlands.[12] Spanish glass decorated with rays is in the Instituto Amatller de Arte Hispánico, Barcelona,[13] and the Hispanic Society of America, New York.[14]

Similar rays, called San Bernardino rays after the flames surrounding the monogram *IHS* (abbreviated from the Greek form of Jesus' name) on the tablet Saint Bernardino of Siena (1380–1444) carried when he preached, were also painted on Italian majolica. Majolica jugs with Christ's monogram encircled by rays are depicted in Northern paintings of the last half of the fifteenth century, such as the *Annunciation* in the Germanisches Nationalmuseum, Nürnberg, that is attributed to the workshop of Stefan Lochner (d. 1451)[15] and the still life Hans Memling (ca. 1430 or 1435–1494) painted on the back of his *Portrait of a Young Man* in the collection of Baron Thyssen-Bornemisza, Madrid.[16] The earliest dated examples of majolica decorated with the flame-encircled monogram are two patens (one in the Musée de Cluny, Paris, the other in the Victoria and Albert Museum) inscribed 1475 and 1491, respectively.[17] Majolica painters also used San Bernardino rays without Christ's monogram, for instance on the shoulder of an *albarello* in the Robert Lehman Collection at the Metropolitan Museum that was probably made in Florence about 1470–90[18] and on an apothecary bottle, also in the Metropolitan, that was made in Faenza about 1500.[19]

The form of this goblet is not uncommon in Venetian glass of the first quarter of the sixteenth century. Other examples, with and without ribbing, are in the Museum des Kunsthandwerks, Leipzig;[20] the Victoria and Albert Museum;[21] the Uměleckoprůmyslové Muzeum,[22] the Österreichisches Museum für Angewandte Kunst, Vienna;[23] the Museum für Kunsthandwerk, Frankfurt am Main;[24] the Bernd Hockemeyer collection, Bremen;[25] the Museo Civico d'Arte Antica, Turin;[26] the British Museum;[27] the Muzeum Narodowe, Wroclaw;[28] the Museum für Kunsthandwerk, Dresden;[29] and the J. Paul Getty Museum.[30] Another goblet is in the James A. de Rothschild Collection at Waddesdon Manor,[31] and others were in the Helfried Krug collection, Mülheim an der Ruhr;[32] the Frédéric Spitzer collection, Paris;[33] the Émile Gavet collection, Paris;[34] and the Kunstgewerbemuseum, Berlin.[35]

NOTES:

1. An unidentified oval red-orange paper label printed *539* has been removed and is in the Robert Lehman Collection files.

2. Schmidt 1912, pp. 94, 95, fig. 58; Schmidt 1922, pp. 96, 97, fig. 59; Von Saldern 1965, p. 32, fig. 5.

3. Ex coll. Ferdinand de Rothschild; C. H. Read 1899, p. 27, no. 57; Tait 1979, p. 36, no. 23, colorpl. 2; Tait 1981, pl. 5; Barovier Mentasti 1982, p. 91, fig. 77.

4. J. Paul Getty Museum, 84.DK.512 (ex coll. Émile Gavet, J. E. Taylor, George Eumorfopoulos); Gavet sale 1897, lot 592; Taylor sale 1912, lot 340; Eumorfopoulos sale 1940, lot 223; Corning 1958, pp. 44–45, no. 23; New York 1975, p. 44, no. 38 (then in the collection of Mrs. Leopold Blumka); *JGS* 28 (1986), p. 101, fig. 10.

5. Museo Civico Cristiano, 36 (ex coll. Brozzoni); Mariacher 1965a, p. 19, fig. 5; Venice 1982, pp. 84–85, no. 76.

6. Corning Museum of Glass, 79.3.193 (ex coll. Jerome Strauss, L. de Rothschild, Oscar Bondy); Corning 1955, cover ill., pp. 36, 37, no. 87; *JGS* 22 (1980), p. 105, fig. 15; Venice 1982, pp. 21, 78, 79, no. 67, colorpl. 8.

7. Grubert 1984, p. 29, fig. 8.

8. Uměleckoprůmyslové Muzeum, 9622/1906 (ex coll. Adalbert von Lanna); Jiřík 1934, pp. 81–82, fig. 42; Hetteš 1960, p. 37, fig. 29; Egg 1962, p. 28, pl. 4, fig. 8; Prague 1973, no. 14, fig. 11; Venice 1982, p. 102, no. 110.

9. British Museum, 80,7-1,4 (ex coll. A. W. Franks); Tait 1979, p. 32, no. 11, colorpl. 7.

10. Hermitage, F.468; Clarke 1974, pp. 54–55, no. C11; Barovier Mentasti 1982, p. 74, fig. 57.

11. Victoria and Albert Museum, C.1890-1855, C.135-1873; Honey 1946, p. 61, pl. 23B; Frothingham 1956, fig. 6.

12. Laméris and Laméris 1991, p. 24, pl. 2.

13. Gudiol Ricart and Artíñano 1935, pl. 22; Frothingham 1956, fig. 8.

14. Hispanic Society of America, T352; Singleton 1925, p. 7; Frothingham 1941, pp. 130–31; Mariacher 1954, fig. 144; Frothingham 1956, frontis.; Frothingham 1963, pp. 28–29, 43, fig. 3; Schlosser 1965, p. 134, fig. 109; Gardner 1979, fig. 48.

15. Scheil 1977, no. 142, pls. 67, 68.

16. Ibid., no. 79, pl. 29; Washington, D.C. 1979–81, no. 25, cover ill. (See also Scheil 1977, pp. 57–64, 109–10, and pls. 23, 24, 27, 28, 30, 31, 37, 38.) On the subject of San Bernardino rays, see also Howell 1913, pp. 105–6. I would like to thank David B. Whitehouse for bringing this information to my attention.

17. Ballardini 1933, nos. 2, 10, figs. 2, 9.

18. Metropolitan Museum, 1975.1.1059; Rasmussen 1989, pp. 12–13, no. 6, ill.

19. Metropolitan Museum, 65.6.5; New York 1975, p. 117, no. 128, ill.

20. Museum des Kunsthandwerks, 08.23; *Bulletin AIHV*, no. 7 (1973–76), p. 104, fig. 132; Kämpfer 1978, p. 67 (drawing); Berlin 1981a, p. 11, pl. 1, no. 1.

21. Victoria and Albert Museum, 678-1884 (ex coll. Alessandro Castellani); Honey 1946, pp. 57, 61, pl. 21; Mariacher 1961, pl. 30; Victoria and Albert Museum 1963, pp. 42–43, no. 20, ill.; Brooks 1973, p. 24; Hermelin and Welander 1980, p. 28. This goblet, which has a ribbed bowl and foot and is almost identical to the Lehman glass except that it has a trailed thread above the ribbing on the bowl and no flame decoration, also has a ribbed cover. See also C.409-1854 and C.135-1873; Honey 1946, p. 60, pls. 22C, 23B; Brooks 1973, p. 22; Venice 1982, pp. 82–83, no. 73.

22. Prague 1973, no. 5, fig. 3.

23. Schlosser 1951, p. 9, pl. 5; Schlosser 1965, p. 100, fig. 86.

24. Museum für Kunsthandwerk, X15667/4950, WME32/357; Garnier 1891, p. 91, no. 9, pl. 4; Spitzer sale 1893, lot 1977, pl. 50; Weiss 1971, p. 107; Ohm 1973, pp. 62–63, nos. 115, 116, pl. opp. p. 65; Klesse and Mayr 1987, p. 15, fig. 5.

25. Ex coll. Fritz Biemann; *JGS* 22 (1980), p. 90, fig. 12; Lucerne 1981, p. 153, no. 643; Venice 1982, pp. 78–79, nos. 66, 68.

26. *Bulletin AIHV*, no. 9 (1981–83), p. 29, fig. 1; Barovier Mentasti 1982, p. 53, fig. 32.

27. Ex coll. Ferdinand de Rothschild; Tait 1979, p. 36, no. 23, colorpl. 2; and ex coll. Felix Slade (s.362); Nesbitt 1871, pp. 68–69, fig. 81; Gerspach 1885, p. 119, fig. 63; Lorenzetti 1931, pl. 7; Mariacher 1963, p. 61; Tait 1979, p. 29, no. 3, colorpl. 3.

28. Gasparetto 1958, fig. 30.

29. Museum für Kunsthandwerk, 37.831; *JGS* 10 (1968), p. 185, fig. 30.

30. J. Paul Getty Museum, 84.DK.534 (ex coll. Leopold Blumka); New York 1975, p. 267, no. 263; *JGS* 28 (1986), p. 101, fig. 12.

31. Charleston 1977, pp. 82–86, no. 15, ill.

32. Klesse 1965, pp. 130–31, nos. 75, 76; Lipp 1974, pp. 138, 171, fig. 203; Krug sale 1981–83, part 1, lot 36, and part 2, lot 362.

33. Spitzer sale 1893, lot 2000, pl. 49.

34. Gavet sale 1897, lot 614.

35. Schmidt 1922, p. 67, fig. 36; Rademacher 1933, p. 126, 131–32, 151, fig. 58b; Mariacher 1954, p. 112, fig. 120; Vávra 1954, p. 43, pl. 110; Dreier 1989b, p. 11, fig. 10.

No. 3, *side*

No. 3, *side*

Venice, ca. 1500–1510

3. Jug

1975.1.1172
H. 21 cm. Transparent dark blue nonlead glass. Blown, enameled, gilt.

The jug has a waisted neck with a trailed double-rib collar below the rim, with gilding on the rim and collar; encircling the neck is a continuous polychrome flowering vine in a wide zone flanked by bands of scribed gilt scale decoration, each scale with a white enamel dot, bordered by red and yellow-orange lines and rows of white dots. At the base of the neck is a trailed ring in turquoise blue, with the remains of gilding. The globular body is painted in enamels with a frieze in which three centaurs aim bows and arrows in a field of elaborate foliate scrollwork with flowers and fantastic animals' heads, on a green and brown grassy ground above a scribed, gilt, and enameled scale band like those on the neck. The applied gilt loop handle is attached to pads at the top and bottom and drawn out into a grooved tail at the bottom. The flared pedestal foot has an underfolded gilt rim and is decorated with alternating yellow-orange and white enamel ovals. Large rough pontil mark under the foot. Painted in white under the foot: Co(?) *1057*.[1]

Cracks in the body around the lower terminal of the handle; small cracks in the foot rim (in the making, as there is gilding inside the cracks); the gilding worn.

Longwave fluorescence. Glass: no visible fluorescence. Enamels: white = pinkish tan, red-orange = dark red, yellow-orange = dark orange, green = greenish yellow, turquoise blue = slightly brighter greenish yellow, brown = brown, dark blue = inky blue; turquoise blue trailed band = inky blue. Gilding: scummy tan. *Shortwave fluorescence.* Glass: no visible fluorescence. Enamels: white = brilliant bluish white; red-orange, yellow-orange, turquoise blue, and brown = varying degrees of dark orange; blue and green = black. Gilding: on the collar, foot rim, and top of foot = dark orange; on the scale band and handle = no visible fluorescence.

PROVENANCE: [Saemy Rosenberg, Stiebel and Co., Paris]; Oscar Bondy, Vienna; Otto Hopfinger, New York; [Blumka Gallery, New York].

EXHIBITED: Corning 1958, pp. 33–35, no. 10, colorpl. 5; Cincinnati 1959, p. 42, no. 535, ill.; New York 1984.

LITERATURE: Bondy n.d., p. 51, no. 193 (1057); Winchester 1958, frontis.; Szabo 1975, p. 105; Charleston 1977, p. 88, under no. 16; Hayward 1982, p. 16.

No. 3, *front*

No. 3, *back*

A strong, fairly uniform turquoise blue underlayer is evident where the gilding is worn on this jug, particularly on the trailed ring at the base of the neck and on the foot rim, where the gilding is almost gone. The blue might have been an enamel undercoat for the gilding, but it is more likely that the glass was "stained" by the gold during firing. The neck was probably straight-sided when the enameling and gilding were applied; the oval form of the enamel dots at the top resulted from slight flaring of the rim during the firing process. The enameling was applied before the handle was attached; the decoration may be seen projecting from beneath the handle attachments. The trailed ring at the top rim is of the same profile as that on the foot rim of No. 1. The shear mark on top of the handle is similar to that on No. 5.

This spectacular jug is one of the masterpieces of the Robert Lehman Collection. Of the numerous parallels in both form and decoration, the closest is a blue jug in the Victoria and Albert Museum, London (Fig. 3.1), that is not only similarly shaped and constructed but also has similar gilt scale bands, vines with cushion-shaped flowers, and enamel ovals around the foot.[2] Enameled foliate scrollwork like this is also found on several other glasses, among them a pilgrim flask in the Louvre, Paris (Fig. 3.2),[3] a colorless conical goblet in the Corning Museum of Glass (Fig. 3.3),[4] and a blue footed bowl in the Museo Civico Cristiano, Brescia.[5] The flowering vine on the bowl of a blue covered goblet also in Brescia (Fig. 3.4) is enameled in the same palette as the decoration on the Lehman jug, and both pieces have the same haphazard scribing on the outlines of the gilt scales; they could be from the same hand or shop.[6]

No. 3, *detail of top of handle*

No. 3, *detail of neck*

Analogous shapes and decoration can also be found in colorless glass. Two jugs in the Museo Vetrario, Murano, one with spiral vines on the neck and body,[7] the other with a band of enameled and gilt scales on the neck,[8] have the same form of handle, with a projecting lower terminus, but the necks are rather taller and more cylindrical. There is also a closely related jug in the Rijksmuseum, Amsterdam, with male grotesques on the front and other figures on the sides,[9] and there are two others in the Louvre, Paris, one with stylized foliate decoration on the body (Fig. 3.5),[10] the other with a blue handle.[11] Other colorless jugs of related form are decorated only with gilt scales; one in the Hermitage, Saint Petersburg, for example, has an overall gilt scale pattern.[12] A frieze of three centaurs, each holding a shield and a feathered dart, amid leafy scrollwork decorates a Venetian goblet in the James A. de Rothschild Collection at Waddesdon Manor that Charleston has dated to the early sixteenth century.[13] A colorless spouted ewer once in the Frédéric Spitzer collection, Paris,[14] and a goblet in the Louvre[15] have related enameling.

No. 3, *detail of bottom of handle*

Fig. 3.1 Jug. Victoria and Albert Museum, London. By courtesy of the Board of Trustees of the Victoria and Albert Museum

Fig. 3.3 Goblet. Corning Museum of Glass, Bequest of Jerome Strauss

Fig. 3.2 Pilgrim flask. Musée du Louvre, Paris. Photograph: Réunion des Musées Nationaux

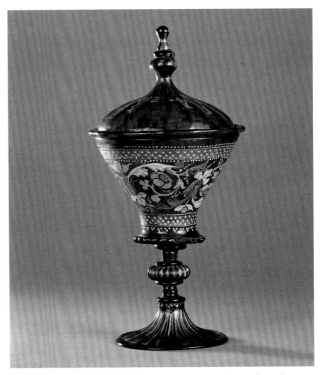

Fig. 3.4 Covered goblet. Museo Civico Cristiano, Brescia. Photograph: Fotostudio Rapuzzi, Brescia. By courtesy of the Civici Musei d'Arte e Storia di Brescia

Fig. 3.5 Jug. Musée du Louvre, Paris. Photograph: Réunion des Musées Nationaux

NOTES:

1. The following labels have been removed and are now in the Robert Lehman Collection files: Unidentified: rectangular white paper label with *193* printed in black and *25* written in pencil (probably while the jug was in Robert Lehman's possession); oval orange paper label printed *537* in black; rectangular tan paper label printed *442* in black; rectangular white paper label with printed blue frame and *K Ků / 483* written in blue ink; rectangular blue paper label printed ANNEXE / N° *530*, with illegible stamp superimposed. Oscar Bondy collection: small oval paper label with *G / Z. 21.* printed in black and *O/27* written in red. Robert Lehman collection: rectangular gold metallic paper label printed *64* in black; circular white paper label typed *64.* in black.

2. Victoria and Albert Museum, C.273-1874; Nesbitt 1878, p. 55; Honey 1946, p. 60, pl. 22B; Frothingham 1956, fig. 3; Gasparetto 1958, fig. 24; Mariacher 1963, p. 50; Brooks 1973, p. 25; Barovier Mentasti 1982, p. 71, fig. 50.

3. Louvre, OA7566.

4. Corning Museum of Glass, 73.2.191 (ex coll. Jerome Strauss); Venice 1982, pp. 92–93, no. 90.

5. Museo Civico Cristiano, 38; Venice 1982, p. 72, no. 61; Brescia 1987, pp. 111, 114, no. 2b.

6. Museo Civico Cristiano, 94; *Bulletin AIHV*, no. 9 (1981–83), p. 34, fig. 1; Venice 1982, pp. 72–73, no. 62; Mianni, Resini, and Lamon 1984, p. 75; Brescia 1987, pp. 111, 113, no. 1b.

7. Museo Vetrario, 1895, div. II D, n. 15; Lorenzetti [1953], pl. 47; Gasparetto 1958, fig. 37; Mariacher 1961, pl. 27; Mariacher 1964, pl. 6; Reggio Calabria 1967, fig. [7]; Mariacher [1970]a, pp. 108, 109, fig. 49; Mariacher and Causa Picone 1972, p. 40, pl. 50; Barovier Mentasti 1982, p. 61, fig. 42; Columbus 1983, p. 14, fig. 2; Zecchin 1987–89, vol. 1, p. 263.

8. Museo Vetrario, 1895, cl. VI, n. 1004; Gasparetto 1958, pl. 37; Mariacher [1966], p. 109, fig. 47; Venice 1982, p. 96, no. 96; Mianni, Resini, and Lamon 1984, p. 76. The projection at the base of the handle is also to be found on a pitcher in the Victoria and Albert Museum (C.681-1884 [ex coll. Alessandro Castellani]; Honey 1946, pp. 57–60; Corning 1958, pp. 60, 61, no. 48; Venice 1982, pp. 102–4, no. 112) and on a spouted jug, with the arms of the Nürnberg families Ebner von Eschenbach and Führer von Heimendorf, in the Uměleckoprůmyslové Muzeum, Prague (9622/1906 [ex coll. Adalbert von Lanna]; Jiřík 1934, pp. 81–82, fig. 42; Hetteš 1960, p. 37, fig. 29; Egg 1962, p. 28, pl. 4, fig. 8; Prague 1973, no. 14, fig. 11; Venice 1982, p. 102, no. 110).

9. Rijksmuseum, 17522; Isings 1966, p. 63, frontis., fig. 44; Lipp 1974, pp. 62, 63, figs. 27–29.

10. Louvre, R104.

11. Louvre, OA3366 (ex coll. Frédéric Spitzer, Debruge Duménil, Soltykoff et Saint-Seine); Labarte 1847, pp. 691, 699–700, no. 1280; Garnier 1891, p. 91, no. 11, pl. 6; Spitzer sale 1893, lot 1979, pl. 49.

12. Kachalov 1959, fig. 62; Barovier Mentasti 1982, p. 58, fig. 38.

13. Charleston 1977, pp. 87–89, no. 16. Charleston described the Lehman jug as "dating probably from the late fifteenth century."

14. Garnier 1891, pp. 91–92, no. 12, pl. 6.

15. Bellanger 1988, p. 319.

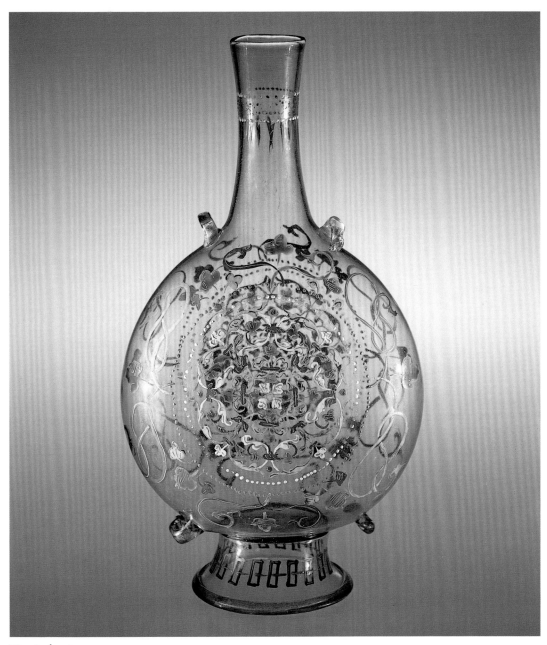

No. 4, *front*

Venice, ca. 1500–1525

4. Pilgrim flask

1975.1.1167

H. 31.4 cm. Colorless (slightly tan) nonlead glass. Blown, enameled, gilt.

Around the tall, slightly waisted neck is a band of scribed gilt scales, each with an opaque blue enamel dot, flanked by a row of white enamel dots above and white dots and dark red vertical dashes below. A circular pattern of entwined vines and trefoil flowers in gilt and blue, red, and white enamel decorates each of the two flattened sides of the bulbous ovoid body. Two gilt loop handles are attached to each side, at the top and bottom. A ring of red enamel rectangles linked with blue enamel dashes encircles the hollow pedestal foot, which has a trailed rim with traces of gilding. Two rough pontil marks, one over the other, under the foot.[1]

Chip on the foot rim; the foot etched inside.

No. 4, *back*

No. 4, *detail of neck*

Longwave fluorescence. Glass: strong yellow-green. Enamels: white = tan, amber = orange, red = dark red, blue = dark blue. *Shortwave fluorescence.* Glass: faint, creamy. Enamels: white = brilliant bluish white, amber = dark red, red = inky blue, blue = inky blue.

PROVENANCE: Otto Hopfinger, New York; [Blumka Gallery, New York].

EXHIBITED: Corning 1958, pp. 54–55, no. 38, ill.; Cincinnati 1959, p. 42, no. 546.

LITERATURE: Szabo 1975, p. 106; Roffia and Mariacher 1983, p. 173, under no. 41.

The forming of the flask was essentially completed before the enamels and gilding were applied. The handles were gilded after they were applied; the gilding does not pass under the handles.

There are numerous parallels in glass, pottery, and metal for the form of this flask, which is probably based on Syrian prototypes. Many of the glass examples attributed to Venetian workshops have identifiable coats of arms of Italian and German noble families. Related pilgrim flasks, so called because of their similarity to the flasks pilgrims used to carry water, are customarily dated to the waning years of the fifteenth and the first quarter of the sixteenth century. Among the earliest datable examples are two flasks in the Museo Civico, Bologna, that bear the arms of Bentivoglio and Sforza and may have been made at the time of the marriage of Alessandro Bentivoglio and Ippolita Sforza in 1492.[2] The enameled decoration on those flasks is, however, chaste by comparison with that on the Lehman flask and shares no apparent stylistic similarities with it.

Enameled decoration similar to this covers one side of a *lattimo* pilgrim flask now in the Hermitage, Saint Petersburg (Fig. 4.1).[3] The opposite side of the Hermitage flask depicts Apollo and Cyparissus, after a woodcut in the 1497 Venetian edition of Ovid's *Metamorphoses* (fol. 85v) or perhaps after Benedetto Montagna's engraving of about 1515–20, which corresponds closely to the woodcut. Interlaced scrollwork much like that on the sides of the Lehman flask was used on a flask in the Corning Museum of Glass with the arms of Della Rovere beneath a bishop's miter[4] and on another in the Wallace Collection, London (Fig. 4.2), that bears the arms of Wilhelm von Rappoltstein or de Ribaupierre of Alsace and those of Christof Philipp, first Count Liechtenstein (d. 1547), as borne from 1523 to 1526.[5] (Von Liechtenstein married Von Rappoltstein's daughter Margaretha in 1516.)

Linked rectangles like those on the foot of the Lehman flask are found on several other pilgrim flasks. The band of scale pattern on the neck is also a common motif; it appears, for example, on a flask in the Toledo Museum of Art.[6]

NOTES:

1. The following labels have been removed: Unidentified: bright orange oval paper label printed *545*. Robert Lehman collection: rectangular gold metallic paper label printed *36*. Metropolitan Museum: rectangular gummed white paper label with *L.58.73.53* (a loan number) typed in red. (The last two labels are in the Robert Lehman Collection files.)
2. Museo Civico, 1364, 1365; Mariacher 1954, fig. 42; Frothingham 1956, fig. 17; Gasparetto 1958, fig. 21; Bologna 1959, pp. 48–49, no. 125, pl. 19; Gasparetto 1960a, p. 124, fig. 29; Mariacher 1963, p. 64; Mariacher 1964, pl. 5; Mariacher [1966], p. 119, fig. 52; Omodeo [1970], p. 16, fig. 14; Mariacher and Causa Picone 1972, p. 43, pl. 57; *Bulletin AIHV*, no. 9 (1981–83), p. 124, fig. 3; Barovier Mentasti 1982, p. 62, fig. 43. A flask in the Bernd Hockemeyer collection, Bremen (ex coll. Fritz Biemann), bears only the arms of Bentivoglio; see Lucerne 1981, pp. 28, 153, no. 646, pl. F20; Venice 1982, pp. 87, 89, no. 81.

Fig. 4.2 Pilgrim flask. Wallace Collection, London. By permission of the Trustees of the Wallace Collection

3. Hermitage, F.468 (ex coll. Basilevsky); Kachalov 1959, fig. 61; Clarke 1974, pp. 43–44, 54–55, no. C11; Barovier Mentasti 1982, p. 74, fig. 57.
4. Corning Museum of Glass, 59.3.19.
5. Wallace Collection, XXV B95 (acquired from Carraud *fils* in 1868); Wallace Collection 1920, no. 95; Von Saldern 1965, pp. 32, 35, fig. 7; Savage 1965, p. 58, ill.; Charleston 1977, p. 91, under no. 17. I am grateful to Suzanne Gaynor of the Wallace Collection for sharing her catalogue notes with me.
6. Toledo Museum of Art, 48.225 (ex coll. Walker); Hutton 1963, p. [3]; Toledo Museum of Art 1969, p. 47.

Fig. 4.1 Pilgrim flask. Hermitage, Saint Petersburg

No. 5, *front*

No. 5, *side*

Venice, 1513–34

5. Armorial jug

1975.1.1170

H. 19.8 cm. Colorless (slightly gray) nonlead glass. Blown, enameled, gilt.

The jug has a trefoil mouth and a flared rim, below which are a trailed collar, rib, and plain gilt band. Encircling the base of the waisted neck is a band of scribed gilt scales, each with a red enamel dot, framed by blue lines and rows of red-and-white dots. On the front of the globular body are the canting arms of the Medici: or, six roundels in orle, five gules, the one in chief azure, charged with three fleurs-de-lys or; surmounted by the papal tiara and the crossed keys, one in blue, the other in yellow (for argent and or), on white looping cords with red and yellow tassels. On either side is a red enamel roundel containing a yellow quatrefoil and set amid elaborate scroll-work. The applied loop handle is attached to convex pads at the top and bottom, where it is drawn out into a projecting tail. The foot has a trailed ring, and its underside has a slight kick. Two rough pontil marks, one over the other, under the foot. Painted in bright red-orange under the foot: L.56.31.56 (a Metropolitan Museum loan number).[1]

Slight etching inside the jug; the center of the armorial shield probably repaired, possibly by further enameling; tiny chip on the foot rim; normal wear on the base ring.

Longwave fluorescence. Glass: strong yellow-green. Enamels: white = pink, red = red, orange = red-orange (with a bright yellowish smudge at the center of the shield), yellow = red-orange, green = dark green, blue = dark blue. *Shortwave fluorescence.* Glass: faint, creamy. Enamels: white = pinkish purple (with a strong halo), red = dark red, yellow = orange (with a bright yellow smudge at the center of the shield), orange = red-orange, green = dark green, blue = inky blue.

PROVENANCE: John Edward Taylor, London (Taylor sale 1912, lot 347; sold to Andrade); [Blumka Gallery, New York].

EXHIBITED: Corning 1958, pp. 50–51, no. 32, ill.; Cincinnati 1959, p. 42, no. 544.

LITERATURE: Szabo 1975, pp. 105–6; Hayward 1982, p. 16.

24

No. 5, *detail of base of neck*

As is the case with many other glass pieces bearing the Medici arms, the yellow-orange enamel on the shield is heavily pitted. This flaw might be mistakenly construed as evidence that the Medici arms were a later addition, but it is more likely that the enameler had technical problems with the yellow enamel, which was extremely difficult to fire successfully. The yellow-orange of the shield was painted first, leaving the five balls in reserve. The handle was made separately and attached to hot bits of glass applied to the body of the jug. The shear mark at its top is similar to that on No. 3.

This jug and the tazza discussed under No. 6 are part of a large group of glass tableware bearing the arms of a Medici pope, either Leo X (Giovanni de' Medici; 1475–1521, r. 1513–21) or Clement VII (Giulio de' Medici; 1478–1534, r. 1523–34).[2] Determining which of the two popes ordered the pieces and whether they constitute one or more services has not been possible. The range in quality of the enameling, from moderately high to mediocre, and the variations in the details of the arms suggest that they were probably made over a number of years.[3]

Fig. 5.1 Jug. Musée du Louvre, Paris. Photograph: Réunion des Musées Nationaux

Fig. 5.2 Jug. Private collection, the Netherlands. Reproduced from Frides Laméris and Kitty Laméris, *Venetiaans en façon de Venise glas, 1500–1700* (Amsterdam: Antiek Lochem, 1991), pl. 5

The greatest number of pieces with the Medici arms are dishes, with and without trumpet feet and with either plain bowls like that of No. 6 or, more often, radial or swirled ribbing. Two other glass jugs have survived, one in the Louvre, Paris (Fig. 5.1),[4] the other in a private collection in the Netherlands (Fig. 5.2).[5] Both have a trailed blue handle and a trailed blue band around the neck, and on both the enameled decoration on the sides is different from that on the Lehman jug. On the jug in the Netherlands the foot is an applied blue pad, but the jug in the Louvre has a trailed colorless foot ring like that on our jug. The handles on the crossed keys of Saint Peter on the Louvre jug are closed trefoils, as here; the keys on the jug in the Netherlands have round handles. All three jugs have a band of gilt scale pattern around the neck. The red circles enclosing yellow quatrefoils that decorate the sides of the Lehman jug appear on none of the other glass objects with the Medici arms, but similar motifs were used on other enameled pieces of the first half of the sixteenth century, for example a jug in the Louvre (see Fig. 3.5)[6] and another in the Museo Vetrario, Murano.[7]

Glass jugs of this form are not altogether uncommon. One example is in the Bernd Hockemeyer collection, Bremen,[8] there is another in the British Museum, London,[9] and still others were once owned by Émile Gavet[10] and Frédéric Spitzer[11] in Paris. The shape is related to that of late fifteenth-century pottery jugs with pinched pouring spouts. A majolica jug bearing the shield of the Medici with a lion's mask, the personal device of Leo X, is in the Victoria and Albert Museum, London.[12]

NOTES:

1. The following labels have been removed and are in the Robert Lehman Collection files: Unidentified: oval bright orange paper label printed *543* in black. J. E. Taylor collection: circular white paper label with *J. E. TAYLOR / COLLECTION* printed in a ring and *347 / 2* written in faded brown ink. Robert Lehman collection: rectangular gold metallic paper label printed *14* in black.

2. See No. 6, notes 2–12.

3. The keys are sometimes nearly fully revealed, as here and on No. 6, sometimes half obscured by the shield. The handles of the keys may be closed trefoils, as here and on Fig. 5.1; open trefoils, as on No. 6; or open rings. The colors of the keys are also sometimes reversed, and the crowns on the tiara are sometimes outlined with black, as on No. 6.

4. Louvre, R111.

5. Ex coll. Fritz Biemann (B544); *JGS* 13 (1971), pp. 140–41, fig. 35; Laméris and Laméris 1991, p. 27, pl. 5.

6. Louvre, R104.

7. Museo Vetrario, 1895, cl. VI, n. 1004; Gasparetto 1958, pl. 37; Mariacher [1966], p. 109, fig. 47; Venice 1982, p. 96, no. 96; Mianni, Resini, and Lamon 1984, p. 76.

8. Galerie Fischer sale 1937, lot 528, pl. 35; Klesse and Von Saldern 1978, p. 305, no. 256; Lucerne 1981, p. 154, no. 647.

9. British Museum, s.396 (ex coll. Felix Slade); Nesbitt 1871, pp. 77–78; Tait 1979, pp. 30–31, no. 8.

10. Gavet sale 1897, lot 585; Miller von Aichholz sale 1925, lot 44, pl. 9.

11. Spitzer sale 1893, lot 2049, pl. 50.

12. Victoria and Albert Museum, C.1715-1855; Victoria and Albert Museum 1963, pp. 50–51, no. 24; Rackham (1940) 1977, no. 334; Rasmussen 1989, p. 21.

Venice, 1513–34

6. Armorial tazza

1975.1.1190
H. 5.8 cm, diam. of rim 23.1 cm. Colorless (slightly gray) nonlead glass. Blown, enameled, gilt.

The shallow, circular bowl has curved sides; below the rim on the exterior is a band of scribed gilt scales, each with a red-and-white enamel dot, flanked by rows of blue and red-and-white enamel dots, and on the interior, in the center, is a large enameled Medici coat of arms, as on No. 5, below the papal tiara and the crossed keys (the colors reversed), here attached to red and yellow cords with tassels. The short trumpet foot has an underfolded rim. Two rough pontil marks, one over the other, under the foot. Painted in bright red-orange under the foot: *L.56.31.60* (a Metropolitan Museum loan number).

Normal wear on the foot.

Longwave fluorescence. Glass: strong yellow-green. Enamels: white dots = pinkish white, white crown = pink, blue = dark blue, red = red, yellow-orange = dark red. *Shortwave fluorescence.* Glass: faint, creamy. Enamels: white dots and crown = strong bluish white, blue = inky blue, red = gray-green, yellow-orange and yellow = dark red.

PROVENANCE: Otto Hopfinger, New York; [Blumka Gallery, New York].

EXHIBITED: Corning 1958, pp. 50–51, no. 31, ill.; Cincinnati 1959, p. 42, no. 545.

LITERATURE: Szabo 1975, p. 106; sale, Sotheby's, London, 23 February 1976, under lot 181; Hayward 1982, p. 16; Venice 1982, p. 106, under no. 121; Roffia and Mariacher 1983, p. 174, under no. 45.

The longwave ultraviolet fluorescence of the white enamel in the papal crown is different from that in the dots in the band near the rim of this tazza (which is not the case on No. 5). This difference is not in itself sufficient reason to suspect that the arms were added recently. It could have resulted from the enamel on the rim overheating when the glass was fired to fuse the enamels in the coat of arms, or some of the gold leaf may have dissolved into the white enamel, coloring it slightly pink and causing the longwave ultraviolet fluorescence to change. The strong oval forms of the enamel dots on the border and the noticeable granulation of the gilding indicate the extent to which the bowl was flared after the enamel dots were applied. That the bowl was more or less straight-sided, or cylindrical, when the enamels were applied explains the somewhat stiff execution of the arms, which would have been considerably harder to reach than the much more cleanly executed gilt scale band on the exterior. The yellow enamel is also slightly rough, a defect found on many of the glass objects decorated with the Medici papal arms. It is likely that the center of the bowl was not heated adequately to melt the yellow enamel.

Like No. 5, this tazza is one of a large group of pieces from a service or services of glass tableware made for either Pope Leo X or Pope Clement VII between 1513 and 1534. Most of the surviving pieces are bowls or footed tazzas, all with the Medici arms but with considerable variation in the details of the papal tiara and the crossed keys that surmount the shield.[1] A tazza like this one, with a plain bowl and a trumpet foot, is in the Metropolitan Museum.[2] Two other tazzas with plain bowls are in the J. Paul Getty Museum, Malibu,[3] and the British Museum,

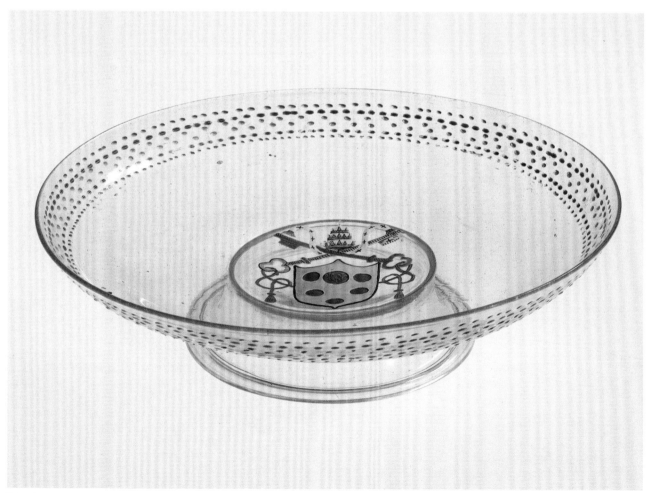

No. 6

No. 6, *shield in center of bowl*

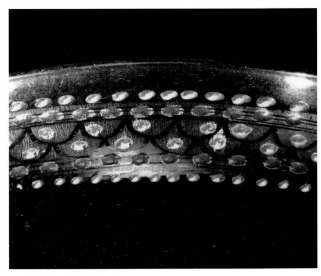

No. 6, *detail of rim*

London;[4] and yet another was in the Émile Gavet collection, Paris.[5] Many more of the tazzas have bowls with radial or swirled ribbing. There are examples in the Louvre, Paris (Fig. 6.1),[6] the Corning Museum of Glass;[7] the Kunstsammlungen der Veste Coburg;[8] the Victoria and Albert Museum, London;[9] the Metropolitan Museum (four examples);[10] and the Kunstmuseum Düsseldorf.[11] Another was on the London art market in 1971.[12]

NOTES:

1. See No. 5, note 3.
2. Metropolitan Museum, 53.225.109 (ex coll. Julia A. Berwind).
3. J. Paul Getty Museum, 84.DK.655; sale, Sotheby's, London, 23 February 1976, lot 181, ill.; Venice 1982, pp. 107, 108, no. 122.
4. Ex coll. Felix Slade; Nesbitt 1871, p. 72, no. 372.
5. Gavet sale 1897, lot 610.
6. Louvre, R100.
7. Corning Museum of Glass, 57.3.44; Comstock 1957, pp. 205, 206; Corning 1958, pp. 50–51, no. 33; Corning Museum of Glass 1958, p. 38, no. 33; Winchester 1958; Corning Museum of Glass 1974, p. 38, no. 39; Venice 1982, pp. 105–6, no. 118. The Corning example has no foot, but an area on the base was ground down, indicating that the stem and foot were removed.
8. Kunstsammlungen der Veste Coburg, HA295.
9. Victoria and Albert Museum, C.171-1936 (ex coll. Wilfred Buckley); Buckley 1926, p. 35, pl. 6B.
10. Metropolitan Museum, 91.1.1450 (ex coll. Edward C. Moore); 17.190.555 (ex coll. Charles Mannheim, J. Pierpont Morgan; Molinier 1898, no. 95 or 96; Corning

Fig. 6.1 Tazza. Musée du Louvre, Paris. Photograph: Réunion des Musées Nationaux

1958, pp. 52–53, no. 34; Venice 1982, pp. 106–8, no. 121); 17.190.557 (ex coll. Charles Mannheim, J. Pierpont Morgan; Molinier 1898, no. 95 or 96; Corning 1958, p. 53, no. 34); and 53.225.95 (ex coll. Julia A. Berwind).
11. Kunstmuseum, 1975-1A; Ricke 1980, no. V-9; Venice 1982, pp. 106, 107, no. 119.
12. Sale, Sotheby's, London, 28 June 1971, lot 164, ill.; Venice 1982, p. 108, under no. 122.

Venice, ca. 1500–1525

7. Armorial tazza

1975.1.1189
H. 5.8 cm, diam. of rim 23.6 cm. Colorless (slightly gray) nonlead glass. Blown, enameled, gilt.

The shallow, circular bowl has curved sides and a slightly depressed center. On the exterior just below the rim is a band of overlapping scribed gilt ovals, each containing a ring of white enamel dots encircling a single white dot, the band flanked above by two rows of enamel dots, white over blue, and below by a row of gilt stripes between a row of blue dots and a row of white dots arranged more or less in triangles. On the interior below the scale band are six gilt and enameled quatrefoil motifs with red-and-yellow centers and petals of green, yellow, and blue dots highlighted with yellow-orange arcs. At the center on the interior is an unidentified enameled shield within a gilt and enameled foliate wreath, each leaf of which is embellished with a green enamel dot, tied with red enamel bands and four scribed gilt bands with blue and white dots: or, a cross azure, charged with five mullets of eight points or, in the first and the fourth quarter an eagle's head sable. The short pedestal foot has a gilt underfolded rim. Rough pontil mark under the foot.[1]

Short annealing crack on the foot near the pontil mark; normal wear on the foot rim.

Longwave fluorescence. Glass: creamy yellowish. Enamels: white = pinkish tan, yellow-orange = strong purplish red (very reflective of UV), blue = dark blue, red = dark red, green = black. *Shortwave fluorescence.* Glass: faint, creamy. Enamels: white = purplish white, yellow-orange = dark orange, blue = dark blue, green = dark blue, red = dark red. Gilding: strong greenish gray.

PROVENANCE: Rothschild (Galerie Fischer sale 1937, lot 482, pl. 32); Otto Hopfinger, New York; [Blumka Gallery, New York].

The enamels were applied over the gilding. The strong oval form of the enamel dots and the granulation of the gilding near the rim indicate that the rim was flared considerably after the gilding and enamels were applied. The dots in the wreath inside the bowl are circular (see detail

No. 7

No. 7, *shield in center of bowl*

No. 7, *detail of rim*

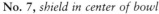ills.). The red and yellow enamel dots in the quatrefoil motifs are granular, apparently because they were not heated enough to fuse them. The wear on the gilding on the foot rim is probably due to its being underfired when the enamels on the bowl were fired; it is not cold gilding.

A large number of tazzas and bowls with enameled coats of arms are known. Early sixteenth-century Venetian tazzas like this one, with similar enameled decoration, gilt scale borders, and gilt wreath designs, are in the British Museum, London;[2] the Metropolitan Museum (two examples);[3] the Museo Vetrario, Murano;[4] the Victoria and Albert Museum, London (six examples);[5] and the New Orleans Museum of Art.[6] Two others were in the Émile Gavet collection, Paris.[7] On most of these tazzas, as on this one, the red and yellow enamels are gritty and underfired, and the gilding on the foot is less well fired than that on the rim.

Because so many of the shields on these objects are crudely painted and badly fired, and because so few of them have been identified,[8] Honey has suggested that they were later additions.[9] The theory that shields were added in the nineteenth century to genuine Renaissance dishes is difficult to accept on technical grounds, however. The bowls of tazzas like this were flared considerably while they were being fired to fuse the enamels. The gilding

and enamels were applied after the tazza was blown and cooled slowly to anneal the glass and reduce strains. The bowl was at that point much more straight sided, so that the enameler was forced to reach awkwardly inside a fairly narrow cylinder to paint the coat of arms. This tazza's bowl, for example, was probably originally about eighteen centimeters in diameter and slightly less in height, judging by the transition of curvature in its center. Furthermore, the enamels themselves were extremely powdery and fragile until they were fired. They tended to flow unevenly from the brush and were easily smudged. The gold leaf, by contrast, was presumably applied to a fixative, making it much easier to work with and allowing designs like the wreath on this tazza to be carefully scribed.

After being gilded and enameled, the tazza was carefully reheated in the annealing oven and attached with a tiny wad of molten glass to a pontil in the center of the foot, directly under the shield. The bowl was then introduced carefully into the glory hole. When the tazza was eventually subjected to the full heat of the furnace, the rim reached the highest temperature. Because the pontil conducted heat away from the glass, the bottom of the bowl and the foot, the area where the pontil was attached, were the coolest parts of the dish. The enamels in the shield were thus the least likely to fuse adequately, and the gilding on the foot was less well fired than that on the rim.

That it would be extremely dangerous to heat Renaissance glass to the firing temperature of enamels is another reason to doubt that the shields on these tazzas are recent additions. Reheating the Lehman tazza without shattering the glass would in fact be impossible, for it has a short crack in the foot that emanates from a large stone alongside the pontil mark. Although we cannot of course be certain when this crack appeared, the glass is most likely to have cracked during the annealing process, after the enameling was fired. There is no evidence to suggest that the tazza was ever fired in a kiln, and it is highly unlikely that anyone would have used a pontil to fire the coat of arms in the late nineteenth century or after. Moreover, neither the Lehman tazza nor the related tazzas that have been examined show any inconsistency between the ultraviolet fluorescence of the enamels on the rim and that of those inside the bowl.

Gilt foliate wreaths similar to that on the Lehman tazza were used to embellish a pale amethyst beaker excavated

in the 1980s in Great Tower Street in London that has been dated to the late fifteenth or early sixteenth century.[10] Wreaths like this are also found on a blue beaker in the British Museum[11] and an extraordinary goblet in the Tiroler Landesmuseum Ferdinandeum, Innsbruck (Fig. 7.1), on which an intricate inscription is painted in enamel on an elaborate pattern of interlaced bands.[12]

NOTES:

1. The following labels have been removed and are in the Robert Lehman Collection files: Unidentified: rectangular blue and white paper label printed *ANNEXE* / *N°* in white and *516* in black. Robert Lehman collection: circular white paper label with *25.* typed in black; rectangular gold metallic paper label printed *25* in black.

2. British Museum, S.373 (ex coll. Felix Slade; with the arms of the Colombini of Siena); Nesbitt 1871, p. 72, no. 373; Tait 1979, p. 34, no. 16.

3. Metropolitan Museum, 81.8.171 (ex coll. James Jackson Jarves; with an unidentified coat of arms), 17.190.556 (ex coll. Charles Mannheim, J. Pierpont Morgan; with an unidentified coat of arms); Molinier 1898, no. 97.

4. Museo Vetrario, cl. VI, n. 477 (with the arms of the Zaguri of Venice); Gasparetto 1958, p. 84, fig. 47; Venice 1982, p. 100, no. 105.

5. Victoria and Albert Museum, C.2476-1910 (ex coll. Salting; with the arms of the Venturini[?]); C.175-1936 and C.5497-1859 (both with arms variously identified as Foscarini impaling Barberini or Gridacci impaling del Nero of Florence); C.5504-1859 (ex coll. J. Soulages; with an unidentified coat of arms; see Honey 1946, p. 61, pl. 23C); C.5489-1859 (ex coll. J. Soulages; with an unidentified coat of arms; see Nesbitt 1878, p. 73; Corning 1958, pp. 58–59, no. 46); C.176-1936 (ex coll. Wilfred Buckley; with the arms of Frederico da Sanseverino, cardinal priest from 1489 to 1517, or Antonio III Sanseverino, cardinal priest from 1527 to 1543; see Buckley 1939, p. 247, no. 134, pl. 23).

6. New Orleans Museum of Art, B248A (ex coll. Melvin Billups; with the arms of France); Corning 1962, p. 27, no. 37.

7. Gavet sale 1897, lots 612, 617 (with arms identified as those of the Grimani of Venice and the Sforza of Cotignola, respectively).

8. A note in the Robert Lehman Collection files incorrectly identifies the arms on this tazza as those of the city of Florence.

9. Honey 1946, p. 61.

10. See Meyer 1992, p. 64. I am indebted to Wendy Evans of the London Museum for bringing this recent discovery to my attention.

11. Tait 1991, p. 158, fig. 199.

12. Mariacher 1963, p. 51.

Fig. 7.1 Goblet. Tiroler Landesmuseum Ferdinandeum, Innsbruck

Venice, ca. 1500–1525

8. Tazza

1975.1.1191
H. 6.1 cm, diam. of rim 25.1 cm. Colorless (slightly gray) nonlead glass. Blown, enameled, gilt.

The shallow, circular bowl has curved sides. On the exterior just below the rim is a band of scribed gilt scales, each with a red-and-white enamel dot, flanked by two rows of blue-and-white dots and two rows of red-and-white dots. In the center of the bowl, in a roundel framed by ragged blue and white circles and a ring of white dots, a man in a red coat, yellow leggings, blue boots, and a yellow and blue hat sits next to a tree, with a bull lying on the grass beside him. The pedestal foot has an underfolded rim. Two rough pontil marks, one over the other, under the foot.[1]

Long arc-shaped annealing crack on the foot; normal wear on the foot rim.

Longwave fluorescence. Glass: strong yellow-green. Enamels: white = pinkish white, blue = dark blue, orange = dark orange, green = light green, gray = gray, red = red. *Shortwave fluorescence.* Glass: faint, creamy. Enamels: white = bright bluish white, yellowish ground = muddy yellow-green, blue = muddy blue, orange = muddy orange, green = muddy green, gray = muddy gray, red = muddy red.

PROVENANCE: Eugen Miller von Aichholz, Vienna (Miller von Aichholz sale 1925, lot 37, pl. 6); Otto Hopfinger, New York; [Blumka Gallery, New York].

The dots on the rim are oval, indicating the degree to which the rim was flared after the enamels were applied. Most of the enamels in the roundel, particularly the yellow, which is flaking off, are underfired and granular. The green is bubbled and pockmarked, probably because it was overheated, essentially to its boiling point. The bull is backed with gray enamel that is visible from the underside. There are brown specks under the green enamel.

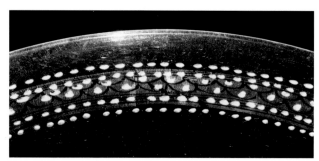

No. 8, *detail of rim*

No. 8, *detail of center of bowl*

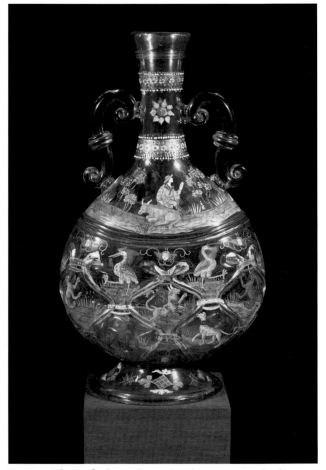

Fig. 8.1 Pilgrim flask. Wadsworth Atheneum, Hartford, J. Pierpont Morgan Collection

No. 8

A great deal of Renaissance Venetian glass with enameled pastoral scenes or animals in roundels has survived (see also No. 14). A scene very much like that on the Lehman tazza encircles the upper part of the body of a monumental pilgrim flask in the Wadsworth Atheneum, Hartford (Fig. 8.1).[2] A tazza with a plain bowl (that is, without ribbing) with a male figure astride a hippocampus is in the Victoria and Albert Museum, London,[3] and others with depictions of animals are in the Louvre, Paris (with deer);[4] the Uměleckoprůmyslové Muzeum, Prague (with a swan);[5] the Museo Civico d'Arte Antica, Turin (with a stork);[6] the Museum für Kunsthandwerk, Frankfurt am Main (with a doe);[7] the Royal Museum of Scotland, Edinburgh (with a doe resting in the sun's rays);[8] the Museo Nazionale della Ceramica "Duca di Martina," Naples (with a bird in the sun's rays);[9] and a private collection in Switzerland (with a pelican in the sun's rays).[10] Four such tazzas – two with lions, one with a horse, and one with two grotesques – were once, like the Lehman tazza, owned by Eugen Miller von Aichholz in Vienna and have not been published since his collection was sold in 1925.[11] The tazza with grotesques was in the collection of Émile Gavet in Paris in the nineteenth century, along with another similar example, with a fantastic bird

basking in the sun's rays, whose present whereabouts are also not known.[12]

NOTES:
1. A rectangular gold metallic paper label printed 27 in black (Robert Lehman collection) has been removed and is in the Robert Lehman Collection files.
2. Wadsworth Atheneum, 1917.336 (ex coll. J. Pierpont Morgan); Wadsworth Atheneum 1958, p. 40; Perrot 1968, p. 430, fig. 8; Lanmon 1978, pp. 16, 17, no. 1; *Glass Collections* 1982, ill. p. 69.
3. Victoria and Albert Museum, c.2478.1910 (ex coll. Frédéric Spitzer); Garnier 1891, p. 101, no. 55; d'Hondt [1893?], p. 105; Spitzer sale 1893, lot 2036, pl. 50.
4. Louvre, OA1976 (ex coll. Campana).
5. Gavet sale 1897, lot 589; Miller von Aichholz sale 1925, lot 60, pl. 12; Hetteš 1960, pp. 34–35, fig. 7; Prague 1973, no. 12, fig. 9.
6. Museo Civico, 133VE; Mallè 1971, pp. 32, 33, fig. 6.
7. Museum für Kunsthandwerk, 13445/5882; Ohm 1975, p. 16, no. 11.
8. Royal Museum of Scotland, 1961.478; *JGS* 5 (1963), p. 147, fig. 29.
9. *Bulletin AIHV*, no. 9 (1981–83), p. 177, fig. 1.
10. Gavet sale 1897, lot 589.
11. Miller von Aichholz sale 1925, lots 33, 42, 54, 46, pl. 6.
12. Gavet sale 1897, lots 583, 587.

Venice, ca. 1500

9. Bowl

1975.1.1176

H. 4.9 cm; diam. of rim 15.6 cm. Transparent dark blue nonlead glass. Blown, enameled, gilt.

Around the exterior of the shallow, circular bowl, which has curved sides and an everted rim, runs a band with two rows of scribed gilt scales, each embellished with three enamel dots (red, green, and blue) and outlined with curved rows of white dots, those in the lower row scraped with a six-toothed "comb"; the scale band is flanked above and below by a row of white dots arranged in triangles and a row of blue dots on gilt framing lines. At the bottom on the interior is a scribed gilt stylized flower composed of a central ring of blue dots enclosing scattered blue and white dots, two rows of rounded petals outlined with curved rows of white dots, and a row of pointed petals, all framed with a ring of blue enamel dots and a ring of white dots arranged in triangles on gilt bands. The bowl has a slight convex kick at its center and a trailed foot ring. Two rough pontil marks, one above the other, on the underside. Painted on the underside: L.56.31.65 (a Metropolitan Museum loan number) in red-orange; 21 in black.[1]

The gilding worn and scaling slightly on the exterior, heavily worn on the interior; wear on the foot rim.

Longwave fluorescence. Glass: dark greenish blue. Enamels: white = dark purplish tan, blue = dark blue, red = dark blue, green = dark blue. Gilding: bright yellowish, scummy. *Shortwave fluorescence.* Glass: muddy, opaque gray surface fluorescence. Enamels: white = strong light bluish white, blue = dark blue, red = inky blue, green = inky blue. Gilding: none.

PROVENANCE: Princes of Liechtenstein, Vaduz and Vienna(?);[2] Frédéric Spitzer, Paris (Spitzer sale 1893, lot 1992, ill.); Otto Hopfinger, New York; [Blumka Gallery, New York].

EXHIBITED: Corning 1958, pp. 56–57, no. 43, ill.; Cincinnati 1959, p. 42, no. 536.

LITERATURE: Garnier 1891, p. 94, no. 24, pl. 5; Roffia and Mariacher 1983, p. 173, under no. 38.

The gilding on the scale band on this bowl was very thickly applied, and the enamel dots are slightly oval. Although it is hard to see in the photograph, there are clearly two rough pontil marks on the underside. One scar overlaps the other slightly.

No. 9

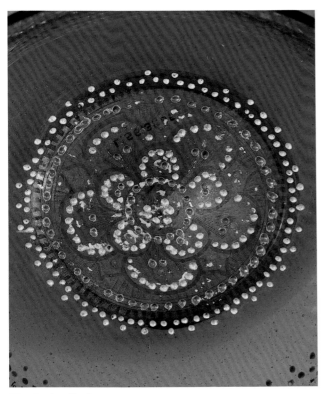

No. 9, *detail of center*

No. 9, *double pontil mark on underside*

No. 9, *detail of side*

The bowl has several Venetian parallels, all in colored glass with scale bands on the sides. Blue glass bowls with similar decoration are in the British Museum, London;[3] the Museo Civico d'Arte Antica, Turin;[4] the Museo Poldi Pezzoli, Milan;[5] the Museo Nazionale di San Martino, Naples;[6] and the Musée Jacquemart-André, Paris.[7] The elegant decoration lavished on such bowls implies that they were not simply small serving bowls but had far more important functions. For example, the Lehman bowl is similar in shape and size to the *lattimo* marriage bowl (*coppa nuziale*) known as the Rothschild bowl in the Corning Museum of Glass (Fig. 9.1)[8] and its companion in the Kunsthistorisches Museum, Vienna (Fig. 9.2).[9]

The elaborate stylized floral motif inside the Lehman bowl appears on a bowl in the Louvre, Paris (Fig. 9.3),[10] and on several other sixteenth-century Venetian glass bowls and tazzas, among them pieces in the Corning Museum of Glass;[11] the Bernd Hockemeyer collection, Bremen;[12] the Museo Nazionale di San Martino;[13] the Museum für Kunsthandwerk, Frankfurt am Main;[14] and the Victoria and Albert Museum, London.[15]

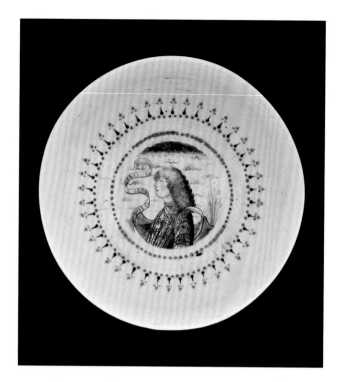

Fig. 9.1 Bowl (side and top views). Corning Museum of Glass

Fig. 9.2 Bowl (side and top views). Kunsthistorisches Museum, Vienna

NOTES:

1. The following labels have been removed and are in the Robert Lehman Collection files: Unidentified: oval orange paper label printed *547* in black. Robert Lehman collection: rectangular gold metallic paper label printed *46* in black.

2. According to a note in the Robert Lehman Collection files, this bowl was once in the collection of the princes of Liechtenstein, but that claim has not been verified.

3. British Museum, s.367 (ex coll. Felix Slade); Nesbitt 1871, p. 71, colorpl. 14, 2; no. 367; Vávra 1954, colorpl. 26; Tait 1979, pp. 34–35, no. 18.

4. Museo Civico d'Arte Antica, 169VE; Mallè 1971, pp. 28–29, fig. 3.

5. Museo Poldi Pezzoli, 1223; Mariacher 1961, pl. 32; Mariacher 1963, p. 46, figs. A, B; Mariacher 1964, pl. 3, bottom; *Bulletin AIHV*, no. 9 (1981–83), p. 58, fig. 1;

Fig. 9.3 Bowl. Musée du Louvre, Paris. Photograph: Réunion des Musées Nationaux

Barovier Mentasti 1982, p. 73, fig. 53; Roffia and Mariacher 1983, p. 173, no. 38, pl. 38; Zecchin 1987–89, vol. 2, p. 34.

6. Museo Nazionale di San Martino, 743; Causa Picone 1967, pp. 28–30; *Bulletin AIHV*, no. 9 (1981–83), p. 171, fig. 1.
7. Omodeo [1970], p. 20, fig. 20.
8. Corning Museum of Glass, 76.3.17 (ex coll. Albert von Parpart, Rothschild); Von Parpart sale 1884, lot 436; Clarke 1974, p. 51, no. C5; Charleston 1980a, pp. 86–87, no. 35; *Glass Collections* 1982, pp. 50–51, fig. F; Strasser and Spiegl 1989, p. 29, fig. 29.
9. Kunsthistorisches Museum, 9052 (ex coll. Gustav von Benda); Clarke 1974, pp. 50–51, no. C4; Venice 1982, p. 97, no. 100.
10. Louvre, OA1103.
11. Corning Museum of Glass, 51.3.117 (ex coll. Eugen Miller von Aichholz); Corning 1955, p. 28, no. 20; Corning 1958, pp. 52–54, no. 36; Gardner 1979, p. 32, pl. 7.
12. Ex coll. Fritz Biemann; Lucerne 1981, p. 154, no. 653.
13. Museo Nazionale di San Martino, 772; Causa Picone 1967, pp. 36–37.
14. Ohm 1973, p. 65, no. 120.
15. Victoria and Albert Museum, C.172-1936 (ex coll. Wilfred Buckley); Buckley 1926, pp. 35–36, pl. 7A; Buckley 1939, p. 247, no. 130, pl. 22.

Venice, ca. 1500–1525

10. Footed bowl

1975.1.1185
H. 17 cm, diam. of rim 26.7 cm. Transparent dark blue nonlead glass. Blown, enameled, gilt.

The exterior of the rounded sides of the circular bowl, which has an everted, outfolded rim with traces of gilding, is decorated with six rows of scribed gilt scales, each scale scraped with a six-toothed "comb," embellished with three enamel dots (blue, green, and red), and outlined with curved rows of pink dots; the band of scale pattern is framed above and below by a row of pink enamel dots arranged in triangles and a row of blue enamel dots on gilt framing lines. Stylized leaves painted in thick green enamel and emanating from a brick-red enamel band encircle the tall, trumpet-shaped pedestal foot, which has a trailed rim. Two large rough pontil marks, one over the other, under the foot. Painted in red-orange on the underside of the bowl: L.56.31.52 (a Metropolitan Museum loan number).[1]

Light wear on the top and side of the bowl rim; the gilding worn and heavily rubbed; heavy wear on the foot rim.

Longwave fluorescence. Glass: none (purple reflection). Enamels: pink = tan, red = dark red, green = tan, blue = dark blue.
Shortwave fluorescence. Glass: none. Enamels: pink = brilliant bluish white, red = dark tan, green = black, blue = black.

PROVENANCE: Rothschild (Galerie Fischer sale 1937, lot 495, pl. 37); Otto Hopfinger, New York; [Blumka Gallery, New York].

EXHIBITED: Corning 1958, pp. 55–57, no. 40, ill.; Cincinnati 1959, p. 42, no. 539; New York 1983–84; New York 1984.

LITERATURE: Davidson 1958, ill.; Roffia and Mariacher 1983, p. 173, under no. 42; Klesse and Mayr 1987, under no. 11.

No. 10

Judging by the very slight transition in the shapes of the enamel dots, from circular to slightly oval at the rim, and the fact that the gilt scale band shows very little granulation, there was little inflation or flaring after the enameling and gilding were applied to the bowl.

Bowls of this form were made in Venice from at least the mid-fifteenth century onward, in both colorless (see No. 11) and colored glass decorated with enameled scenes or with gilt and enameled scale or diaper patterns. Among them are the famous blue "Barovier" *coppa nuziale* (mar-

riage bowl) of about 1460–70 in the Museo Vetrario, Murano, which is decorated with enameled scenes traditionally attributed to Angelo Barovier,[2] and the blue bowl of about 1490–1500 in the Cleveland Museum of Art, which has a frieze of putti playing musical instruments.[3] Colored glass bowls with gilt and enameled scale bands like that on the Lehman bowl are in the Louvre, Paris (Fig. 10.1);[4] the Victoria and Albert Museum, London (Fig. 10.2);[5] and the Hermitage, Saint Petersburg (Fig. 10.3).[6] Two others were sold in Paris in the late 1800s, one from the collection of Émile Gavet,[7] the other from the collection of Frédéric Spitzer.[8] A similar bowl deco-

No. 10, *detail of side of bowl*

Fig. 10.1 Footed bowl. Musée du Louvre, Paris. Photograph: Réunion des Musées Nationaux

rated with a diaper rather than a scale pattern is in the Metropolitan Museum.[9] When it is not heavily rubbed, as it is here, the gilding on these colored bowls stands out dramatically.

Similar bands of gilt and enameled scales were also used to decorate small bowls (see No. 9), goblets, and ewers made of colored glass.[10]

NOTES:

1. The following labels have been removed and are in the Robert Lehman Collection files: Unidentified: oval orange paper label printed *546* in black; circular white paper label printed *829* in black. Robert Lehman collection: rectangular gold metallic paper label printed 2 in black; circular gummed paper label with 2. typed in black.
2. Museo Vetrario, cl. VI, n. 1; Venice 1982, pp. 74–78, no. 65.
3. Cleveland Museum of Art, 60.38 (ex coll. Charles Stein, Maurice de Rothschild); ibid., p. 81, no. 71. For another such bowl, see Mariacher 1963, p. 56.
4. Louvre, R34 (ex coll. Rothschild).
5. Victoria and Albert Museum, c.164-1936 (ex coll. Alessandro Castellani, Lebeuf de Montgermont, Wilfred Buckley); Castellani sale 1884, lot 415; L[ebeuf] de M[ontgermont] sale 1891, lot 273; Buckley 1939, p. 246, no. 123, pl. 20.
6. Hermitage, K.2062.
7. Gavet sale 1897, lot 621.
8. Garnier 1891, p. 92, no. 16, pl. 5; Spitzer sale 1893, lot 1984, pl. 49.
9. Metropolitan Museum, 17.190.731 (ex coll. Charles Mannheim, J. Pierpont Morgan); Molinier 1898, no. 92.
10. See, for example, Venice 1982, pp. 78–79, no. 66 (a blue goblet in the Bernd Hockemeyer collection, Bremen), and p. 79, no. 69 (a blue ewer in an unnamed private collection).

Fig. 10.2 Footed bowl. Victoria and Albert Museum, London. By courtesy of the Board of Trustees of the Victoria and Albert Museum

Fig. 10.3 Footed bowl. Hermitage, Saint Petersburg

Venice, ca. 1500–1525

11. Footed bowl

1975.1.1186
H. 16.4 cm, diam. of rim 25.4 cm. Colorless (strong grayish tan), bubbly nonlead glass. Blown, enameled, gilt.

The deep, circular bowl has rounded sides and a slightly everted, outfolded gilt rim. The exterior is decorated with a wide scribed gilt band with six rows of scales, those in the lower five rows scraped with a six-toothed "comb," decorated with blue, green, and red dots and outlined with curved rows of pink dots; the scale band is flanked by rows of white dots arranged in triangles and rows of blue dots on gilt framing lines. The heavy, trumpet-shaped pedestal foot has a trailed, gilt rim. Rough pontil mark under the foot. Painted in red-orange under the foot: *L.56.31.53* (a Metropolitan Museum loan number).[1]

Heavy wear on the interior and rim of the bowl and on the foot rim.

Longwave fluorescence. Glass: strong yellow-green. Enamels: white = tan, pink = tan, red = inky blue, blue = inky blue, green = inky blue. *Shortwave fluorescence.* Glass: faint orange-tan. Enamels: white = brilliant bluish white, pink = stronger bluish white, red = dark red, blue = dark inky blue, green = dark green.

PROVENANCE: Otto Hopfinger, New York; [Blumka Gallery, New York].

EXHIBITED: Cincinnati 1959 (not in catalogue).

No. 11, *detail of side of bowl*

The gilding is unusually heavy. The gilding on the foot was poorly fired and is wearing off. Many of the white dots have a pinkish tint, presumably because the gold leaf dissolved into the enamel during firing. The oval dots on the scale border and rim indicate that the bowl was narrower when the enamels were applied.

A relatively common form in Renaissance Venetian enameled glass, this bowl has several recorded parallels. Similar bowls and tazzas are in the Metropolitan Museum;[2] the Museo Vetrario, Murano (two examples);[3] the Museo Civico, Brescia;[4] the Victoria and Albert Museum, London;[5] the Corning Museum of Glass;[6] the British Museum, London;[7] the Württembergisches Landesmuseum, Stuttgart;[8] the Museo Poldi Pezzoli, Milan (two examples);[9] and a private collection in Basel.[10] The present location of two others, one of them formerly in the Alessandro Castellani collection, Rome, and the Lebeuf de Montgermont collection, is unknown.[11]

NOTES:
1. A rectangular gold metallic paper label printed *3* in black (Robert Lehman collection) has been removed and is in the Robert Lehman Collection files.
2. Metropolitan Museum, 17.190.549 (ex coll. Charles Mannheim, J. Pierpont Morgan); Molinier 1898, no. 93.
3. Museo Vetrario, cl. VI, n. 63 (with unidentified arms); and cl. VI, n. 477 (with the arms of the Zaguri of Venice); Lorenzetti [1953], pl. 49; Mariacher 1954, p. 52, fig. 43; Gasparetto 1958, p. 84, fig. 47; Mariacher 1964, pl. 4; Schack 1976, p. 231, fig. 109; Venice 1982, p. 100, no. 105.
4. Museo Civico, 41; Brescia 1987, pp. 111, 116, no. 4b.
5. Victoria and Albert Museum, C.163-1936 (ex coll. Wilfred Buckley); Buckley 1939, p. 246, no. 122, pl. 21; Savage 1965, fig. 29.
6. Corning Museum of Glass, 60.3.88.
7. Ex coll. Felix Slade; Nesbitt 1871, pp. 71, 72, no. 370, fig. 84; Vávra 1954, p. 99, fig. 85.
8. Ex coll. Ernesto Wolf; Klesse and Mayr 1987, no. 11.
9. Roffia and Mariacher 1983, p. 173, nos. 42, 43, pls. 42, 43.
10. Basel 1988, no. 3.
11. Lubin [1959?], pp. [22–23]; L[ebeuf] de M[ontgermont] sale 1891, lot 273.

No. 11

Venice, ca. 1500–1525

12. Footed bowl

1975.1.1197

H. 16.2 cm, diam. of rim 27.9 cm. Colorless (purplish gray) nonlead glass. Blown, pattern molded, enameled, gilt.

Around the lower half of the rounded sides of the circular bowl, which has a slightly everted, outfolded rim, are twelve molded ribs with gilding along their entire length; above the ribs on the exterior is a band of three rows of scribed gilt scales, each embellished with three enamel dots (blue, green, and red) and outlined with curved rows of white dots, those in the lower two rows scraped with a five-toothed "comb"; the scale band is flanked above and below by a row of blue dots on gilt framing lines and a row of white dots arranged in triangles. The trumpet-shaped pedestal foot has sixteen ribs, with traces of gilding, and a trailed foot rim. Two rough pontil marks, one over the other, under the foot.[1]

Small bubble broken inside the bowl, which is etched; heavy wear on the bowl rim, the foot rim, and the gilding on the foot.

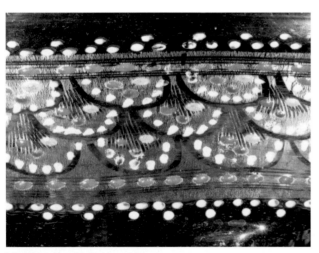

No. 12, *detail of side of bowl*

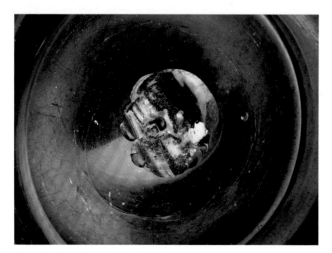

No. 12, *double pontil mark under foot*

Fig. 12.1 Footed bowl. Musée National de la Renaissance, Château d'Écouen. Photograph: Réunion des Musées Nationaux

Longwave fluorescence. Glass: brilliant yellow-green. Enamels: white = pinkish tan, red = dark red, blue = black, green = dark blue. Gilding: scummy. *Shortwave fluorescence.* Glass: faint orange-tan. Enamels: white = strong bluish white, red = inky blue, blue = inky blue, green = inky green. Gilding: nothing.

PROVENANCE: Otto Hopfinger, New York; [Blumka Gallery, New York].

LITERATURE: Haynes 1959, fig. 14b(?).

The ribbing on the bowl was formed on a second gather that ends at the tops of the ribs. The enamel dots in the scale band are slightly oval and the gilt band is granular, indicating that there was some shaping of the rim after the decoration was applied. The double pontil mark is especially clear on this bowl. The first pontil scar is concave; the second left glass behind and is slightly off center.

A number of Venetian footed bowls like Nos. 12 and 13, with vertical (rather than swirled) molded ribbing and enameled decoration, have been recorded. One of the most important of them is a bowl in the Musée National de la Renaissance, Château d'Écouen (Fig. 12.1), that bears the arms of Catherine de Médicis (1519–1589) impaled by the arms of France and can presumably be dated to the middle of the sixteenth century, perhaps to 1533, the year of her marriage to the duke of Orléans,

No. 12

who became King Henry II of France in 1547.[2] Other examples are in the Louvre, Paris;[3] the Museo Vetrario, Murano;[4] the Museo Civico d'Arte Antica, Turin;[5] the Rheinisches Landesmuseum, Bonn;[6] the Museo Civico Cristiano, Brescia;[7] the National Museums and Galleries on Merseyside, Liverpool;[8] the Vito Manca collection, Perugia;[9] the Österreichisches Museum für Angewandte Kunst, Vienna;[10] the Kunstgewerbemuseum, Berlin;[11] the Kunstindustrimuseet, Copenhagen;[12] the Victoria and Albert Museum, London;[13] the Museum Boymans-van Beuningen, Rotterdam;[14] the Musée du Verre, Liège;[15] the Metropolitan Museum (four examples);[16] and the Kunstsammlungen der Veste Coburg.[17] Still others were formerly in the Kunstgewerbemuseum, Berlin;[18] the A. de Frey collection, Paris;[19] the Helfried Krug collection, Mülheim;[20] the Eugen Miller von Aichholz collection, Vienna;[21] the Frédéric Spitzer collection, Paris;[22] the Max Strauss collection, Vienna;[23] and the Somzée collection, Brussels(?).[24]

NOTES:

1. The following labels have been removed and are in the Robert Lehman Collection files: Robert Lehman collection: rectangular gold metallic paper label printed 79 in black; gummed circular white paper label with 79. typed in black. Metropolitan Museum: rectangular white paper label with L.56.31.75 (a loan number) typed in red.

2. Musée National de la Renaissance, R100; "Le verre," *Métiers d'art*, no. 8 (July 1979), p. 12; Erlande-Brandenburg 1987, p. 177, fig. 52; Bellanger 1988, p. 323.

3. Louvre, R9, R15 (ex coll. Rothschild; R15 probably also ex coll. Adalbert von Lanna); see Lanna sale 1911, lot 700, pl. 62.

4. Lorenzetti [1953], pl. 50; Barovier Mentasti 1982, p. 68, fig. 47.

5. Museo Civico d'Arte Antica, 129 VE; Mallè 1971, p. 34, fig. 10.

6. W. Bremen 1964, pp. 368–71, no. 180; Fritz 1964, p. 22, fig. 5.

7. Museo Civico Cristiano, 37 (ex coll. Brozzoni); Mariacher 1965a, p. 19; Venice 1982, p. 85, no. 77; Brescia 1987, pp. 111, 115, no. 3b.

8. National Museums and Galleries on Merseyside, 10.8.76.1; Gatty 1883, no. 201; Liverpool 1979, p. 38, no. D1.
9. Mariacher 1971, p. 25, no. 34.
10. Schlosser 1951, p. 9, pl. 3; Mariacher 1963, p. 60.
11. Kunstgewerbemuseum, 1976,11; Dreier 1989b, pp. 46–47, no. 15, pl. 8.
12. Boesen 1950, fig. 8.
13. Victoria and Albert Museum, C.5492-1859.
14. Isings 1966, p. 65, fig. 47.
15. Musée du Verre, Baar 1058 (ex coll. Frédéric Spitzer, Armand Baar); Garnier 1891, p. 93, no. 19; Spitzer sale 1893, lot 1986; Liège 1958, pp. 126, 127, no. 260; *Bulletin AIHV*, no. 5 (1967–70), p. 75, fig. 78; Philippe 1973, p. 28, fig. 4.

16. Metropolitan Museum, 81.8.172 (ex coll. James Jackson Jarves), 91.1.1420 (ex coll. Edward C. Moore), 91.1.1432 (ex coll. Edward C. Moore), 17.190.553 (ex coll. J. Pierpont Morgan).
17. Kunstsammlungen der Veste Coburg, HA284.
18. Schmidt 1912, p. 94, fig. 57; Schmidt 1922, p. 96, fig. 58.
19. De Frey sale 1933, lot 179, pl. 19.
20. Klesse 1973, pp. 102, 103, no. 472; Krug sale 1981–83, part 1, lot 40.
21. Miller von Aichholz sale 1925, lot 56, pl. 14.
22. Garnier 1891, p. 93, no. 20; d'Hondt [1893?], p. 88; Spitzer sale 1893, lot 2033, pl. 49.
23. Strauss sale 1920, pl. 2; Strauss sale 1925, lot 346.
24. Somzée sale 1904, lot 1185, pl. 85.

Venice, ca. 1500–1525

13. Footed bowl

1975.1.1184
H. 18 cm, diam. of rim 29.4 cm. Colorless (slightly gray) nonlead glass. Blown, pattern molded, enameled, gilt.

Around the lower half of the rounded sides of the deep, circular bowl, which has a slightly everted, outfolded rim, are twelve molded ribs with gilding along their entire length. Above the ribs on the exterior is a band of two rows of scribed gilt scales, each embellished with an enamel dot (blue, green, or red, arranged to form diagonal rows of matching colors) and outlined with curved rows of white dots, those in the lower row scraped with a six-toothed "comb"; the scale band is flanked above and below by a row of blue dots on gilt framing lines and a row of white dots arranged in triangles. The trumpet-shaped pedestal foot has sixteen ribs, with traces of gilding, and a trailed foot rim. Two rough pontil marks, one over the other, under the foot. Painted in red-orange under the foot: L.56.31.75 (a Metropolitan Museum loan number).[1]

Bubble broken at the end of one rib; thin, irregular bubble broken inside the bowl; heavily etched band inside the bowl at the level of the gilt band; heavy wear on the bowl and foot rims.

Longwave fluorescence. Glass: brilliant yellow-green. Enamels: white = pinkish, green = dark green, blue = dark blue, red = dark red. *Shortwave fluorescence.* Glass: faint, creamy, slightly orange. Enamels: white = strong bluish white, blue and red = inky blue, blue = inky blue, green = inky green. Gilding on ribs: bluish white.

PROVENANCE: Otto Hopfinger, New York; [Blumka Gallery, New York].

The ribbing on the bowl was formed on a second gather that ends at the tops of the ribs.

No. 13, *detail of side of bowl*

Except that the gilt scale band is narrower, in form and details this bowl is almost identical to No. 12. For a discussion of similar bowls, see No. 12.

NOTE:
1. A round white paper label with 1. typed in black (Robert Lehman collection) has been removed and is in the Robert Lehman Collection files.

No. 13

Venice, ca. 1500–1525

14. Tazza

1975.1.1188
H. 6.1 cm, diam. of rim 22.8 cm. Colorless (slightly gray),
bubbly nonlead glass. Blown, pattern molded, enameled, gilt.

The shallow, circular bowl has an everted rim, an underfolded
edge, and rounded sides with twenty ribs. On the exterior just
below the edge is a band of scribed gilt ovals, each containing a
ring of pink enamel dots encircling a single red dot, flanked by
two rows of light blue dots and two rows of white dots, with
additional red dots below arranged with the white to form
triangles. A trailed colorless thread encircles the exterior above
the ribbing. In the center of the bowl, in a roundel framed with
a gilt border and a ring of white enamel dots, a fabulous
horned animal, painted in white enamel with pink highlights,
stands amid polychrome foliage, his right leg resting on a leafy
cornucopia. The pedestal foot has an underfolded rim. Two
rough pontil marks, one over the other, under the foot.[1]

Normal wear on the foot rim.

Longwave fluorescence. Glass: strong yellow-green. Enamels:
white = pinkish, yellow-orange = dark red, pink = purplish,
turquoise = dark blue, blue = dark blue, green = dark green.
Shortwave fluorescence. Glass: faint, creamy. Enamels: white
= bright bluish white, yellow-orange = orange, pink = bright
bluish white, the animal = purple, the foliage = dark red and
dark blue.

PROVENANCE: Émile Gavet, Paris (Gavet sale 1897, lot 593);
John Edward Taylor, London (Taylor sale 1912, lot 341);
George Eumorfopoulos, London (Eumorfopoulos sale 1940,
lot 216); Otto Hopfinger, New York; [Blumka Gallery, New
York].

Fig. 14.1 Tazza. British Museum, London. By courtesy of the
Trustees of the British Museum

EXHIBITED: London 1930, no. 9551; Corning 1958, pp. 52–53,
no. 35, ill.; Cincinnati 1959, p. 42, no. 541, ill.; New York
1975, p. 58, no. 61, ill.

LITERATURE: H. Read 1926, pp. 190, 191, fig. 6; Tait 1979, p.
31, under no. 9; Roffia and Mariacher 1983, p. 176, under no.
73.

No. 14, *detail of center of bowl*

No. 14, *detail of rim*

No. 14

The dots on the rim are oval and the gilding is granulated, indicating that the rim was flared after the enamels were fired. Nearly all of the light blue enamel dots in
the border are missing, leaving shiny pockmarks in their
places. The ribbing was molded on a second gather of
glass, which stops at the tops of the ribs.

Venetian footed bowls and tazzas with twenty radial ribs
and enameled decoration are relatively rare. Bowls with
forty molded ribs are far more common (see Nos. 1, 15,
16). The closest parallel to this tazza in both form and
(albeit less detailed) decoration is a tazza in the British

Museum, London (Fig. 14.1), that has a twenty-ribbed
bowl with a unicorn in a roundel at its center.[2] A stylized
enameled rosette and a border of gilt and enameled rings
decorate a related tazza in the Metropolitan Museum.[3]

NOTES:
1. The following labels have been removed and are in the Robert Lehman Collection files: Unidentified: oval orange paper
   label, printed 544 in black. Robert Lehman collection: rectangular gold metallic paper label printed 23 in black.
2. British Museum, s.378 (ex coll. Felix Slade); Nesbitt 1871,
   p. 73; Tait 1979, p. 31, no. 9.
3. Metropolitan Museum, 53.225.94 (ex coll. Julia A.
   Berwind).

Venice, ca. 1500–1525

15. Bowl

1975.1.1177
H. 4.6 cm, diam. of rim 21.6 cm. Colorless (slightly gray) and transparent bright green nonlead glass. Blown, pattern molded, enameled, gilt.

The shallow, circular bowl has curved sides; an everted, underfolded rim with a trailed green thread at the edge of the fold; and molded radial ribbing (forty ribs) on the bottom that extends partway up the sides. On the exterior just below the rim is a band of scribed gilt scales (arranged horizontally), those in the center with red dots and those on the edges with white dots. Above the scale band are a row of blue dots on gilt framing lines and a row of white dots; below it are a row of blue dots on a thin gilt band, a row of gilt rectangles, and a row of white and red dots arranged in triangles. A trailed colorless thread encircles the bowl above the squared ends of the ribbing. The bowl has a slight kick in the center and a trailed foot ring. Rough pontil mark on the underside.[1]

Slight wear on the rim; heavy wear on the foot ring.[2]

Longwave fluorescence. Glass: strong yellow-green. Enamels: white = pink, blue = purple, red = dark red. *Shortwave fluorescence.* Glass: strong, creamy. Enamels: white = strong bluish white, blue = dark inky blue, red = dark inky blue.

PROVENANCE: Oscar Bondy, Vienna(?); Otto Hopfinger, New York; [Blumka Gallery, New York].

EXHIBITED: Corning 1958, pp. 48–49, no. 30, ill.; Cincinnati 1959, p. 42, no. 540.

LITERATURE: Roffia and Mariacher 1983, p. 173, under no. 44; Klesse and Mayr 1987, under no. 8.

Fig. 15.1 Piero di Cosimo, *Madonna and Child*. Royal Collections, Stockholm

No. 15, *detail of rim*

No. 15, *top view*

No. 15

Although the ribs on this bowl seem at first glance to be spaced equally, there are actually slight variations. Scholars might be able to group related objects more accurately if they were to compare these variations on forty-ribbed bowls; bowls with identical variations in spacing were probably made in the same mold. The three bowls with forty ribs in the Robert Lehman Collection (Nos. 1, 15, 16) were patterned in three different molds. The ribbing on this bowl was formed on a second gather of glass that ends at the tops of the ribs. The dots at the rim are oval, indicating that it was flared after the enamel was applied.

Low, ribbed bowls like Nos. 15 and 16, on trailed foot rings and with rounded sides and either vertical or everted rims, are fairly common in Renaissance Venetian enameled glass. Such a bowl appears in the *Madonna and Child* in the Royal Collections, Stockholm, that Piero di Cosimo (ca. 1462–1521?) painted in the early sixteenth century (Fig. 15.1).[3] Similar bowls with forty radial ribs are in the Uměleckoprůmyslové Muzeum, Prague;[4] the Metropolitan Museum (two examples);[5] the Museo Civico

d'Arte Antica, Turin;[6] the Museo Civico, Bologna;[7] the Pinacoteca Ambrosiana, Milan;[8] the Kunstgewerbemuseum, Berlin;[9] Württembergisches Landesmuseum, Stuttgart;[10] the Kunstsammlungen der Veste Coburg (two examples);[11] the Kunstmuseum Düsseldorf;[12] the Museum für Kunsthandwerk, Frankfurt am Main;[13] the Victoria and Albert Museum, London (two examples);[14] the Museo Vetrario, Murano (two examples);[15] the Museum Boymans-van Beuningen, Rotterdam;[16] the Otto Dettmers collection, Bremen;[17] and a private collection in the Netherlands.[18] Another was in the Frédéric Spitzer collection, Paris.[19]

Forty-rib molds were also used on the bowls of tazzas. Two forty-ribbed tazzas that can be dated to the first quarter of the sixteenth century are in the British Museum, London. One, on a trumpet foot, bears the arms of Leonardo Loredan as doge (1501–21).[20] The other, on a low spreading foot, bears two coats of arms that have been identified as those of Fabricio Caretto, who was grand master of the Order of Saint John of Jerusalem from 1513 to 1521, and Musio Costanzo of Naples, who was admiral of the Order of Saint John and died in 1547.[21]

NOTES:

1. A rectangular gold metallic paper label printed *65* in black and a gummed circular paper label typed *68.* in black (both Robert Lehman collection) have been removed and are in the Robert Lehman Collection files. The *i8* once painted in white inside the bowl, perhaps while it was in the Bondy collection, is no longer visible.

2. A note in the Robert Lehman Collection files says that this bowl has "traces of gilding on the ribs"; there is no evidence of that gilding now.

3. Douglas 1946, pp. 74, 76, 86, 118, pl. 56.

4. Uměleckoprůmyslové Muzeum, 9629/1906 (ex coll. Adalbert von Lanna); Hetteš 1960, p. 34, fig. 4; Prague 1966–67, p. 42; Prague 1973, no. 10, fig. 7; Venice 1982, p. 89, no. 84.

5. Metropolitan Museum, 81.8.162 (ex coll. James Jackson Jarves), 53.225.99 (ex coll. Julia A. Berwind).

6. Museo Civico d'Arte Antica, 9VE (483); Mallè 1971, pp. 35–36, fig. 8.

7. Bologna 1959, p. 49, pl. 20, no. 127; Zecchin 1987–89, vol. 2, p. 35.

8. Zecchin 1987–89, vol. 2, p. 37.

9. Kunstgewerbemuseum, 1976,64 (ex coll. Walter F. Smith, Jr.); Dreier 1989b, p. 48, no. 16.

10. Ex coll. Ernesto Wolf; Klesse and Mayr 1987, no. 8.

11. Kunstsammlungen der Veste Coburg, HA283, HA287.

12. Kunstmuseum, 1940-29; Heinemeyer 1966, p. 77, no. 216; Jantzen 1960, p. 13, no. 3.

13. Museum für Kunsthandwerk, X17887/5008; Ohm 1973, p. 67, no. 124.

14. Ex coll. Wilfred Buckley; Buckley 1926, p. 36, figs. 8A, 8B; Honey 1946, p. 62, pl. 32C.

15. Zecchin 1957, p. 26; Zecchin 1987–89, vol. 1, p. 274.

16. Ex coll. Bodenheim; Van Gelder and Jansen 1969, p. 64, no. 47; Schrijver 1980, p. 41, fig. 18.

17. Düsseldorf 1968–69, p. 28, no. 60.

18. Laméris and Laméris 1991, pp. 48, 49, no. 3.

19. Garnier 1891, p. 93, no. 20, pl. 7; Spitzer sale 1893, lot 1988, pl. 50.

20. Lorenzetti 1931, pl. 8; Mariacher 1954, p. 57, fig. 48; Mariacher 1963, p. 63.

21. British Museum, s.374 (ex coll. Felix Slade); Nesbitt 1871, pp. 72–73; Tait 1979, pp. 30–31, no. 7.

Venice, ca. 1500–1525

16. Bowl

1975.1.1178

H. 3.3 cm, diam. of rim 19.4 cm. Colorless (slightly gray) and transparent amethyst nonlead glass. Blown, pattern molded, enameled, gilt.

The shallow, circular bowl has an everted, underfolded rim and molded radial ribbing (forty ribs) on the bottom that extends partway up the sides. On the exterior below the rim is a band of scribed gilt linked circles, each with a ring of pink enamel dots encircling a red dot. Above the band are a row of blue dots on gilt framing lines and a row of white dots; below it are a row of blue dots on a thin gilt band, a row of gilt rectangles, and a row of white dots arranged in triangles. A trailed amethyst thread encircles the bowl above the ribbing. The bowl has a slight kick in the center and a trailed foot ring. Two rough pontil marks, one above the other, on the underside.[1]

Broken in thirty-one pieces and several tiny fragments, with many chips and seven slightly larger pieces lost and about half the amethyst thread lost; restored in 1989.

Longwave fluorescence. Glass: brilliant yellow-green; amethyst thread = gray. Enamels: white = tan, blue = dark bluish purple, red = dark red. *Shortwave fluorescence.* Glass: faint, creamy; amethyst thread = nothing. Enamels: white = strong bluish white, blue = inky dark blue, red = inky dark blue.

PROVENANCE: Otto Hopfinger, New York; [Blumka Gallery, New York].

The ribbing on this bowl is very sharply defined. It was formed on a second gather that ends at the tops of the ribs.

For a discussion of similar bowls, see No. 15.

NOTE:

1. A rectangular gold metallic paper label printed *66* in black and a gummed circular paper label typed *66.* in black (both Robert Lehman collection) have been removed and are in the Robert Lehman Collection files.

No. 16

No. 16, *top view*

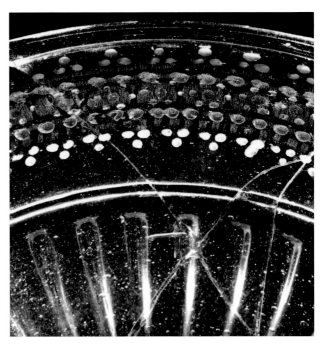

No. 16, *detail of rim*

Venice, ca. 1500–1525

17. Tazza

1975.1.1187

H. 5.3 cm, diam. of rim 23.1 cm. Colorless (slightly tan) nonlead glass. Blown, pattern molded, enameled, gilt.

On the exterior of the shallow, circular, diamond-molded bowl (twenty diamonds in a row) with slightly curved sides is a band of scribed gilt scales, each with a blue dot and framed by gilt linear bands and rows of white dots arranged in triangles. The short, trumpet-shaped pedestal foot has an underfolded rim. Two rough pontil marks, one over the other, under the foot.[1]

Chips on the rim; the gilding worn; wear on the foot rim.

Longwave fluorescence. Glass: strong yellow-green. Enamels: white = tan, blue = dark reddish purple. *Shortwave fluorescence.* Glass: faint, creamy. Enamels: white = brilliant bluish white, blue = dark inky blue.

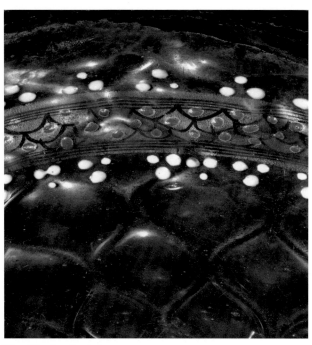

No. 17, *detail of rim*

PROVENANCE: Otto Hopfinger, New York; [Blumka Gallery, New York].

EXHIBITED: Corning 1958, pp. 62–63, no. 51, ill.; Cincinnati 1959, p. 42, no. 547.

The oval enamel dots indicate that the bowl was flared after the gilding and enamels were applied.

Related tazzas with diamond-molded bowls and enameled decoration are in the British Museum, London;[2] the Toledo Museum of Art (see Fig. 1.4);[3] the Victoria and Albert Museum, London;[4] and the Louvre, Paris (three examples). Another is in a private collection in the Netherlands,[5] and two others were in the Émile Gavet collection, Paris,[6] and the Eugen Miller von Aichholz collection, Vienna.[7]

NOTES:

1. The following labels have been removed and are in the Robert Lehman Collection files: Unidentified: oval bright orange paper label printed *548* in black. Robert Lehman collection: rectangular gold metallic paper label printed *24* in black. Metropolitan Museum: gummed rectangular white paper label typed *L.58.73.59* (a loan number) in red.
2. British Museum, s.376 (ex coll. Felix Slade); Nesbitt 1871, p. 73, no. 376; Tait 1979, p. 33, no. 14.
3. Toledo Museum of Art, 32.1; Garnier 1891, p. 101, no. 58; d'Hondt [1893?], p. 108; Spitzer sale 1893, lot 2037, pl. 49; Hutton 1963, p. [3]; Toledo Museum of Art 1969, p. 47.
4. Victoria and Albert Museum, C.2478-1910 (ex coll. Frédéric Spitzer); Garnier 1891, p. 92, no. 13, pl. 7; Spitzer sale 1893, lot 1981, pl. 49.
5. Laméris and Laméris 1991, p. 25, pl. 3.
6. Gavet sale 1897, lot 605.
7. Miller von Aichholz sale 1925, lot 48, pl. 10.

No. 17

Venice, ca. 1500–1525

18. Goblet

1975.1.1198

H. 32 cm, diam. of rim 8.2 cm. Colorless (slightly grayish tan) nonlead glass. Blown, pattern molded, enameled, gilt.

The tall, slightly flared, cylindrical bowl has a flared and folded flange at the base and a rounded bottom. Below the rim is a band of scribed gilt linked circles, each with a ring of pink enamel dots encircling either a dark red or a light blue dot, flanked above by a row of white dots and below by a band of gilt pelmets with dark red dots and a band of white dots and light blue dots arranged in triangles. At the base of the bowl is a band of scribed gilt scales, each with a light blue dot, flanked above by a row of pink dots and below by a band of gilt pelmets with dark red enamel dots and a band of pink dots and light blue dots arranged in triangles. Another band of scribed gilt scales, each with a green enamel dot, decorates the flange at the base. The stem has a short capstan, above a hollow gilt knop with fifteen slightly swirled ribs, above a short, straight section. The fifteen vertical ribs on the trumpet-shaped pedestal foot stop short of the trailed rim. Two rough pontil marks, one over the other, under the foot.[1]

The gilding worn; heavy wear on the foot rim but almost none on the rim of the bowl, which presumably once had a cover.

Longwave fluorescence. Glass: strong yellow-green. Enamels: white = tan, pink = brownish, red = red, blue = dark blue. *Shortwave fluorescence.* Glass: creamy. Enamels: white = strong bluish white, pink = strong bluish white, red = black, blue = soft blue. Gilding: scummy areas on ribs, perhaps the remnants of gilding.

PROVENANCE: Eugen Miller von Aichholz, Vienna (Miller von Aichholz sale 1925, lot 52, pl. 9); Frederic Neuburg, Vienna(?);[2] Otto Hopfinger, New York; [Blumka Gallery, New York].

No. 18, *detail of rim*

The form of the bowl did not change substantially after the enamel and gilding were applied. The enamel dots at the rim are circular, and the gilding is not granulated. Some of the enameling has flaked off, presumably because the firing was not adequate to make it adhere. The rim on the bowl is unusually thick. The two rough pontil marks, one over the other, can be clearly seen on this goblet.

No. 18, *detail of bottom of bowl*

No. 18, *double pontil mark under foot*

No. 18

The form and proportion of this glass, with its tall, slender, cylindrical bowl, suggests that it, like No. 19, may have been intended as a reliquary. Reliquary glasses of related proportion can be found in the Museo Vetrario, Murano (see Figs. 19.1, 19.3);[3] the J. Paul Getty Museum, Malibu;[4] the Corning Museum of Glass (see Fig. 19.5);[5] the British Museum, London (see Fig. 19.2);[6] and a private collection in Basel.[7] Vertical ribbing similar to that on the Lehman glass, stopping short of the foot rim, decorates a goblet in the Hermitage, Saint Petersburg (Fig. 18.1),[8] as well as one in the Österreichisches Museum für Angewandte Kunst, Vienna,[9] and another in the Kunstsammlungen der Veste Coburg.[10]

NOTES:
1. The following labels have been removed and are in the Robert Lehman Collection files: Unidentified: circular white paper label inscribed *400*(?) in pencil and *20* (no longer visible) in faded brown ink. Robert Lehman collection: rectangular gold metallic paper label printed *59* in black.
2. According to a note in the Robert Lehman Collection files, this glass was once in the Neuberg collection, but it is not included in Schmidt 1931.
3. See No. 19, note 2.
4. Corning 1958, p. 37, no. 14.
5. Corning Museum of Glass, 79.3.183, 79.3.226 (both ex coll. Jerome Strauss).
6. See No. 19, note 3.
7. Basel 1988, no. 5.
8. Hermitage, F.472; Kachalov 1959, fig. 64.
9. Schlosser 1951, p. 9, pl. 5; Schlosser 1965, p. 100, fig. 86.
10. Kunstsammlungen der Veste Coburg, HA35; Netzer 1986, fig. 1.

Fig. 18.1 Goblet. Hermitage, Saint Petersburg

Venice, ca. 1500

19. Goblet

1975.1.1163

H. 21.6 cm, diam. of rim 7.6 cm. Colorless (slightly gray) and transparent dark blue nonlead glass. Blown, pattern molded, gilt.

The cylindrical, straight-sided bowl has a flared, folded flange at the base and a flat bottom. The stem is formed of a colorless, slightly tapered, solid shank with a rounded disk at the base that is mounted on a gilt blue hollow ovoid knop with twelve ribs and a colorless capstan below it. The gilt blue trumpet-shaped pedestal foot also has twelve ribs, and a trailed colorless rim. Small rough pontil mark under the foot. Crudely scratched on the top of the foot: *Ň 4*; painted in white under the foot: *455*.[1]

Slight wear on the foot rim; probably once had a cover, now missing.

Longwave fluorescence. Colorless glass: strong yellow-green. Blue glass: faint olive green. *Shortwave fluorescence.* Colorless glass: faint, creamy. Blue glass: nothing (muddy greenish fluorescence on the underside of the foot).

PROVENANCE: Eugen Miller von Aichholz, Vienna (Miller von Aichholz sale 1925, lot 35, pl. 5); Otto Hopfinger, New York; [Blumka Gallery, New York].

EXHIBITED: Corning 1958, pp. 36–37, no. 13, ill.; Cincinnati 1959, p. 42, no. 537; New York 1984.

LITERATURE: Venice 1982, p. 104, under no. 115; Roffia and Mariacher 1983, p. 173, under no. 40; Dreier 1989b, p. 51, under no. 21.

No. 19

Similar goblets are in the Museo Vetrario, Murano (Figs. 19.1, 19.3; the latter with a diamond-molded, rather than ribbed, foot and knop);[2] the British Museum, London (Fig. 19.2; with a folded, rather than trailed, foot ring);[3] the Victoria and Albert Museum, London (Fig. 19.4; also with a folded foot rim);[4] the Corning Museum of Glass (Fig. 19.5);[5] the Kunstsammlungen der Veste Coburg;[6] and the Museo Poldi Pezzoli, Milan.[7] The form of the stem, with colorless sections above and below a gilt blue ribbed knop, is echoed on a bowl in the Toledo Museum of Art that is decorated with an enameled processional scene.[8]

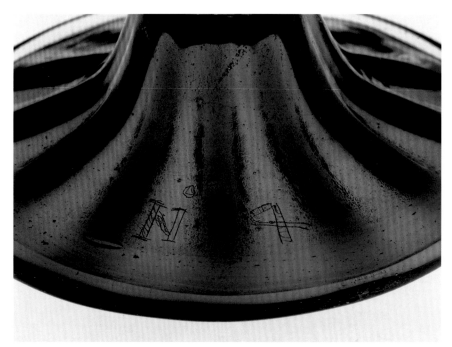

No. 19, *inscription on foot*

Fig. 19.1 Covered goblet. Museo Vetrario, Murano

Fig. 19.2 Covered goblet. British Museum, London.
By courtesy of the Trustees of the British Museum

Fig. 19.3 (left) Covered goblet. Museo Vetrario, Murano. Reproduced from Giulio Lorenzetti, *Murano e l'arte del vetro soffiato: Guida del Museo Vetrario di Murano* (Venice, [1953]) Fig. 19.4 (center) Goblet. Victoria and Albert Museum, London. By courtesy of the Board of Trustees of the Victoria and Albert Museum Fig. 19.5 (right) Goblet. Corning Museum of Glass, Bequest of Jerome Strauss

The protruding, folded flange at the base of the bowl suggests that this glass originally had a cover with a matching folded rim. Like No. 18, it may have been used as a reliquary. One of the goblets in Murano (Fig. 19.3) and the goblet in the British Museum (Fig. 19.2) have covers surmounted by crosses. (The cover now associated with the other goblet in Murano [Fig. 19.1] is probably not original.) The number diamond-engraved on the top of the foot of the Lehman goblet implies that it was one of a series of glasses for which specific identification was deemed important, reinforcing the idea that it is a reliquary. None of the related goblets, however, have numbers inscribed on their feet.

NOTES:

1. The following labels have been removed and are in the Robert Lehman Collection files: Unidentified: oval orange paper label printed *538* in black. Robert Lehman collection: rectangular gold metallic paper label printed *58* in black; circular gummed paper label typed *58.* in black. Metropolitan Museum: rectangular gummed paper label typed *L.58.73.60* (a loan number) in black.

2. Museo Vetrario, 1859, div. II D, no. 2; cl. VI, nn. 1006, 1014; Mariacher 1961, pl. 33; Mariacher [1966], p. 110, fig. 48; Mariacher [1970]a, p. 112, fig. 50; Mariacher [1970]b, pp. 22, 24, fig. 7; Mariacher and Causa Picone 1972, p. 41, pl. 52; Barovier Mentasti 1982, p. 54, fig. 35; Venice 1982, pp. 104–5, no. 115; Columbus 1983, p. 15, no. 3. For the second example, see Lorenzetti [1953], pl. 11; Gasparetto 1958, fig. 59.

3. British Museum, S.532 (ex coll. Felix Slade); Mariacher 1963, p. 69. Tait does not, however, accept an early date for this goblet; he believes it was made in the nineteenth century (conversation with the author, 1992).

4. Victoria and Albert Museum, C.698-1893 (ex coll. Frédéric Spitzer); Garnier 1891, p. 99, no. 48; d'Hondt [1893?], p. 83; Honey 1946, p. 61, pl. 23A; Mariacher 1954, fig. 40; Gasparetto 1958, fig. 43; Mariacher 1961, pl. 34; Mariacher 1964, pl. 5.

5. Corning Museum of Glass, 79.3.226 (ex coll. Jerome Strauss).

6. Kunstsammlungen der Veste Coburg, HA135.

7. Museo Poldi Pezzoli, 1211; Roffia and Mariacher 1983, p. 173, no. 40, fig. 40.

8. Toledo Museum of Art, 40.119 (ex coll. George Eumorfopoulos); H. Read 1926, p. 189, pl. opp. p. 187; Hutton 1963, p. [1]; Toledo Museum of Art 1969, p. 43.

Probably Venice, probably late nineteenth century

20. Goblet

1975.1.1209

H. 18.7 cm, diam. of rim 12.3 cm. Transparent brownish nonlead glass. Blown, enameled, gilt.

The hexagonal, tapered, straight-sided bowl has two gilt framing lines and a row of gray enamel dots at the rim; gilt lines follow the angles of the sides, which end in rounded arcs forming panels at the bottom of the bowl. On each of the six sides is an enameled and gilt armorial shield: azure, a saltire or between three stars of four points or, in base a gauntleted fist holding a sword or; or, a cross potent between four crosslets gules; sable, a pile or between two fleurs-de-lys or; gules, a pale or charged with a column argent on a base gules, between two keys palewise, the dexter or and ward in chief, the sinister or and ward in base, a chief or charged with a double-headed eagle sable; or, a pile gules charged with a pale argent; or, a fess azure, in chief a lion passant sable. The short

gilt stem is formed of a disk on a short neck and an inverted baluster knop flared at the base. The circular foot has an underfolded gilt rim. Tiny rough pontil mark under the foot. Painted in red-orange under the foot: L.56.31.71 (a Metropolitan Museum loan number).[1]

Wear on the corners of the bowl and on the foot rim. The entire lower half of the bowl may once have been gilt, and the tiny flecks of gilding around the shields suggest that there may have been additional gilt decoration on the sides. The slight but distinct haze on the lower part of the sides may be what remains of sizing applied before the gilding.

Longwave fluorescence. Glass: faint tan. Enamels: white = strong white, blue = light gray-blue, red = tan, black = gray. Gilding: tan. *Shortwave fluorescence.* Glass: faint, slightly

No. 20, *details of shields on bowl*

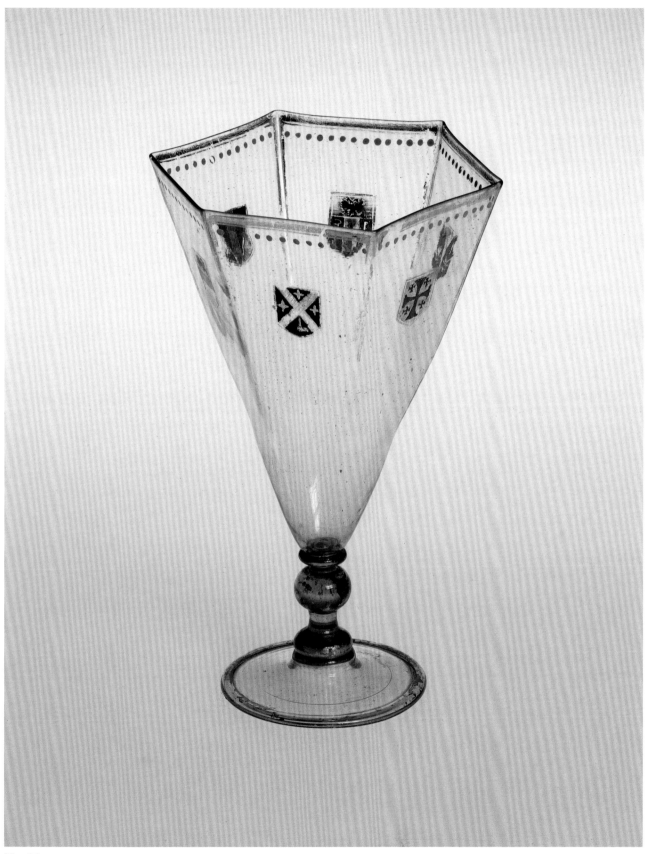

No. 20

brownish orange. Enamels: white dots = bluish white, white in armorials = faint white, blue = pea green, red = red-orange, black = pea green. Gilding: muddy pea green.

PROVENANCE: J. Rosenbaum, Frankfurt am Main(?);[2] [N. V. Int. Antiquiteten-handel, Amsterdam]; Oscar Bondy, Vienna; Otto Hopfinger, New York; [Blumka Gallery, New York].

EXHIBITED: Corning 1958, pp. 62–63, no. 52, ill.; Cincinnati 1959, p. 43, no. 553, ill.

LITERATURE: Bondy n.d., p. 51, no. 194.

The enameling on this goblet was apparently fired in a muffle kiln rather than on a pontil. The thick part of the stem did not get hot enough to fuse the gilding, and it is flaking noticeably now.

I know of no close parallels for the form of this goblet.[3] Venetian *cristallo* glasses made in the late nineteenth and early twentieth centuries frequently have a noticeable brownish tint like this glass (sixteenth- to seventeenth-century Venetian glasses are typically relatively colorless). That the gilding appears to be gold paint rather than gold leaf also raises suspicion that the Lehman goblet was made in Venice in the late nineteenth century.[4] Fur-

thermore, the inexplicable wear on the gilding on the shields and the rim implies that someone took great pains to make the glass look "old." That the gilding on the stem, which should have received the greatest amount of wear, has survived is further evidence of the goblet's late date and indicates as well that it probably spent its life in a collector's cabinet rather than being used.

The coats of arms have eluded identification. It may be that they are fictitious.

NOTES:
1. A rectangular gold metallic paper label printed *63* in black (Robert Lehman collection) has been removed and is in the Robert Lehman Collection files.
2. Rosenbaum's ownership has not been verified.
3. The only related glass that has come to my attention is a blue goblet in the J. Paul Getty Museum, Malibu (Corning 1958, pp. 102–3, no. 111). The Getty glass is hexagonal, but the bowl is slenderer than that of the Lehman goblet, and it has a molded lion-mask stem and a much taller foot. It is decorated with a stylized foliate design in enamel and gilt.
4. According to a note in the Robert Lehman Collection files, Mariacher examined this glass in May 1964 and suggested that "it might have been made in Florence where some fugitive Venetian glass-blowers manufactured excellent glass-ware in the mid-XVI century."

Façon de Venise, probably South Germany or the Tyrol (possibly Hofglashütte at Innsbruck), 1592

21. Armorial goblet

1975.1.1218

H. 22.3 cm, diam. of rim 12.4 cm. Colorless (strong gray) nonlead glass. Blown, enameled, gilt.

Below the rim of the large ovoid bowl is a band of scribed gilt scales, each with a blue enamel dot, flanked by rows of white dots. On the sides are three large coats of arms with elaborate gold shields (two with caryatids at the sides), red enamel scrolls, and blue-and-white striped cords, surrounded by green vines and red-and-blue flowers: The arms of Madrutz of the Tyrol: quarterly, 1 and 4 argent, an eagle sable, crowned and armed or, 2 and 3 quarterly with inescutcheon, 1 and 4 bendy of six, gules and azure, fimbriated or, 2 and 3 per chevron sable and argent, the argent striated sable with a chevron gules overall; inescutcheon: sable, a cross or between four roundels or. The arms of Welsperg of the Tyrol: quarterly, with inescutcheon, 1 and 4 sable, a lion or standing on a double mount argent, 2 and 3 gules, a fess dancetty argent; inescutcheon: quarterly argent and sable. And an unidentified coat of arms with *1592* written in white enamel above it: sable, a fess argent charged with a lion's head sable, tongue gules. Stylized lilies of the valley with red-and-white flowers

and blue and green foliage fill the spaces between the arms. Two pale green lines encircle the bowl just above its base, which is decorated with green arcades and alternately red-and-white and red-and-blue enameled gadroons. The bulbous, hollow, inverted baluster stem is attached to a merese edged with blue and white dots; on the stem is a band of inverted scribed gilt scales, each with a blue enamel dot, framed above by a row of white enamel dots and below by a row of tan enamel dots, and, at its flared base, a ring of blue and white dots. The circular foot has an underfolded rim and is decorated with a band of scribed circles highlighted with rings of tan or blue enamel dots and framed by two rows of tan dots. Two rough pontil marks, one above the other, under the foot.[1]

The gilding worn, especially on the stem and foot; slight wear on the rim of the bowl; wear on the foot rim.

Longwave fluorescence. Glass: yellowish olive green. Enamels: white = pinkish tan, red = dark red, blue = purple, green = greenish, black = black, tan = tan. *Shortwave fluorescence.* Glass: faint greenish orange. Enamels: white = strong bluish

No. 21

white, red = black, blue = dark inky blue, black = dark blue, tan = tan.

PROVENANCE: Von Forstner, Halle an der Saale(?);[2] Frederic Neuburg, Vienna; Otto Hopfinger, New York; [Blumka Gallery, New York].

EXHIBITED: New York 1985.

LITERATURE: Schmidt 1931, pp. 42–44, 64, no. 42, pl. 15.

There was no further manipulation of the bowl or the foot after the enamels and gilding were applied: in the scale border on the rim and in the annular band on the foot the gilding is not shattered and the enamel dots are consistently circular. Except in certain areas, such as the lion's head, the gilding on the coats of arms is painted; the scale bands and the ring on the foot are gold leaf. Most of the gilding on the foot has been rubbed off, whereas the gilding on the rim is nearly pristine. Because the goblet was held by a pontil attached underneath the foot to fire the enamels, the rim of the bowl reached a higher temperature than the foot.

Two of the three shields on this imposing glass have been identified as the arms of South Tyrolean nobility: the arms with the crowned Tyrolean eagles belong to the barons von Madrutz (Madruzzo in Italian); those with the standing lions to the barons von Welsperg.[3] Three of the Fürstbischofs, or prince bishops, who ruled the bishopric of Trent and Brixen in the Tyrol between 1027 and 1802 were members of the Madrutz family. The first was Cardinal Christoph von Madrutz, who became bishop in 1542 and ruled until 1578. A *Stangenglas* with his arms that can be dated before 1578 and that Egg has tentatively attributed to the Hall in Tyrol glasshouse of Johann Chrysostomus Höchstetter (in operation 1569–99) is in the Österreichisches Museum für Angewandte Kunst, Vienna (Fig. 21.1).[4] It has a simple gilt scale border similar to that on the Lehman glass. Christoph was succeeded as bishop by his nephew Cardinal Ludwig M. von Madrutz, who was in turn succeeded by his nephew Cardinal Carl Emanuel von Madrutz (d. 1653). The Madrutz were made barons in 1541 and counts in 1618,

No. 21, *shield on bowl*

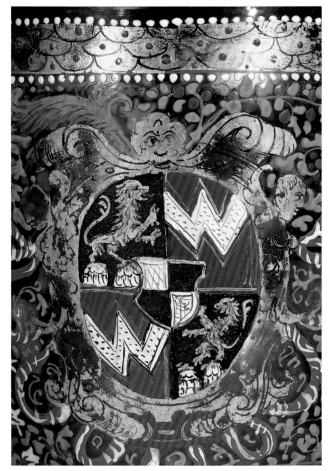

No. 21, *shield on bowl*

No. 21, *detail of stem*

No. 21, *detail of foot*

No. 21, *shield on bowl*

No. 21, *foliage on bowl*

Fig. 21.1 *Stangenglas.* Österreichisches Museum für Angewandte Kunst, Vienna

Fig. 21.2 Goblet. British Museum, London. By courtesy of the Trustees of the British Museum

three of them became knights of the Golden Fleece, and they married into such other illustrious families as the Medici, Braganza, Bourbon, Orsini, Gonzaga, and Hohenem.

The arms on the Lehman goblet may be those of Johannes Täufer von Madrutz (Gianbattista de Madruzzo), who was born 21 June 1564 in Calavino, the son of Nikolas von Madrutz, "gentleman of Madrutsch, Avio, and Brenntony, Marquis of Sorriano and Gallese, Knight of the Golden Fleece, Governor of Pavia, General and Warlord of Emperor Charles V and King Philip II of Spain, Commander of the Imperial Guards," and his second wife, Diana, countess Arco di Arco. Johannes Täufer was famous in his own right as a doctor of law, count of the Court of Lateran, and *eques auratus* in Rome. His stepbrother Cardinal Ludwig von Madrutz made him *comes palatinatus* of Trent in 1594, and Archduke Maximilian of Tyrol recognized the title in 1608, adding "von und zu Ebenheim."

The barons von Welsperg, whose castle is in the Gsieser Tal between Bruneck and Toblach, about twenty kilometers north of Trent, trace their ancestry to Ulrich I von Welsperg (1269–1294), who is said to have been a descendant of Otto Welf von Welsperg (1070–1090). The family was awarded the coat of arms and baronial title in 1539. In 1567, when the rank was reaffirmed, six members of the family (five of them brothers) are recorded, and another is listed in 1571; determining which of them might have been associated with this goblet has proved impossible. No marriages between the Welsperg and Madrutz families have been recorded. The third coat of arms remains unidentified.

A goblet in the British Museum, London (Fig. 21.2), that is enameled on one side with an unidentified coat of arms and on the other with a full-length figure of a woman in a blue dress holding a black fan is practically identical to the Lehman goblet in both form and proportions.[5] The band of gilt and enameled scale pattern that encir-

Fig. 21.3 Goblet. Grünes Gewölbe, Dresden. Photograph: Staatliche Kunstsammlungen Dresden

century after that. Whether late sixteenth-century enameled glasses like the Lehman goblet and those related to it were produced in Venice for Northern customers or whether they were made in local Austrian, German, and Bohemian glasshouses, by Venetian or native glassmakers, has therefore long been a subject for debate. A pair of *Stangengläser* in the group at the British Museum bear the arms of the Praun and Roming families of Nürnberg and are decorated with portraits of Jacob Praun and Clara von Roming, who were married in 1589. Tait has noted that the figure of the woman appears to have been copied from a woodcut by Tiziano Vecellio in *Habiti antichi et moderni*, a book of costumes published in Venice in 1590.[11] This, he says, lends credence to the view Schmidt advanced in 1911, that in the late sixteenth century the Venetians may still have been making such enameled glasses for German clients. Tait convincingly argues for a Venetian origin for the goblet with the commedia dell'arte characters, which "would seem to be a curious subject for a German patron to commission from a local South German glasshouse or, indeed, for such a glasshouse to produce for general sale." The origin of the armorial glasses in the group, he says, "has yet to be proved."[12]

Neither the form nor the dense enameled decoration, particularly the stylized lilies of the valley, on the Lehman goblet is typically Venetian. The capacious ovoid bowl and the exaggerated inverted baluster stem are paralleled in a series of glasses that have been associated with South German and Tyrolean glasshouses. A goblet dated 1602 in the Grünes Gewölbe, Dresden (Fig. 21.3),[13] with a speckled bowl and decorated with an enameled eagle and the monogram of Joachim Friedrich von Brandenburg and Katherina von Küstein, has been attributed to the Saxon factory at Grimnitz. Glasses of closely related form but with unfired painted decoration or diamond-point decoration, or both, that have generally been attributed to Hall or the Hofglashütte at Innsbruck (see No. 25) are in the Germanisches Nationalmuseum, Nürnberg;[14] the Uměleckoprůmyslové Muzeum, Prague (Fig. 21.4);[15] the Österreichisches Museum für Angewandte Kunst, Vienna;[16] and the Kunsthistorisches Museum, Vienna (two examples).[17]

Similarly dense enameled designs, but not the lilies of the valley, were used on some of the *façon de Venise* glasses in a group customarily attributed to Innsbruck and to Barcelona. Examples are in the Victoria and Albert Museum, London;[18] the Musée des Arts Décoratifs, Paris;[19] the British Museum (Fig. 21.5);[20] the Museo Vetrario, Murano;[21] the Museo Civico d'Arte Antica,

cles its rim is also nearly identical to the band on the Lehman glass, sketchily scribed and with no attempt at shading the scales with combed lines. Scale bands treated in much the same way appear on glasses in the Kunstmuseum Düsseldorf;[6] the Museum für Angewandte Kunst, Cologne;[7] and the Kunstgewerbemuseum, Berlin;[8] and similar borders embellish the rims of seven other glasses in the British Museum – three goblets and four *Stangengläser*.[9] Two of those goblets and all four *Stangengläser* are decorated with enameled Germanic armorial shields and full-length portraits of men and women. Painted on the third goblet are three male figures that Tait has identified as Pantaloon, Harlequin, and the Doctor of the commedia dell'arte.[10] Elaborate floral enameling like that on the Lehman goblet appears on none of these glasses.

Gilding and enameling on glass began to go out of fashion in Italy after the mid-sixteenth century, though it continued to be popular in the north for more than a

Fig. 21.4 Covered goblet. Uměleckoprůmyslové Muzeum, Prague

Fig. 21.5 Covered goblet. British Museum, London. By courtesy of the Trustees of the British Museum

Turin;[22] the Bernd Hockemeyer collection, Bremen;[23] the Rijksmuseum, Amsterdam;[24] the Louvre, Paris;[25] and the Bayerisches Nationalmuseum, Munich.[26] Related enameled decoration on glasses associated with Barcelona usually does not include the red and dark blue that were used on the Lehman glass.[27]

That the enameling and gilding were applied to this glass after it was fully shaped, and that the overlapping of the leaves forming the gilt ring on the foot is not radial and is rather less controlled than on earlier sixteenth-century Venetian glasses, might be evidence against its having been made in Venice (though it could be that over the course of the years the Venetian glassmakers changed or forgot the techniques their predecessors had used more than fifty years before). It is also true that the intricate decoration on this goblet, or that on the related group in the British Museum, could not have been flared

after it was applied with anything less than disastrous results.

In the unpublished catalogue of the Frederic Neuburg collection he prepared in 1931, Schmidt theorized that this goblet could have been made in Ljubljana, Villach, Graz, Trent, or Ala, where *façon de Venise* glasshouses are known to have been operating at the end of the sixteenth century. No glasses from any of those factories have been documented, however.[28] In a discussion of the spread of enameling to glasshouses in Bohemia and the German states, Charleston has commented that "there is usually no danger of identifying as Venetian a glass enamelled in Germany or Bohemia in the decades on either side of 1600. To distinguish between the glasses made in different centres in those areas, however, is very much more difficult, and often impossible with the criteria at present established."[29]

68

NOTES:

1. The following labels have been removed and are in the Robert Lehman Collection files: Unidentified: circular white paper label with *15 / 34* written in ink. Frederic Neuburg collection: circular white paper label with *Neuburg No. 79* (*Neuburg No.* printed, *79* written in ink). Robert Lehman collection: circular white paper label typed *61*.

2. In his catalogue of the Neuburg collection Schmidt (1931, p. 64, no. 42) says this glass was "aus Sammlung Baron von Forstner, Halle a/S." The provenance has not been otherwise documented.

3. I am indebted to Ludwig Igálffy v. Igály of Vienna for identifying the arms of Madrutz and Welsperg and providing the historical information on the families. On the Madrutz, he consulted Bergmann 1858 and Indermauer 1924; on the Welsperg family, see Kneschke 1852–54, vol. 2, p. 660. See also Schmidt 1931, pp. 42–44, 64, no. 42.

4. Österreichisches Museum für Angewandte Kunst, F158 (ex coll. J. Zöllner, A. Überbacher); Innsbruck 1959, p. 11, fig. 3; Egg 1962, p. 82, pl. 31, fig. 72; Schlosser 1965, colorpl. 8. Egg suggested that the arms on this glass were cold-painted and cold-gilt; in fact, the enameling and gilding were fired.

5. British Museum, s.853 (ex coll. Felix Slade, Ralph Bernal); Gasparetto 1958, p. 286, fig. 89; Tait 1979, p. 43, no. 40, colorpl. 12.

6. Kunstmuseum, 1940-30 (ex coll. J. Jantzen); Jantzen 1960, p. 15, no. 10, pl. 4; Heinemeyer 1966, p. 60, no. 156.

7. Museum für Angewandte Kunst, F164; Schmidt 1922, p. 200; Cologne [1961], no. 177, fig. 6; Klesse 1963, p. 115, no. 236; Von Saldern 1965, pp. 46, 47, fig. 29; Klesse and Reineking von Bock 1973, p. 165, no. 333; Lipp 1974, pp. 58, 159–60, figs. 15, 16; Baumgärtner 1977b, fig. 2.

8. Kunstgewerbemuseum, 1972,40; Dreier 1989b, pp. 43–44, no. 11, pl. 10.

9. British Museum, s.852, s.845, s.846, 55.12-1.132, s.839, s.842, 55.12-1.131; Tait 1979, pp. 42–46, nos. 38, 39, 41–44.

10. British Museum, s.852; ibid., p. 42, no. 38, colorpl. 13.

11. British Museum, s.845, s.846; ibid., pp. 42–43, no. 39.

12. Ibid., pp. 27–28. See also Schmidt 1911, p. 249; W. King 1929.

13. Grünes Gewölbe, N106; Schmidt 1914, pl. 1; Von Saldern 1965, pp. 222–23, fig. 387.

14. Germanisches Nationalmuseum, GL156; Strasser and Spiegl 1989, pp. 30, 34, fig. 35 (as South Germany, 1600–1620).

15. Uměleckoprůmyslové Muzeum, z-106/37; Bernt [1951?], p. 50, no. 25; Vávra 1954, p. 55, fig. 136; Egg 1962, p. 62, pl. 19, fig. 42 (as Hofglashütte, Innsbruck).

16. Österreichisches Museum für Angewandte Kunst, F.155; Von Saldern 1965, pp. 48, 49, fig. 32.

17. Kunsthistorisches Museum, 3363, 3372; Egg 1962, figs. 56, 60. These two glasses are part of a group that Egg believes were probably made by Antonio Montano, a Venetian glassmaker who worked in Hall from 1572 to 1590; see ibid., pp. 67–71, pls. 25–27, figs. 56–62.

18. Victoria and Albert Museum, C.234-1936 (ex coll. Wilfred Buckley); Buckley 1939, p. 252, no. 192, pl. 51; Frothingham 1941, fig. 46 (as Spanish, late sixteenth or early seventeenth century); Schack 1976, p. 222, fig. 89.

19. Musée des Arts Décoratifs, 16.905; Frothingham 1941, fig. 47 (as Spanish, late sixteenth or early seventeenth century).

20. Ibid., fig. 48 (as Spanish, late sixteenth or early seventeenth century).

21. Mariacher 1954, fig. 145 (as Barcelona, fifteenth century); Mariacher [1970]a, pp. 141, 142, fig. 67; Mariacher [1970]b, pp. 25, 27, fig. 8.

22. Museo Civico d'Arte Antica, 4VE (174); Mallè 1971, pp. 56–57, figs. 35, 36.

23. Ex coll. Fritz Biemann; Lucerne 1981, p. 155, no. 657, pl. F21.

24. Rijksmuseum, NMII648; Frothingham 1941, fig. 45 (as Spanish, late sixteenth or early seventeenth century); Schrijver 1964, pl. 17a; Schlosser 1965, p. 138, fig. 113; Lipp 1974, pp. 123, 169, fig. 171; Schack 1976, p. 222, fig. 90.

25. Louvre, OAII34 (ex coll. Sauvgeot).

26. Bayerisches Nationalmuseum, 62/55; Rückert 1982, pp. 88–89, no. 150, pl. 6.

27. Schmidt 1912, p. 369, fig. 216; Schmidt 1922, p. 381, fig. 231; Gudiol Ricart and Artíñano 1935, pls. 9–11, fig. 123; Frothingham 1941, frontis., figs. 38–44, pl. 2; Gudiol Ricart 1941, figs. 36, 42, nos. 35–63; Frothingham 1956, figs. 12–16, 18–22, 24, 25; Frothingham 1963, pp. 37–39, colorpl. A, figs. 4–9; Fritz 1964, p. 22, fig. 6; Mariacher 1964, pl. 12; Mariacher [1966], pp. 140, 141, figs. 64, 65; Causa Picone 1967, pp. 78–80; Mariacher [1970]a, pp. 138, 140, fig. 66; Weiss 1971, p. 86; Corning Museum of Glass 1974, p. 57, no. 67; Charleston 1980a, pp. 102–3, no. 43; *Bulletin AIHV*, no. 9 (1981–83), p. 171, fig. 2b; Venice 1982, pp. 110–11, nos. 127–30; Rodriguez Garcia 1987, pp. 421–29.

28. See Schmidt 1931, p. 44.

29. Charleston 1977, p. 27; see also Von Saldern 1965, pp. 159–60.

Façon de Venise, probably Bohemia, late
sixteenth century

22. Goblet

1975.1.1153

H. 15.2 cm, diam. of rim 5.5 cm. Gray nonlead glass. Blown,
mold blown, enameled, gilt.

Below the cylindrical rim of the globular bowl is a ring of tiny
white enamel dots, followed by a plain gilt band, two rows of
alternating blue and white dots flanking gilt diamonds, a plain
gilt band, a row of gilt diamonds flanked by two rows of white
dots, a wider band of scribed gilt scales embellished with red
and blue dots arranged in slanted rows, a row of white dots,
and a row of blue dots. A merese separates the bowl from the
baluster stem, which consists of a short, straight section; a
hollow ovoid knop mold blown with lion masks in relief
separated by swags of dots and stylized florets, with sixteen
ribs above and ten below; and a flared base decorated with
white enamel dots. The circular foot has an underfolded rim.
Two rough pontil marks, one over the other, under the foot.[1]

The gilding nearly worn off and mainly evident as ghost
patterns; slight wear on the rim of the bowl; normal wear on
the foot rim.

Longwave fluorescence. Glass: strong yellow-orange. Enamels:
white = tan, red = dark red, blue = dark blue. *Shortwave
fluorescence.* Glass: faint orange. Enamels: white = bluish
white, red = dark blue, blue = blue.

PROVENANCE: Princes of Liechtenstein, Vaduz and Vienna(?);[2]
Otto Hopfinger, New York; [Blumka Gallery, New York].

Gilding remains on the scale band on this goblet only
under the enamel dots and outlining the scale pattern,
where the lines of the scales appear as a heavier gold,
suggesting that the scales were scratched with a diamond
before the gilding was applied.

Among the many glass fragments found in 1957 in the
drain of a house facing the north side of the cathedral
of Saint Vitus in Prague were several molded lion-mask
stems, one of them preserved along with half the bowl of
a *filigrana* goblet now in Prague Castle that bears the arms
and name of Georg Pontanus de Breitenberg, canon and
later provost of the Prague Chapter, and the date 1595.[3]
Hetteš proposed that the glass from the find was pro-

duced either at the glasshouse at Bubeneč, on the northern edge of Prague, or at the Schürers' glasshouse at
Broumy, southeast of the city. The Schürers, the most
renowned of the glassmakers who in the sixteenth century were displaced from Saxony by the growing mining
industry, came to own seventeen of the many new glassworks established in Bohemia and Moravia to compete
with Venetian manufacturers for the local trade.[4] An
enameled and gilt tazza with a mold-blown lion-mask stem
in the Fritz Biemann collection, Zurich, that is dated 1599
has also been attributed to Bohemia.[5] See also No. 44.

The glass material of this goblet and that of No. 23
apparently have a similar chemical composition: when
illuminated with longwave ultraviolet light the glass of
both goblets emits an orangish light. They may, therefore, have been made in the same region, if not the same
factory. The orange fluorescence of these glasses probably results from the decolorizer used, presumably manganese.

NOTES:
1. A rectangular gold metallic paper label printed *11* in black
   and a circular white paper label typed *11.* (both Robert
   Lehman collection) have been removed and are now in the
   Robert Lehman Collection files.
2. According to the Blumka Gallery files, this goblet was once
   in the collection of the princes of Liechtenstein, but that
   provenance has not been otherwise documented.
3. Hetteš 1963, p. 38, fig. 1, and see also pp. 46, 48, figs. 6:va,b,
   11. See also Hejdová 1981, which includes an analysis of the
   Bohemian glass fragments, many of them similar to the
   Prague finds, that were excavated in 1958–61 at the Rejdice
   glasshouse in northeastern Bohemia, which was founded by
   Paul Schürer, Jr., in the 1570s.
4. Hetteš 1963, pp. 40–41, 52–53; see also Hejdová 1981, pp.
   18–19.
5. *JGS* 29 (1987), p. 114, fig. 7.

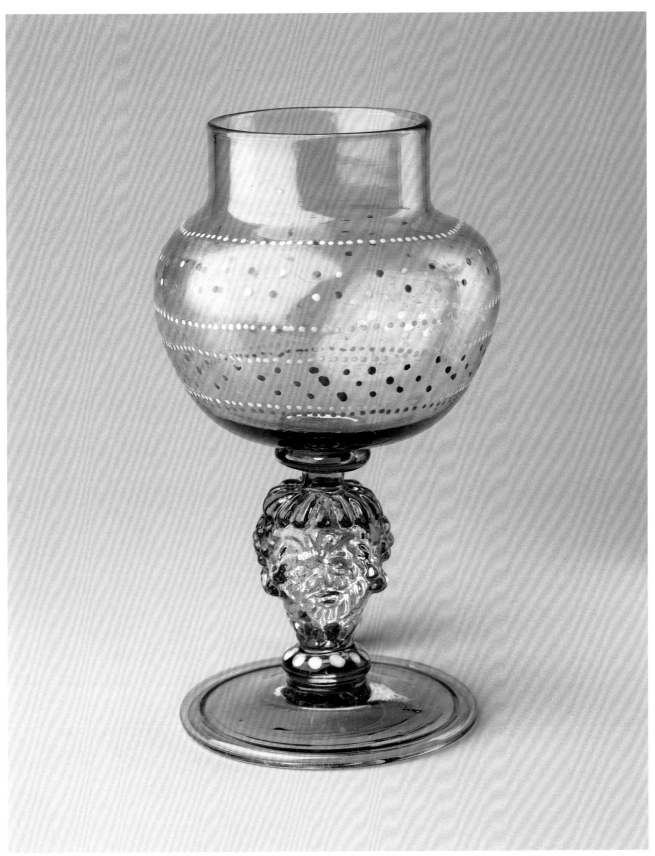

No. 22

Façon de Venise, probably Bohemia, late
sixteenth century

23. Goblet

1975.1.1202

H. 16.3 cm, diam. of rim 6.1 cm. Gray-green nonlead glass.
Blown, pattern molded, enameled, gilt.

The inverted pear-shaped bowl has a short cylindrical rim
decorated with a row of white enamel dots above a plain gilt
band and three horizontal white lines. A wide band of stylized
white vines and scrolls, with three white lines below it,
encircles the shoulder of the bowl, and its sides are molded
into twelve rounded panels decorated with alternating blue
and white vertical serpentine lines. The stem is composed of
two small ball knops. The tall, trumpet-shaped foot has an
underfolded rim. Rough iron red annular pontil mark under
the foot.[1]

Broken bubble in the base of the bowl; normal wear on the
foot rim; bruise on the foot near the pontil mark.

Longwave fluorescence. Glass: strong yellow-orange. Enamels:
white = tan and (where thick) purple, blue = gray-blue.
Shortwave fluorescence. Glass: faint orange. Enamels: white =
strong bluish white, blue = dark blue.

PROVENANCE: Princes of Liechtenstein, Vaduz and Vienna (?);[2]
Otto Hopfinger, New York; [Blumka Gallery, New York].

So-called iron pontil marks like the one on this glass
result from the buildup of iron oxide on the tip of the
pontil. When the oxide builds up sufficiently, the wad of
glass on the end separates from the pontil, carrying some
of the iron oxide with it. The single large pontil mark
evident here probably hides an earlier mark. The diameter of the pontil rod was .7 cm.

Foliate scrollwork like that on the shoulder of this goblet was used on a Saxon *Humpen* in the Uměleckoprůmyslové Muzeum, Prague (Fig. 23.1), that is dated 1585
and has been attributed to the Heidelbach glasshouse[3]
and on a goblet in the Corning Museum of Glass that
has been dated to the late sixteenth century and attributed to Bohemia or the Tyrol (Fig. 23.2).[4] Related white
enameled decoration also appears on glass fragments
found in 1957 in the drain of a house in Prague that
Hetteš believes were made in a local Bohemian glasshouse in the late sixteenth or early seventeenth century
(see also No. 22).[5] A late sixteenth-century Bohemian
goblet in the Ernesto Wolf collection, São Paulo and Paris
(Fig. 23.3),[6] and another (dated 1594) in the Uměleckoprůmyslové Muzeum,[7] both decorated with hunting
scenes, share with the Lehman goblet the enameled
sinusoidal motifs and the double-ball-knop stem and
high trumpet foot. Similarly shaped stems and feet were

found in 1957 in the house drain in Prague[8] and in
1958–61 in the excavations of the glasshouse founded in
the 1570s at Rejdice in northeastern Bohemia.[9]

The fluorescence of this glass matches that of No. 22,
which indicates that they may have been manufactured
in the same region.

NOTES:
1. A rectangular gold metallic paper label printed 6 in black
   and a circular white paper label typed 6. (both Robert Lehman collection) have been removed and are now in the Robert Lehman Collection files.
2. According to the Blumka Gallery files, this goblet was once
   in the collection of the princes of Liechtenstein, but that
   provenance has not been otherwise documented.
3. Uměleckoprůmyslové Muzeum, 9.892; Vávra 1954, no. 145,
   pl. 58; Von Saldern 1965, pp. 161, 162, fig. 295; Baumgärtner
   1977b, p. 42, fig. 9; Drahotová 1980, p. 79; Haase 1988,
   pp. 294, 379, no. 3, pl. 4, fig. 6; Hejdová and Drahotová
   1989, pp. 65, 96, 180, no. 45.

No. 23, *detail of bowl*

No. 23

Fig. 23.1 *Humpen*. Uměleckoprůmyslové Muzeum, Prague

Fig. 23.3 Goblet. Collection of Ernesto Wolf, São Paulo and Paris. Reproduced from Brigitte Klesse and Hans Mayr, *European Glass from 1500–1800* (Vienna: Kremayr und Scheriau, 1987), no. 45

Fig. 23.2 Goblet. Corning Museum of Glass, Gift of Jerome Strauss

4. Corning Museum of Glass, 68.3.51 (ex coll. Jerome Strauss); Haynes 1959, fig. 35b.
5. Hetteš 1963, p. 49, figs. 16, 17.
6. Klesse and Mayr 1987, no. 45. For related goblets, see also Schmidt 1931, p. 42, no. 40; Von Saldern 1965, p. 170, figs. 309, 310; Hejdová and Drahotová 1989, pp. 66, 99, 180, no. 48.
7. Uměleckoprůmyslové Muzeum, 10.398; Hetteš 1963, pp. 49–50, 52, fig. 25.
8. Ibid., p. 46, fig. 6:11a–d.
9. Hejdová 1981, pp. 24, 25, figs. 7, 8.

Façon de Venise, Germany or Silesia (possibly Petersdorf, Fritz Heckert factory), late nineteenth century

24. Double cup (*Doppelscheuer*)

1975.1.1154a,b

H. 15.5 cm, h. without cover 11.6 cm, diam. of cup 8.1 cm, diam. of cover 6.7 cm. Colorless (slightly gray) nonlead glass. Blown, enameled, gilt.

The cup has a cylindrical, slightly flared rim and a thistle-shaped bowl. Below the rim is a gilt band with enameled stylized flowers with white petals and red centers, flanked by rows of white and blue enamel dots; at the base of the neck is a red enamel band highlighted with yellow dots; and the bulbous body is decorated with a row of red-and-white dots; a row of blue dots; a wide band of scribed gilt scales, each with white outlines, blue, green, and red dots, and scraped horizontal lines; a row of tiny blue dots; a scribed gilt dentil band; and a row of red-and-white dots. The applied handle has a large, rounded attachment at the body and a flattened, scrolled end and is gilt on the bottom, with white and red florets along the underside and red and yellow-on-blue florets on the edges of the scrolled end. The tall, trumpet-shaped pedestal foot has an underfolded rim and is decorated with three rows of white and yellow-green dots; two rows of blue and two rows of white dots; and, near the rim, a band of scribed gilt scales, each with a red-and-white dot.

The domed cover has a tapered, straight-sided rim that fits inside the rim of the cup and an applied flared finial in the form of a pedestal foot with an outfolded rim. It is decorated with a band of scribed gilt scales, like those on the cup, that is flanked by rows of red-and-white dots and rows of tiny blue dots on gilt bands. The finial, or foot, is gilt on the inside and on the rim and is decorated with two rows of white dots flanking a row of pale green dots; on its flattened center, within a red ring with yellow dots, are two coats of arms amid stylized white foliage and with *1518* written above in white: sable, an arrow or in bend sinister between two stars of six points or; argent, three rams' horns conjoined by a trefoil or.

The two-part, form-fitting wooden case is covered with dark brown leather and lined with gray suede, with metal hooks and eyes attached around the edge.

Rough pontil mark under the foot of the cup; large ring-shaped rough pontil mark inside the cover. Painted in bright red-orange under the foot of the cup: *L.56.31.54* (a Metropolitan Museum loan number). Painted in black on the pontil mark on the cover: *985*. On the bottom of the case, a rectangular pale blue paper label printed *M Keezer & Fils / Amsterdam / No.* in black and typed *260L / E*, and a triangular paper label with a printed blue frame and *7.* written in black ink.

Cup: tiny chip on the rim; the foot and another small piece broken from the bowl and cemented; tiny fragments missing; the inside cloudy, with a white scum that scrapes off easily; unconvincing wear on the foot. Cover: tiny chip on the rim; the gilding worn; the inside cloudy, like the cup; almost no wear on the rim of the cover and none on the rim of the finial (foot). Case: water-stained and warped.

Longwave fluorescence. Glass: pale greenish. Enamel: white = magenta and (on the coats of arms) bright yellow, green =

strong yellow, red = dark red-orange, blue = faint light blue, yellow = strong amber. *Shortwave fluorescence.* Glass: brilliant bluish white (perhaps a surface bloom) and (inside the bowl) a dark purple reflection. Enamel: white (on both body and coat of arms) = purple, blue = black, green = black, yellow-orange = faint orange, red = black. The enamel dots show a strong halo. Gilding: strong tan.

PROVENANCE: [M. Keezer en Fils, Amsterdam (260L/E)]; Adalbert von Lanna, Prague (Lanna sale 1911, lot 708, pl. 59); Kurz, Vienna(?);[1] Frederic Neuburg, Vienna; Otto Hopfinger, New York; [Blumka Gallery, New York].

EXHIBITED: Cincinnati 1959 (not in catalogue).

LITERATURE: Schmidt 1931, pp. 4–5, 21, no. 2, pl. 2; London 1968b, under no. 211; Szabo 1975, p. 106; Tait 1979, p. 41, under no. 35; Barovier Mentasti 1982, p. 71; *Glass Collections* 1982, p. 111; Hayward 1982, p. 16; Dreier 1989b, p. 46, under no. 14; Tait 1991, pp. 18–19, fig. 12.

Gold leaf was used for all the gilding on the cup and cover. The gilding was applied before the enameling. The very controlled parallel horizontal scribed lines on the gilt scales were scraped on after the enamel dots were applied, and perhaps after the gilding and enameling were fired. The handle was applied before the gilding and enameling. The gold foil is not shattered, and the enamel dots are consistently circular, indicating that there was no manipulation of the form after the gilding and enameling were applied. The gilding at the foot rim of the cup is slightly granular, perhaps because it rested on the floor of the kiln while it was being fired.

Drinking vessels like this, called double mazers, or *Doppelscheuern*, were popular in northern Europe in the fourteenth, fifteenth, and sixteenth centuries. They were originally made of wood, but the form was imitated in silver, rock crystal, and glass. An example made of mazerwood embellished with a silver-gilt crown, handle, and foot that probably dates to the sixteenth century was in the collection of Mrs. Ernest Brummer in 1975.[2] Another, of maplewood and copper-gilt, that has been attributed to Germany and dated to the late fifteenth or sixteenth century is in The Metropolitan Museum of Art (Fig. 24.1).[3]

No. 24, *shields on top of cover*

No. 24, *detail of cover*

No. 24, *detail of handle*

No. 24, *detail of foot*

No. 24

No. 24, *case*

Fig. 24.1 *Doppelscheuer.* The Metropolitan Museum of Art, New York, Gift of J. Pierpont Morgan, 1917 (17.190.363)

A rock crystal *Doppelscheuer* that was probably supplied with enameled silver-gilt mounts in Nürnberg in 1484 or 1485 is in the Kunsthistorisches Museum, Vienna,[4] and the Metropolitan Museum also has a rare example made of jasper and mounted in silver-gilt that has been attributed to sixteenth-century Germany.[5]

Glass *Scheuern* were produced in the late fifteenth and sixteenth centuries both in Venice and north of the Alps. Gilt and enameled Venetian examples are in the Victoria and Albert Museum, London,[6] and the Kunstgewerbemuseum, Berlin.[7] A *millefiori* cup made in Venice in the late fifteenth century was in the Kunstgewerbemuseum but was lost during World War II.[8] A German *Scheuer* (without its cover) of opaque red glass dated to the sixteenth century is in the Karl Amendt collection, Krefeld (Fig. 24.2),[9] and a number of *Scheuern* made of green glass (*Waldglas*, or forest glass) have survived.[10]

In his sermon on glass and glassmaking, the fifteenth in a series of sermons on mining, metallurgy, and mineralogy that were published as *Bergpostilla, oder Sarepta* in 1562, Johann Mathesius (1504–1565), a pastor in Jáchymov (Joachimsthal) in northwestern Bohemia, described the purpose of these "double cups and covered presentation vessels." Before a prince or a gentleman drank from the cup, a servant would pour some of the drink into the cover, "and first taste that no poison be in it, then discard the rest, and, while the gentleman drinketh, hold up the cover."[11]

The Lehman cup can be grouped with four other similar or nearly identical *Doppelscheuern*, in the British Museum, London (Fig. 24.3);[12] the Corning Museum of Glass (Fig. 24.4);[13] the Západočeské Muzeum, Plzeň (Fig. 24.5);[14] and a private collection in Stockholm.[15] All four, like the Lehman cup, bear two coats of arms that have been identified as those of the Scharff family of Nürnberg and the Hörlin family of Augsburg.[16]

The cup in the British Museum (Fig. 24.3) is identical to the Lehman cup except that there is gilding on the yellow enamel, the pontil mark on the cup is ring-shaped (like that on the cover of the Lehman cup), and the tip of the handle appears to have been rolled around a slender glass rod. Like the Lehman cup, it bears the date 1518 above the shields on the cover. It also has a slightly iridescent whitish accretion on the inside, and the gilt scales on the body were scraped with parallel lines, but those on the cover and foot were not.

The bottom half of the cup in Corning (Fig. 24.4) is decorated with the same scale pattern as are those in New York and London (and, like the London cup, its handle appears to have been rolled around a glass rod),

Fig. 24.2 *Scheuer*. Collection of Karl Amendt, Krefeld. Reproduced from Erwin Baumgartner and Ingeborg Krueger, *Phönix aus Sand und Asche* (Munich: Rheinisches Landesmuseum Bonn, 1988), no. 475

Fig. 24.3 *Doppelscheuer*. British Museum, London, Rothschild Bequest. By courtesy of the Trustees of the British Museum

Fig. 24.4 *Doppelscheuer*. Corning Museum of Glass

Fig. 24.5 *Doppelscheuer*. Západočeské Muzeum, Plzeň. Reproduced from Dagmar Braunová, *Renesanční a barokní emailované sklo* (Plzeň, 1980), no. 30a, b

79

Fig. 24.6 Goblet. Present location unknown. Reproduced from Stuttgarter Kunstauktions-haus Dr. Fritz Nagel, *Europäisches Formglas 15.–19. Jahrhunderts* (5 October 1990), pl. 64

on all three cups are also different from what one finds on sixteenth-century gilt Venetian glasses, on which the scales are scribed more or less vertically (see, for example, Nos. 9–13). The cloudy white substance coating the inside of all three cups may have been sprayed on to make them look "old."

That the *Doppelscheuern* in London, Corning, and New York are in fact historicizing glasses made at the end of the nineteenth century may be confirmed by the reported existence of a fifth such cup in Stockholm that is said to bear the mark of the Fritz Heckert factory in Petersdorf, Silesia, which was founded in 1866. Although I was unable to examine the Stockholm cup, I did test the fluorescence of an enameled beaker in the collection of Rudolf von Strasser in Pelham Manor, New York, that is a signed product of the Heckert factory from the late nineteenth century. The fluorescence, of both the glass and the enamels, matches that of the Lehman and Corning cups. I was also unable to examine the *Doppelscheuer* in Plzeň (Fig. 24.5), which also bears the date 1518, but it appears to be nearly identical to the Lehman and Corning cups. It is likely, therefore, that all five of these glasses are copies of a lost, early *Doppelscheuer*.

The enameled decoration on a goblet of late nineteenth-century manufacture, but "dated" 1656, that was on the art market in Stuttgart in 1990 (Fig. 24.6) is in many ways similar to that on the five *Scheuern*, particularly in the gilt and enameled scale borders.[17]

but the lid is covered with a very different geometric design, and the date enameled above the shields is 1512. With the 1512 cup the Corning Museum also acquired a second cover, with the same geometric pattern but without the finial, or foot, and with a single unidentified coat of arms and the date 1615. When the glass of the cup and both covers was exposed to ultraviolet light they were found to fluoresce the same brilliant bluish white as the Lehman cup and cover, and the enamels on both cups and all three covers fluoresce identically, under both longwave and shortwave ultraviolet light. The Corning cup and covers were also sprayed with a whitish accretion.

The existence of the two covers, one "dated" 1615, when *Doppelscheuern* had already gone out of fashion in northern Europe, for the cup in Corning is alone enough to cast serious doubts on the date enameled on its mates in London and New York. The brilliant bluish white fluorescence of the Lehman and Corning cups and covers adds to those doubts; none of the sixteenth-century Venetian and *façon de Venise* glasses I have submitted to ultraviolet light showed that color fluorescence. The very controlled parallel horizontal lines scribed on the gilt scales

NOTES:

1. Kurz of Vienna is included in the provenance of the cup given in Schmidt 1931, p. 21, no. 2.

2. New York 1975, p. 48, no. 47.

3. Metropolitan Museum, 17.190.363 (ex coll. J. Pierpont Morgan); Los Angeles–Chicago 1970, pp. 234–35, no. 111. For other examples made of wood, see Garnier 1891, p. 31, no. 85, pl. 15; Spitzer sale 1893, lot 1783, pl. 46; W. Dexel 1943, p. 62, figs. 212, 213; Schiedlausky 1956, p. 59, no. 27; Kohlhaussen 1959; Kohlhaussen 1960; W. Dexel 1973, pp. 168, 219, figs. 141, 142, 320; T. Dexel 1986, pp. 80–81, figs. 71a,b.

4. Lamm 1929–30, vol. 1, no. 3, pl. 86; vol. 2, p. 237; Von Falke 1930, p. 129, fig. 17; Loewenthal 1934, p. 45, fig. 1; Kohlhaussen 1960, pp. 38–39, fig. 13.

5. Metropolitan Museum, 17.190.364 (ex coll. Albert Oppenheim, J. Pierpont Morgan); Breck and Rogers 1929, p. 128, fig. 74.

6. Victoria and Albert Museum, c.1890–1855 (without a handle or a cover).

7. Kunstgewerbemuseum, 1978,5; *JGS* 21 (1979), p. 120, fig. 7; Dreier 1989b, pp. 45–46, no. 14, colorpl. 9.

8. Schmidt 1912, p. 85, fig. 50; Schmidt 1922, p. 87, fig. 51; Dreier 1989b, p. 9, fig. 5.

9. Bonn–Basel 1988, p. 382, no. 475.

10. See Schmidt 1912, p. 142, fig. 75; Schmidt 1922, pp. 145, 147, fig. 76; Hessisches Landesmuseum 1935, p. 64, pl. 44, no. 374; W. Dexel 1939, p. 280; W. Dexel 1943, p. 62, fig. 211; Cologne [1961], no. 59; Klesse 1963, p. 63, no. 84; Rademacher 1963, pp. 124–25, 150, pl. 56; Isings 1966, fig. 37; Weiss 1971, p. 137, top; Klesse and Reineking von Bock 1973, p. 101, no. 155; Kämpfer 1978, p. 66, figs. 42, 43; T. Dexel 1986, pp. 80–81, fig. 71C; Bonn–Basel 1988, pp. 381–85. Three green glass *Doppelscheuern* also appear in Albert Bouts's painting *The Last Supper*, which is dated to the early sixteenth century (Palais des Beaux-Arts, Brussels, 542; Chambon 1955, pl. M, d).

11. "Die zwifachen scheiren und die verdackte Credentzen sein / darauss die / so Fürsten und Herrn bey dem trincken stehen / etwas in deckel schencken / und zuvor kosten / das kein gifft darin sey / und das ubrige wegkschwencken / und weil der Herr trincket / den deckel in die höhe halten" (Mathesius [1562] 1927, fol. 18). On Mathesius, see also Hetteš 1963, pp. 41–42, and Charleston 1977, pp. 26–27.

12. British Museum, Waddesdon Bequest 59 (ex coll. Ferdinand de Rothschild); C. H. Read 1899, p. 27, pl. 15, no.

59; C. H. Read 1927, p. 13, no. 59; Gasparetto 1958, pp. 86, 284, fig. 50; Von Saldern 1965, p. 35, n. 63; London 1968b, pp. 154–55, no. 211; Tait 1979, pp. 40–41, no. 35; Hollister 1981, p. 224, fig. 2; Tait 1991, pp. 18–19, fig. 11.

13. Corning Museum of Glass, 80.3.38a–c; *JGS* 23 (1981), p. 98, fig. 25; Tait 1991, pp. 18–19, figs. 13, 14.

14. Západočeské Muzeum, 427; Braunová 1980, p. 106, pl. 30a,b. I am indebted to Olga Drahotová of the Uměleckoprůmyslové Muzeum, Prague, for bringing this glass to my attention.

15. According to the owner, the cup in Stockholm bears the mark of the Heckert factory in Petersdorf. I have been unable to reach him to confirm its resemblance to the other four cups or to obtain a photograph.

16. See Tait 1979, pp. 40–41, no. 35. In 1991 (p. 18) Tait said that the arms identified as those of the Scharff family may be copied from the arms of Seuthe of Augsburg. Schmidt (1931, pp. 4–5, 21) identified the arms as belonging to the Seutter and Hörnlin families and cited the marriage of Joachim Seutter and Affra Hörnlin in 1518.

17. Friedleben sale 1990, lot 607, pl. 64.

Venetian or *façon de Venise*, probably Innsbruck, possibly Venice, about 1570; possibly Hall in Tyrol, mid- to late sixteenth century

25. Dish

1975.1.1180

H. 8.3 cm, diam. of rim 27.5 cm. Colorless (gray) nonlead glass. Blown, reverse painted, gilt (unfired).

The shallow, circular dish has an underfolded rim and curved sides with twelve large lobes, each decorated in gilding with a large rectangle framed with dots and lines and filled with delicate scrolled vines, with swag borders above and below. Reverse painted on the slightly convex center is a scene representing Apollo and the Muses. The sides flare at the bottom to form a broad, folded foot that is decorated with a gilt ropework border. Small rough pontil mark centered on the underside. Painted in bright red-orange under the foot: *L.58.73.65* (a Metropolitan Museum loan number).

Flaking paint and some wear on the gilding; no evidence of repainting; normal wear on the base rim.

Longwave fluorescence. Glass: strong yellow-green. Paint: no evidence of repainting. *Shortwave fluorescence.* Glass: creamy orange. Paint: no evidence of repainting.

PROVENANCE: Frédéric Spitzer, Paris (Spitzer sale 1893, lot 1993); John Edward Taylor, London (Taylor sale 1912, lot 199; sold to Seligmann); Leopold Hirsch, London; A. de Frey, Paris; Otto Hopfinger, New York; [Blumka Gallery, New York].

EXHIBITED: Corning 1958, pp. 66, 67, no. 57, ill.; Cincinnati 1959, p. 42, no. 548.

LITERATURE: Gerspach 1885, p. 161, fig. 77; Garnier 1891, p. 94, no. 25; d'Hondt [1893?], p. 17; Szabo 1983, p. 24, fig. 30; Dreier 1989b, p. 43, under no. 10; Ryser 1991, p. 59, fig. 50.

The decoration was probably produced by temporarily affixing a print to the inside of the dish and tracing the outlines on the underside with black paint. The colors were then added to fill in the outlines, just as if the print were being tinted. There is some modeling of the figures

No. 25

in the paint layer. No metal foil was used to highlight the paint.

The source for the reverse-painted scene on the Lehman dish appears to have been the central group of figures in Marcantonio Raimondi's engraving of about 1517–20 (Fig. 25.1)[1] after a lost preparatory drawing by Raphael for his fresco *Parnassus* in the Stanza della Segnatura in the Vatican. In the fresco, which was begun in 1508, Raphael replaced the figure of Apollo playing the lyre with an image of him playing a *lira da braccio*, removed the tree trunk that in the print partly hides the head of the Muse to Apollo's right, and altered the poses of the Muses at the far left and far right.[2]

The same scene, seemingly copied from the same source, appears on two large Venetian glass dishes, one in the Museo Vetrario, Murano (Fig. 25.2),[3] the other in the Uměleckoprůmyslové Muzeum, Prague (Fig. 25.3),[4] and on a reverse-painted glass panel in the Frieder Ryser col-

lection, Bern, that has been attributed to Hall in Tyrol or Innsbruck and dated to about 1570–90 (Fig. 25.4).[5] The same group (with the figure of Apollo reversed but the Muses in the same direction as here) also decorates a majolica plate, formerly in the collection of F. von Parpart, Berlin, that is dated 1540 and bears the arms of Xanto Avelli di Rovigo of Urbino[6] and (with the entire scene reversed) a late sixteenth-century trilobed majolica basin in the Minneapolis Institute of Arts (Fig. 25.5).[7]

Attributing this dish to a specific glasshouse and the painting to a specific artist is far more difficult than identifying the source of the design. The vocabulary of the gilt ornament on the sides of the dish is echoed on three reverse-painted glasses in the Bayerisches Nationalmuseum, Munich, a large dish dated 1536 (Fig. 25.6) and two ewers of about 1535–38 (Fig. 25.8) that have been identified as products of the Hall in Tyrol glasshouse of Wolfgang Vitl and were perhaps painted by Paul Dax.[8] Dax is documented as producing decorated glass

No. 25, *top view*

No. 25, *detail of side*

No. 25, *detail of foot*

Fig. 25.1 Marcantonio Raimondi (after Raphael), *Parnassus*

("geschmelzt arbait im glaswerch") at the Hall factory in 1538; he died in Innsbruck in 1561.⁹ A reverse-painted plate with related decoration is in the Bernd Hockemeyer collection, Bremen (Fig. 25.7).¹⁰ The painting on the plate

has also been attributed to Paul Dax, but the date inscribed on it, 1526, precludes its having been made at the Hall glasshouse, which was in operation from 1534 to 1635. Wolfgang Vitl founded the Hall factory and

Fig. 25.2 Dish. Museo Vetrario, Murano

Fig. 25.3 Dish. Uměleckoprůmyslové Muzeum, Prague. Reproduced from Karel Hetteš, *Old Venetian Glass* (London: Spring Books, 1960), fig. 50

oversaw its production of "Venetian" glass until 1540. From 1540 to 1569 the glasshouse was managed by Sebastian Höchstetter, and he was succeeded by his brother Johann Chrysostomus Höchstetter, who ran the factory until 1599.[11] It is possible, of course, that the plate was made in Venice but decorated in the Tyrol, or that the artisan who painted it and the related objects worked first in Venice and later moved to the Tyrol.

Glasses with unfired painted and gilded decoration were also being produced in Venice in the sixteenth century,

Fig. 25.4 Glass panel. Collection of Frieder Ryser, Bern

Fig. 25.5 Majolica basin. Minneapolis Institute of Arts, The John R. Van Derlip Fund

Fig. 25.6 Dish. Bayerisches Nationalmuseum, Munich

Fig. 25.7 Plate. Collection of Bernd Hockemeyer, Bremen.
Photograph courtesy of Fritz Biemann, Zurich

and a number of reverse-painted objects that can be related to the Lehman dish have survived. In addition to the two large dishes with Apollo and the Muses, there are a jug and a bowl in the Severočeské Muzeum, Liberec;[12] a dish in the Metropolitan Museum;[13] and other exam-

Fig. 25.8 Ewer. Bayerisches Nationalmuseum, Munich

ples in the Uměleckoprůmyslové Muzeum;[14] the Museo Civico d'Arte Antica, Turin;[15] the Corning Museum of Glass;[16] the Museum für Kunsthandwerk, Frankfurt am Main;[17] the Musée National de la Renaissance, Château d'Écouen;[18] and the Österreichisches Museum für Angewandte Kunst, Vienna.[19] Another was in the Kunstgewerbemuseum, Berlin, and was lost during World War II,[20] and Émile Gavet of Paris owned two others, one of which was later in the collection of Max Strauss in Vienna.[21]

The gray tint in the glass of the Lehman dish allies it with objects produced in the glasshouse at Hall or at nearby Innsbruck, most of which have a gray or honey-colored tint. So far as I know, however, its shape is paralleled only in Venetian dishes. Venetian twelve-lobed *vetro a retorti* dishes without further decoration can be found in the Hermitage, Saint Petersburg (Fig. 25.9);[22] the Victoria and Albert Museum, London;[23] the Museo Civico, Bologna;[24] the Museo Civico di Storia ed Arte ed Orto Lapidario, Trieste;[25] and the Louvre, Paris.[26] Another was formerly in the collections of Max Strauss, Vienna, and Antoine Seilern, London.[27]

Even more closely related to the Lehman dish are two twelve-lobed *vetro a retorti* dishes in the Museo Civico d'Arte Antica, Turin (see Fig. 25.10),[28] that are decorated with reverse-painted portraits of a woman who has been identified as Philippine Welser (1527–1580). Philippine

Fig. 25.9 Dish. Hermitage, Saint Petersburg

Welser, whose portrait also appears on a circular dish in the Bayerisches Nationalmuseum,[29] married Archduke Ferdinand of Tyrol in 1557. If the portraits are indeed of Philippine Welser, it is likely that the Lehman dish was also made after the late 1550s, either in Venice or, perhaps, in the Hofglashütte that Archduke Ferdinand (1520–1595) set up in 1570 near Ambras, his palace at

Fig. 25.10 Dish. Museo Civico d'Arte Antica, Turin. Photograph: Archivio Fotografico dei Musei Civici di Torino

Innsbruck. The archduke, son of Emperor Ferdinand I and younger brother of Maximilian II, departed Prague in 1563 and became regent of the Tyrol in 1568. The glasshouse was staffed with artisans supplied by the Venetian Signoria.[30] See also No. 26.

NOTES:

1. Oberhuber 1978, p. 244, no. 247; Lawrence (Kans.)–Chapel Hill–Wellesley 1981–82, pp. 155–57. A contemporary copy of Marcantonio's print by an anonymous artist also exists, but it is in the opposite direction; see Oberhuber 1978, p. 245, no. 247B-II.

2. See Pope-Hennessy 1970, pp. 94–100, figs. 82–84.

3. Museo Vetrario, cl. VI, n. 50 (ex coll. Museo Correr); Museo Correr 1909, p. 83, no. 487; Gasparetto 1958, fig. 60; Mariacher 1959a, colorpl. 4; Venice 1982, pp. 132–33, no. 178.

4. Uměleckoprůmyslové Muzeum, Z209 (ex coll. Lobkowicz); Hetteš 1960, p. 41, fig. 50; Prague 1973, no. 125.

5. Ryser collection, HGL504; Ryser 1991, p. 56, fig. 44.

6. See von Parpart (F.) sale 1912, lot 172, pl. 10.

7. Minneapolis Institute of Arts, 90.100; *Arts* 14, no. 2 (February 1991), cover ill.

8. Bayerisches Nationalmuseum, G551 (Fig. 25.6), G517, G515 (Fig. 25.8); Jiřík 1934, fig. 41; Egg 1962, pp. 25–28, pl. 3, figs. 6, 7; Kämpfer and Beyer 1966, p. 277, pls. 87, 89; Rückert 1982, pp. 79–81, nos. 130–32, colorpls. 4, 5, pls. 31, 32.

9. See Zedinek 1927, pp. 99–100.

10. Ex coll. Fritz Biemann (130); *JGS* 29 (1987), p. 115, fig. 6.

11. See Egg 1962 and Strasser and Spiegl 1989, pp. 11–13, 159–67.

12. Severočeské Muzeum, 549; Hetteš 1960, pp. 37–38, fig. 32; Prague 1973, no. 130, fig. 31; Venice 1982, pp. 132–33, no. 180.

13. Metropolitan Museum, 53.225.113 (ex coll. Julia A. Berwind), with a painted scene of the conversion of Saint Paul in the center on the underside and gilt tendril patterns on the sides.

14. Uměleckoprůmyslové Muzeum, 2596/1888; Prague 1973, no. 126.

15. Museo Civico d'Arte Antica, V.O.181 (3052); Mariacher 1959a, p. 78; Mariacher 1961, colorpl. 59; Mariacher 1963, pl. opp. p. 104; Mariacher [1970]a, pp. 125, 126, fig. 58; Mallè 1971, pp. 40–41, fig. 19; Barovier Mentasti 1982, p. 77, fig. 61.

16. Corning Museum of Glass, 57.3.43; Corning 1958, p. 66, no. 56.

17. Museum für Kunsthandwerk, 6761/5266/358; Mariacher 1960, p. 32, pl. 59; Ohm 1973, p. 65, no. 119.

18. Musée National de la Renaissance, 80EN11013. For three other dishes in the Musée National (79EN2148, 79EN2162, 79EN2687) that are reverse painted in different styles, see Ennès 1982, p. 31, and Marandel et al. 1982, p. 21.

19. Österreichisches Museum für Angewandte Kunst, F178 (ex coll. Kaiserl. Rat Dr. A. Jele); Bucher 1888, p. 57, no. 571, pl. 5. The decoration in the center was repainted, probably in the seventeenth century.

20. Schmidt 1912, p. 98, fig. 61; Schmidt 1922, pp. 100, 101, fig. 62; Lorenzetti 1931, pl. 5; Gasparetto 1958, fig. 56; Dreier 1989b, p. 8, fig. 3 (all of whom describe another related dish, decorated with two Prophets[?], that was also lost during World War II from the Kunstgewerbemuseum and of which no photograph has survived).
21. Gavet sale 1897, lots 595, 627; Strauss sale 1920, pl. 4.
22. Hermitage, F.772.
23. Photographed by the author, 1975.
24. Bologna 1959, p. 50, pl. 21, no. 132.
25. Mariacher 1960, p. 21, fig. 17.
26. Louvre, 79 EN2159.
27. Strauss sale 1925, lot 247; London 1974, pp. 16–17, no. 25; Seilern sale 1982, lot 248.
28. Museo Civico d'Arte Antica, v.o.181-3050 (Mariacher 1963, p. 76; identified as being in Stuttgart); v.o.180-3051 (Mariacher 1961, colorpl. 47; Mariacher [1966], p. 125, fig. 56; Mallè 1971, pp. 41–42, fig. 420; Mariacher and Causa Picone 1972, p. 45, pl. 60; Barovier Mentasti 1982, p. 80, fig. 64; Marandel et al. 1982, p. 17, fig. 1).
29. Bayerisches Nationalmuseum, G547; Rückert 1982, p. 82, no. 134.
30. See Egg 1962; Fleming and Honour 1977, p. 397; Strasser and Spiegl 1989, pp. 11–13, 159–67; and Tait 1991, pp. 172–74.

Venetian or *façon de Venise*, probably Innsbruck, possibly Venice, about 1570; possibly Hall in Tyrol, mid- to late sixteenth century

26. Tazza

1975.1.1192
H. 7.5 cm, diam. of rim 25.3 cm. Colorless (slightly gray) nonlead glass. Blown, reverse painted, gilt (unfired).

The shallow, circular bowl has a trailed double ring at the rim and two additional trailed rings midway down the curved sides. Above the trailed rings is a gilt border of serpentine lines and triple radial dashes; in the wide band below the rings are four reverse-painted roundels, each with a head in right profile on a dark blue background outlined in white, alternating with four gray grotesque figures blowing horns they hold in their outstretched arms, amid foliate scrolls of gilt and green leaves outlined with gold and with a gilt meander border above and a dotted band below. The four heads, a woman with fruit and flowers in her hair, a bearded man with red-and-white helmet and collar, a woman with her hair drawn back and tied with leaves and flowers, and a bacchic head wearing a leafy wreath, may represent the Four Seasons. The roundels and the grotesques are backed with silver foil and dark gray paint. The trumpet-shaped pedestal foot has an underfolded rim. Rough pontil mark under the foot.[1]

The glass in mint condition, with normal wear; considerable loss of the reverse-painted decoration, particularly the gilding; no evidence of repainting.

Longwave fluorescence. Glass: cloudy gray-green. Paint: black (on the back) and white (the grotesques and the rims of roundels); no evidence of repainting. *Shortwave fluorescence.* Glass: faint, greenish. Paint: nothing; no evidence of repainting.

PROVENANCE: Otto Hopfinger, New York; [Blumka Gallery, New York].

The black outlines of the decoration were painted first. They were then inpainted with translucent colors, backed with silver foil, and covered with gray paint to seal the surface.

Gray grotesques, four heads in roundels, and colored vines nearly identical to those on this dish (and also backed with gray paint and silver foil) decorate the spectacular dish in the Bayerisches Nationalmuseum, Munich (Fig. 25.6), that has been attributed to the Hall in Tyrol glasshouse of Wolfgang Vitl and to the glass painter Paul Dax.[2] But similar decoration was also used on the plate in the Bernd Hockemeyer collection, Bremen (Fig. 25.7), that is dated 1526 and thus could not have been made at the Hall factory, which Vitl set up in 1534 (see No. 25).[3]

A tazza of similar form reverse painted with the arms of Derr and Dietherr(?) of Nürnberg but with no surviving decoration on the rim is in the Victoria and Albert Museum, London.[4] Other tazzas of similar form are in the Kunstsammlungen der Veste Coburg[5] and the Louvre, Paris.[6]

Venetian glassmakers also produced tazzas of this shape and used similar decorative motifs. A sixteenth-century Venetian tazza like this is in the Uměleckoprůmyslové

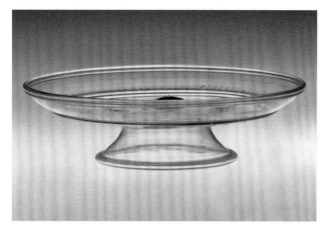

No. 26, *side view*

Fig. 26.1 Tazza. The Metropolitan Museum of Art, New York, Gift of Julia A. Berwind, 1953 (53.225.93)

No. 26, *roundel on bowl*

No. 26, *roundel on bowl*

No. 26, *roundel on bowl*

No. 26, *roundel on bowl*

No. 26

Muzeum, Prague.[7] Another, in the Metropolitan Museum (Fig. 26.1), has reverse-painted red, white, and green disks, yellow latticework, and related vines and leaves.[8] A Venetian *calcedonio* ewer in the Museum für Kunsthandwerk, Frankfurt am Main, has related gilt borders,[9] as does a covered goblet in the Kunstsammlungen zu Weimar.[10]

NOTES:

1. A rectangular gold metallic paper label printed *28* in black and a circular white paper label typed *28.* (both Robert Lehman collection) have been removed and are in the Robert Lehman Collection files.
2. Bayerisches Nationalmuseum, G551; Rückert 1982, p. 79, no. 130, colorpl. 4.
3. Ex coll. Fritz Biemann (130); *JGS* 29 (1987), p. 115, fig. 6.
4. Victoria and Albert Museum, C.331-1936 (ex coll. Wilfred Buckley); Buckley 1939, p. 260, no. 263, fig. 62.
5. Kunstsammlungen der Veste Coburg, HA425.
6. Louvre, R86.
7. Uměleckoprůmyslové Muzeum, Z-106/60-1947 (ex coll. Hossner, Eugen Miller von Aichholz); Miller von Aichholz sale 1925, lot 60; Hetteš 1960, pp. 34–35, fig. 7; Prague 1973, no. 12, fig. 9.
8. Metropolitan Museum, 53.225.93 (ex coll. Julia A. Berwind).
9. Museum für Kunsthandwerk, 6772/351; Schmidt 1912, p. 81, fig. 47; Schmidt 1922, p. 83, fig. 48; Fuchs 1956, p. 33, no. 26; Mariacher 1963, p. 109 (mistakenly located in the Victoria and Albert Museum, London); Weiss 1971, p. 124; Ohm 1973, cover, p. 60, no. 108, pl. opp. p. 64; T. Dexel 1983, p. 281, no. 366.
10. See Hörning [1978], no. 3.

Venice or *façon de Venise*, northern Europe, possibly
the Southern Netherlands, seventeenth century

27. Tazza

1975.1.1195

H. 9.4 cm, diam. of rim 29.5 cm. Colorless (slightly tan) and
transparent turquoise blue nonlead glass. Blown, trailed,
diamond-point (scratch) engraved.

The flat, circular top has a rounded, upturned rim; around the
edge on the underside is a wide band of diamond-point
engraved flowers and foliage, and inside that is a trailed,
nipped blue chain flanked by two trailed, milled colorless
threads. The waisted trumpet-shaped pedestal foot is bulbous
at the top and has a trailed colorless thread around the middle
and an underfolded rim. Rough pontil mark under the foot.

Mint condition; normal wear.

Longwave fluorescence. Strong yellow-green. *Shortwave
fluorescence.* Faint, creamy.

PROVENANCE: Albert Pollak, Vienna(?);[1] Otto Hopfinger, New
York; [Blumka Gallery, New York].

EXHIBITED: New York 1979–80.

Judging by the number that survive, a great many tazzas
like this must have been produced in both Venice and
northern Europe in the seventeenth and early eighteenth
centuries. That they exist in a variety of sizes suggests
that they were designed to be arranged on the table in
stacks, or pyramids, probably holding decorative arrays
of dishes of sweetmeats.

No. 27

Fig. 27.1 Tazza. Rosenborg Castle, Copenhagen

A similar tazza that was given to King Frederick IV of Denmark during his visit to Venice in 1708–9 is in Rosenborg Castle, Copenhagen (Fig. 27.1).[2] Other examples, most of them with diamond-point decoration (ranging from relatively crude to highly competent), are in the Corning Museum of Glass (Fig. 27.2);[3] the Victoria and Albert Museum, London;[4] the Museo Vetrario, Murano;[5] the British Museum, London;[6] the Metropolitan Museum;[7] the Museo de Artes Decorativas, Barcelona;[8] the Bayerisches Nationalmuseum, Munich;[9] the Museo Nazionale di San Martino, Naples;[10] the Württembergisches Landesmuseum, Stuttgart;[11] the Museum

für Kunsthandwerk, Frankfurt am Main;[12] the Kestner-Museum, Hannover;[13] the Hermitage, Saint Petersburg (three examples); the Musée du Verre, Liège;[14] and a private collection in the Netherlands.[15] Another was owned by Max Strauss in Vienna,[16] and yet another was in the Kunstgewerbemuseum, Berlin, and was lost during World War II.[17]

NOTES:

1. According to a note in the Robert Lehman Collection files, this tazza was once owned by Albert Pollak, but the provenance has not been otherwise verified.
2. Rosenborg Castle, 224; Boesen 1960, no. 97-98.
3. Corning Museum of Glass, 51.3.239 (ex coll. Maurice Bompard, Russell C. Veit); Corning 1955, p. 29, no. 21; Corning 1958, pp. 92, 93, no. 97; Corning Museum of Glass 1958, p. 38, no. 34; Corning Museum of Glass 1974, p. 38, no. 40.
4. Victoria and Albert Museum, C.180-1936 (ex coll. Wilfred Buckley); Buckley 1926, p. 40, pl. 18; Buckley 1939, pp. 247–48, pl. 25, no. 138; Honey 1946, p. 63, pl. 25D; Mariacher [1976?], pl. 8.
5. Museo Vetrario, cl. VI, n. 536; Venice 1982, p. 163, no. 250; Murano 1983, p. 17, no. 32; Mianni, Resini, and Lamon 1984, p. 79. For another tazza in the same museum, see Mariacher 1954, p. 81, fig. 79; Mariacher 1963, p. 92; Mariacher 1964, pl. 10; Mariacher 1965b, p. 97; Reggio Calabria 1967, fig. [26]; Mariacher [1970]b, pp. 40, 41, fig. 17; Barovier Mentasti and Toninato 1983, p. 21.
6. British Museum, S.544 (ex coll. Felix Slade; London 1968b, p. 168, no. 234), S.543 (ex coll. Felix Slade; Nesbitt 1871, p. 100, fig. 159, no. 543; Tait 1979, pp. 134, 135, no. 232).
7. Metropolitan Museum, 81.8.179, 81.8.182 (both ex coll. James Jackson Jarves); McNab 1960, p. 93, fig. 3.
8. Ex coll. Plandiura; Gudiol Ricart 1941, no. 77; Frothingham 1963, p. 40, pl. 11A, B.
9. Bayerisches Nationalmuseum, G.556; Rückert 1982, pp. 68–69, no. 97, pl. 24.
10. Museo Nazionale di San Martino, 811; Causa Picone 1967, pp. 71–73; Mariacher [1976?], pl. 9.
11. Ex coll. Ernesto Wolf; Klesse and Mayr 1987, nos. 32, 33.
12. Museum für Kunsthandwerk, WME2/5014; Ohm 1973, p. 68, no. 129.
13. Kestner-Museum, 1930,103; Mosel 1957, p. 49, no. 17, pl. 6; Mosel 1979, p. 54, no. 13 (17), pl. 5.
14. Musée du Verre, Baar 611 (ex coll. Armand Baar).
15. Laméris and Laméris 1991, pp. 88, 89, no. 65.
16. Strauss sale 1920, pl. 13.
17. With the arms of Maria Madalena Chieregata; Schmidt 1912, pp. 99–100, fig. 62; Schmidt 1922, pp. 101–2, fig. 63; Dreier 1989b, p. 8, fig. 4.

Fig. 27.2 Tazza. Corning Museum of Glass

Venice, late sixteenth century

28. Covered bowl

1975.1.1214a,b

H. with cover 11.2 cm, diam. of cover 20.3 cm. Colorless (gray) nonlead glass. Blown, molded, diamond-point (scratch) engraved.

The shallow, circular bowl has a convex center and curved sides decorated with diamond-point engraved swags of tiny circles and an undulating vine with stylized flowers. The low, domed cover has a folded rim and a tapered brim that fits inside the bowl rim. On top of the cover is an applied merese surmounted by a ribbed (seven ribs) ball finial and a smaller ball knop; a ring of diamond-point decoration (clusters of grapes?) encircles the base of the finial, and the exterior of the cover is decorated with diamond-point engraved stylized flowers on a vine that undulates around two scorpions, two dogs, and two parrotlike birds. Small rough pontil mark on the underside of the bowl; another inside the cover. Painted in gray under both pieces: *O. B. 104i* (Oscar Bondy collection); painted in bright red-orange on the underside of the bowl: *L.58.73.56 A/B* (a Metropolitan Museum loan number).[1]

Normal wear on the bottom of the bowl and the rim of the cover.

Longwave fluorescence. Strong yellow-green. *Shortwave fluorescence.* Faint, creamy.

PROVENANCE: [Leopold Blumka, Vienna]; Oscar Bondy, Vienna; Otto Hopfinger, New York; [Blumka Gallery, New York].

EXHIBITED: Corning 1958, pp. 88–90, no. 91, ill.; Cincinnati 1959, p. 42, no. 552.

LITERATURE: Bondy n.d., p. 49, no. 178 (1041).

No. 28

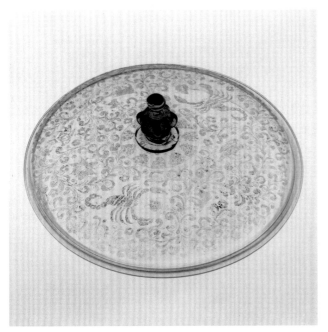

No. 28, *cover*

No. 28, *detail of rim*

The style of the diamond-point engraving on this bowl is characteristic of the late sixteenth century. The outlines of the design elements were drawn first, then filled in with nervous, parallel hatching. Rather than flowing continuously, the vines start and stop in short segments. Except for the symmetrical positioning of the two scorpions on the cover, there seems to have been little planning of the composition.

Similar diamond-point decoration appears on a two-handled covered bowl in the Museo Civico Cristiano, Brescia (Fig. 28.1);[2] a bucket or situla in the Umělecko-průmyslové Muzeum, Prague;[3] a tazza and a bowl in the Museo Vetrario, Murano;[4] a plate in the Musée National de la Renaissance, Château d'Écouen;[5] and a two-handled bowl in the Victoria and Albert Museum, London.[6]

NOTES:

1. The following labels have been removed: Unidentified: oval orange paper label printed *558* in black (in Robert Lehman Collection files). Oscar Bondy collection: rectangular white paper label with *129* printed in black and *BO* written in faded brown ink (not in file).
2. Museo Civico Cristiano, 148; Mariacher 1965a, p. 21, fig. 7; Mariacher 1965b, no. 51; Mariacher [1976?], pl. 5; Venice 1982, p. 129, no. 173.
3. Ex coll. Adalbert von Lanna; Hetteš 1960, p. 40, fig. 39.
4. For the tazza, see Lorenzetti [1953], pl. 17; Gasparetto 1958, p. 286, fig. 80. For the bowl (cl. VI, n. 1127), see Lorenzetti [1953], frontis. and pl. 8; Mariacher 1954, p. 66, fig. 58;

Mariacher 1964, pl. 11; Reggio Calabria 1967, fig. [10]; Mariacher [1970]a, pl. 5; Mariacher [1970]b, p. 38, fig. 15; Mariacher [1976?], pl. 6; Venice 1982, pp. 128, 129, no. 171.
5. Pelliot 1930, p. 303, fig. 1.
6. Ex coll. Wilfred Buckley; Buckley 1926, p. 37, pl. 10B.

Fig. 28.1 Covered bowl. Museo Civico Cristiano, Brescia. Photograph: Fotostudio Rapuzzi, Brescia. By courtesy of the Civici Musei d'Arte e Storia di Brescia

Façon de Venise, probably northern Europe, probably the Netherlands or France, or possibly Venice, early seventeenth century

29. Wineglass

1975.1.1205
H. 13.1 cm. Colorless (slightly purplish gray), bubbly nonlead glass. Blown, diamond-point (scratch) engraved.

Below the slightly everted rim of the tall, ovoid bowl is a band of diamond-point engraved stylized flowers flanked by scroll-work borders; below the band are four scratched sprigs (two tulips, a rose, and a carnation) with hatched petals and leaves. The stem is a slender inverted baluster, and the circular foot is decorated with four sprays of scratched stylized flowers. Tiny rough pontil mark under the foot.[1]

Slight wear on the foot rim.

Longwave fluorescence. Strong yellow-green. *Shortwave fluorescence.* Faint, creamy.

PROVENANCE: Otto Hopfinger, New York; [Blumka Gallery, New York].

Attributing this wineglass with any certainty to a particular manufacturing center is difficult. A similar glass in the Museo Vetrario, Murano (Fig. 29.1),[2] has been attributed to Venice; two others in the Musée du Verre, Liège (see Fig. 29.2), have been attributed to France.[3] Although the diamond-point decoration on this glass is cruder, the similarity of its fluorescence to that of No. 28 suggests that it too may have been made in Venice.

NOTES:
1. A rectangular gold metallic paper label printed *18* in black and a circular white gummed paper label typed *18.* in black (both Robert Lehman collection) have been removed and are in the Robert Lehman Collection files.
2. Barovier Mentasti 1982, p. 120, fig. 106.
3. Musée du Verre, Baar 816 (Fig. 29.2), Baar 817 (both ex coll. Armand Baar).

Fig. 29.1 Wineglass. Museo Vetrario, Murano

Fig. 29.2 Wineglass. Musée du Verre, Liège

No. 29

Venice or *façon de Venise*, probably the Southern
Netherlands, late sixteenth to early seventeenth century

30. Beaker

1975.1.1149
H. 19.8 cm. Colorless (slightly tan) nonlead glass. Blown,
ice-glass technique, trailed, gilt.

The tapered cylindrical beaker has an allover surface of
fractured ice glass and a flared, gilt rim. The flattened foot
rim is trailed and milled. Slight kick in the bottom with a rough
pontil mark.[1]

Normal wear on the top and foot rims.

Longwave fluorescence. Strong yellow-green. *Shortwave
fluorescence.* Faint tan.

PROVENANCE: Otto Hopfinger, New York; [Blumka Gallery, New
York].

The term ice glass refers to glass objects with a crackled
surface that gives the impression of fractured ice. The
effect is simple to produce, although the technique is de-
manding. A gather of molten glass on the end of the
blowpipe is dipped in water. The outer surface cools
quickly and shatters, and (if the gather is not left in the
water too long) the inner part remains molten. The object can then be shaped by normal means. The temperature of the glass must be carefully controlled during the
shaping process, however; if the crackled outer surface
becomes too hot it will begin to melt and the edges will
begin to soften. Apsley Pellatt (1791–1863), who worked
at the Falcon Glassworks in London, illustrated the ice-
glass technique in 1849.[2]

More beakers have survived than perhaps any other
form of ice glass. A glass nearly identical to this one in
the Kunstmuseum Düsseldorf (Fig. 30.1) has been attributed to the Southern Netherlands and dated to the late
sixteenth century.[3] Other late sixteenth- or seventeenth-
century examples, some with gilding, some with molded
prunts (either "pearls" or lion or human masks) on the
sides, are in the Musées Royaux d'Art et d'Histoire,
Brussels (Fig. 30.2);[4] the Musée du Verre, Liège;[5] the
Kunstsammlungen der Veste Coburg;[6] the Österreichisches
Museum für Angewandte Kunst, Vienna;[7] the British Museum, London;[8] the Musée National de la Renaissance,
Château d'Écouen;[9] the Rijksmuseum, Amsterdam (six

Fig. 30.1 Beaker. Kunstmuseum Düsseldorf. Photograph:
Walter Klein, Düsseldorf

Fig. 30.2 Beaker. Musées Royaux d'Art et d'Histoire,
Brussels

No. 30

examples);[10] the Museum Boymans-van Beuningen, Rotterdam;[11] the A. J. Guépin collection, the Netherlands;[12] the Toledo Museum of Art;[13] the Kunstgewerbemuseum, Berlin;[14] the Hermitage, Saint Petersburg;[15] the Victoria and Albert Museum, London;[16] the Musée des Antiquités, Rouen;[17] and another private collection in the Netherlands.[18] Three others were formerly in the collections of Max Strauss, Vienna;[19] Uwe Friedleben, Hannover;[20] and Karl Thewalt, Cologne.[21]

NOTES:

1. A rectangular gold metallic paper label printed *60* in black and a circular white paper label typed *60.* (both Robert Lehman collection) have been removed and are in the Robert Lehman Collection files.
2. Pellatt 1849, pp. 116–17.
3. Kunstmuseum Düsseldorf, P1972.4; *JGS* 15 (1973), pp. 190, 191, fig. 21.
4. Berryer 1957, p. 58, fig. 20.
5. Musée du Verre, Baar 542 (ex coll. Armand Baar); Liège 1958, pp. 158, 159, no. 373; Venice 1982, pp. 135–38, no. 187.
6. Kunstsammlungen der Veste Coburg, HA543; Netzer 1986, fig. 4.
7. Schlosser 1965, p. 114, fig. 99.
8. British Museum, S.700 (ex coll. Felix Slade); Bohn 1857, p. 290, no. 2804; Nesbitt 1871, p. 123, no. 700; London 1968b, p. 147, no. 196; Savage [1975], p. 32.
9. Ennès 1982, p. 25.
10. Van Gelder 1955, p. 39, pl. 11.5; Schrijver 1964, pl. 17d; Van Gelder and Jansen 1969, p. 65, nos. 68, 73; Schrijver 1980, p. 120, fig. 93.
11. Van Gelder 1955, p. 39, pl. 11.1.
12. Delft 1970, p. 9, no. 14, fig. 9.
13. Toledo Museum of Art, 13.423 (ex coll. Julius H. W. Campe); Toledo Museum of Art 1969, p. 50.
14. Kunstgewerbemuseum, 1976.22 (ex coll. Walter F. Smith, Jr.); Dreier 1989b, pp. 77–78, no. 58.
15. Kachalov 1959, fig. 65.
16. Victoria and Albert Museum, C.208-1936 (ex coll. Wilfred Buckley; without prunts); Buckley 1939, p. 250, no. 166, pl. 33; Gardner 1979, p. 37, fig. 24. For another beaker, with prunts on the sides, in the Victoria and Albert Museum, see Chambon 1955, p. 313, no. 34, pl. 9.
17. Bellanger 1988, p. 39.
18. Laméris and Laméris 1991, pp. 36, 94, 95, no. 76, pl. 14.
19. Strauss sale 1925, lot 238.
20. T. Dexel 1977, p. 91, no. 63; T. Dexel 1983, p. 132, no. 76.
21. Thewalt sale 1903, lot 472, pl. 7.

Venice or *façon de Venise*, early seventeenth century

31. Pitcher

1975.1.1213

H. 12.5 cm. Colorless (gray) and transparent dark blue-green nonlead glass. Blown, ice-glass technique, trailed.

The squat, bulbous body has an allover fractured ice-glass surface and a flared rim edged with dark blue-green trailing and pincered into a trefoil to form a rounded pouring spout. The applied, flattened strap handle has two ribs and curls outward at its lower end, and the flattened foot ring is trailed. Slight kick in the bottom with a rough pontil mark.[1]

Normal wear on the rim and the foot ring.

Longwave fluorescence. Strong yellow-green. *Shortwave fluorescence.* Faint tan.

PROVENANCE: Otto Hopfinger, New York; [Blumka Gallery, New York].

EXHIBITED: Corning 1958, pp. 94, 95, no. 99, ill.; Cincinnati 1959, p. 43, no. 557.

LITERATURE: Revi 1967, p. 64; Roffia and Mariacher 1983, p. 187, under no. 194.

For a description of the ice-glass technique, see No. 30.

Philip II of Spain owned sixty-five examples of ice glass in 1564.[2] A "bucket in ice glass with a thread of gold" was listed in the inventory taken in Murano before the sale in 1570 of glass left behind by the master glassmaker Bortolo d'Alvise, who in 1569 had left Venice for Florence, at the invitation of Grand Duke Cosimo I.[3] A wide variety of forms were produced in ice glass, but I know of only one related pitcher, in the Kunstsammlungen der Veste Coburg.[4]

NOTES:

1. The following labels have been removed and are in the Robert Lehman Collection files: Unidentified: oval orange paper label printed *559* in black. Robert Lehman collection: rectangular gold metallic paper label printed *15* in black; circular white paper label typed *15.*
2. Klein and Lloyd 1989, p. 78.
3. "Sechielo a giazo con un fil d'oro." Cited in Barovier Mentasti 1982, pp. 101, 102, fig. 89. See also Tait 1991, pp. 165–66.
4. Kunstsammlungen der Veste Coburg, HA552.

No. 31

Venice, ca. 1500

32. Footed bowl

1975.1.1196

H. 18.6 cm, diam. of rim 28.4 cm. Translucent red nonlead glass with multicolored marbling on the exterior. Blown.

The circular bowl has rounded sides and an everted rim with an outfolded edge. The trumpet-shaped pedestal foot has a trailed (or folded?) rim. Rough pontil mark under the foot.[1]

Normal wear on the foot and bowl rims; slight wear in the bottom of the bowl.

Longwave fluorescence. Interior: dark red-brown. Exterior: faint tan marbling on dark red-brown. *Shortwave fluorescence.* Interior: muddy gray. Exterior: dark brown marbling on muddy gray.

PROVENANCE: Sale, Sotheby's, London, 17 November 1953, lot 59; [Arthur Churchill Ltd., London]; Otto Hopfinger, New York; [Blumka Gallery, New York].

EXHIBITED: Corning 1958, pp. 16, 63, no. 53, colorpl. 2; Cincinnati 1959, p. 42, no. 542.

LITERATURE: Churchill 1953, p. 33, fig. 23; Haynes 1959, fig. 18b.

Book 2 of Antonio Neri's *Arte vetraria*, the famous treatise on the art of glassmaking published in Florence in 1612, is devoted to "the different ways of making chalcedony glass with the colors of agate and oriental jaspers." Neri gives three recipes for preparing "calcidonio"

glass by adding metallic compounds to "well cleaned glass made from cullet of crystal vessels and cristallino, or at least used white glass, since pristine glass fritt never before used cannot yield chalcedony glass."[2] The first recipe (as translated by Christopher Merret in 1662) continues:

> Let the glass boil, and settle 24 hours at least, then make a little glass body of it, which put in the furnace many times, and see if the glass be enough, and if there be on the outside toyes of Blew, and Sea-green, Red, Yellow, and all colours . . . and it hath some waves, such as Calcidony, Jaspers, Oriental Agats have, and that the body kept within be as to the sight as red as fire. Now as soon as it is made and perfected, it is wrought into vessels always variegated.[3]

"Thus," Jean Haudicquer de Blancourt added in 1699, "you may perfectly imitate Agat, oriental Chalcedony, with the Fairest and most Beautifull Colours, and wavings, so lively and full, that it will seem as if nature her self could not arrive to the like perfection, or art imitate it."[4]

Fig. 32.1 Footed bowl. Pinacoteca Civica Tosio-Martinengo, Brescia. Photograph: Fotostudio Rapuzzi, Brescia

No. 32, *top view*

No. 32

Vessels made of *calcedonio*, or marbled, glass were mentioned in an inventory taken at the factory of Giovanni Barovier in Venice in 1496.[5] The 1542 inventory of glass belonging to King Henry VIII lists "thre Bolles of glasse jasper colour withowte covers two of them having feete."[6] A *calcedonio* ewer appears in the right foreground of *The Gathering of the Manna* (National Gallery of Art, Washington, D.C.), a painting by Bachiacca (1494–1557) that is dated to between 1540 and 1555.[7]

The reddish tint to the Lehman bowl dates it to about the turn of the sixteenth century. Trumpet-footed *calcedonio* bowls like this, all attributed to Venice and dated to the late fifteenth or early sixteenth century, are in the Österreichisches Museum für Angewandte Kunst, Vienna;[8] the J. Paul Getty Museum, Malibu;[9] the Kunstgewerbemuseum, Berlin;[10] the Pinacoteca Civica Tosio-Martinengo, Brescia (Fig. 32.1);[11] the Museo Civico d'Arte Antica, Turin;[12] the Corning Museum of Glass;[13] and the British Museum, London.[14] Similarly shaped marbled bowls, but with trailed foot rings, can be found in the Victoria and Albert Museum, London;[15] the Kunstsammlungen der Veste Coburg;[16] and the Österreichisches Museum für Angewandte Kunst.[17]

NOTES:

1. The following labels have been removed: Unidentified: oval orange paper label printed *550* in black; fragmentary rectangular white paper label with *2 smaller in the / Briti Musm.2* written in brown ink. Metropolitan Museum: rectangular gummed white paper label typed *L.58.73.62* (a loan number) in red. Robert Lehman collection: rectangular gold metallic paper label printed *78* in black.

2. Quoted and translated in Neri (1612) 1980, introduction by Barovier Mentasti, pp. LVI–LVII.

3. Neri 1612, book 2, chap. 42, pp. 39–40 (English translation by Christopher Merret, 1662): "Si lasci il vetro quocere, e riposare al meno hore ventiquattro, poi se ne faccia una boccietta, & si rinfuocoli più volte nella fornace, & si cavi fuora, e si vegga se il vetro sta a ragione, e se da fuori scherzi d'aierino, di verde, d'acqua marina, di rosso, di giallo, e di tutti i colori, con scherzi, & onde bellissime, come fa il Calcidonio, Diaspro, & Agata Orientale, e che la boccia guardata dentro all'Aria sia rossa, come un fuoco, all'hora come a fatto e stagionato, si lavori in vasi sempre lisci, & non riformati, che non vengano bene, e questi di diverse sorti." See also Neri 1612 (1662), pp. 59–62, 70–85.

4. Neri (1612) 1699 (English translation of the French edition of 1697), p. 98. When Christopher Merret translated Neri's work into English in 1662 he added lengthy comments of his own. In 1697, without giving due credit to either Neri or Merret, Haudicquer de Blancourt incorporated the Neri-Merret text (derived from a Latin translation printed in Amsterdam in 1668), with his own elaborations, into his *De l'art de la verrerie*. An English translation of Haudicquer de Blancourt's text was published in London in 1699. See Barovier Mentasti in Neri (1612) 1980, introduction, pp. LX–LXII.

5. See Zecchin 1968, pp. 105–9.

6. Hartshorne 1897, p. 464.

7. National Gallery of Art, 1952.5.4(791); Nikolenko 1966, p. 59, fig. 71. Spouted ewers different in form from the one in the painting are in the Victoria and Albert Museum, London (c.1828–1855; Honey 1946, pp. 57–58, pl. 20A; Mariacher 1961, colorpl. 38; Isings 1966, fig. 42); the Museo Nazionale del Bargello, Florence (Mariacher 1954, p. 54, fig. 45; Mariacher [1966], p. 136, fig. 62; Mariacher [1970]a, pp. 136, 138, fig. 64); the Museum für Kunsthandwerk, Frankfurt am Main (6772/351; Schmidt 1912, p. 81, fig. 47; Schmidt 1922, pp. 83, 84, fig. 48; Fuchs 1956, p. 33, no. 26; Mariacher 1963, p. 109 [incorrectly located in the Victoria and Albert Museum]; Weiss 1971, p. 124; Ohm 1973, cover ill., p. 60, no. 108, pl. opp. p. 64; T. Dexel 1983, p. 281, no. 366); and the Cleveland Museum of Art (85.141; *JGS* 28 [1986], p. 100, fig. 9).

8. Österreichisches Museum für Angewandte Kunst, 2414 (ex coll. Max Strauss); Strauss sale 1925, lot 254; Schlosser 1951, pp. 5, 12, pl. 43; Mariacher 1963, p. 109. The museum also has a marbled glass bowl with a flared foot (Schlosser 1965, p. 115, fig. 100).

9. J. Paul Getty Museum, 84.DK.660 (ex coll. Fritz Biemann); Düsseldorf 1968–69, p. 28, no. 59; Gateau 1974, pp. 65, 125; Klesse and Von Saldern 1978, pp. 106, 107, no. 43; Lucerne 1981, p. 157, no. 661; Venice 1982, p. 94, no. 93; Biemann sale 1984, lot 48.

10. Kunstgewerbemuseum, 1975,46; *JGS* 19 (1977), p. 171, fig. 15; Dreier 1989b, cover ill., pp. 54–56, no. 26.

11. Zecchin 1987–89, vol. 2, p. 225.

12. Museo Civico d'Arte Antica, 163VE; Mariacher 1960, pl. 40; Mallè 1971, p. 37, fig. 13.

13. Corning Museum of Glass, 59.3.23.

14. British Museum, O.A.51110.

15. Victoria and Albert Museum, 5574-1859; Honey 1946, p. 57, pl. 20C.

16. Kunstsammlungen der Veste Coburg, HA729.

17. Schlosser 1965, p. 115, fig. 100.

No. 33

Probably Venice, probably late nineteenth century

33. Bowl

1975.1.1183
H. 3.8 cm, diam. of rim 14.4 cm. Translucent amber nonlead glass with multicolored marbling on the exterior. Blown.

The shallow, circular bowl has curved sides. Slight kick in the bottom with a rough pontil mark.[1]

Slight wear on the base.

Longwave fluorescence. Interior: nothing. Exterior: tan marbling. *Shortwave fluorescence.* Interior: muddy gray. Exterior: cream marbling on brownish tan.

PROVENANCE: Otto Hopfinger, New York; [Blumka Gallery, New York].

EXHIBITED: New York 1983–84.

Assigning a specific date to this small bowl is difficult. Its simple form is not necessarily early (but see No. 28), however, and the lack of wear, the amber background color (rather than reddish, as No. 32), and the strong marbling suggest that it probably dates to the last half of the nineteenth century, when the making of *calcedonio* glass was revived in Venice (see No. 35).

No. 33, *bottom view*

NOTE:
1. The following labels have been removed and are in the Robert Lehman Collection files: Unidentified: circular white paper label with a printed blue frame and *185/6* written in pencil. Robert Lehman collection: rectangular gold metallic paper label printed *76* in black; circular white paper label typed *76*.

Venice (possibly Salviati), late nineteenth century

34. Vase

1975.1.1200

H. 20.3 cm. Opalescent bluish white and marbled multicolored brownish nonlead glass (strong brownish marbling on the exterior, faint bluish marbling on the interior). Blown, trailed.

The amphora-shaped vase has an ovoid body and a waisted neck encircled by a trailed angular ring. The two trailed loop handles have folded projections near where they are attached to the ring at the neck. The body tapers to a marbled merese above a trumpet-shaped pedestal foot that is brownish underneath. Marbleized cream-colored rough pontil mark under the foot.[1]

Small open bubble on the side (a manufacturing defect); slight wear on the foot rim.

Longwave fluorescence. Inside: vase = reddish tan, foot = dark brown. Outside: marbled red-brown and tan. *Shortwave fluorescence.* Inside: vase = faint blue, foot = pea green. Outside: strong marbled bluish white with tan swirls.

PROVENANCE: Otto Hopfinger, New York; [Blumka Gallery, New York].

EXHIBITED: New York 1983–84.

The intensity of the marbling identifies this vase as a late nineteenth-century interpretation of a classical form. A ewer in the Gemeentemuseum, The Hague,[2] and one in the Museo Vetrario, Murano, that was made by Lorenzo Radi in about 1856 (Fig. 34.1)[3] display similar marbled veining, as does a neoclassical vase in the Corning Museum of Glass (Fig. 34.2) that was made by Antonio Salviati (1816–1890), probably in the late nineteenth century.[4] Radi had already been experimenting with marbled and veined glass when he and Salviati became partners in 1859. That year Salviati founded the Venetian glass factory specializing in enameled glass and mosaics that was known by various names over the next thirty years. Salviati played a key role in the revival of the Venetian glass industry in the nineteenth century, producing ornamental and table glass in Renaissance styles as well as imitations of ancient Roman glass (see also Nos. 40, 49–51, 73, 80).[5]

NOTES:
1. A rectangular gold metallic paper label printed 74 in black and a circular white paper label typed 74. (both Robert Lehman collection) have been removed and are in the Robert Lehman Collection files.
2. The Hague 1972, p. 16, no. 71, pl. 18.
3. Murano 1978, pp. 7, 26, no. 125, pl. 2.
4. Corning Museum of Glass, 71.3.161 (ex coll. Frederick Carder, Gladys Welles).

Fig. 34.1 Ewer. Museo Vetrario, Murano

Fig. 34.2 Vase. Corning Museum of Glass, Bequest of Gladys C. Welles

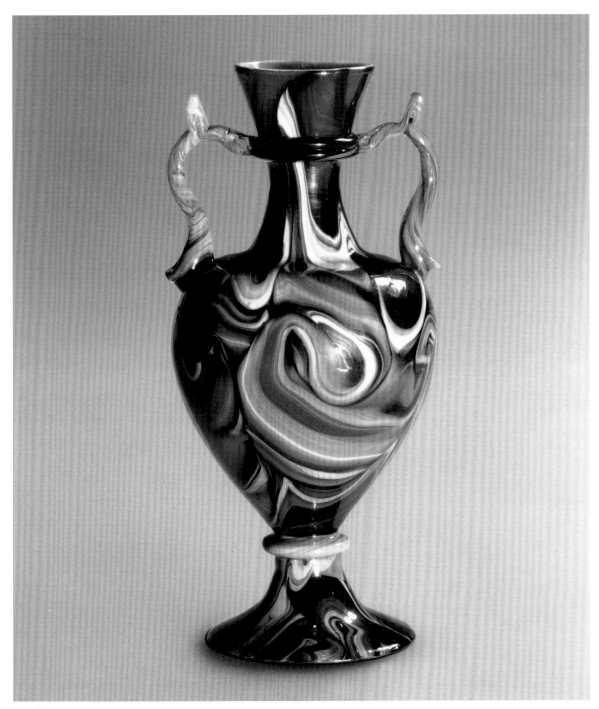

No. 34

5. See Barovier Mentasti 1982, pp. 200–222; Klein and Lloyd 1989, pp. 182–83; Sarpellon et al. 1989, pp. 13–17; and Tait 1991, pp. 202–3. According to Barovier Mentasti and Sarpellon et al., the company was known as Salviati Dott. Antonio fu Bartolomeo from 1859 to 1866(?). In 1866 Salviati formed the Società Anonima per Azioni Salviati & C., which was established in London and had its factory in Murano. In 1872 the name was changed to the Venice and Murano Glass and Mosaic Company Limited (Salviati & C.), infor-mally the Compagnia Venezia e Murano, and that name continued to be used after 1877, when Salviati formed two firms, Salviati & C. (specializing in enamels and mosaics) and Salviati Dr. Antonio (specializing in blown glass), both headed by him. After 1877 various members of the Barovier and Camozzo families played increasingly important roles in the Salviati glassworks. In 1883 ownership of the Salviati furnace was transferred to the two families. In 1896 the company was renamed Artisti Barovier.

Venice (probably Giuseppe Barovier), late
nineteenth century

35. Vase

1975.1.1602
H. 8.2 cm, diam. of rim 5.9 cm. Translucent amber nonlead
glass with multicolored marbling on the exterior. Blown.

The urnlike vase has a bulbous, waisted body with a cup-
shaped rim and two applied inverted loop handles that curl at
the upper terminals. A merese separates the body from the
trumpet-shaped pedestal foot, which has an underfolded rim.
Ring-shaped pontil mark under the foot.[1]

Mint condition; no wear.

Longwave fluorescence. Interior: red-brown. Exterior: red-
brown. *Shortwave fluorescence.* Interior: strong bluish white.
Exterior: slight marbling on strong bluish white.

PROVENANCE: Otto Hopfinger, New York; [Blumka Gallery, New
York].

EXHIBITED: New York 1983–84.

Fig. 35.2 Vase. Museo Vetrario, Murano

Small urns like this were made in Venice in the late seventeenth and eighteenth centuries, usually of opaque white
or colorless glass, as parts of large and elaborate table
settings designed to imitate formal gardens.[2]

Calcedonio was popular in the late fifteenth and early
sixteenth centuries and was also made in the seventeenth
and early eighteenth centuries. It was produced again in
the mid-nineteenth century as part of the revival of Venetian glassmaking that was stimulated by the opening

Fig. 35.1 Vases. Barovier collection, Murano. Photograph courtesy of Rosa Barovier Mentasti, Venice

No. 35

of the Museo Vetrario in Murano in 1861.[3] A key figure in the Muranese revival was Giuseppe Barovier (1853–1942), who in 1868, when he was just fifteen years old, was described as "a young man with much drive, whose work, admirable for his age, revealed extraordinary genius."[4] Among the many objects Barovier created based on ancient Greek and Roman prototypes are two small footed vessels, one of *calcedonio* glass (Fig. 35.1), that like the Lehman vase echo the form of a *kantharos*.[5]

A larger urn in the Museo Vetrario, of nearly the same form but in black glass with metallic spangles (Fig. 35.2), was made by Francesco Ferro e Figlio, a Venetian glass-house in operation in the last quarter of the nineteenth century.[6] A similar vase in the Metropolitan Museum, of olive green glass with colored spangles, has been attributed to Salviati's Compagnia Venezia e Murano (see No. 34) and dated to about 1875.[7]

NOTES:

1. The following labels have been removed and are in the Robert Lehman Collection files: Unidentified: rectangular white paper label with a printed blue and white dotted frame and *3800*(?) written in brown ink and *4071* written in light gray ink. Robert Lehman collection: rectangular gold metallic paper label typed *85* in black; rectangular white paper label printed *85.* in black.

2. See, for example, Mariacher 1965b, pp. 61, 67, 68; Isings 1966, fig. 118.

3. See Barovier Mentasti 1974.

4. Zanetti 1868, quoted and translated in Barovier Mentasti 1974, p. 117.

5. Barovier Mentasti 1974, p. 118, fig. 12.

6. Gasparetto 1960b, p. 31, no. 20, pl. 7a; Murano 1978, p. 28, no. 216, fig. 61; Berlin 1981b, pp. 20, 34, 35, no. 65, fig. 23; Barovier Mentasti 1982, p. 216, fig. 219; Venice 1982, p. 234, no. 446.

7. Metropolitan Museum, 81.8.74 (ex coll. James Jackson Jarves).

Northern Europe, probably Bohemia or Germany, possibly early sixteenth century, probably late nineteenth century

36. Jug

1975.1.1173
H. 22.9 cm. Transparent dark blue nonlead glass. Blown, pattern molded, trailed.

Twenty-four vertical ribs reaching almost to the rim decorate the globular body and cylindrical, straight-sided neck. The applied loop handle has a small pincered thumbpiece at the top and lacks a decorative terminal at the bottom, where it is poorly attached. The coil-wound foot has a pincered rim. Rough pontil mark under the foot. Painted in white under the foot: *7009.* (unidentified).[1]

Slight wear on the neck rim; some wear on the bottom of the foot rim; heavy wear in places on the sides of the points on the foot rim and along the ribs; Y-shaped crack through the bottom. Stain on the top of the handle from a metal mount for a missing (probably pewter) cover.

Longwave fluorescence. Nothing. *Shortwave fluorescence.* Nothing.

PROVENANCE: Hans Wilczek, Burg Kreuzenstein; Otto Hopfinger, New York; [Blumka Gallery, New York].

LITERATURE: Walcher-Molthein 1926, p. 45, fig. 19.

Jugs in this form were made in the sixteenth and seventeenth centuries in Venice, northern Europe, and possibly Spain, first in stoneware and rock crystal, and, ultimately, in glass. Two such jugs made of stoneware in the Rhineland in the sixteenth century are in the Hetjens-Museum/Deutsches Keramikmuseum, Düsseldorf.[2] The shape of the Lehman jug is especially close to that of a rock crystal jug in the Österreichisches Museum für Angewandte Kunst, Vienna, that can also be dated to the sixteenth century.[3] Several similarly shaped glass jugs, with similar handles, that have been dated to the sixteenth and seventeenth centuries have survived. Examples are in the Louvre, Paris;[4] the Museum für Angewandte Kunst, Cologne (Fig. 36.1);[5] the Art Institute of Chicago (Fig. 36.2);[6] the Victoria and Albert Museum, London;[7] the Uměleckoprůmyslové Muzeum, Prague;[8] the Corning Museum of Glass;[9] and a private collection in Stuttgart.[10] Three others were on the art market in the 1980s, two in London (see Fig. 36.3),[11] the other first in London and then in Bissendorf.[12]

Pincered feet like that on the Lehman jug are found more frequently on drinking glasses.[13] An example made in northern Italy, Switzerland, or southern Germany in the thirteenth or fourteenth century is in the Corning Museum of Glass.[14] That all of the points have survived

unbroken on the Lehman jug is extraordinary, though not unknown. Similar feet have survived undamaged on many drinking glasses dating from the thirteenth to the late fifteenth century, but it is somewhat surprising that the points on a pincered foot rim on such a large object could remain in pristine condition for more than four centuries.

The pattern of wear on the Lehman jug is also disturbing. While wear would be expected on the bottoms of the projecting points on the foot rim, on the neck rim, and on the ribs at the widest point of the curved sides, the jug should be relatively untouched everywhere else. The wear on the sides of the foot rim projections and on long, curved stretches of the ribs is distinctly odd and could not have occurred in the course of normal use. Indeed, it is my opinion that the jug was probably made in the late nineteenth century and then intentionally "worn" to make it appear older than it in fact is. (One could surmise that the pewter cover was removed because it would give the piece away.) A nineteenth-century date would explain the remarkable condition of the fragile foot. And such a weak, poorly applied handle might have been thought sufficient on a jug that was never intended to be filled.

NOTES:
1. The following labels have been removed and are in the Robert Lehman Collection files: Unidentified: rectangular white paper label with a serrated edge, a printed double-line blue frame, and *356.* written in red ink. Robert Lehman collection: rectangular gold metallic paper label printed *70* in black and a circular white paper label typed *70.* (not in file).
2. Düsseldorf–Oldenburg 1979–80, p. 35, nos. 44, 46.
3. Strohmer 1947, pp. 10–15. For other examples of rock crystal jugs, see Lamm 1929–30, vol. 2, pl. 83; Von Falke 1930; and Loewenthal 1934.
4. Louvre, 66EN2721.
5. Museum für Angewandte Kunst, F347; Cologne [1961], no. 107; Klesse 1963, p. 126, no. 268; Klesse and Reineking von Bock 1973, p. 125, no. 223.
6. Art Institute of Chicago, 1927.1005 (ex coll. Jacques Mühsam); Schmidt 1914–26, vol. 1, p. 81, no. 409; Tait 1967, pp. 109–10, fig. 33.
7. Victoria and Albert Museum, 1609-1855.
8. I am grateful to Olga Drahotová of the Uměleckoprůmyslové Muzeum for bringing this example to my attention.
9. Corning Museum of Glass, 89.3.10.

No. 36

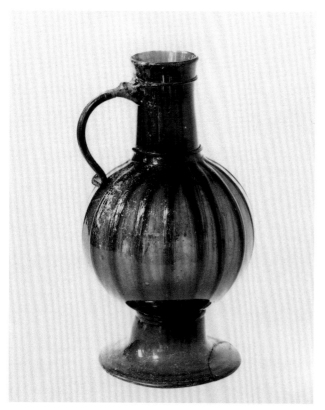

Fig. 36.1 Jug. Museum für Angewandte Kunst, Cologne.
Photograph: Rheinisches Bildarchiv, Cologne

Fig. 36.2 Covered jug. Art Institute of Chicago, Gift of Julius
and Augusta N. Rosenwald

Fig. 36.3 Covered jug. Present location unknown. Photograph
courtesy of Sheppard and Cooper Ltd, London

10. Lohr am Main 1984, pp. 71, 72, fig. 2.
11. One was offered for sale at Sotheby's, London, 6 October
    1992, lot 28 (and see also Battie and Simon 1991, p. 75);
    the other was offered for sale at Christie's, London, 25
    November 1986, lot 223.
12. Ex coll. Hollingworth Magniac; sale, Sotheby's, London,
    24 November 1986, lot 162, ill.; Reinhard Scholtissek,
    Bissendorf (*Kunst und Antiquitäten*, no. 2 [1988], p. 119).
13. See, for example, Bonn–Basel 1988, pp. 181–82, nos. 149,
    150; pp. 186–87, nos. 155–59; pp. 195–204, nos. 168–83;
    pp. 207–17, nos. 188–203; pp. 232–35, nos. 223–28; pp.
    297–98, nos. 339–42; p. 332, no. 398; pp. 337–40, nos.
    403–8; pp. 342–43, nos. 411–13; pp. 347–48, no. 420;
    p. 351, no. 429; pp. 365–66, nos. 450, 451, 453. Pincered
    feet like these are also found on bowls; see ibid., pp. 281,
    283–85, nos. 319–23; p. 429, nos. 539–41.
14. Corning Museum of Glass, 87.3.33 (ex coll. Fritz Biemann);
    Venice 1982, p. 68, no. 48; Corning Museum of Glass 1987,
    pp. 5, 21; Bonn–Basel 1988, pp. 200–201, no. 178.

Northern Europe, probably Germany,
seventeenth century

37. Inkwell

1975.1.1220
H. 6.3 cm. Transparent dark green glass. Blown, pattern
molded.

The globular, ribbed body (sixteen ribs) has a waisted neck,
a flared, inward-folded rim, and an applied loop handle with a
pincered lower terminal. Slight kick in the bottom with a
rough pontil mark.[1]

Normal wear on the base.

Longwave fluorescence. Strong yellow-green. *Shortwave
fluorescence.* Faint tan.

PROVENANCE: Otto Hopfinger, New York; [Blumka Gallery,
New York].

The function of vessels like this was a subject for specu-
lation (they were variously called spittoons or inkwells)
until 1982, when Rückert reported conclusively that they
were inkwells: in an altarpiece made in 1756 for the
Premonstratensian cloister at Windberg in the Bavarian
forest, identical objects sit with carved wooden pens on
consoles near columns laden with books.[2] A number of
such inkwells exist. There are seven examples in the
Bayerisches Nationalmuseum, Munich (see Fig. 37.1),[3]
and others are preserved in the Museum für Angewandte
Kunst, Cologne;[4] the Museum für Kunsthandwerk, Frankfurt am Main;[5] the Badisches Landesmuseum, Karlsruhe;[6]
and a private collection in Brunswick.[7]

No. 37

Fig. 37.1 Inkwell. Bayerisches Nationalmuseum, Munich

NOTES:

1. A rectangular gold metallic paper label printed *20* in black
   (Robert Lehman collection) has been removed and is in the
   Robert Lehman Collection files.
2. Rückert 1982, p. 127, under no. 276.
3. Bayerisches Nationalmuseum, B1050, NN788, 63/73, 13/98,
   13/97, G1340 (Fig. 37.1); NN789; ibid., pp. 127–28, nos.
   276–82, pls. 80, 81.
4. Museum für Angewandte Kunst, F493; Cologne 1960, no.
   326; Cologne [1961], no. 95; Klesse 1963, p. 70, no. 106;
   Klesse and Reineking von Bock 1973, p. 109, no. 177.
5. Museum für Kunsthandwerk, 7445/4896; Ohm 1973, p.
   117, no. 262.
6. Badisches Landesmuseum, Heine Collection; Karlsruhe 1971,
   p. 14, no. 4.
7. T. Dexel 1983, p. 300, no. 401.

Probably northern Europe, probably Germany,
late seventeenth century

38. Cruet

1975.I.1175
H. 14 cm. Transparent amber and opaque white nonlead glass.
Blown, trailed, combed.

The cruet, of amber glass with trailed and combed opaque
white looping, has a globular body, a tall cylindrical neck with
a flared rim, an applied S-shaped spout, and a loop handle that
was attached first at the bottom, then curled at the upper attachment. Deep kick in the bottom with a rough pontil mark.[1]

The tip of the spout broken (in manufacture); normal wear on
the base.

Longwave fluorescence. Amber glass: dark brown reflection.
Opaque white glass: magenta. *Shortwave fluorescence.* Amber
glass: metallic purple reflection. Opaque white glass: strong
bluish white.

PROVENANCE: Otto Hopfinger, New York; [Blumka Gallery, New
York].

The white wave pattern was produced by trailing a thread
of white glass in a continuous spiral around the amber
glass body. While it was still molten, the white glass was
combed upward like cake icing.

The form and decoration of this cruet have their roots
in Islamic glass. Attributing it to a particular center is
difficult because glasses in similar colors and with similar looped decoration were manufactured in Venice, Germany, England, and probably other areas as well during
the seventeenth and eighteenth centuries. An amber bottle with opaque white threading that is attributed to Venice or Germany and dated to the eighteenth century is in
the Metropolitan Museum (Fig. 38.1).[2] The Corning Museum of Glass owns an amber jug with trailed and combed
white looping that was probably made in England in the
seventeenth century (Fig. 38.2).[3]

NOTES:
1. A rectangular gold metallic paper label printed 77 in black
   (Robert Lehman collection) has been removed and is in the
   Robert Lehman Collection files.
2. Metropolitan Museum, 83.7.161 (ex coll. Henry G.
   Marquand).
3. Corning Museum of Glass, 79.2.161 (ex coll. Jerome Strauss).

Fig. 38.1 Bottle. The Metropolitan Museum of Art, New
York, Gift of Henry G. Marquand, 1883 (83.7.161)

Fig. 38.2 Jug. Corning Museum of Glass, Gift of the Ruth
Bryan Strauss Memorial Foundation

No. 38 *(enlarged)*

Façon de Venise, probably Barcelona, ca. 1500

39. Spouted jug

1975.1.1174
H. 25.1 cm. Transparent dark blue and opaque white nonlead glass. Blown, pattern molded, trailed.

The jug has a flared, cup-shaped rim with trailed white threading, a tapered neck with a trailed angular collar, and an ovoid body with molded ribbing (eighteen ribs) pincered into diamonds and trailed white threading forming white dashes on the ribs and thin concentric lines above. The applied, curved, ribbed (eighteen ribs) spout has a trailed white tip and a trailed collar around the neck. The applied ribbed (three ribs) strap handle has two rounded ears drawn up to form a thumbpiece and a long, pointed terminal at the base. The domed, ribbed (fourteen ribs), trumpet-shaped pedestal foot has trailed white dashes on the ribs and a flared, underfolded rim. Rough pontil mark under the foot.[1]

Lower tip of the handle broken and missing; short lengths of white threading broken and missing at the base of the neck; lower edge of the handle broken at the side; broken bubble at the base of the spout; traces of yellow paint on the side of the neck; normal wear on the foot rim.

Longwave fluorescence. Blue glass: slightly cloudy white. White glass: pink. *Shortwave fluorescence.* Blue glass: nothing. White glass: brilliant bluish white.

PROVENANCE: Rothschild (Galerie Fischer sale 1937, lot 486, pl. 37); Oscar Bondy, Vienna; Otto Hopfinger, New York; [Blumka Gallery, New York].

EXHIBITED: New York 1983–84.

The white trailing on the foot and on the body of this ewer, though applied separately, was treated in the same way. The initial gather of glass was inserted into a deeply ribbed mold. The ribbed gather was then trailed with a continuous thread of white glass that melted into the outer parts of the ribs but spanned the spaces between

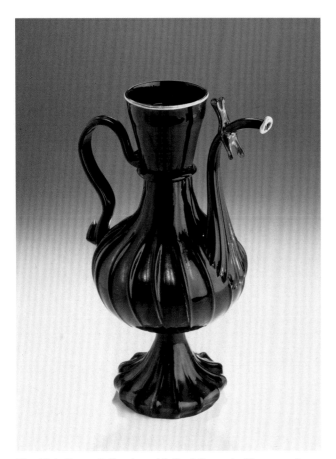

Fig. 39.1 Ewer. Collection of J. Krul, Brussels. Photograph courtesy of Sheppard and Cooper Ltd, London

Fig. 39.2 Spouted jug. Collection of Bernd Hockemeyer, Bremen. Reproduced from Brigitte Klesse and Axel von Saldern, *500 Jahre Glaskunst: Sammlung Biemann* (Zurich: ABC Verlag, 1978), no. 260

No. 39

Fig. 39.3 Spouted jug. Museo Poldi Pezzoli, Milan

Fig. 39.4 Spouted jug. Museo Civico d'Arte Antica, Turin.
Photograph: Archivio Fotografico dei Musei Civici di Torino

Fig. 39.5 Basin. Museo de Artes Decorativas, Barcelona

them. When the gather was inflated, the threading broke over the gaps, and as the form got larger and larger the short strips of white threading on the ribbing became farther and farther apart. (Note how the threading at the top of the foot, where the expansion was least, is a continuous, though wavy, band.)

Sixteenth-century ewers, basins, and other glasses with similar checkered white trailing have survived in both Italian and Spanish collections. It could be that the distinctive decorating technique originated in Italy and was later adopted in Barcelona.

The shape of this ewer's ribbed body, foot, and spout is echoed in an amethyst glass ewer in the J. Krul collection, Brussels, that is thought to have been made in Barcelona about 1580 (Fig. 39.1).[2] Spouted jugs in blue glass with checkered trailing are in the Bernd Hockemeyer collection, Bremen (Fig. 39.2),[3] and the Museo Poldi Pezzoli, Milan (Fig. 39.3).[4] Another, from Castello di Cereseto, is in the Museo Civico d'Arte Antica, Turin (Fig. 39.4).[5] Blue or colorless basins with similar decoration are in the Instituto Amatller de Arte Hispánico, Barcelona; the

Museo de Artes Decorativas, Barcelona (Fig. 39.5);⁶ the Museo Vetrario, Murano (two examples);⁷ the Museo Poldi Pezzoli;⁸ the Museu Arqueologic-Artistic Episcopal, Vich, Spain;⁹ and the Vito Manca collection.¹⁰ The basin in Vich has been attributed to Cadalso, in the province of Madrid, where glass was being made in the early sixteenth century.

Trailed white threading like this was also used on other objects made of both colored and colorless glass. A colorless goblet is in the Corning Museum of Glass.¹¹ A blue *almorratxa* (sprinkler vessel) is in the José Gudiol Ricart collection;¹² and two other Spanish *almorratxas* are in the Instituto Amatller de Arte Hispánico¹³ and the Museo de Artes Decorativas.¹⁴

NOTES:

1. The following labels have been removed and are now in the Robert Lehman Collection files: Unidentified: rectangular paper label with a blue frame and *Aiguiere / en Verre Bleu Venise(?) / XVIᵉ siecle* written in ink. Oscar Bondy collection: oval white paper label with *G / z. 48* printed in black and *0/32* written in red ink. Robert Lehman collection: rectangular gold metallic paper label printed *75* in black; circular white paper label typed *75*.
2. Ex coll. Lord Astor of Hever; *International Ceramics* (published by the *Antique Collector*), 1986, cover ill.

3. Ex coll. Fritz Biemann, Kofler; Klesse and Von Saldern 1978, p. 307, no. 260; Lucerne 1981, p. 155, no. 656; Venice 1982, p. 102, no. 109.
4. Museo Poldi Pezzoli, 1269; Roffia and Mariacher 1983, pp. 174–75, 221, no. 55, fig. 58.
5. Museo Civico d'Arte Antica, 147VE (acquired from Pietro Accorsi, 1933; ex coll. Sangiorgi); Mariacher 1961, pl. 41; Mariacher 1967, pp. 46, 222; Mallè 1971, pp. 43–44, fig. 22; Barovier Mentasti 1982, p. 87, fig. 75; Turin 1982–83, pp. 72–74, 101, no. 33.
6. Museo de Artes Decorativas, 23674; Gudiol Ricart 1941, no. 86A.
7. Museo Vetrario, cl. VI, n. 483 (ex coll. Maglione, Naples); Mariacher 1954, p. 327; Gasparetto 1958, p. 284, fig. 46; Mariacher 1959a, p. 39, fig. c, colorpl. 3; Gasparetto 1960a, p. 121, fig. 28; Mariacher 1963, ill. opposite p. 80; Barovier Mentasti 1982, p. 89, fig. 76; Venice 1982, p. 102, no. 111. For the second example, see Mariacher 1963, p. 65.
8. Museo Poldi Pezzoli, 1250; *Bulletin AIHV*, no. 9 (1981–83), p. 58, fig. 2; Roffia and Mariacher 1983, p. 175, fig. 55, no. 56.
9. Gudiol Ricart and Artíñano 1935, pl. 25, no. 1; Frothingham 1963, pp. 26, 33, 57, 60–65.
10. Mariacher 1971, p. 26, no. 35.
11. Corning Museum of Glass, 63.3.37; *JGS* 6 (1964), p. 160, fig. 20. The glass is heavily crizzled.
12. Gudiol Ricart and Artíñano 1935, pp. 180–81, no. 161.
13. Ex coll. Prats; Gudiol Ricart 1941, no. 32A.
14. Ibid., pl. 105C.

Venice (probably Pauly e Cie or Salviati), late nineteenth century

40. Footed vessel (saltcellar?)

1975.1.1164

H. 10.3 cm, diam. of rim 9 cm. Topaz-tinted nonlead glass. Blown, pattern molded, applied and impressed parts, gilt.

Below the underfolded rim of the flared, double-ogee bowl is a row of prunts (alternately small, undecorated wads of glass and molded, slightly larger gilt berry prunts) flanked above and below by two trailed threads incorporating gold foil in the glass. The twelve vertical ribs that decorate the lower part of the bowl were formed on a second gather that ends at the tops of the ribs. A merese separates the bowl from the two flattened gilt knops, with sixteen spiral ribs, that form the stem. The trumpet-shaped pedestal foot has sixteen vertical ribs and is embellished with a ring of tiny molded and applied gilt berry prunts, two circuits of trailed threading incorporating gold foil, and a trailed rim. Small rough pontil mark inside the bowl.¹

Mint condition; almost no wear.

Longwave fluorescence. Glass: faint yellow-green. *Shortwave fluorescence.* Glass: strong bluish white.

PROVENANCE: Otto Hopfinger, New York; [Blumka Gallery, New York].

The technique of incorporating gold foil within the glass material (rather than applying it on the surface) is of nineteenth-century origin, and the strong brownish tint to the glass also dates this small dish, which may have been intended as a saltcellar, to the late 1800s.

A diamond-molded saltcellar of similar shape and with similar gilding that has been dated to the late nineteenth century is in the Uměleckoprůmyslové Muzeum, Prague.² Molded ribbing, trailed threading, and berry prunts like those on the Lehman glass decorate a tall goblet, also of smoky topaz-colored glass, in the Toledo Museum of Art (Fig. 40.1) that Klesse believes was also made in the late nineteenth century, perhaps in Murano.³ Another goblet with similar decorative elements (Fig. 40.2) has been published as the work of Pauly e Cie of Venice.⁴ The Lehman glass is likely to have been made in Venice by

No. 40

Fig. 40.1 Goblet. Toledo Museum of Art, Toledo, Ohio, Purchased with funds from the Libbey Endowment, Gift of Edward Drummond Libbey

either Pauly e Cie or in the glasshouse Antonio Salviati founded in 1859 (see No. 34).

NOTES:

1. The following labels have been removed and are in the Robert Lehman Collection files: Unidentified: remains of a paper label with illegible inscription. Robert Lehman collection: rectangular gold metallic paper label printed *81* in black; fragment of a rectangular white paper label with a printed blue dotted frame and *81.* written in black ink, *11571* in pencil (no longer visible), and *5200* in brown (now blue) ink (the last two numbers unidentified).
2. I thank Olga Drahotová for bringing this saltcellar to my attention during my visit to the Uměleckoprůmyslové Muzeum in 1991.
3. Toledo Museum of Art, 58.23; *JGS* 1 (1959), p. 110, fig. 21 (as German, about 1600). Klesse's opinion is noted on the Toledo Museum of Art catalogue card.
4. Marangoni 1927, p. 104.

Fig. 40.2 Goblet. Present location unknown. Reproduced from Guido Marangoni, ed., *Enciclopedia delle moderne arti decorative italiane* (Milan: Casa Editrice Ceschina, 1927), vol. 3, p. 104

Venice or *façon de Venise*, probably sixteenth century

41. Stemmed cup(?)

1975.1.1151

H. 14.9 cm, diam. of rim 9.2 cm. Colorless (slightly grayish tan) nonlead glass. Blown, pattern molded, trailed, gilt.

The shallow ovoid bowl has a trailed ring below the rim and heavy angular molded radial ribbing (twelve ribs), with traces of gilding, on the bottom half. The two columnar sections of the stem bracket a hollow gilt ribbed knop (sixteen ribs) sandwiched between flared mereses (or trailed disks?). The domed trumpet foot has a trailed rim. Small rough pontil mark under the foot. Remains of a number painted in red-orange under the foot (now mostly scraped off and illegible).[1]

Normal wear on the rim of the bowl (which cracked in manufacture but was successfully healed by reheating in the glory hole), on the side of the trailed ring, and on the foot rim; broken bubble inside the bowl; the gilding heavily worn.

Longwave fluorescence. Glass: strong yellow-green. Gilding: nothing. *Shortwave fluorescence.* Glass: orange-tan. Gilding: white.

PROVENANCE: Albert Pollak, Vienna(?);[2] Otto Hopfinger, New York; [Blumka Gallery, New York].

I know of no parallels for this glass. The trailed ring could have been a seat for a missing cover, but if so the cover was seldom used or was lost very soon, for there is no wear on the top of the thread. (The heaviest wear is on the foot rim.) Trailed rings as seats for covers were relatively common in the eighteenth century, but they are not so common on early sixteenth-century Venetian or *façon de Venise* glasses. The trailed foot rim is, however, consistent with sixteenth-century practices. The proportions of the dome of the foot are unusual, suggesting that it might have been intended as a finial rather than as a foot — perhaps to hold something else, such as a small tray.

NOTES:
1. The following labels have been removed and are in the Robert Lehman Collection files: Unidentified: rectangular white paper label with a serrated edge, a printed blue meander border, and 457 written in blue ink. Robert Lehman collection: rectangular gold metallic paper label printed 7 in black; circular white paper label typed 7. in black (the 7 crossed out and 41. written in blue ink above it).
2. According to the Blumka Gallery files this cup was owned by Albert Pollak.

No. 41

Venice, seventeenth century

42. Wineglass

1975.1.1160

H. 12.3 cm. Colorless (slightly gray) nonlead glass. Blown.

The shallow, cup-shaped bowl has curved sides. The hollow stem is composed of five flattened ball knops of descending size, a short ovoid knop, and, at the base, a spreading disk. The sloping foot has an underfolded rim. Small rough pontil mark under the foot. Painted in orange under the foot: [ ].73.[ ]3 (a fragmentary Metropolitan Museum loan number).[1]

Etched inside the bowl; normal wear on the rim and foot.

Longwave fluorescence. Strong yellow-green. *Shortwave fluorescence.* Faint tan.

PROVENANCE: Otto Hopfinger, New York; [Blumka Gallery, New York].

EXHIBITED: Corning 1958, no. 101, ill.; Cincinnati 1959, no. 550.

LITERATURE: Corning 1958, under nos. 92, 102.

Several glass objects with bulbous stems like the one on this wineglass are depicted in early seventeenth-century drawings by Jacopo Ligozzi (1547–1626) in the Uffizi, Florence.[2] Some of the many surviving seventeenth-century Venetian wineglasses with similar stems are decorated with diamond-point engraving; others have taller, funnel-shaped bowls. Examples are in the J. Paul Getty Museum, Malibu (Fig. 42.1);[3] the Museo Vetrario, Murano;[4] the Corning Museum of Glass;[5] the Museum für Angewandte Kunst, Cologne;[6] and a private collection in Brunswick.[7]

A coin of Pope Innocent XI (1676–89) was inserted in the uppermost ball knop of the stem of a goblet in the Corning Museum of Glass (Fig. 42.2).[8] Other later versions of this glass, dating from the end of the seventeenth century or the beginning of the eighteenth century, have combed trailed threading on the bowls. One such glass is in the Kunstmuseum Düsseldorf (Fig. 42.3),[9] and there is another in the Österreichisches Museum für Angewandte Kunst, Vienna.[10]

NOTES:
1. A rectangular gold metallic paper label printed *39* in black (Robert Lehman collection) has been removed and is in the Robert Lehman Collection files.
2. Cited in Corning 1958, p. 97, under no. 101.
3. J. Paul Getty Museum, 84.DK.541 (ex coll. Oscar Bondy, Silberman, Leopold Blumka); ibid., p. 90, no. 92; *JGS* 28 (1986), p. 107, fig. 31.

Fig. 42.1 (left) Wineglass. J. Paul Getty Museum, Malibu Fig. 42.2 (center) Goblet. Corning Museum of Glass, Gift of the Ruth Bryan Strauss Memorial Foundation Fig. 42.3 (right) Wineglass. Kunstmuseum Düsseldorf. Photograph: Walter Klein, Düsseldorf

No. 42

4. Museo Vetrario, cl. VI, n. 65; Murano 1983, pp. 16, 17, no. 31. See also Gasparetto 1958, p. 285, fig. 62, another example in the Museo Vetrario.
5. Corning Museum of Glass, 58.3.194.
6. Museum für Angewandte Kunst, F36; Cologne [1961], no. 210; Klesse 1963, p. 99, no. 189; Klesse and Reineking von Bock 1973, p. 145, no. 278.

7. T. Dexel 1986, pp. 138, 139, fig. 168.
8. Corning Museum of Glass, 79.3.459 (ex coll. Henry Brown, Jerome Strauss); Corning 1958, pp. 96–97, no. 102.
9. Kunstmuseum, 17671; Heinemeyer 1966, p. 89, no. 262.
10. Österreichisches Museum für Angewandte Kunst, 5607; Bucher 1888, p. 65, pl. 5, no. 5607.

Probably *façon de Venise*, northern Europe, possibly Venice, late sixteenth to mid-seventeenth century

43. Goblet

1975.1.1156
H. 20.3 cm. Colorless (slightly gray) nonlead glass; silvered metal fittings. Blown, pattern molded.

The conical, straight-sided bowl has twelve ribs. A merese separates the bowl from a hollow stem composed of a short, cylindrical section above an angular inverted baluster that is set into a silvered metal collar with a flared basal glass disk. The conical foot has an underfolded rim. A tiny brass screw penetrates the foot and stem and is secured under the foot by a square brass nut. Rough pontil mark under the foot.[1]

Heavily crizzled; the stem broken and repaired with metal fittings, probably in the nineteenth century.[2]

Longwave fluorescence. Strong yellow-green. *Shortwave fluorescence.* Apparently gray, but the surface fluoresces strong yellowish white due to the accumulated dirt and lint on the rough crizzled surface.

PROVENANCE: Otto Hopfinger, New York; [Blumka Gallery, New York].

Fig. 43.1 Goblet. Museo Vetrario, Murano

The heavy crizzling of this glass suggests a northern European origin. While not unknown in Italian glass, crizzling seems to have been mainly a northern problem. A related glass is in the Museo Vetrario, Murano (Fig. 43.1).[3] The bowl of another, fitted with a mid-seventeenth-century Dutch silver windmill and whistle, is in the Corning Museum of Glass (Fig. 43.2).[4]

NOTES:
1. A rectangular gold metallic paper label printed *12* in black (Robert Lehman collection) has been removed and is in the Robert Lehman Collection files.
2. A note in the Robert Lehman Collection files suggesting that "the flat foot was broken and repaired probably still in the 16th century" is incorrect.
3. Zecchin 1987–89, vol. 2, p. 121.
4. Corning Museum of Glass, 79.3.360 (ex coll. H. A. Steengracht, William R. Hearst, Jerome Strauss); Corning 1955, pp. 58–59, no. 152.

Fig. 43.2 Fragment of a goblet. Corning Museum of Glass, Bequest of Jerome Strauss

No. 43

Façon de Venise, northern Europe, sixteenth century

44. Wineglass

1975.1.1158

H. 18.5 cm. Colorless (strong greenish gray) nonlead glass. Blown, mold blown.

The wide, conical bowl has slightly incurved sides. The tall stem is composed of a merese; an angular knop; a slender true baluster above a mold-blown ovoid knop decorated in relief with two lions' heads with swags and stylized flowers between them and ribbing above and below (fourteen ribs above, ten below); and, above the small, disk-shaped foot, a capstan. Rough pontil mark under the foot.[1]

Normal wear on the foot and rim.

Longwave fluorescence. Strong yellow-green. *Shortwave fluorescence.* Orangish tan.

PROVENANCE: Otto Hopfinger, New York; [Blumka Gallery, New York].

The lion-mask stem was formed in a full-size two-part mold; the mold seams run through the swags at the sides.

Drinking glasses with molded lion-mask stems were common products of Venetian and *façon de Venise* glasshouses throughout Europe in the sixteenth and early seventeenth centuries (see also No. 22). The Roman art-ist Giovanni Maggi included a drawing of a wineglass with a lion-mask stem (Fig. 44.1) in his *Bichierografia* (Uffizi, Florence), which is dated 1604 (see also No. 54).[2] A diamond-engraved wineglass with a similarly shaped lion-mask stem (Fig. 44.2) that is inscribed *Barbara Potters 1602* and was probably made in Sir Jerome Bowes's glasshouse at Blackfriars (London) is in the Victoria and Albert Museum, London.[3] In 1602 Bowes held a patent of monopoly from the queen to produce Venetian-style glass at his Blackfriars glassworks, which he set up in 1596.[4] The Victoria and Albert Museum also has in its collection a tazza with a related stem (Fig. 44.3).[5] Other glasses with baluster stems decorated with molded lion masks are in the British Museum, London;[6] the Haags Gemeentemuseum, The Hague;[7] the Corning Museum of Glass;[8] the Museum für Kunsthandwerk, Frankfurt am Main;[9] and the Germanisches Nationalmuseum, Nürnberg.[10] Another was formerly in the Vecht collection, Amsterdam.[11]

Attributing these glasses to a specific area in Europe, much less to a particular glasshouse, is almost always

Fig. 44.1 Giovanni Maggi, sketch of a wineglass. Reproduced from Maggi, *Bichierografia* (1604; reprinted Florence: Studio per Edizioni Scelte, 1977), vol. 2, p. 190

No. 44, *detail of stem*

No. 44

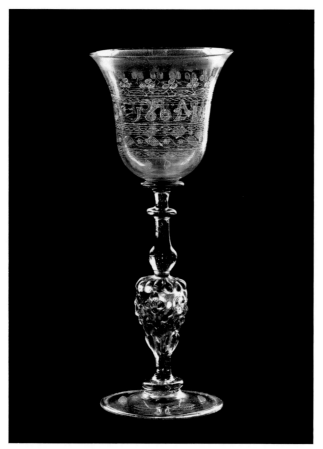

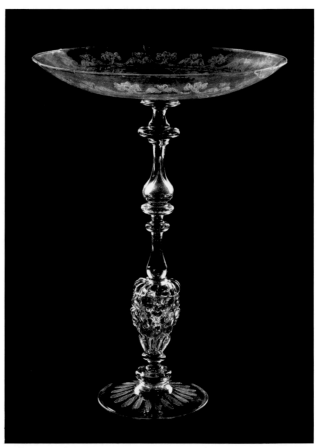

Fig. 44.2 Wineglass. Victoria and Albert Museum, London. By courtesy of the Board of Trustees of the Victoria and Albert Museum

Fig. 44.3 Tazza. Victoria and Albert Museum, London. By courtesy of the Board of Trustees of the Victoria and Albert Museum

impossible. Their origins may ultimately be identified only by studying the individual characteristics of the molds in which they were made and comparing them with lion-mask stems that can be firmly attributed, through either controlled excavations at glasshouse sites or clear documentation. The task is a formidable one, however, given the number of lion-mask stems that have survived.

NOTES:

1. A rectangular gold metallic paper label printed *30* in black and a circular white paper label typed *30.* (both Robert Lehman collection) have been removed and are in the Robert Lehman Collection files.
2. Maggi (1604) 1977, vol. 2, p. 190.
3. Victoria and Albert Museum, c.575-1925; Honey 1947, no. 13; Gasparetto 1958, p. 286, fig. 94 (right); Isings 1966, pp. 71–76, fig. 54 (center); London 1978, p. 13, no. 5; Charleston 1980b, pp. 81, 85, fig. 28; Charleston 1984, pl. 14d.
4. See Charleston 1980b, pp. 79–81.
5. Victoria and Albert Museum, c.344-1936 (ex coll. Wilfred Buckley); Buckley 1939, pp. 260–61, no. 275, fig. 81; Honey 1946, p. 64, pl. 27B. For another glass with a related stem, also now in the Victoria and Albert Museum, see Buckley 1926, p. 37, pl. 10A.
6. Nesbitt 1871, pp. 88, 89, no. 473, fig. 131.
7. Van Gelder and Jansen 1969, p. 64, no. 49.
8. Corning Museum of Glass, 79.3.489 (ex coll. Jerome Strauss; Frothingham 1963, pp. 42–43, pl. 28b), 79.3.323 (ex coll. Jerome Strauss; Churchill 1951, pp. 14, 15, figs. 16, 17; Haynes 1959, pl. 38a,b).
9. Museum für Kunsthandwerk, 7004/4994; Weiss 1971, p. 114; Ohm 1973, p. 70, no. 134.
10. Heikamp 1986, p. 153, fig. 135.
11. Vecht sale 1938, lot 28.

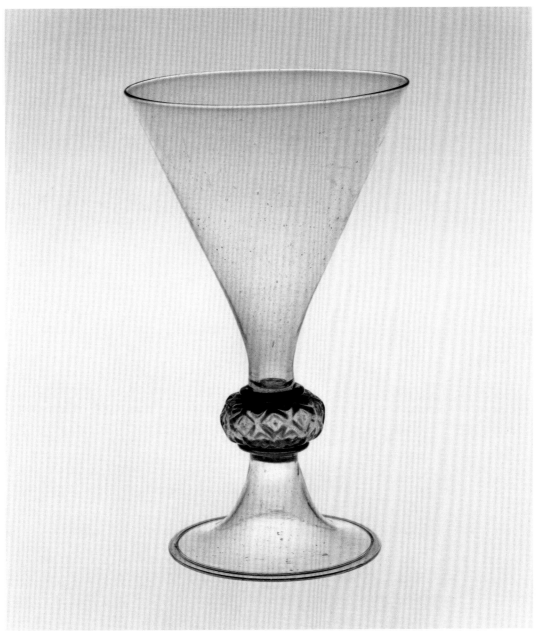

No. 45

Façon de Venise, probably Hall in Tyrol or France,
sixteenth century

45. Goblet

1975.1.1157
H. 23.9 cm, diam. of rim 14.6 cm. Colorless (dark gray)
bubbly nonlead glass. Blown, pattern molded, gilt.

The goblet has a conical, straight-sided bowl, waisted slightly
at the bottom, and a hollow ovoid gilt stem knop, molded in a
diamond pattern (ten diamonds in a row, each with a raised
"eye") separated from the stem and foot by mereses. The
trumpet-shaped pedestal foot has an underfolded rim. Rough
pontil mark under the foot.[1]

Normal wear on the foot rim.

Longwave fluorescence. Glass: strong yellow-green. *Shortwave
fluorescence.* Glass: faint brownish orange.

PROVENANCE: Probably Stift Heiligenkreuz, Vienna (Galerie Fischer sale 1937, lot 506, pl. 35); Otto Hopfinger, New York;
[Blumka Gallery, New York].

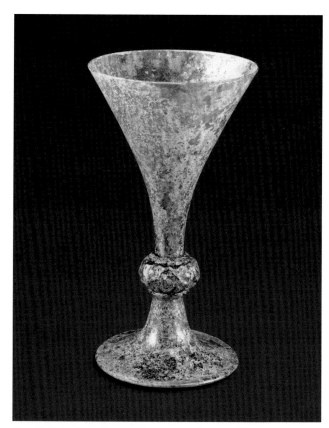

Fig. 45.1 Goblet. Germanisches Nationalmuseum, Nürnberg. Reproduced from Clementine Schack, *Die Glaskunst* (Munich: Keysersche, 1976), fig. 242A. Photograph courtesy of the Corning Museum of Glass

Fig. 45.2 Goblet. Present location unknown. Photograph courtesy of Sotheby's, London

Several related *façon de Venise* goblets, with or without the molded knop, some with pattern-molded bowls, have been attributed to either Hall in Tyrol or France and dated to the sixteenth century. A goblet with a diamond-molded bowl and knop is in the Germanisches National-museum, Nürnberg (Fig. 45.1).[2] The Corning Museum of Glass owns two examples,[3] and there are others in the Österreichisches Museum für Angewandte Kunst, Vienna (with the arms of Matthäus Lang von Wellenburg, prince archbishop of Salzburg from 1519 to 1540);[4] the Victoria and Albert Museum, London;[5] the Kunstmuseum Düsseldorf;[6] the Pilkington Glass Museum, Saint Helens, Merseyside;[7] the Museo Civico di Storia ed Arte ed Orto Lapidario, Trieste;[8] the Museo Civico, Milan;[9] the Rijksmuseum, Amsterdam (two examples); the J. Paul Getty Museum, Malibu;[10] the Tiroler Landesmuseum Ferdinandeum, Innsbruck;[11] the Vito Manca collection;[12] the New Orleans Museum of Art;[13] the Musée des Arts Décoratifs, Paris;[14] and a private collection in Basel.[15] Another was on the art market in London in 1990 (Fig.

45.2).[16] A goblet with a molded knop similar to that on the Lehman glass was excavated at Southampton in a 1500–1550 context.[17]

Goblets of this form, copied from a glass with a diamond-molded bowl and stem in the Germanisches Nationalmuseum (probably Fig. 45.1), were included in the illustrated catalogues of the Rheinische Glashütten-Actien-Gesellschaft in Ehrenfeld bei Köln in 1881, 1886, and 1888.[18] The copies, one of which, of gold-ruby glass, is in the Württembergisches Landesmuseum, Stuttgart,[19] are inferior to the original sixteenth-century goblets in the quality of both the glass and the molding, however.

NOTES:

1. A rectangular gold metallic paper label printed *13* in black (Robert Lehman collection) has been removed and is in the Robert Lehman Collection files.
2. Germanisches Nationalmuseum, G27; Schack 1976, p. 284, fig. 242A.
3. Corning Museum of Glass, 56.3.109; Corning 1958, pp. 46, 47, no. 26; Corning Museum of Glass 1958, p. 39, no.

35; Corning Museum of Glass 1974, p. 39, no. 41. See also 79.3.998 (ex coll. Jerome Strauss); Haynes 1959, pl. 24A (probably the Strauss glass).

4. Zedinek 1927, pl. 87. The coat of arms is painted but unfired.

5. Victoria and Albert Museum, C.216-1936 (ex coll. Wilfred Buckley); Buckley 1939, p. 251, no. 174, pl. 39; Honey 1946, p. 68, pl. 35A; Charleston 1952, pp. 157, 158, fig. 6; Vávra 1954, p. 92, pl. 221; Gasparetto 1958, p. 287, fig. 109.

6. Kunstmuseum, 17684; Egg 1962, pp. 38, 40, pl. 7, fig. 13; Heinemeyer 1966, p. 54, no. 134, pl. 5.

7. Pilkington Glass Museum, 2784 (ex coll. Henry Brown, Walter F. Smith); JGS 11 (1969), p. 114, fig. 29.

8. Mariacher 1960, p. 15, fig. 11; Bulletin AIHV, no. 9 (1981–83), p. 108, fig. 3.

9. Mariacher 1963, pl. 68c.

10. J. Paul Getty Museum, 84.DK.545; JGS 28 (1986), p. 106, fig. 27.

11. Innsbruck 1959, fig. 2.

12. Mariacher 1971, p. 31, no. 44.

13. New Orleans Museum of Art, no. 31A (ex coll. Melvin Billups).

14. Bellanger 1988, p. 469.

15. Basel 1988, no. 6.

16. Sale, Sotheby's, London, 10–11 October 1990, lot 60.

17. Perth and Coleman-Smith 1975, pp. 218–20, no. 1525.

18. See Schäfke 1979, pp. 74–75, 112–13, 182–83, nos. 149, 158, 444.

19. Schack 1976, p. 284, fig. 242B.

Venice, probably late sixteenth century, possibly early twentieth century

46. Vase

1975.1.1168
H. 28.5 cm. Colorless (topaz-tinted) nonlead glass. Blown, pattern molded, trailed.

The vase has a flattened, circular body and a conical neck with a trailed rigaree collar. A merese separates the body from a hollow, ribbed (sixteen ribs), bulbous knop stem. The conical foot has an underfolded rim. Rough pontil mark under the foot.[1]

Internal etching and staining; normal wear on the foot.

Longwave fluorescence. Olive green. *Shortwave fluorescence.* Orange.

PROVENANCE: Albert Pollak, Vienna; probably Hans Makarts; probably Max Strauss, Vienna (Strauss sale 1925, lot 236, ill.[?]); Otto Hopfinger, New York; [Blumka Gallery, New York].

Dating vases of this form is difficult. Among the several Venetian and *façon de Venise* examples with either ribbed or plain stem knops that have been dated confidently to the sixteenth or seventeenth century are vases in the Museo Vetrario, Murano (Fig. 46.1);[2] the Musée du Vin, Château Mouton-Rothschild, Pauillac;[3] the Bayerisches Nationalmuseum, Munich;[4] the Museo de Artes Decorativas, Barcelona;[5] the Kunstsammlungen der Veste Coburg;[6] the Museum für Kunsthandwerk, Frankfurt am Main;[7] the Museo d'Arte Industriale e Galleria "Davia-Bargellini," Bologna;[8] and the Musée du Verre, Liège (with enameled coats of arms). Vases with similar flattened bodies were also produced in Barcelona in the sixteenth century, but the Spanish glasses are often more ovoid in shape and have taller necks, sometimes with applied handles, and smaller, higher feet separated from the body only by a merese, without the bulbous stem knop.[9]

Vases like this were also made in Venice in the 1920s. The vase illustrated in Figure 46.2 was made in 1922 as part of the "classics" line produced at the Venetian glasshouse Cappellin-Venini, which Paolo Venini (1895–1959) established in 1921, appointing the painter Vittorio Zecchin (1878–1947) as artistic and technical director.[10] In 1926 Bellini Brothers, a New York importer, advertised a nearly identical Venini vase as a reproduction of an original piece in the Museo Vetrario in Murano.[11] The Lehman vase is probably an early version of the form dating to the late sixteenth century, as evidenced by the etching and staining on the interior and the wear on the foot, as well as the rather crude flattening of the sides

No. 46

Fig. 46.1 Vase. Museo Vetrario, Murano

Fig. 46.2 Vase (left). Cappellin-Venini, Venice. Photograph courtesy of Venini, Venice

and attachment of the foot. Its slight amber tint is somewhat unusual for a late sixteenth-century glass, but the color is not as strong as is typical of topaz-tinted copies made in the early 1900s.

NOTES:

1. The following labels have been removed and are in the Robert Lehman Collection files: Unidentified: circular white paper label with *574*(?) written in black ink. Albert Pollak collection: rectangular white paper label with a serrated edge and a printed border of blue triangles on three sides and with *A. POLLAK. / 6ii.* written in faded brown ink. Robert Lehman collection: rectangular gold metallic paper label printed *53* in black; circular white paper label typed *53*.
2. Mariacher 1963, p. 74, fig. C.
3. Bernier 1962, pp. 28, 29.

4. Bayerisches Nationalmuseum, G532; Morin-Jean 1913, p. 268, fig. 347A; Rückert 1982, p. 53, no. 42, pl. 10.
5. Museo de Artes Decorativas, 23417.
6. Kunstsammlungen der Veste Coburg, HA178.
7. Museum für Kunsthandwerk, 12248/5192; Museum für Kunsthandwerk 1956, no. 134; Ohm 1973, p. 67, no. 126.
8. Omodeo [1970], p. 119, fig. 9.
9. Enameled examples are in the Hispanic Society of America, New York, and the Victoria and Albert Museum, London (Frothingham 1963, pp. 37–38, colorpl. A, pl. 4). See also Lanna sale 1911, lot 797, pl. 59; Frothingham 1941, pp. 132, 133, frontis., fig. 43; Gudiol Ricart 1941, fig. 54; Lorenzetti [1953], pl. 18; Frothingham 1956, pp. 25, 26, figs. 15, 16, 18; Isings 1966, p. 72, fig. 55.
10. Murano 1977, p. 19, no. 158, fig. 63. See also Tait 1991, p. 14.
11. Advertisement in *International Studio* 85 (December 1926), p. 83. For other twentieth-century copies, see Mariacher 1954, p. 148, fig. 157; Gasparetto 1958, p. 288, fig. 149; and Deboni 1989, p. 35.

Façon de Venise, possibly Spain, Barcelona,
seventeenth century

47. Sprinkler bottle(?)

1975.1.1145
H. 15.2 cm. Colorless (purplish gray) and opaque white
nonlead glass. Blown, pattern molded, trailed.

The ribbed (twenty ribs) bottle has a conical body and a neck
shaped into a bulbous knop, an ovoid knop, and a tapered
section below the flared rim, the knops and rim decorated with
trailed opaque white rings. The body and conical base are
open at the bottom. The flared foot has a trailed opaque white
rim. Rough pontil mark under the foot.[1]

Normal wear on the foot rim.

Longwave fluorescence. Colorless glass: moderate yellow-green.
Opaque white glass: strong pink. *Shortwave fluorescence.*
Colorless glass: faint gray-blue. Opaque white glass: strong
bluish white.

PROVENANCE: Otto Hopfinger, New York; [Blumka Gallery, New
York].

The neck, body, base, and foot were formed of one gather
and blown into a ribbed mold. The hole in the base,

presumably meant to be closed with a cork, was formed
while the glass was hot, rather than being drilled when it
was cool.

I was able to identify only one other bottle of this type, a
bottle in the Instituto Amatller de Arte Hispánico, Barcelona, that is attributed to Barcelona and dated to the
seventeenth century. It too is ribbed and has an opening
in the bottom, and it was formed of grayish colorless
glass.

NOTE:
1. A rectangular gold metallic paper label printed *19* in black
(Robert Lehman collection) has been removed and is in the
Robert Lehman Collection files.

Northern Europe, probably Germany,
seventeenth century

48. Beaker

1975.1.1219
H. 26.4 cm. Colorless (slightly purplish gray) nonlead glass.
Blown, pattern molded.

The slightly waisted cylindrical beaker has spirally ribbed
(sixteen ribs) sides and a trailed foot ring. Conical kick in the
base with a rough pontil mark. Painted under the foot in
white: 5; in creamy white: x (both unidentified).[1]

Normal wear on the rim and foot; heavy white scum on the
underside and on the foot ring.

Longwave fluorescence. Strong greenish. *Shortwave fluorescence.*
Strong yellowish cream.

PROVENANCE: Hans Wilczek, Burg Kreuzenstein; Otto Hopfinger, New York; [Blumka Gallery, New York].

LITERATURE: Walcher-Molthein 1926, p. 67, fig. 48; Klesse 1965,
p. 42, under no. 40.

The molded ribbing on this beaker is unusual in that it
stops at the lower edge and does not continue onto the
base.

The form of this beaker can be traced to the pole-shaped
German *Stangengläser* of the sixteenth century. Glasses
like this but with trailed horizontal threading, called
Passgläser, were used for drinking contests; a drinker was
required to drink precisely to the next line, or *Pass*, or be
forced to try again.

Ribbed beakers of this form with trailed foot rings are
rare. Among the few close parallels to this beaker that
appear in the literature are glasses in the Württembergisches Landesmuseum, Stuttgart (Fig. 48.1);[2] the Gewerbemuseum der LGA im Germanischen Nationalmuseum,

Fig. 48.1 Beaker. Württembergisches Landesmuseum, Stuttgart

Fig. 48.2 Beaker. Gewerbemuseum der LGA im Germanischen Nationalmuseum, Nürnberg. Reproduced from Walter Dexel, *Das Hausgerät Mitteleuropas*, 2d ed. (Brunswick and Berlin: Klinkhardt und Biermann, 1973), fig. 620

Nürnberg (Fig. 48.2);[3] and the Museen der Stadt Regensburg.[4] Another was in the Helfried Krug collection, Mülheim an der Ruhr.[5] Many more beakers of this type have foot rims that are folded extensions of the bowls.[6]

NOTES:

1. A rectangular gold metallic paper label printed *71* in black and a circular white paper label typed *71.* (both Robert Lehman collection) have been removed and are in the Robert Lehman Collection files.
2. Württembergisches Landesmuseum, G606; W. Dexel 1939, p. 417; W. Dexel 1973, p. 306, fig. 619.

3. W. Dexel 1939, pl. 29; W. Dexel 1950, p. 61, fig. 109; W. Dexel 1973, p. 306, fig. 620; T. Dexel 1977, p. 88, no. 56; T. Dexel 1983, p. 141, no. 98.
4. Museen der Stadt Regensburg, K(b)1960/56 (ex coll. Brauser); Baumgärtner 1977a, p. 28, no. 37.
5. Klesse 1965, pp. 42–43, no. 40; Krug sale 1981–83, part 2, lot 319.
6. Four such beakers are in the Museum für Kunsthandwerk, Frankfurt am Main (5888/4872, 5672/4878, x7816/4879, x14894/4920; Ohm 1973, pp. 111–12, nos. 246–49), and there is another in the Historisches Museum, Basel (1905.79; Basel 1982, pp. 12–13, no. 3).

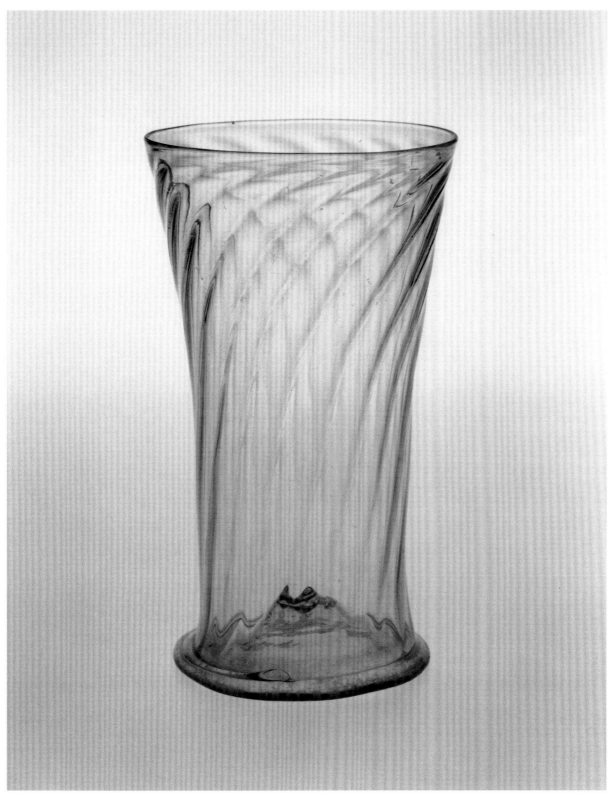

No. 48

Probably Venice (probably Salviati), late
nineteenth century

49. Bottle

1975.1.1150
H. 33.5 cm. Colorless (slightly gray) and opaque white nonlead
glass; pewter mount. Blown, *vetro a fili*, trailed.

Cemented to the top of the bottle's long, cylindrical neck is a
pewter mount with a threaded sleeve for a screw cap. Two
trailed colorless rigaree collars decorate the neck, and seventeen slender white threads standing in relief run the full length
of the neck and the globular body. Slight kick in the bottom.
No pontil mark.[1]

Slight wear on the base; short crack in the bottom, extending
from a stone; pewter screw cap missing.

Longwave fluorescence. Colorless glass: strong yellow-green.
Opaque white glass: orange-pink. *Shortwave fluorescence.*
Colorless glass: faint, purplish. Opaque white glass: faint,
purplish.

PROVENANCE: Otto Hopfinger, New York; [Blumka Gallery,
New York].

The white canes were probably applied to this vessel either by rolling the gather on a marver on which the canes
were laid or by blowing the gather into a mold in which
the canes were placed upright along the sides. Although
it may be of eighteenth-century date, the pewter mount
was most likely added to the bottle some time after it
was made, perhaps recently. Not only has the sleeve been
tampered with, but the mount is cemented to the cylindrical rim. Such mounts are usually held in place by flared
rims, and there is no evidence that this bottle's neck was
broken and the pewter mount moved down.

White stripes like these decorate a bottle in the Metropolitan Museum[2] and a beaker in the Victoria and Albert Museum, London,[3] that have been dated to the seventeenth century or eighteenth century. And the same
striping technique was used on a number of other
seventeenth-century objects. Examples are in the Museo
Nazionale della Ceramica "Duca di Martina," Villa
Floridiana, Naples;[4] the Museo del Settecento Veneziano,
Ca'Rezzonico, Venice;[5] the Musée du Verre, Liège (three);
the Museo Poldi Pezzoli, Milan;[6] the Hermitage, Saint
Petersburg (two);[7] the Kunstmuseum Düsseldorf;[8] and a
private collection.[9] Another was owned by Helfried Krug
in Mülheim an der Ruhr.[10] A group of late sixteenth-
century glass vessels attributed to Barcelona also have
similar white threading standing in slight relief.[11]

A white-striped bottle in the same form as the Lehman bottle that was in the Uwe Friedleben collection in

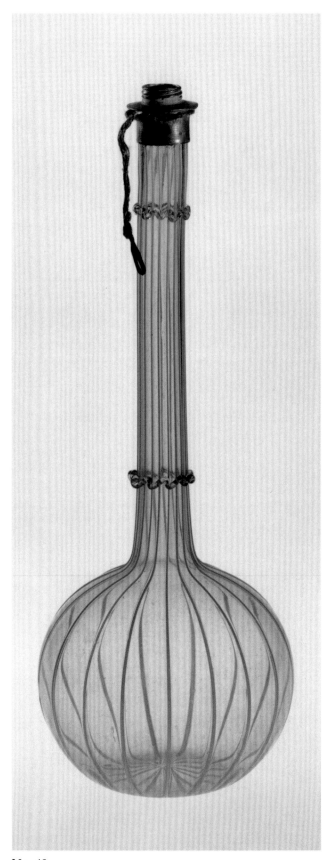

No. 49

Fig. 49.1 Bottle. The Metropolitan Museum of Art, New York, Gift of James Jackson Jarves, 1881 (81.8.283)

Fig. 49.2 Bottle. Corning Museum of Glass

Hannover has been attributed to seventeenth- or eighteenth-century Spain.[12] I suspect, however, that like the only other close parallels I know of – one, with a glass stopper, in the Metropolitan Museum (Fig. 49.1);[13] one in the Corning Museum of Glass (Fig. 49.2);[14] and one in the Museo Vetrario, Murano[15] – it may be a late nineteenth-century product. Bottles of nearly identical form in four different sizes and with glass stoppers are illustrated in a catalogue of Antonio Salviati's glasshouse, the Compagnia Venezia e Murano (see No. 34), that was probably issued in the 1880s (Fig. 49.3).[16]

NOTES:
1. The following labels have been removed and are in the Robert Lehman Collection files: Unidentified: circular white paper label with *715*. written in gray ink and crossed out; rectangular white paper label with a perforated edge, a printed blue geometric meander border, and *380* written in blue ink; rectangular white paper label with *3980* written in pencil. Robert Lehman collection: rectangular gold metallic paper label printed *43* in black; circular white paper label typed *43*.
2. Metropolitan Museum, 81.8.282 (ex coll. James Jackson Jarves).

3. Victoria and Albert Museum, C.5241-1901; Honey 1946, p. 64, pl. 29C; Honey 1947, fig. 10.
4. Omodeo [1970], p. 76, fig. 61.
5. Ex coll. Gatti Casazza; Murano 1981, pp. 20, 32, no. 51, fig. 29.
6. Museo Poldi Pezzoli, 1268; Roffia and Mariacher 1983, p. 180, no. 114, fig. 110.

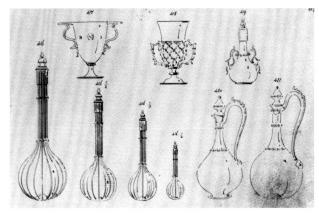

Fig. 49.3 Venice and Murano Glass and Mosaic Company (Salviati e C.), catalogue (1880s). Reproduced from Clementine Schack, *Die Glaskunst* (Munich: Keyersche, 1976), fig. 22. Photograph courtesy of the Corning Museum of Glass

7. Carbonnier 1893, p. 99, no. 282; Mikhailova 1970, nos. 6, 7, pl. 4.
8. Kunstmuseum, 17676; Heinemeyer 1966, p. 84, no. 243.
9. Mariacher 1963, p. 94.
10. Klesse 1973, pp. 128, 129, no. 509; Krug sale 1981–83, part 1, lot 29.
11. See Gudiol Ricart and Artíñano 1935, pls. 15, 16; Frothingham 1941, figs. 30, 33; Gudiol Ricart 1941, nos. 11, 12, 24, 31, 33, 66, 68, 70, 71, 91, 103; Frothingham 1956, fig. 32; Frothingham 1963, pp. 31, 38, 40–43, 49, pls. 12–15A, 16, 17.

12. Friedleben sale 1990, lot 193. I was not able to examine this bottle.
13. Metropolitan Museum, 81.8.283a,b (ex coll. Henry G. Marquand).
14. Corning Museum of Glass, 64.3.27 (ex coll. Wadsworth Atheneum, Hartford).
15. Ryley 1902, p. 271.
16. Schack 1976, p. 65, fig. 22.

Venice (probably Salviati), late nineteenth century

50. Vase

1975.1.1201

H. 17 cm. Transparent topaz-tinted and opaque brownish white nonlead glass. Blown, pattern molded, *vetro a fili*, trailed.

The pointed ovoid bowl is decorated with seventeen vertical brownish white stripes and two trailed rigaree bands flanking four applied wads of glass. Below are two applied, pointed "ears." At the base of the bowl is a trailed rigaree collar. The stem is formed of a ribbed (sixteen ribs), hollow, flattened ball knop on a short capstan; a thin disk with a trailed rigaree edge; a capstan; a ribbed (sixteen ribs), hollow, ovoid knop; and a smaller, ribbed (sixteen ribs) basal knop. The sloping foot does not have a folded rim. Small rough pontil mark under the foot.[1]

The tips of the applied "ears" broken and two tiny chips at the top of the stem (handles probably missing); very little wear on the foot rim.

Longwave fluorescence. Topaz glass: yellow-green. Opaque white glass: orange. *Shortwave fluorescence*. Topaz glass: bluish white. Opaque white glass: strong purplish white.

PROVENANCE: Otto Hopfinger, New York; [Blumka Gallery, New York].

The color and the fluorescence of the glass of this vase and No. 51 are the same.

The applied "ears" were probably the upper attachments of loop handles that ran to the ribbed knop at the top of the stem, where, indeed, there are two tiny chips. A catalogue published by Antonio Salviati's Venetian glasshouse (see No. 34) in the last quarter of the nineteenth century illustrates a vase with loop handles (Fig. 50.1) similar to the type that might have been used on the Lehman vase.[2]

NOTES:
1. The following labels have been removed and are in the Robert Lehman Collection files: Unidentified: tiny squarish white paper label with a typed 4 and 89. written in black ink (probably while the vase was in Robert Lehman's possession). Robert Lehman collection: rectangular gold metallic paper label printed 89 in black.
2. Sarpellon et al. 1989, fig. 384.

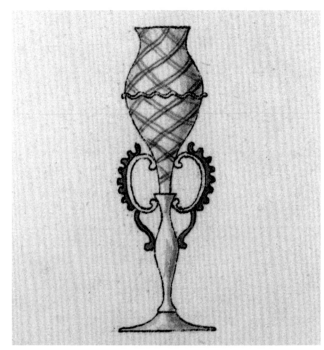

Fig. 50.1 Salviati Dr. Antonio, Venice, catalogue (late 1800s), no. 384. Collection of Paolo Zancopé, Venice. Reproduced from Giovanni Sarpellon et al., *Salviati, il suo vetri e i suoi uomini, 1859–1987* (Venice: Stamperia di Venezia, 1989)

No. 50

Venice (probably Salviati), late nineteenth century

51. Covered sweetmeat dish

1975.1.1215a,b
H. 30.2 cm. Topaz-tinted and opaque brownish white nonlead glass. Blown, pattern molded, *vetro a fili.*

The cover is shaped into four bulges of decreasing size, larger near the folded rim and tapered brim and smaller at the top below the finial, a ribbed (sixteen ribs), hollow, flattened ball knop mounted on a short capstan and a wide disk and topped by a dumbbell finial on a merese. The bowl is similarly shaped and has a flared rim. Twelve vertical brownish white stripes decorate the bowl and cover. The stem is formed of a merese, a short capstan, and a ribbed (sixteen ribs), hollow, pointed ovoid knop set into a capstan. The sloping foot does not have a folded rim. Small rough pontil marks inside the cover, inside the bowl, and under the foot. Painted in white under the foot: *B.i045* (Bondy collection).[1]

Almost no wear; tiny chip on the foot rim.

Longwave fluorescence. Topaz glass: yellow-green. Opaque white glass: orange. *Shortwave fluorescence.* Topaz glass: bluish white. Opaque white glass: strong purplish white.

PROVENANCE: [E. and A. Silverman, Vienna]; Oscar Bondy, Vienna; Otto Hopfinger, New York; [Blumka Gallery, New York].

LITERATURE: Bondy n.d., p. 49, no. 181 (1045).

The color and the fluorescence of the glass of this dish and No. 50 are the same. The brownish white stripes, formed of flattened tubes, stop at the rim of the cover and do not run onto the brim.

Fig. 51.1 Covered sweetmeat dish. Corning Museum of Glass

Fig. 51.2 Covered goblet. The Metropolitan Museum of Art, New York, Rogers Fund, 1951 (51.68ab)

No. 51

Fig. 51.3 Sweetmeat dish. Musée du Verre, Liège

Fig. 51.4 Sweetmeat dish. Museo de Artes Decorativas, Barcelona

Like several comparable glasses, in the Corning Museum of Glass (Fig. 51.1),[2] the Museo Vetrario, Murano, and elsewhere, this sweetmeat dish is a nineteenth-century imitation of a seventeenth-century glass, most likely of Venetian origin. Antonio Salviati's Venetian glasshouse (see No. 34) produced many such imitations in the late nineteenth century. A shallow "champagne" glass with a bowl decorated with stripes like those on the Lehman dish was among the glasses Salviati's firm the Compagnia Venezia e Murano exhibited at the Exposition Universelle in Paris in 1878.[3]

Similarly shaped and decorated seventeenth-century drinking glasses and dishes that have been attributed to Venice or the Netherlands survive in the Metropolitan Museum (Fig. 51.2);[4] the Musée du Verre, Liège (Fig. 51.3);[5] the Cecil Higgins Museums and Art Gallery, Bedford, England;[6] and the Musées Royaux d'Art et d'Histoire, Brussels.[7] Another was formerly in the Joan. d'Huyvetter collection.[8] The nineteenth-century versions are also distinctly similar to striped glass vessels made in Barcelona in the sixteenth century, an example of which is in the Museo de Artes Decorativas, Barcelona (Fig. 51.4).[9]

NOTES:

1. The following labels have been removed and are in the Robert Lehman Collection files: Unidentified: two rectangular white paper labels (one very faded) with cut corners, reverse-printed borders of white dots on blue and inner framing lines, both with *K Ku (Ka?)* / *515* written in faded blue ink; rectangular white paper label printed *175* in bold black, with indecipherable handwritten numbers and letters, one crossed out in orange pencil. Oscar Bondy collection: rectangular brown paper label with *DECKEL* / *ZU.125* / *BO* written in brown ink. Robert Lehman collection: rectangular gold metallic paper label printed *50* in black; circular white paper label typed *50*.
2. Corning Museum of Glass, 59.3.44a,b.
3. See Barovier Mentasti 1982, p. 205, fig. 205.
4. Metropolitan Museum, 51.68a,b (ex coll. Mr. and Mrs. Russell C. Veit); sale, Parke-Bernet, New York, 2 May 1951, lot 138, ill.
5. Musée du Verre, Baar 1372 (ex coll. Sambon, Armand Baar); Liège 1958, pp. 147, 148, no. 325.
6. Savage [1975], p. 13, upper left.
7. Berryer 1957, p. 65, fig. 25.
8. D'Huyvetter sale 1829, lot 4, pl. 19.
9. Museo de Artes Decorativas, 23680; Gudiol Ricart 1941, pl. 27.

No. 52

Venice or *façon de Venise*, possibly Saxony, second
half of the sixteenth or early seventeenth century

52. Tazza

1975.1.1193

H. 13.2 cm, diam. of rim 20.3 cm. Colorless (gray-green tint)
and opaque white nonlead glass. Blown, *vetro a retorti*, trailed,
pincered.

The rounded sides of the shallow, circular bowl are decorated
with a repeat pattern of widely spaced stripes and twisted
canes standing in low relief on the outer surface: a white
stripe, a multispiral cane, a white stripe, a twisted cane with
two pairs of threads encircling a single white thread (all the
twists descending clockwise). In the center of the bowl is a
large wad of glass with a broken projection on top. The stem is
composed of a thin merese, a hollow inverted baluster knop
with white stripes, a collar cemented into a cuff striped with
twisted canes, and a separate colorless bulbous knop with five
trailed and pincered colorless wings. The stem is mounted on a

domed foot with a terraced base knop and a polished rim.
Painted in white in reverse under the foot: *J.156.*[1]

The foot, the rim of which is ground and chipped, and the
collar at the base of the stem are not original and were taken
from two different glasses, probably of late nineteenth-century
German origin. A rod has been inserted into the foot and up
into the stem and cemented in place.

Longwave fluorescence. Tazza, colorless glass: faint greenish
yellow; opaque white twists and stripes: orange. Collar:
orange. Foot: strong greenish. *Shortwave fluorescence.* Tazza,
colorless glass: faint, purplish; opaque white glass: twists =
strong bluish white, stripes = purple. Collar: faint light purple. Foot: white.

No. 52, *top view*

Fig. 52.1 Tazza. Österreichisches Museum für Angewandte Kunst, Vienna

PROVENANCE: Otto Hopfinger, New York; [Blumka Gallery, New York].

The colorless gather forming the bowl of this tazza was probably rolled on a marver on which the canes were laid out, then heated to fuse the canes to the surface, and finally pincered at the end to bring the canes together at the center.

Glasses produced by the same technique have been attributed to Saxon and other *façon de Venise* glasshouses and dated to the late sixteenth or early seventeenth century. A tazza in the Österreichisches Museum für Angewandte Kunst, Vienna (Fig. 52.1), has a similar large rough scar inside the bowl.[2] Two examples are in the Museum für Kunsthandwerk, Schloss Pillnitz, Dresden, one with alternating solid and twisted canes (Fig. 52.2) and the other with all solid canes.[3]

NOTES:
1. A rectangular gold metallic paper label printed 42 in black and a circular white paper label typed 42. (both Robert Lehman collection) have been removed and are in the Robert Lehman Collection files.
2. Österreichisches Museum für Angewandte Kunst, KHM330 (ex coll. Schloss Ambras, Innsbruck); Schlosser 1951, p. 11, pl. 33.
3. Museum für Kunsthandwerk, 37832, 39039; Dresden 1975, p. 37, nos. 10, 11; Berlin 1981a, p. 30, no. 38.

Fig. 52.2 Tazza. Museum für Kunsthandwerk, Schloss Pillnitz, Dresden. Photograph: Staatliche Kunstsammlungen Dresden

No. 53

Venice or *façon de Venise*, first half of the
sixteenth century

53. Tazza

1975.1.1216

H. 11.4 cm, diam. of rim 16.2 cm. Colorless (slightly gray) and opaque white nonlead glass. Blown, *vetro a retorti*, pincered.

The rounded sides of the shallow, circular bowl are decorated with opaque white twisted canes and white stripes in low relief on the outer surface: two trailed multispiral twists encircle the sides and alternating stripes and radial twists nipped to form diamonds cover the flat center. The stem has two colorless mereses at the top; a hollow section composed of two bulbous knops, a large ovoid knop, and a dumbbell knop, all covered with vertical opaque white stripes; and a colorless merese at the bottom. The trumpet-shaped pedestal foot, also with

vertical opaque white stripes, has an underfolded rim. Small rough pontil mark under the foot.[1]

Normal wear on the foot rim.

Longwave fluorescence. Colorless glass: strong yellow-green. Opaque white twists and stripes: strong yellow-green. *Shortwave fluorescence.* Colorless glass: purplish. Opaque white glass: twists = strong bluish white, stripes = purplish.

PROVENANCE: Otto Hopfinger, New York; [Blumka Gallery, New York].

No. 53, *top view*

Fig. 53.1 Tazza. British Museum, London. By courtesy of the Trustees of the British Museum

EXHIBITED: Corning 1958, pp. 70, 71, no. 64, ill.; Cincinnati 1959, p. 43, no. 558, ill.

LITERATURE: Venice 1982, p. 122, under no. 161; Roffia and Mariacher 1983, p. 180, under no. 112; Klesse and Mayr 1987, under no. 12.

The threads and twists were probably applied to the outer surface of this tazza using the technique described in No. 52. The trailed twists running around the circumference were added separately (see also No. 54).

Several stemmed tazzas with a similar "nipt-diamond-waies" pattern, formed of either opaque white twists or plain white stripes or both, have been dated to the late sixteenth or early seventeenth century. Tazzas with nipped twists are in the British Museum, London;[2] the Corning Museum of Glass;[3] the Museum Willet-Holthuysen, Amsterdam;[4] the Museo Poldi Pezzoli, Milan;[5] and a private collection.[6] The British Museum also has a tazza with nipped white stripes (Fig. 53.1),[7] as does the Victoria and Albert Museum, London,[8] and another was at Nystad Antiquairs in Amsterdam in the 1960s.[9] A tazza with both nipped twists and nipped stripes is in the

Kunstsammlungen der Veste Coburg.[10] The same technique was also used on drinking glasses, one example of which is in the Victoria and Albert Museum.[11]

NOTES:
1. The following labels have been removed and are in the Robert Lehman Collection files: Unidentified: oval orange paper label printed *554* in black. Robert Lehman collection: rectangular gold metallic paper label printed *68* in black; circular white gummed paper label typed *68* (not in file). Metropolitan Museum: rectangular white paper label typed *L.58.73.54* (a loan number) in red.
2. British Museum, s.674 (ex coll. Felix Slade); Nesbitt 1871, p. 119, no. 674, fig. 211; Tait 1979, p. 70, no. 93.
3. Corning Museum of Glass, 64.3.6.
4. Van Gelder and Jansen 1969, p. 63, no. 46.
5. Roffia and Mariacher 1983, pp. 180, 246, no. 113, pl. 112.
6. Venice 1982, p. 122, no. 161.
7. British Museum, s.598 (ex coll. Felix Slade); Nesbitt 1871, p. 108, no. 598; Tait 1979, p. 67, no. 86.
8. Victoria and Albert Museum, c.189-1936; Buckley 1926, pp. 38–39, pl. 14A; Sanctuary 1957, pp. 14–15.
9. Schrijver 1964, pl. 8b; Schrijver 1980, p. 46, fig. 21.
10. Kunstsammlungen der Veste Coburg, HA357.
11. Ex coll. Wilfred Buckley; Buckley 1926, p. 39, pl. 15B.

Venice or *façon de Venise*, probably the Southern
Netherlands or Germany, late sixteenth or early
seventeenth century

54. Boot glass

1975.1.1207
H. 23.3 cm. Colorless (slightly tan) and opaque white nonlead
glass. Blown, *vetro a retorti*, trailed, applied and impressed
parts, gilt.

The boot-shaped drinking vessel has a flared rim, a rounded
calf, a tapered ankle, and a rounded toe. Two rings of trailed
opaque white twists flanked by pairs of slender opaque white
threads encircle the calf, and the lower portion of the boot is
decorated with raised vertical opaque white stripes and
multispiral twists, with a trailed colorless zigzag along the
outside of the calf and an applied gilt molded berry prunt
pincered flat to form a spur on the heel. A trailed rim forms
the edge of the flat sole. Rough pontil mark under the heel.

Normal wear on the side of the calf and on the foot rim.

Longwave fluorescence. Colorless glass: light yellow-green.
Opaque white stripes and twists: slightly pink. *Shortwave
fluorescence.* Colorless glass: faint, creamy. Opaque white
glass: stripes = purple, twists = strong bluish white.

PROVENANCE: Otto Hopfinger, New York; [Blumka Gallery,
New York].

EXHIBITED: New York 1979–80.

LITERATURE: Strasser and Spiegl 1989, p. 184, under no. 27.

The stripes and twists were probably applied to this glass
using the technique described under No. 52. The rounded
toes of Nos. 54 and 55 were formed by applying a blob
of molten colorless glass over the striped gather, then
blowing it out; as the stripes expanded outward into the
toes they became thinner and fainter.

Drinking glasses in a wide variety of novel forms were
popular in the late sixteenth and seventeenth centuries
in both northern Europe and Italy. Shoes and boots like
the two in the Robert Lehman Collection (see also No.
55) and those in the Rudolf von Strasser collection, Pelham
Manor, New York (Fig. 54.1);[1] the Museum für Kunst
und Gewerbe, Hamburg;[2] the Cinzano Collection,
London;[3] the Karl Ruhmann collection, Vienna;[4] the
Musées Royaux d'Art et d'Histoire, Brussels;[5] and the
Corning Museum of Glass[6] were common, but other
shapes were also devised to amuse drinkers and to test
their skill. "No drinking vessel can be either big enough
or beautiful and unusual enough for us Germans," Moses
Pflacher commented in 1589 in his "Sermon on the Cost
of Wine."

No. 54, *detail of side*

We drink from apes and priests, from monks and nuns,
from lions and bears, from ostriches and cats, and from
the Devil himself; I will not and dare not even men-
tion the obscene wine bibbers who drink to each other
from tankards, dishes, pots, lids, shoes, boots, wash-
basins, and even in a sybaritic manner from urinals
and chamber pots.[7]

Among the 1,600 drinking vessels in ingenious forms
sketched by the Roman artist Giovanni Maggi in the four
codices of his *Bichierografia* (Uffizi, Florence), dated 1604
and dedicated to the famous collector Cardinal Del
Monte, is a sketch of a boot similar to the Lehman glasses
(Fig. 54.2).[8]

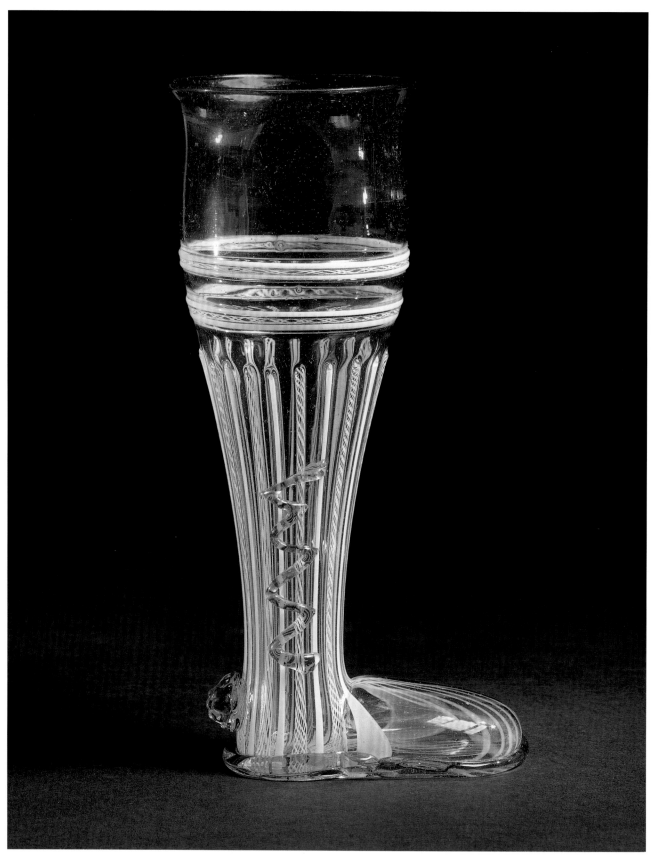

Fig. 54.1 Boot glass. Collection of Rudolf von Strasser, Pelham Manor, New York

Fig. 54.2 Giovanni Maggi, sketch of a boot glass. Reproduced from Maggi, *Bichierografia* (1604; reprinted Florence: Studio per Edizioni Scelte, 1977), vol. 2, p. 150

NOTES:

1. Strasser collection, SR118; Strasser and Spiegl 1989, pp. 184–85, no. 27.
2. Museum für Kunst und Gewerbe, 1919-272.
3. Lazarus [1973?], n.p.; Lazarus 1978, no. 32.
4. Schlosser 1965, p. 157, fig. 129.
5. Chambon 1955, p. 316, no. 53, pl. 17; Mariacher 1964, pp. 103, 104, fig. 56.
6. Corning Museum of Glass, 70.3.326.
7. "Uns Teutschen kann man die Trinkgeschirr nicht gross genug, sondern auch nicht schön und seltsam genug machen. Man trinkt aus Affen und Pfaffen, Mönch und Nonnen,

Löwen und Bären, Straussen und Käuzen und aus dem Teufel selbst: Ich will und mag nichts sagen von den unflätigen Weinzapfen, die aus Kannen, Schüssel, Häfen, Hüten, Schuhen, Stiefeln, Handbecken und gar auf ein sybaritische Weis aus den Matulis (= Nachtgeschirren) und Harnkachel einander zutrinken" (Pflacher, "Weinthewre oder Bericht aus Gottes Wort, woher und auss was Ursachen die jetzige Weinthewrung entstanden," quoted in Schiedlausky 1956, p. 47, and in part in Von Saldern 1965, p. 28).
8. Maggi (1604) 1977, vol. 1, p. 150.

Venice or *façon de Venise*, probably the Southern Netherlands or Germany, late sixteenth or early seventeenth century

55. Boot glass

1975.1.1208
H. 25.1 cm. Colorless (gray) and opaque white nonlead glass. Blown, *vetro a retorti*, trailed, applied and impressed parts, gilt.

The boot-shaped drinking vessel has a flared rim, a rounded calf, a tapered ankle, and a rounded toe and is decorated overall with vertical opaque white stripes alternating with multispiral twists. Along the outside of the calf are four

applied impressed gilt prunts with stylized floral molding consisting of four heart-shaped petals alternating with four smaller oval petals around a central raised dot. A trailed strap runs across the instep and around the heel, where there are the remains of a trailed and pincered spur. A trailed rim forms the edge of the flat sole. Rough pontil mark under the heel.[1]

Normal wear on the foot rim; the spur broken and mostly missing.

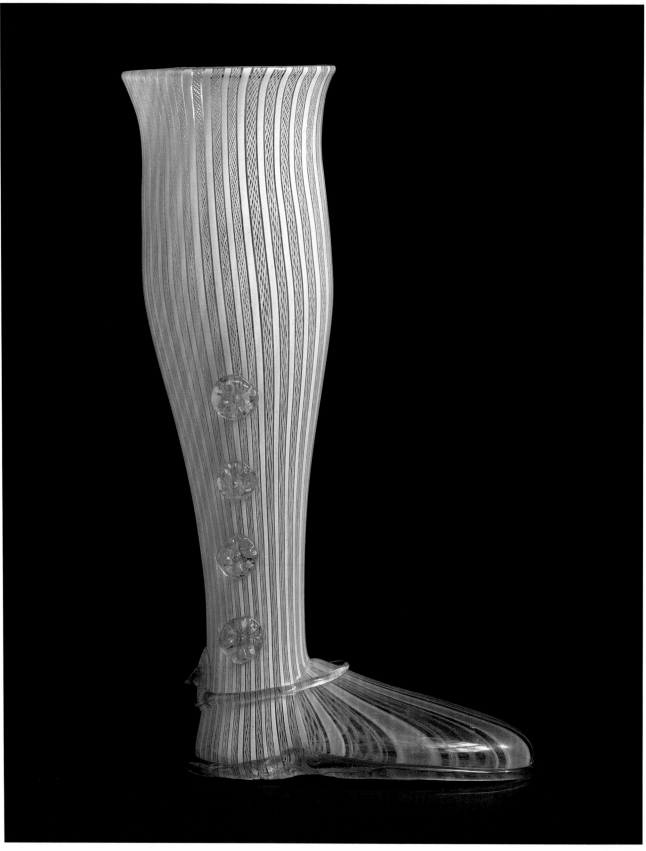

No. 55

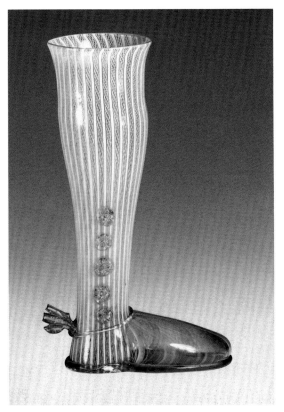

Fig. 55.1 Boot glass. Kunstsammlungen der Veste Coburg

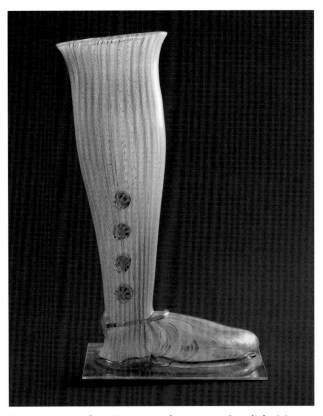

Fig. 55.2 Boot glass. Kunstgewerbemuseum, Staatliche Museen Preussischer Kulturbesitz, Berlin

No. 55, *detail of side*

Longwave fluorescence. Colorless glass: faint yellow-green. Opaque white stripes and twists: pinkish orange. *Shortwave fluorescence.* Colorless glass: faint orange. Opaque white glass: stripes = purplish pink, twists = strong bluish white.

PROVENANCE: Probably Adalbert von Lanna, Prague (Lanna sale 1911, lot 863, pl. 61[?]); Otto Hopfinger, New York; [Blumka Gallery, New York].

LITERATURE: Dreier 1989b, p. 68, under no. 46(?); Strasser and Spiegl 1989, p. 184, under no. 27.

The opaque white stripes are flattened "tubes" of opaque white on colorless cores, and the opaque white twists were also gathered on colorless cores. The stripes and twists are fainter on the blown-out toe; for a description of how the toe was formed, see No. 54.

Some boot-shaped vessels were made in colorless glass;[2] others were decorated with plain opaque white or colored stripes. Glass boots like Nos. 54 and 55, with opaque white stripes and twists, seem to have survived in greater numbers. Boot glasses with *vetro a retorti* decoration are in the Kunstsammlungen der Veste Coburg (Fig. 55.1);[3] the Kunstgewerbemuseum, Berlin (Fig. 55.2);[4] and the Museo Poldi Pezzoli, Milan (without the trailed strap at the ankle).[5] Another similar example is in the Victoria and Albert Museum, London,[6] and two others were in the Joan. d'Huyvetter collection.[7] A boot glass with blue and white spiral stripes and twists was offered for sale by Reinhard Scholtissek, Schledehausen, in 1988.[8]

Petal-molded prunts like these are also found on northern European "unbreakable" *Waldglas* drinking glasses that have been dated to the 1650s, an example of which is in the Corning Museum of Glass.[9]

NOTES:

1. A rectangular gold metallic paper label printed *56* in black and a circular white paper label typed *56.* in black (both Robert Lehman collection) have been removed and are in the Robert Lehman Collection files.

2. See, for instance, Museo Poldi Pezzoli, 1183; Roffia and Mariacher 1983, pp. 177–78, no. 89, fig. 87.

3. Kunstsammlungen der Veste Coburg, a.s.615. I am indebted to Anna-Elizabeth Theuerkauff-Liederwald of Berlin for drawing my attention to this related glass and for sharing her catalogue notes with me.

4. Kunstgewerbemuseum, 1972,39; Dreier 1989b, pp. 67–68, no. 46. A similar glass was destroyed during World War II (see Kunstgewerbemuseum 1937, p. 111, no. 74).

5. Museo Poldi Pezzoli, 1171; Omodeo [1970], p. 91, fig. 24; Roffia and Mariacher 1983, p. 177, no. 88, fig. 88.

6. Victoria and Albert Museum, c.5227-1901.

7. D'Huyvetter sale 1829, lots 1, 5, pl. 19.

8. *Weltkunst* 58, no. 17 (1 September 1988), p. 2503.

9. Corning Museum of Glass, 79.3.617; *Antiques* 42 (August 1941), p. 82; Corning 1955, p. 42, no. 98.

Venice or *façon de Venise*, late sixteenth century

56. Drinking horn

1975.1.1169

L. 35.5 cm. Colorless (slightly gray) and opaque white nonlead glass. Blown, *vetro a retorti*, trailed.

The long, curved, tapered horn, circular in cross section, is open at the wide end and closed at the narrow end with a colorless disk and knob. It is covered with pairs of opaque white stripes alternating with single multispiral twists. Two trailed milled collars with loops for suspension encircle the wider half of the horn, and attached near the wide open end is a trailed grooved strap handle with a pincered thumbpiece and a curled lower terminal. No pontil mark.[1]

The rim cracked off and the edge grozed; several chips on the rim, one fairly large; the thumbpiece on the handle chipped. Probably missing a metal cover.

Longwave fluorescence. Colorless glass: strong yellow-green. Opaque white twists and stripes: yellow-green. *Shortwave fluorescence.* Colorless glass: faint, slightly greenish. Opaque white glass: twists = tan, stripes = brighter tan.

PROVENANCE: Frederic Neuburg, Vienna; Otto Hopfinger, New York; [Blumka Gallery, New York].

EXHIBITED: New York 1979–80.

LITERATURE: Schmidt 1931, pp. 6, 23, no. 6, pl. 4.

The opaque white stripes, flattened "tubes" of opaque white on colorless cores, and the twists, opaque white

No. 56, *detail of side and handle*

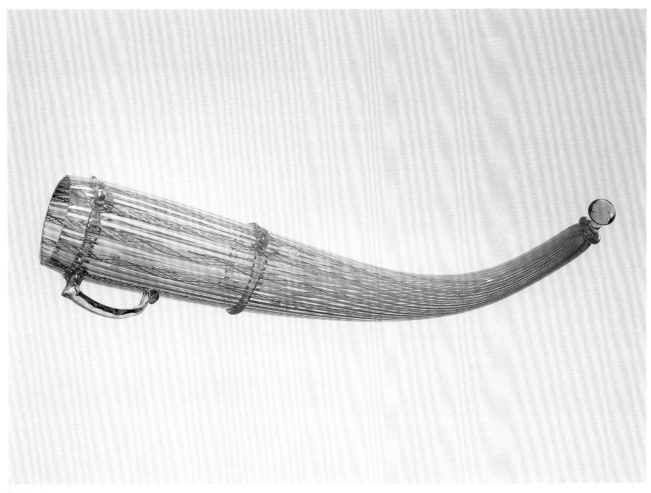

No. 56

with some noticeably dark gray tinted threads, were picked up on an inner gather of colorless glass. The fluorescence demonstrates, however, that unlike those on the other examples of *vetro a retorti* in the Robert Lehman Collection (except Nos. 66 and 68), the twists and stripes on this horn are coated inside and out with layers of colorless glass. (The opaque white twists usually lie on the exterior of the canes and fluoresce brilliant bluish white.)

Animal horns have probably been used as drinking vessels almost continuously from prehistoric times. Glass drinking vessels in the shape of horns were used during the Roman Empire, and they continued to be made and used by Frankish tribes in northern Europe after the fall of Rome in the fifth century.[2] In the sixteenth and seventeenth centuries horns were but one of a wide array of

amusingly shaped glass vessels used for drinking (see also Nos. 54, 55). Drinking vessels in the form of "cors de chasse" were being manufactured at the Colinet glassworks in Beauwelz in the Southern Netherlands in what is now Belgium in the early seventeenth century.[3]

Glass horns necked down to be closed with a cork or stopper were also used by hunters to hold powder and shot, but the open end on the Lehman horn shows no evidence that it was ever cut down. Other glass horns with pewter screw caps appear to have been intended as liquor flasks; one such horn is in the Österreichisches Museum für Angewandte Kunst, Vienna,[4] and another was on the art market in Switzerland in 1937.[5]

The Lehman drinking horn was probably originally fitted with a hinged metal cover like those that survive on the striped glass horns in the Louvre, Paris (Fig. 56.1);[6]

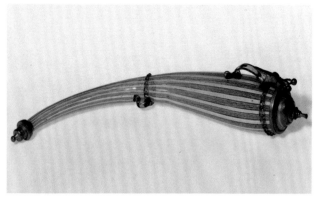

Fig. 56.1 Drinking horn. Musée du Louvre, Paris. Photograph: Réunion des Musées Nationaux

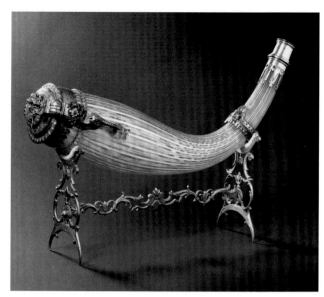

Fig. 56.3 Drinking horn. Kunstgewerbemuseum, Staatliche Museen Preussischer Kulturbesitz, Berlin

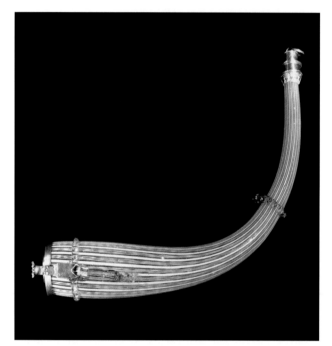

Fig. 56.2 Drinking horn. Corning Museum of Glass, Gift of Jerome Strauss

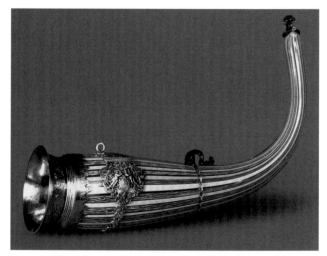

Fig. 56.4 Drinking horn. Württembergisches Landesmuseum, Stuttgart. Reproduced from Brigitte Klesse and Hans Mayr, *European Glass from 1500–1800* (Vienna: Kremayr und Scheriau, 1987), no. 16

the Corning Museum of Glass (Fig. 56.2);[7] and the Kunstgewerbemuseum, Berlin (Fig. 56.3).[8] A striped horn in the Württembergisches Landesmuseum, Stuttgart, has a silver-gilt rim and a colorless glass button finial on the curved tip (Fig. 56.4).[9] Other horns in *vetro a retorti* with metal fittings are in the Historisches Museum der Pfalz mit Weinmuseum, Speyer,[10] and the Kunsthistorisches Mu-

seum, Vienna.[11] Another was sold from the collection of a Mr. E. Joseph of London in 1890.[12]

Drinking horns were also made of color-spattered glass; an example attributed to seventeenth-century France is in the Louvre.[13] A diamond-point engraved Dutch drinking horn dated 1659 is in the Corning Museum of Glass (Fig. 56.5);[14] other sixteenth- or seventeenth-century

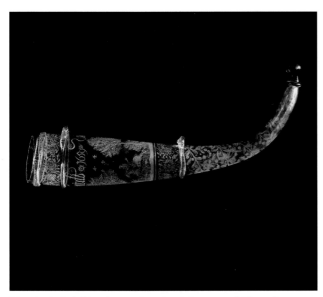

Fig. 56.5 Drinking horn. Corning Museum of Glass, Bequest of Jerome Strauss

examples with diamond-engraved decoration are in the Prinsenhof, Delft;[15] the Rijksmuseum, Amsterdam;[16] and the Musée National de la Renaissance, Château d'Écouen.[17] Drinking horns made in the same period of clear, undecorated glass are in the Metropolitan Museum;[18] the Vleeshuis, Antwerp;[19] the Wadsworth Atheneum, Hartford;[20] the Museum für Angewandte Kunst, Cologne;[21] the Cinzano Collection, London;[22] the Corning Museum of Glass;[23] the Kestner-Museum, Hannover;[24] the Musée National de Céramique, Sèvres;[25] the Musée de Douai, La Chartreuse;[26] the British Museum, London;[27] and the Museum of Fine Arts, Boston.[28] The present location of another undecorated horn is unknown.[29]

NOTES:

1. The following labels have been removed and are in the Robert Lehman Collection files: Unidentified: circular white paper label with 7 written in black ink; triangular white paper label outlined in blue with 7 written in black ink (not in file). Frederic Neuburg collection: torn circular white paper label with double black framing lines and *NEUBURG. / No* printed in black and *8* written in black ink.

2. See, for example, Morin-Jean 1913, p. 159, fig. 212; Evison 1955, pp. 159–95; Fuchs 1956, fig. 11; Fremersdorf 1961, pls. 41–44; *JGS* 4 (1962), p. 141, no. 12; Schlosser 1965, p. 32, fig. 21; Mariacher and Causa Picone 1972, p. 34, fig. 43; Périn 1972, p. 69, fig. 1-2; Evison 1975, pp. 74–87; Savage [1975], p. 29; Kämpfer 1978, fig. 34; Charleston 1984, p. 7, pl. 2a.

3. *Journal d'Amand Colinet* (1607), cited in Chambon 1955, p. 314, under no. 43.

4. Schlosser 1965, p. 156, fig. 128.

5. Galerie Fischer sale 1937, lot 504, pl. 35.

6. Louvre, OA1084.

7. Corning Museum of Glass, 66.3.30 (ex coll. Jerome Strauss); Corning 1955, p. 57, no. 149.

8. Kunstgewerbemuseum, K320a,b; Dreier 1989b, pp. 69–70, no. 47, colorpl. 16.

9. Ex coll. Ernesto Wolf; Klesse and Mayr 1987, no. 16.

10. Ibid., under no. 16.

11. Kunsthistorisches Museum, 2676; ibid.

12. Joseph sale 1890, lot 939.

13. Bellanger 1988, p. 314.

14. Corning Museum of Glass, 79.3.298 (ex coll. Frederic Neuburg, Jerome Strauss); Schmidt 1931, pp. 93, 101, no. 80, pl. 26; Corning 1955, p. 57, no. 150; *JGS* 22 (1980), p. 106, fig. 22.

15. Van Gelder 1955, no. 3, pl. 15; Van Gelder and Jansen 1969, p. 67, no. 102.

16. Van Gelder 1955, no. 2, pl. 15; Van Gelder and Jansen 1969, p. 67, no. 101. For another drinking horn in the Rijksmuseum, see Buckley 1929, p. 15, no. 12, pl. 9.

17. Gerspach 1885, p. 297, fig. 144.

18. Metropolitan Museum, 83.7.210 (ex coll. Henry G. Marquand).

19. *Bulletin AIHV*, no. 5 (1967–70), pp. 26, 27, fig. 2.

20. Wadsworth Atheneum, 1956.3468 (ex coll. Edith Van Gerbig); Lanmon 1978, p. 28, no. 20.

21. Museum für Angewandte Kunst, F219; Cologne [1961], no. 158; Klesse 1963, p. 90, no. 163; Klesse and Reineking von Bock 1973, p. 136, no. 253.

22. Lazarus 1974, n.p.

23. Corning Museum of Glass, 63.3.22.

24. Kestner-Museum, W.M.V.39; Mosel 1979, p. 69, no. 59 (45).

25. Morin-Jean 1913, pp. 269–70, fig. 349.

26. Bellanger 1988, p. 316.

27. British Museum, 55,12-1,153 (ex coll. Ralph Bernal); Bohn 1857, p. 300, no. 2937; Buckley 1929, p. 15, pl. 9; Chambon 1955, p. 314, no. 43, pl. 13; Van Gelder 1955, p. 27, pl. 15; London 1968b, p. 141, no. 184.

28. Museum of Fine Arts, 57.214; *Glass Collections* 1982, p. 19.

29. Tillman 1973, no. 3.

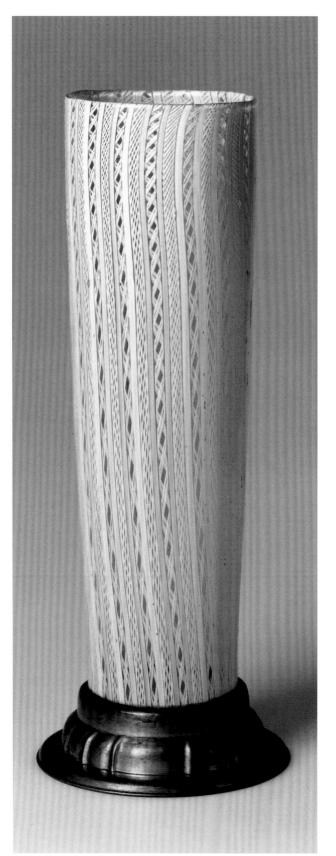

No. 57

Façon de Venise, probably the Southern Netherlands, possibly Bohemia or Saxony, late sixteenth century

57. Beaker (*Stangenglas*)

1975.1.1165
H. 27.4 cm. Colorless (slightly gray) and opaque white nonlead glass; pewter mount. Blown, *vetro a retorti*.

The cylindrical body has a flat bottom and straight sides decorated with vertical opaque white stripes alternating with multispiral opaque white twists or canes enclosing two pairs of double-spiral threads. The cast and turned pewter foot has a rounded collar above a domed and spirally gadrooned base and a flared foot rim. Rough pontil mark on the bottom of the glass. Painted in white inside the mount: 3.[1]

Foot rim missing (probably replaced with the pewter mount in the late nineteenth century).

Longwave fluorescence. Colorless glass: strong pinkish yellow. Opaque white twists and stripes: strong pinkish yellow. *Shortwave fluorescence*. Colorless glass: purple. Opaque white glass: twists = strong bluish white, stripes = pinkish purple.

PROVENANCE: Albert Pollak, Vienna; Otto Hopfinger, New York; [Blumka Gallery, New York].

EXHIBITED: New York 1979–80.

The twists and stripes were presumably applied by rolling the colorless gather on a marver on which the canes were laid out side by side, then heating it to fuse the canes to the surface (the same technique that was probably used on Nos. 52–56 and 58–61). Opaque white

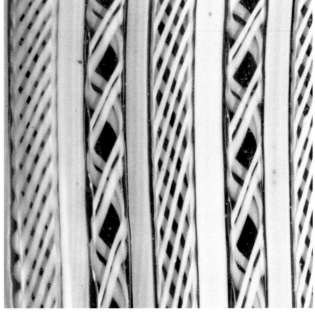

No. 57, *detail of side*

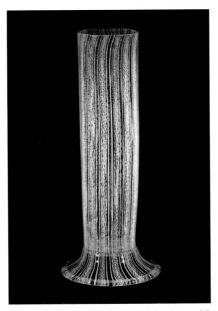

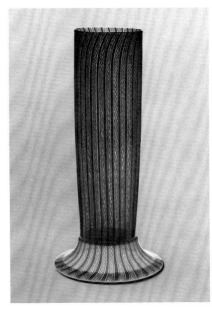

Fig. 57.1 (left) Beaker. Kunstmuseum Düsseldorf. Photograph: Walter Klein, Düsseldorf Fig. 57.2 (center) Beaker. Corning Museum of Glass Fig. 57.3 (right) Beaker. Musée du Louvre, Paris. Photograph: Réunion des Musées Nationaux

stripes separate the twisted canes in all but one place, which may be where two different twists placed at the ends of the row of canes on the marver came together. The *Stangenglas* is a standard Germanic form that derives from fifteenth-century prototypes of greenish *Waldglas* and continued to be popular until the end of the seventeenth century. *Stangengläser* were often made

in colorless glass – sometimes enameled, painted, or diamond-point engraved – or worked in the ice-glass technique. They were also decorated with nipped opaque white stripes or made in *vetro a reticello* or *vetro a retorti*, with the twists arranged either spirally or, as here, vertically. Several *vetro a retorti* beakers with vertical stripes and twists like those on the Lehman glass (and with flared

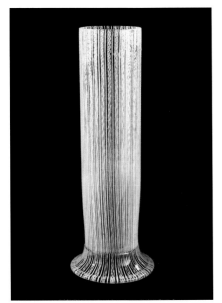

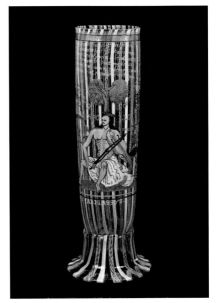

Fig. 57.4 (left) Beaker. Pilkington Glass Museum, Saint Helens, England Fig. 57.5 (center) Covered beaker. Hermitage, Saint Petersburg Fig. 57.6 (right) Beaker. Corning Museum of Glass, Gift of Edwin J. Beinecke

feet like the one the Lehman glass must originally have had) have been attributed to the Southern Netherlands, Bohemia, or Saxony and dated to the late sixteenth century. Examples are in the Kunstmuseum Düsseldorf (Fig. 57.1);[2] the Corning Museum of Glass (Fig. 57.2);[3] the Louvre, Paris (Fig. 57.3);[4] the Pilkington Glass Museum, Saint Helens, England (Fig. 57.4);[5] the Hermitage, Saint Petersburg (Fig. 57.5);[6] the Österreichisches Museum für Angewandte Kunst, Vienna;[7] the Museum für Kunsthandwerk, Frankfurt am Main;[8] the Württembergisches Landesmuseum, Stuttgart;[9] and the Rheinisches Landesmuseum, Bonn.[10] Two others were in the Vecht collection, Amsterdam,[11] and the Joan. d'Huyvetter collection.[12] An unusual *vetro a retorti* beaker with enameled decoration that was made in Saxony in the late sixteenth century is now in the Corning Museum of Glass (Fig. 57.6).[13]

NOTES:

1. The following labels have been removed and are in the Robert Lehman Collection files: Unidentified: circular white paper label with *582* written in gray ink, crossed out, and *471* written over it in purple ink (while the beaker was in the Pollak collection). Albert Pollak collection: rectangular white paper label with a printed blue toothed frame and *A. Pollak / 471* typed in black. Robert Lehman collection: rectangular gold metallic paper label printed *54* in black; circular white paper label typed *54.* in black.
2. Kunstmuseum, 17667; Heinemeyer 1966, p. 81, no. 232 (misnumbered 224).
3. Corning Museum of Glass, 57.3.47.
4. Louvre, 78EN6093.
5. Pilkington Glass Museum, 1968/7/6 (ex coll. Walter F. Smith); Smith sale 1968, lot 880.
6. Hermitage, F486 (Fig. 57.5); see also F223.
7. Schlosser 1951, p. 11, pl. 37.
8. Museum für Kunsthandwerk, V27/4934 (Museum für Kunsthandwerk 1956, p. 154; Frankfurt am Main 1966–67, p. 50, no. 95; Ohm 1973, p. 91, no. 196), 13426/5824 (Ohm 1975, p. 30, no. 50).
9. Ex coll. Ernesto Wolf; Klesse and Mayr 1987, no. 15.
10. Ex coll. Walther Bremen; W. Bremen 1964, pp. 390, 391, no. 207.
11. Vecht sale 1938, lot 26.
12. D'Huyvetter sale 1829, lot 3, pl. 21.
13. Corning Museum of Glass, 57.3.51 (ex coll. Edwin J. Beinecke); Von Saldern 1965, pp. 310–13, no. 46.

Venice, sixteenth century

58. Covered beaker

1975.1.1203a,b
H. with cover 28 cm. Colorless (gray) and opaque white nonlead glass. Blown, *vetro a retorti*.

The straight, tapered sides of the bowl are decorated with vertical opaque white stripes alternating with opaque white twists composed of two pairs of double spiral threads encircling a single vertical thread. Identical stripes and twists decorate the trumpet-shaped pedestal foot, which has an underfolded rim, and the domed cover, which has a folded, projecting rim and a tapered brim that fits inside the beaker rim and is drawn up into a small hollow ball and topped by an applied colorless finial consisting of a small ball knop above two flattened disks. Rough pontil mark under the foot; ring-shaped rough pontil mark inside the cover, around the opening to the hollow ball. Painted in bright orange under the foot: *L.56.31.68A,B* (a Metropolitan Museum loan number).[1]

Normal wear on the foot rim and cover.

Longwave fluorescence. Colorless glass: strong yellow-green. Opaque white twists and stripes: strong pinkish yellow. *Shortwave fluorescence.* Colorless glass: faint brownish. Opaque white glass: twists = strong bluish white, stripes = pinkish purple.

PROVENANCE: Spitzner, Dresden(?);[2] Frederic Neuburg, Vienna; Otto Hopfinger, New York; [Blumka Gallery, New York].

EXHIBITED: Corning 1958, pp. 68, 69, no. 61, ill.; Cincinnati 1959, p. 42, no. 551.

LITERATURE: Schmidt 1931, pp. 6, 23, no. 5, pl. 4.

The beaker and cover were made from different gathers. The bowl and foot each have thirty-three white stripes and twists; the cover has thirty.

A *vetro a retorti* covered beaker much like this one, but without a foot, is represented in the *Crucifixion* painted by Peter Gärtner (Monogrammist P. G.) in 1537 (Walters Art Gallery, Baltimore).[3] A nearly identical beaker in the Museum für Angewandte Kunst, Cologne (Fig. 58.1), has been attributed to Venice and dated to the last half of the sixteenth century.[4] Other close parallels are in the Toledo Museum of Art (Fig. 58.2);[5] the British Museum, London;[6] the Hermitage, Saint Petersburg;[7] the Museum für Kunsthandwerk, Frankfurt am Main (two examples);[8] the Museen der Stadt Regensburg;[9] the Württembergisches

No. 58

No. 58, *detail of side*

Landesmuseum, Stuttgart;[10] and a private collection in Germany.[11] A similarly shaped beaker but with diagonal striping and no cover once belonged to the Sheridans of Frampton Court, Dorset.[12]

NOTES:

1. The following labels have been removed and are in the Robert Lehman Collection files: Unidentified: fragment of a circular white paper label; oval orange paper label with *552* printed in black. Robert Lehman collection: rectangular gold metallic paper label with *52* printed in black.
2. Schmidt's claim in his catalogue of the Neuburg collection (1931, p. 23, no. 5) that this glass was "aus Sammlung Spitzner, Dresden 1916" has not been verified.
3. Walters Art Gallery, 37.246; Walters Art Gallery n.d., p. 76, no. 246 (attributed to Georg Pencz); Corning 1958, p. 20, fig. 2.
4. Museum für Angewandte Kunst, F379; Mariacher 1954, pp. 63, 65, fig. 55; Cologne 1960, no. 331; Cologne [1961], no. 200; Klesse 1963, p. 95, no. 178; Klesse and Reineking von Bock 1973, p. 141, no. 265.
5. Toledo Museum of Art, 13.417; Hutton 1963, no. 2.
6. Ex coll. Felix Slade; Nesbitt 1871, p. 118, no. 666, fig. 208; Vávra 1954, p. 107, fig. 103; Zecchin 1957, p. 19.
7. Kachalov 1959, p. 121.
8. Museum für Kunsthandwerk, 13450/5831, 6190/4930, 246; Ohm 1973, p. 92, no. 200; Ohm 1975, p. 22, no. 26.
9. Museen der Stadt Regensburg, κ(в)1960/78; Baumgärtner 1977a, p. 36, no. 61.
10. Ex coll. Ernesto Wolf; São Paulo 1957, no. 28.
11. Düsseldorf 1968–69, p. 29, no. 62.
12. Sanctuary 1957, pp. 14, 16, fig. 4.

Fig. 58.1 Covered beaker. Museum für Angewandte Kunst, Cologne. Photograph: Rheinisches Bildarchiv, Cologne

Fig. 58.2 Covered beaker. Toledo Museum of Art, Toledo, Ohio, Gift of Edward Drummond Libbey

Venice or *façon de Venise*, possibly Saxony,
mid-sixteenth century

59. Armorial flask

1975.1.1204
H. 18.1 cm. Colorless (slightly gray) and opaque white nonlead
glass. Blown, *vetro a retorti*, enameled, gilt.

The flask has a short, tapered neck with a trailed, colorless,
horizontally ribbed gilt rim and a flattened ovoid body with a
trailed, colorless, gilt oval foot rim. Vertical pairs of opaque
white stripes alternating with either a multispiral twist or a

twist with a pair of double spiral threads encircling a single
vertical thread cover the body and neck, and on the front and
back of the body are two enameled and gilt coats of arms:
gules, a fess argent (Austria) and quarterly, 1 and 4 sable, a
lion or, crowned gules (Pfalz, the Palatinate of the Rhine),
2 and 3 lozengy in bend of argent and azure (Dukedom of
Bavaria). Two rough pontil marks, one over the other, on the
bottom. Painted in bright red-orange on the bottom: *L.56.31.74*
(a Metropolitan Museum loan number).[1]

No. 59, *front*

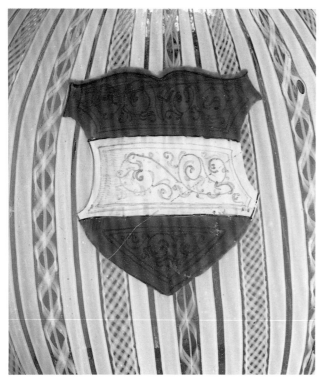

No. 59, *shield on back*

Fig. 59.1 Flask. Österreichisches Museum für Angewandte Kunst, Vienna

A crack in the side with Austrian arms; normal wear on the foot rim; the gilding worn.

Longwave fluorescence. Colorless glass: strong greenish tan. Opaque white twists and stripes: strong greenish tan. Enamels: blue = dark purplish red, red = dark red, white = lavender, black = dark blue. *Shortwave fluorescence.* Colorless glass: faint, bluish. Opaque white glass: twists = strong bluish white, stripes = pinkish purple. Enamels: blue = inky dark blue, red = black, white = lavender, black = black. Gilding: slight orange.

PROVENANCE: William Randolph Hearst, San Simeon, California(?);[2] Otto Hopfinger, New York; [Blumka Gallery, New York].

EXHIBITED: Corning 1958, pp. 70, 71, no. 62, ill.; Cincinnati 1959, p. 43, no. 554; New York 1985.

LITERATURE: Winchester 1958, frontis.

The numerous open bubbles between the opaque white stripes are typical of *vetro a retorti.* As was the case with Nos. 52–58, 60, and 61, the twists and stripes were picked up on the outside of a colorless gather. The gilding on the coats of arms is fused gold "paint"; the gilding on the foot and neck rims is fused gold leaf.

The only recorded parallel for this flask is in the Österreichisches Museum für Angewandte Kunst, Vienna (Fig. 59.1).[3] It has applied molded berry prunts alongside the arms on both sides. Both flasks may have been made on the occasion of the marriage on 4 July 1546 of Albrecht V of Bavaria (1528–1579) to Anna of Austria (1528–1590), daughter of Ferdinand I. The flasks certainly predate two other weddings between the houses of Austria and Bavaria: between Ferdinand II (1578–1637) and Maria Anna von Bayern (1574–1616) on 23 April 1600 and between Johann Wilhelm von Pfalz-Neuburg and Maria Anna of Austria, daughter of Ferdinand III, in 1678.[4]

A covered goblet in the Hermitage, Saint Petersburg (Fig. 59.2), also bears the Bavarian coat of arms.[5] And those arms are incorporated in the arms of Elector Ottheinrich of Pfalz, which appear with the date 1553 on a beaker now in the Württembergisches Landesmuseum, Stuttgart (Fig. 59.3).[6] The Stuttgart beaker is one of a group of drinking glasses with the arms of the counts palatine that were made in the last half of the sixteenth century.[7]

Fig. 59.2 Covered goblet. Hermitage, Saint Petersburg

Fig. 59.3 Beaker. Württembergisches Landesmuseum, Stuttgart

NOTES:

1. The following labels were removed and are in the Robert Lehman Collection files: Unidentified: round orange paper label printed 553 in black. Robert Lehman collection: rectangular gold metallic paper label printed 69 in black.
2. Hearst's ownership has not been verified.
3. Österreichisches Museum für Angewandte Kunst, F168 (ex coll. Forstmeister Koch-Sternfeld, Austria).
4. See Weihrich 1893. I am indebted to Ludwig Igálffy v. Igály of Vienna for his assistance in identifying the possible occasion for which the two flasks were made.
5. Hermitage, K2362; Carbonnier 1893, n.p., ill.
6. Württembergisches Landesmuseum, E749; Schmidt 1911,

pp. 281–82; Von Saldern 1965, pp. 36, 37, fig. 14.
7. Another beaker bearing the date 1553 was in the Schlossmuseum, Berlin, before World War II (Schmidt 1911, pp. 281–82; Schmidt 1912, p. 158, fig. 83 [the arms identified as Pfalz-Lützelsteiner]; Schmidt 1922, p. 161, fig. 85 [the arms identified as those of Pfalzgraf Ottheinrich]). Two glasses dated 1596 are in the Bayerisches Nationalmuseum, Munich (G114, 116 [with the arms of Pfalzgraf Otto Heinrich II von Sulzbach]; Kämpfer and Beyer 1966, p. 281, pl. 125; Rückert 1982, pp. 94–95, nos. 162, 163, pl. 43). Another dated 1596 is in the Mnichovo Hradiště Městské Muzeum, Mnichov (Jiřík 1934, p. 97).

Venice, late sixteenth century

60. Goblet

1975.1.1147

H. 17.6 cm, diam. of rim 10.9 cm. Colorless (slightly gray) and opaque white nonlead glass. Blown, *vetro a retorti*.

The trumpet-shaped bowl is covered with vertical multispiral opaque white twists. A hollow ball knop, also decorated with twists, between two colorless mereses separates the bowl from the trumpet-shaped foot, which is covered with similar twists and has an underfolded rim. Rough pontil mark under the foot. Painted in bright red-orange under the foot: *L.56.31.55* (a Metropolitan Museum loan number).[1]

Normal wear on the bowl rim and the foot rim. Missing a cover.

Longwave fluorescence. Colorless glass: strong yellow-green. Opaque white twists: creamy. *Shortwave fluorescence*. Colorless glass: purple (inside). Opaque white twists: strong bluish white.

PROVENANCE: Spitzner, Dresden(?);[2] Frederic Neuburg, Vienna; Otto Hopfinger, New York; [Blumka Gallery, New York].

EXHIBITED: Cincinnati 1959 (not in catalogue).

LITERATURE: Schmidt 1931, pp. 6, 23, no. 4, pl. 4 (shown with a matching cover).

The same combination of *vetro a retorti* multispiral twists is found on numerous objects in various forms made in the late sixteenth century. Goblets of similar form with a similar arrangement of side-by-side vertical twists are in the National Museums and Galleries on Merseyside, Liverpool (Fig. 60.1);[3] the Kunstsammlungen der Veste Coburg;[4] the Saint Louis Art Museum;[5] the Corning Museum of Glass;[6] the A. J. Guépin collection, the Netherlands;[7] the Württembergisches Landesmuseum, Stuttgart;[8] the Staatliche Galerie Moritzburg, Halle;[9] the Victoria and Albert Museum, London;[10] the Musées Royaux d'Art et d'Histoire, Brussels;[11] the Bernd Hockemeyer collection, Bremen;[12] and the Cinzano Collection, London.[13] The present whereabouts of four others are unknown.[14] Related goblets with either widely spaced or spiral opaque white twists are in the Museum für Kunsthandwerk, Frankfurt am Main;[15] the Gemeentemuseum, The Hague;[16] the Musées Royaux d'Art et d'Histoire;[17] the New Orleans Museum of Art;[18] and the Corning Museum of Glass.[19]

NOTES:

1. The following labels have been removed: Unidentified: circular white paper label with *3* written in brown ink. Frederic Neuburg collection: circular white paper label printed *NEUBURG* and with *No 2* written in black ink. Robert Lehman collection: rectangular gold metallic paper label printed *10* in black.

2. Schmidt's claim in his catalogue of the Neuburg collection (1931, p. 23, no. 4) that this glass was "aus Sammlung Spitzner, Dresden 1916" has not been verified.

3. National Museums and Galleries on Merseyside, 11.8.76.1; Gatty 1883, no. 216; Hurst 1968, p. 19, no. 10; Liverpool 1979, p. 40, no. D5.

4. Maedebach 1970, p. 15; Weiss 1971, fig. p. 113.

5. Saint Louis Art Museum, 93; *Glass Collections* 1982, p. 158.

6. Corning Museum of Glass, 70.3.3; *JGS* 13 (1971), pp. 140, 141, fig. 37.

7. Delft 1970, p. 8, no. 5, fig. 4.

8. Ex coll. Ernesto Wolf; Klesse and Mayr 1987, no. 18.

9. Staatliche Galerie Moritzburg, 18 (ex coll. Bourgeois); Berlin 1981a, pp. 20, 21, no. 20.

10. Victoria and Albert Museum, C.45-1923; Chambon 1955, p. 316, no. 51, pl. 15.

11. Ibid., p. 315, no. 45, pl. 14.

12. Ex coll. Walter F. Smith, Jr., Fritz Biemann; Smith sale 1968, lot 865, ill.; Klesse and Von Saldern 1978, pp. 114, 115, no. 60; Lucerne 1981, p. 159, no. 671; Biemann sale 1984, lot 55, ill.

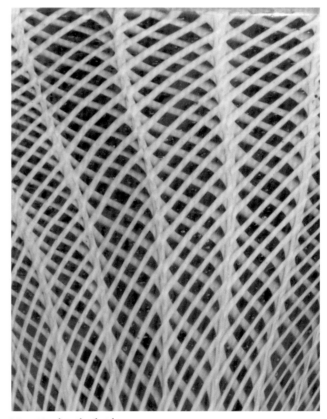

No. 60, *detail of side*

No. 60

Fig. 60.1 Goblet. Board of Trustees of the National Museums and Galleries on Merseyside (Liverpool Museum), Liverpool

13. Lazarus 1974, n.p.; Lazarus 1978, no. 19.

14. Three were formerly in the Schlossmuseum, Berlin (Schmidt 1912, p. 102, fig. 63; Schmidt 1922, p. 104, fig. 64); the Joan. d'Huyvetter collection (d'Huyvetter sale 1829, lot 4, pl. 18); and the Karl Thewalt collection, Cologne (Thewalt sale 1903, lot 494, pl. 7). The fourth is of unknown provenance (Fuchs 1956, p. 33, fig. 27).

15. Museum für Kunsthandwerk, 6777/353; Ohm 1973, p. 75, no. 149.

16. *Bulletin AIHV*, no. 1 (1962), pp. 28–29, fig. 29; Schrijver 1964, pl. 7; Isings 1966, p. 57, fig. 50; Van Gelder and Jansen 1969, p. 63, no. 41; Schrijver 1980, p. 34, fig. 15.

17. Musées Royaux d'Art et d'Histoire, 264; Berryer 1957, p. 60, pl. 41b; Liège 1958, pp. 132, 135, no. 281.

18. New Orleans Museum of Art, B195A (ex coll. Melvin Billups); Corning 1962, p. 28, no. 39.

19. Corning Museum of Glass, 68.3.64, 79.3.371 (both ex coll. Jerome Strauss); Haynes 1959, fig. 27d.

Venice, early seventeenth century

61. Vase

1975.1.1199

H. 26.5 cm. Colorless (slightly gray) and opaque white nonlead glass. Mold blown, *vetro a retorti* and *vetro a reticello*, trailed, molded, gilt.

The vase has a tall, waisted neck with a flared rim and a flattened, ovoid body in the form of a ribbed (thirteen ribs each side) scallop shell covered with swirled *vetro a retorti* opaque white multispiral twists alternating with stripes. Two scrolled handles with multispiral twists are attached to the sides of the trailed double neck ring of colorless glass and rest on colorless pads on the shoulders; applied to each handle is a gilt colorless prunt molded in relief as a human head. A short section of glass with similar twists and stripes has been added at the base of the body and cut to fit a replacement stem, composed of a *vetro a reticello* flattened hollow ball knop flanked by angular colorless mereses, and a trumpet-shaped *vetro a reticello* foot with an underfolded rim. Rough pontil mark under the foot. Painted under the foot in orange: *C252* (not identified); in bright red-orange: *L.56.31.64* (a Metropolitan Museum loan number).[1]

Chip on one handle at the top joint; the body cracked below the opposite handle. The stem and foot are replacements from an unmatching (but probably seventeenth-century) object; a colorless plastic rod is cemented into a hole drilled through the foot and stem and into the bottom of the shell.

Longwave fluorescence. Colorless glass: vase = strong yellow-green, foot = strong greenish yellow. Opaque white twists and stripes: strong greenish yellow. *Shortwave fluorescence.* Colorless glass (vase and foot): purple. Opaque white glass: twists = bluish white, stripes = pinkish purple, *vetro a reticello* threads = strong bluish white. Plastic rod: opaque white.

PROVENANCE: Albert von Parpart, Schloss Hünegg, Lake of Thun, Switzerland (von Parpart [Albert] sale 1884, lot 484); possibly Achille Seillière, Château de Mello, Paris (Seillière sale 1890, lot 262[?]); Karl Thewalt, Cologne (Thewalt sale 1903, lot 510, pl. 7); princes of Liechtenstein, Vaduz and Vienna(?);[2] Otto Hopfinger, New York; [Blumka Gallery, New York].

EXHIBITED: Cincinnati 1959 (not in catalogue).

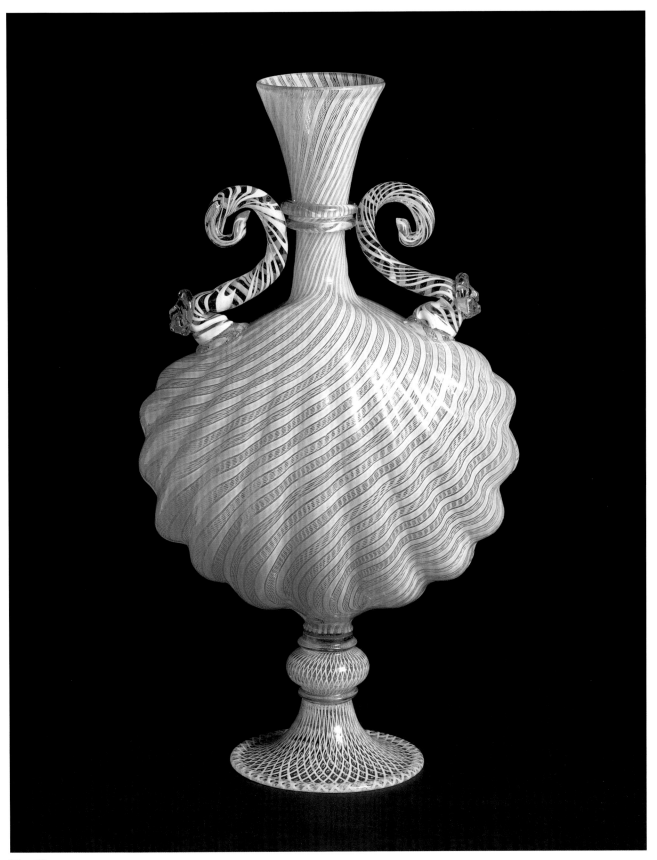

No. 61

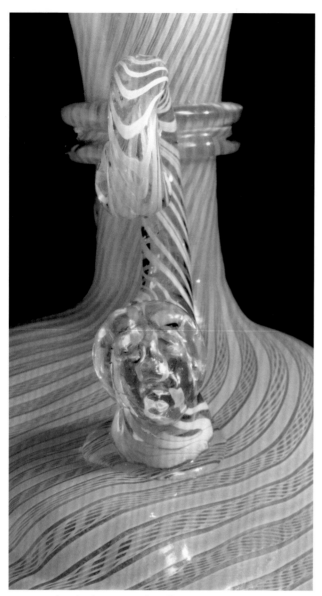

No. 61, *detail of prunt on handle*

No. 61, *detail of handle*

Glass scallop-shell vases were popular in Europe from ancient Roman times until at least the late seventeenth century.[3] During the late sixteenth and seventeenth centuries such vases were produced in both Venetian and *façon de Venise*, especially Spanish, glasshouses. The closest parallel to the Lehman vase is a vase with similar opaque white twists alternating with white stripes and similarly shaped handles that was owned by Antoine Seilern in London (Fig. 61.1).[4] Two other scallop-shell vases of the same form and with related *vetro a retorti*

decoration but with somewhat different handles are in the Toledo Museum of Art (Fig. 61.2; with opaque white twists and stripes)[5] and the Hermitage, Saint Petersburg (Fig. 61.3; with opaque white multispiral twists and opaque blue stripes).[6] All three of those vases have been attributed to seventeenth-century Venice, as have the shell-shaped vases now in the Museo Vetrario, Murano (two examples);[7] the Museo Nazionale di San Martino, Naples;[8] the Museo Poldi Pezzoli, Milan (two examples);[9] the Metropolitan Museum (with gilt masks on the handles);[10]

Fig. 61.1 Vase. Present location unknown. Photograph courtesy of Christie's, London

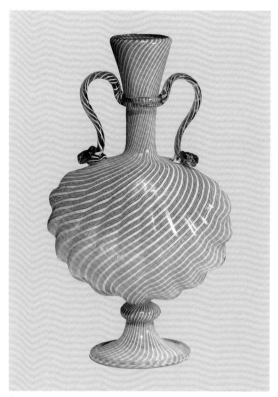

Fig. 61.2 Vase. Toledo Museum of Art, Toledo, Ohio, Gift of Edward Drummond Libbey

Fig. 61.3 Vase. Hermitage, Saint Petersburg

Fig. 61.4 Covered cup or reliquary. Museo Poldi Pezzoli, Milan

Fig. 61.5 Covered vase. Istituto e Museo di Storia della Scienza, Florence. Photograph: Franca Principe, Florence

the Pilkington Glass Museum, Saint Helens, Merseyside;[11] and a private collection in the Netherlands.[12] A vase in the Musée du Verre, Liège,[13] and another in the New Orleans Museum of Art[14] have been attributed to Spanish glasshouses and dated to the seventeenth century.

There are also lamps with shell-shaped bodies; two examples, one in the Museo Nazionale di San Martino,[15] the other in the Museo Nazionale della Ceramica "Duca di Martina," Villa Floridiana, Naples,[16] have been attributed to Spain and dated to the seventeenth century. Giuseppe Recco (1634–1695), a Neapolitan artist who was strongly influenced by his Spanish contemporaries and who died in Spain, depicted a shell-shaped washing bottle in one of his still lifes.[17]

The unusual shape of the handles of the Lehman vase and the distinctive human-mask prunts are found on other objects believed to have been produced in Venice in the late sixteenth or early seventeenth century: a covered cup or reliquary in the Museo Poldi Pezzoli (Fig. 61.4);[18] a covered ice-glass vase in the Istituto e Museo di Storia della Scienza, Florence (Fig. 61.5);[19] and a covered vase

that was in the Kunstgewerbemuseum, Berlin, and was destroyed during World War II.[20] Similar handles also appear on a Venetian *vetro a retorti* vase in the Royal Museum of Scotland, Edinburgh,[21] and on the stem of a Venetian covered goblet that was owned by Adalbert von Lanna in Prague (Fig. 61.6).[22] Other glasses with similar handles that have been attributed to the Hofglashütte in Innsbruck are in the Wallace Collection, London;[23] the Kunstsammlungen der Veste Coburg;[24] and the Uměleckoprůmyslové Muzeum, Prague.[25]

NOTES:

1. The following labels have been removed and are in the Robert Lehman Collection files: Unidentified: torn oval white paper label with a scalloped edge and *163*. written in blue ink. Robert Lehman collection: rectangular gold metallic paper label printed *45* in black.

2. According to a note in the Blumka Gallery files, this vase was once in the collection of the princes of Liechtenstein, but that information has not been verified.

3. For Roman examples, see Morin-Jean 1913, p. 167, fig.

Fig. 61.6 Covered goblet. Present location unknown.
Reproduced from Rudolph Lepke's Kunst-Auctions-Haus,
Berlin, *Sammlung des Freiherrn Adalbert von Lanna, Prag*
(21–28 March 1911), lot 823, pl. 62

218; Bologna 1959, p. 39, no. 102, pl. 13; Fremersdorf
1961, pp. 74–75, pls. 159–65; Kämpfer and Beyer 1966,
p. 267, pl. 15; Kämpfer 1978, p. 34; *Bulletin AIHV*, no. 9
(1981–83), p. 121, fig. 4.

4. Seilern sale 1982, lot 247.
5. Toledo Museum of Art, 13.420; Hutton 1963, p. [6];
Welander-Berggren 1990, p. 50.
6. Hermitage, F482.
7. Museo Vetrario, cl. VI, n. 561 (ex coll. Maglione, Naples;
Museo Correr, Venice; Morin-Jean 1913, p. 268, fig. 347D;
Mariacher 1954, p. 327; Venice 1982, pp. 140, 142, no.
202), cl. VI, n. 541 (ex coll. Maglione, Naples; Museo
Correr; Venice 1982, p. 143, no. 206).
8. Causa Picone 1967, p. 13.
9. Museo Poldi Pezzoli, 1271, 1173; Roffia and Mariacher
1983, p. 184, nos. 155, 156, figs. 152, 154; Zecchin
1987–89, vol. 2, p. 43.
10. Metropolitan Museum, 81.8.106 (ex coll. James Jackson
Jarves).
11. Pilkington Glass Museum, 2788; *JGS* 11 (1969), p. 115,
fig. 34; Savage [1975], p. 34.
12. Laméris and Laméris 1991, p. 29, pl. 7. For yet another
example, see Waring n.d., pl. 4.
13. Musée du Verre, Baar 1611 (ex coll. Armand Baar); Liège

1958, pp. 128, 129, no. 264; *Bulletin AIHV*, no. 5
(1967–70), p. 75, fig. 79; Philippe 1973, p. 29, fig. 6.
14. New Orleans Museum of Art, B450A (ex coll. George S.
McKearin, Melvin Billups); Corning 1962, p. 32, no. 48.
15. Museo Nazionale di San Martino, 940; Venice 1982, p.
154, no. 232.
16. Museo Nazionale della Ceramica, 691; ibid., no. 233.
17. Muzeum Narodowe, Warsaw; reproduced in Marandel et
al. 1982, p. 70.
18. Museo Poldi Pezzoli, 1207; Mariacher 1961, pl. 43;
Mariacher 1967, p. 55; Roffia and Mariacher 1983, p.
177, no. 79, fig. 80.
19. Mariacher 1961, pl. 30; Heikamp 1986, pp. 61, 71, figs.
38, 52.
20. Schmidt 1912, p. 106, fig. 66; Schmidt 1922, p. 108, fig.
67.
21. Royal Museum of Scotland, 1884-44.30.
22. Lanna sale 1911, lot 823, pl. 62.
23. Wallace Collection, IIIE179; Egg 1962, p. 59, no. 11, pl.
16, fig. 33.
24. Kunstsammlungen der Veste Coburg, HA170; ibid., p. 60,
no. 14, pl. 17, fig. 35.
25. Uměleckoprůmyslové Muzeum, 2645; ibid., p. 61, no. 18,
pl. 17, fig. 34.

Venice, late seventeenth to early eighteenth century

62. Goblet

1975.1.1210

H. 19.9 cm, diam. of rim 9.4 cm. Colorless (slightly tan) and opaque white nonlead glass. Blown, *vetro a reticello*.

The tapered, bucket-shaped bowl has a rounded base drawn into a short neck and is crisscrossed with opaque white spiral threads forming rectangular cells, each entrapping a tiny air bubble. Colorless mereses flank the hollow stem, formed into three ball knops of the same *vetro a reticello* as the bowl. The sloping foot, also *vetro a reticello*, has an underfolded rim. Small rough pontil mark under the foot. Painted in bright red-orange under the foot: L.58.73.61 (a Metropolitan Museum loan number).

Normal wear on the bowl and foot rims.

Longwave fluorescence. Strong yellow-green. *Shortwave fluorescence.* Faint purplish.

PROVENANCE: Otto Hopfinger, New York; [Blumka Gallery, New York].

EXHIBITED: Corning 1958, pp. 80–81, no. 79, ill.; Cincinnati 1959, p. 43, no. 556.

I know of only one other *vetro a reticello* glass comparable to this one, a goblet in the New Orleans Museum of Art whose stem is formed into four ball knops, rather than three (Fig. 62.1).[1] Many drinking glasses in other shapes made with the *vetro a reticello* technique have survived, however. Particularly important for dating them are the glasses in Rosenborg Castle in Copenhagen that King Frederick IV acquired during his visit to Venice in 1708–9, among which are several of *vetro a reticello* (see Fig. 62.2).[2]

NOTES:
1. Ex coll. Melvin Billups (B34A), Max Strauss, Schick; Bernt [1951?], p. 56, no. 47 (shown with a cover); Corning 1962, p. 28, no. 40.
2. Rosenborg Castle, 22-14; Boesen 1960, no. 38. See also ibid., nos. 21–37, 39–45.

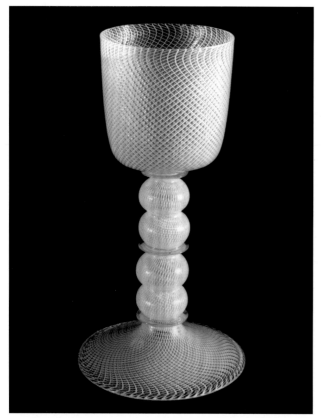

Fig. 62.1 Goblet. New Orleans Museum of Art, Gift of Melvin P. Billups in memory of his wife, Clarice Marston Billups

Fig. 62.2 Goblet. Rosenborg Castle, Copenhagen

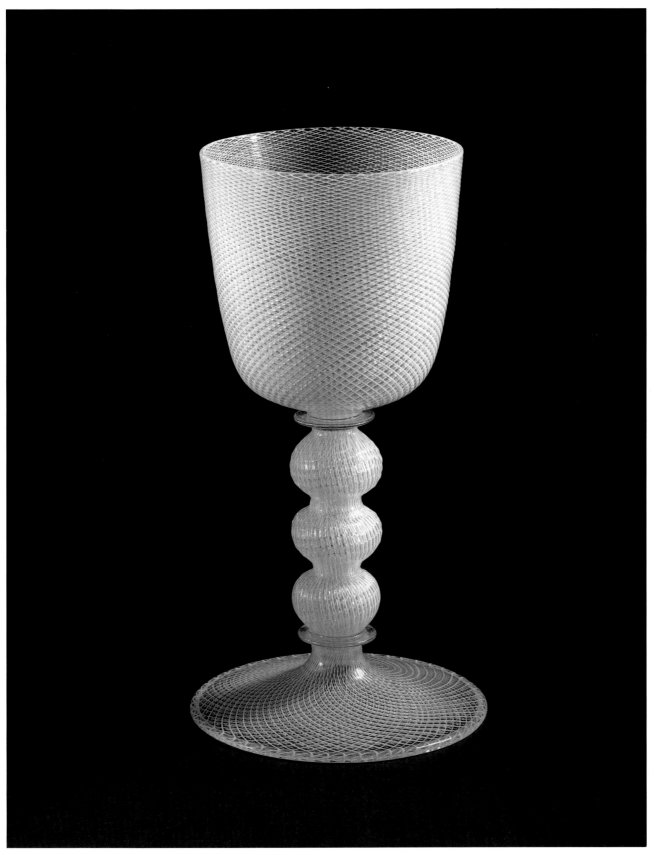

No. 62

Probably Venice, mid-sixteenth century; the mounts probably Augsburg, about 1550–1600

63. Covered goblet

1975.1.1212a,b

H. with cover 34.7 cm. Colorless (slightly gray) and opaque white nonlead glass. Blown, *vetro a reticello*, silver foil; silver-gilt mounts.

The bowl, with a flared rim and a large bulbous midsection above a smaller, waisted bulge, forms a double cyma curve in profile. It is crisscrossed with opaque white spiral threads forming rectangular cells, each entrapping a tiny air bubble, with shattered silver foil within the walls. The stem is a waisted knop above a hollow ovoid knop, both also *vetro a reticello*, above a colorless capstan. Encircling the bowl above and below the large bulbous section are molded silver-gilt straps with scalloped borders connected by four similar vertical straps, the horizontal straps with stylized flowers, the vertical each with a caryatid. A silver-gilt mount of two rings connected by four molded caryatids with elaborately scrolled tails spans the waisted knop and attaches the bowl to the stem. The domed silver-gilt foot, topped by a globular knop decorated with raised gadrooning, has a molded rim and is covered with four repoussé putti heads in scrolled frames interspersed with floral and fruit trophies. The silver-gilt cover is a waisted dome, the top section covered with eight repoussé ovals, four of them enclosing stylized floral motifs, the larger bottom section decorated with repoussé heads, two male and two female, in scrolled panels amid floral bouquets. A cast lion rampant holding an undecorated shield in its paws and secured by a four-pointed nut and a screw to a turned cap surmounts the cover, which has a turned rim and a tapered brim that fits over the glass rim on the goblet. Painted in bright red-orange under the foot: *L.56.31.61A* (a Metropolitan Museum loan number).[1]

The original glass foot missing; the stem undoubtedly broken under the mount. The silver-gilt mounts, on which there are no hallmarks, were presumably added when the glass was broken.

No. 63, *detail of cover*

No. 63, *detail of cover*

No. 63, *detail of cover*

No. 63

No. 63, *detail of band on side of bowl*

Longwave fluorescence. Strong yellow-green. *Shortwave fluorescence.* Faint tan.

PROVENANCE: Rothschild, Vienna(?);[2] Otto Hopfinger, New York; [Blumka Gallery, New York].

EXHIBITED: Corning 1958, pp. 76, 77, no. 73, ill.; Cincinnati 1959, p. 543, no. 555; New York 1985.

I have found only one glass in a shape similar to that of the Lehman piece, a *vetro a retorti* goblet in the J. Paul Getty Museum, Malibu, with silver-gilt mounts that bear an Augsburg inspection mark and an unidentified maker's mark (Fig. 63.1).[3] Venetian and *façon de Venise* objects from the sixteenth century in *vetro a reticello* with silver or gold foil sandwiched between the two layers of glass are rare. Among the few surviving examples are a glass bucket in the New Orleans Museum of Art (Fig. 63.2);[4] a beaker in the British Museum, London;[5] two beakers in the Hermitage, Saint Petersburg (Figs. 63.3, 63.4);[6] and a jug in the Museen der Stadt Regensburg (Fig. 63.5).[7]

No. 63, *detail of stem*

No. 63, *detail of foot*

Fig. 63.1 Covered goblet. J. Paul Getty Museum, Malibu

Fig. 63.2 Bucket. New Orleans Museum of Art, Gift of Melvin P. Billups in memory of his wife, Clarice Marston Billups. Reproduced from Paul Perrot, *A Decade of Glass Collecting* (Corning Museum of Glass, 1962), no. 41

Fig. 63.3 Beaker. Hermitage, Saint Petersburg

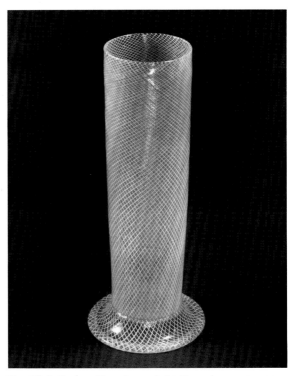

Fig. 63.4 Beaker. Hermitage, Saint Petersburg

Fig. 63.5 Jug. Museen der Stadt Regensburg. Reproduced from Sabine Baumgärtner, *Gläser: Antike, Mittelalter, neuere Zeit* (Karlsruhe: Corona-Verlag, 1977), no. 101

NOTES:

1. The following labels have been removed and are in the Robert Lehman Collection files: Unidentified: two oval orange paper labels, one printed 556 in black and one printed 545 in black; a piece of old masking tape with 556-8 written in pencil (no longer legible). Robert Lehman collection: rectangular gold metallic paper label printed 29 in black.
2. The catalogue of the 1958 Corning exhibition says that the goblet was once in the Rothschild collection in Vienna, but that provenance has not been documented.
3. J. Paul Getty Museum, 84.DK.514.A,B (ex coll. Leopold Blumka); *JGS* 28 (1986), pp. 102–3, fig. 15.
4. New Orleans Museum of Art, 64.170 (with silver foil; ex coll. Agnes Carpenter, Melvin Billups); Corning 1962, p. 29, no. 41.
5. British Museum, U73,10-29,1 (with gold foil); Tait 1979, pp. 40, 41, no. 33; Tait 1991, pp. 170–71, fig. 218.
6. Hermitage, F485, F484 (with gold foil).
7. Museen der Stadt Regensburg, K(B)1960/112 (with gold foil); Baumgärtner 1977a, p. 53, no. 101.

Venice, probably late nineteenth century, possibly late eighteenth century

64. Vase

1975.1.1217
H. 20.5 cm. Colorless (slightly gray) and opaque white nonlead glass. Blown, *vetro a retorti*.

The bowl, oval in cross section, has an inward-sloping rim, rounded shoulders, and tapered, rounded sides. It is formed of opaque white multispiral twists; chaplet twists with intertwined pairs of triple spiral twists, some with central threads; and opaque white stripes. Two sloppily applied white-striped mereses separate the bowl from the awkward, trumpet-shaped pedestal foot with opaque white chaplet twists like those in the bowl. Rough pontil mark inside the bowl.[1]

Long Y-shaped crack through the base of the bowl and the mereses.

Longwave fluorescence. Colorless glass: strong yellow-green. Opaque white twists and stripes: creamy yellow. *Shortwave fluorescence.* Colorless glass: strong bluish white. Opaque white twists and stripes = strong bluish white.

PROVENANCE: Albert Pollak, Vienna(?);[2] Otto Hopfinger, New York; [Blumka Gallery, New York].

The bowl and foot were blown from different gathers of glass (the sequence of canes does not match). The canes were not picked up on a colorless gather, as was the case with Nos. 52–61. Rather, they were laid out side by side, softened and fused to form a solid rectangle, then picked up on a collar of hot glass; the resulting cylinder was then reheated to mask the seam, pincered together at the end to form a bubble, and blown to shape the glass.[3] The mereses were probably made using glass left over on the end of the blowpipe.

The poor workmanship and awkward form, as well as the technique used to pick up the canes, known in Venetian glasshouses as the Pastorelli plate technique, suggest a late nineteenth-century date for this vase. I know of only two other glasses with similar decoration. One, a footed bowl with wide multispiral twists, is in the Museo Vetrario, Murano (Fig. 64.1).[4] The other, a footed bowl with widely spaced olive green twists, was in the collection of Fritz Biemann, Zurich (Fig. 64.2).[5]

No. 64

Fig. 64.1 Footed bowl. Museo Vetrario, Murano

Fig. 64.2 Footed bowl. Present location unknown. Reproduced from Brigitte Klesse and Axel von Saldern, *500 Jahre Glaskunst: Sammlung Biemann* (Zurich: ABC Verlag, 1978), no. 66

NOTES:

1. The following labels were removed and are in the Robert Lehman Collection files: Unidentified: rectangular white gummed paper label with a blue printed geometric meander border and 594 written in black ink; large oval gummed white paper label with 5(?)94 written in greenish brown(?) ink. Robert Lehman collection: rectangular gold metallic paper label printed 5 in black; round white paper label typed 5.

2. According to a note in the Blumka Gallery files, this vase was once owned by Albert Pollak, but the provenance has not been otherwise documented.
3. The technique is illustrated in Tait 1991, pp. 238–39.
4. Mariacher 1961, pl. 49.
5. Klesse and Von Saldern 1978, p. 120, no. 66; Biemann sale 1984, lot 75, ill.

Venice, late seventeenth or early eighteenth century

65. Plate

1975.1.1181

Diam. 48.1 cm. Colorless (slightly gray) and opaque white nonlead glass. Blown, *vetro a retorti*.

The flat, circular plate has an underfolded rim, sloping, slightly curved sides, a rounded booge, and a convex center with a rounded point. It is formed of spirals of opaque white twists in two different patterns – multispiral twists alternating with intertwined pairs of four-ply spiral bands – gathered together at the center. Large rough ring-shaped pontil mark on the back. Painted in bright red-orange on the back: *L.58.73.55* (a Metropolitan Museum loan number).[1]

Mint condition; little wear.

Longwave fluorescence. Colorless glass: strong yellow-green. Opaque white twists: creamy. *Shortwave fluorescence.* Colorless glass: faint purplish. Opaque white twists: strong bluish white.

PROVENANCE: Albert Pollak, Vienna; Otto Hopfinger, New York; [Blumka Gallery, New York].

EXHIBITED: Corning 1958, pp. 76, 77, no. 72, ill.; Cincinnati 1959, p. 42, no. 549 (or No. 67?).

LITERATURE: Hetteš 1960, p. 44, under no. 63; Charleston 1977, p. 102, under no. 21.

So far as I know, this elegant plate has only three counterparts, in the Uměleckoprůmyslové Muzeum, Prague (Fig. 65.1);[2] the Kunstsammlungen zu Weimar (Fig. 65.2);[3] and the Musée National de la Renaissance, Château d'Écouen.

No. 65

No. 65, *detail of center*

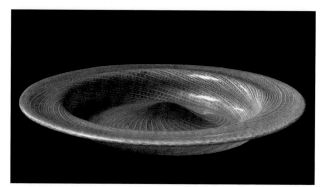

Fig. 65.1 Plate. Uměleckoprůmyslové Muzeum, Prague

Fig. 65.2 Plate. Kunstsammlungen zu Weimar. Photograph: Fotoatelier Louis Held, Weimar

NOTES:

1. A rectangular gold metallic paper label printed *48* in black (Robert Lehman collection) has been removed and is in the Robert Lehman Collection files. The following labels are visible in an old photograph of the plate in the files: Unidentified: illegible circular white paper label. Albert Pollak collection: rectangular white paper label with a printed blue(?) and white toothed border and *A. Pollak / 452* typed in black.

2. Uměleckoprůmyslové Muzeum, 5973; Hetteš 1960, p. 44, no. 63, pl. 63.

3. Kunstsammlungen zu Weimar, A1981; Hörning [1978], no. 33.

No. 66

Venice, mid-seventeenth to early eighteenth century

66. Plate

1975.1.1179

Diam. 26 cm. Colorless (slightly grayish tan) and opaque white nonlead glass. Blown, *vetro a retorti*.

The flat, circular plate has an underfolded rim, sloping sides, a rounded booge, and a slightly convex center. It is formed of radial flattened opaque white twists in a repeated sequence: a multispiral twist, a chaplet twist of six intertwined threads, and a twist with a pair of four-ply spiral bands. Small rough pontil mark on the back. Painted in bright red-orange on the back: L.56.31.57 (a Metropolitan Museum loan number).[1]

Crizzled; slight wear on the base and rim.

Longwave fluorescence. Colorless glass: pale yellowish. Opaque white twists: pinkish purple. *Shortwave fluorescence.* Colorless glass: purple. Opaque white twists: pinkish purple.

PROVENANCE: Otto Hopfinger, New York; [Blumka Gallery, New York].

EXHIBITED: Cincinnati 1959 (not in catalogue).

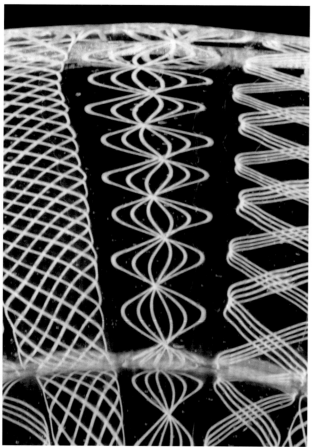

No. 66, *detail of rim*

The plate is markedly ribbed on the back. The opaque white twists were picked up on an inner colorless gather. The fluorescence of the twists indicates, however, that the threads do not lie exposed on the surface of the canes but are covered with a thin layer of colorless glass (as on Nos. 56 and 68).

Vetro a retorti plates like this with a similarly complex arrangement of intricate twists are in the Toledo Museum of Art (Fig. 66.1);[2] the Museo Vetrario, Murano (Fig. 66.2);[3] the Österreichisches Museum für Angewandte Kunst, Vienna (Fig. 66.3);[4] the Kunstgewerbemuseum, Berlin;[5] and the Metropolitan Museum (Fig. 66.4).[6] Twists of comparable complexity also decorate a tazza in Rosenborg Castle, Copenhagen (Fig. 66.5),[7] that is one of a number of *vetro a retorti* vessels that King Frederick IV of Denmark acquired during his visit to Venice in 1708–9.

Drinking glasses and other vessels with complex twists are usually dated to the late seventeenth and early eighteenth centuries.[8] It is often difficult, however, to distinguish between seventeenth- or early eighteenth-century *vetro a retorti* plates incorporating such elaborate twists and late nineteenth-century imitations of them. Similarly crisp twists are found, for example, on the copies of *vetro a retorti* plates pictured in the catalogues of the Rheinische

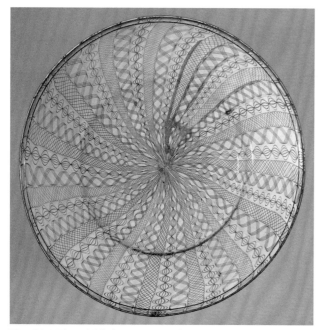

Fig. 66.1 Plate. Toledo Museum of Art, Toledo, Ohio, Purchased with funds from the Libbey Endowment, Gift of Edward Drummond Libbey

Fig. 66.2 Plate. Museo Vetrario, Murano

Fig. 66.3 Plate. Österreichisches Museum für Angewandte Kunst, Vienna

Fig. 66.4 Plate. The Metropolitan Museum of Art, New York, Gift of James Jackson Jarves, 1881 (81.8.138)

Glashütten-Actien-Gesellschaft in Ehrenfeld bei Köln for 1881 and 1886 (Fig. 66.6).⁹ A plate made at Ehrenfeld in 1886 is in the Museum für Angewandte Kunst, Cologne.¹⁰ The Ehrenfeld plates were made in three sizes, with diameters of 28, 22, and 16 centimeters, and are distinguished from earlier examples by the clarity of the colorless glass.

The crizzling of the Lehman plate helps to confirm that it was likely manufactured considerably earlier than the late nineteenth century. Crizzling is a problem that seems to have been experienced in European glasshouses mainly during the latter part of the seventeenth and the early years of the eighteenth century, when glass chemistry was not entirely understood and glassmakers were

Fig. 66.5 Tazza. Rosenborg Castle, Copenhagen

Fig. 66.6 Rheinische Glashütten-Actien-Gesellschaft, Ehrenfeld bei Köln, catalogue (1881). Reproduced from Werner Schäfke, *Ehrenfelder Glas des Historismus* (Cologne: W. König, 1979), no. 170. Photograph courtesy of the Corning Museum of Glass

refining their raw materials to produce truly colorless glass but were removing stabilizing compounds by accident. Crizzling has not been found on Ehrenfeld glass, but it is found from time to time on late nineteenth-century Venetian glass (see No. 69).

NOTES:

1. A rectangular gold metallic paper label printed 22 in black (Robert Lehman collection) has been removed and is in the Robert Lehman Collection files.
2. Toledo Museum of Art, 58.21; *JGS* 1 (1959), p. 109, fig. 19.
3. Museo Vetrario, cl. VI, n. 563 (ex coll. Maglione, Naples; Museo Correr, Venice); Gasparetto 1958, p. 287, fig. 103; Mariacher 1959a, p. 75; Mariacher 1963, p. 101; Barovier Mentasti 1982, p. 127, fig. 116; Marandel et al. 1982, p. 17, fig. 2; Venice 1982, p. 120, no. 158; Barovier Mentasti and Toninato 1983, p. 20; Mianni, Resini, and Lamon 1984, p. 80; Zecchin 1987–89, vol. 1, p. 326.
4. Österreichisches Museum für Angewandte Kunst, 418 (ex coll. Erw. Bar. Schleinitz); Bucher 1888, p. 60, no. 7338; Schlosser 1951, p. 11, no. 38, pl. 38.
5. Kunstgewerbemuseum, K374; Berlin 1965, pp. 90, 93, fig. 30; *Bulletin AIHV*, no. 7 (1973–76), pp. 39, 42, fig. 23; Berlin 1981a, p. 23, no. 24. Another similar plate was in the Kunstgewerbemuseum before World War II; see Schmidt 1912, p. 102, fig. 63; Schmidt 1922, p. 104, fig. 64.
6. Metropolitan Museum, 81.8.138 (ex coll. James Jackson Jarves).
7. Rosenborg Castle, 382; Boesen 1950, fig. 12; Boesen 1960, no. 54. See also Boesen 1960, nos. 51–53, 55–58.
8. See, for example, Ryley 1902, pp. 268, 269; Frothingham 1956, fig. 37; Mallè 1971, pp. 65–66, fig. 50; Tait 1979, p. 76, no. 108; Murano 1981, pp. 19, 30, no. 23; Barovier Mentasti 1982, p. 131, figs. 121, 122; Columbus 1983, p. 22, no. 18; Murano 1983, p. 23, no. 56.
9. Schäfke 1979, pp. 80–81, 162–63, nos. 170, 357.
10. Museum für Angewandte Kunst, F831; Klesse and Reincking von Bock 1973, p. 236, no. 523.

Venice, probably late seventeenth century

67. Plate

1975.1.1182

Diam. 47.5 cm. Colorless (slightly gray), opaque red-brown, and opaque white (slightly gray) nonlead glass. Blown, *vetro a retorti*.

The flat, circular plate has an underfolded rim, sloping sides, a rounded booge, and a slightly convex center. It is formed of alternating swirled dark red-brown stripes and multispiral opaque white twists, gathered together at the center. Rough ring-shaped pontil mark on the back. Painted in bright red-orange on the back: L.56.31.67 (a Metropolitan Museum loan number).[1]

Mint condition; normal wear on the base and rim.

Longwave fluorescence. Colorless glass: strong yellowish. Red-brown glass: dark brick red. Opaque white twists: creamy. *Shortwave fluorescence.* Colorless glass: faint purple. Red-brown glass: nothing. Opaque white twists: strong bluish white.

PROVENANCE: Otto Hopfinger, New York; [Blumka Gallery, New York].

EXHIBITED: Cincinnati 1959, p. 42, no. 549 (or No. 65?).

The twists and stripes of this plate were picked up from a marver on an inner gather of colorless glass. The red-brown stripes, which are noticeably striated and nonuniform, seem to be of iron-red glass.

No. 67, *detail of center*

No. 67

Vetro a retorti incorporating colored threads or stripes was used in the seventeenth and eighteenth centuries to make glasses in many shapes. Venetian examples are a cruet and a mug in the Museo Vetrario, Murano (Figs. 67.1, 67.2);[2] a vase in the Hermitage, Saint Petersburg (Fig. 67.3);[3] two vases in the Österreichisches Museum für Angewandte Kunst;[4] and an *albarello*, two bottles, a bowl, and a ewer in the Victoria and Albert Museum, London.[5]

The size and design of this extraordinary plate are unique among colored *vetro a retorti* glasses. Nothing about its construction or design, however, automatically

relegates it to the realm of late nineteenth-century historical revivals. That the reddish brown stripes seem to be made of iron-red glass tends to support an earlier date, for in the eighteenth century and later the colored threads in *vetro a retorti* were more often made of gold-ruby glass.

The spiraling iron-red enamel stripes on some early eighteenth-century Chinese porcelain, such as a pair of K'ang-hsi bottles sold at Sotheby's in 1990 (Fig. 67.4), may have been meant to replicate the effect of *vetro a retorti* wares like this plate.[6]

Fig. 67.1 Cruet. Museo Vetrario, Murano

Fig. 67.2 Mug. Museo Vetrario, Murano

NOTES:

1. A rectangular gold metallic paper label printed *49* in black (Robert Lehman collection) has been removed and is in the Robert Lehman Collection files.
2. Museo Vetrario, cl. VI, n. 66, cl. VI, n. 1229; Reggio Calabria 1967, fig. [17]; Murano 1981, pp. 20, 33, no. 53; Venice 1982, pp. 196–97, no. 337; Columbus 1983, p. 21, no. 16.
3. Hermitage, F806.
4. Österreichisches Museum für Angewandte Kunst, 3281, 312.
5. Victoria and Albert Museum, C.364-1873, C.323-1884, C.1534-1876, C.1819-1855, C.198-1936.
6. Ex coll. Ava Gardner; Gardner sale 1990, lot 212, ill. Du Boulay 1990 (p. 117, fig. 11) illustrates a similar bottle.

Fig. 67.3 Vase. Hermitage, Saint Petersburg

Fig. 67.4 Bottle. China, K'ang-hsi. Present location unknown. Photograph courtesy of Sotheby's, London

Venice, early eighteenth century

68. Covered bottle

1975.1.1166a,b

H. with cover 17.8 cm. Colorless (slightly gray) and opaque white nonlead glass. Blown, *vetro a retorti*, applied, molded.

The cylindrical, straight-sided bottle is ribbed (forty-four [?] ribs) and has a short cylindrical neck, slightly rounded shoulders, and a flat bottom. It is formed of side-by-side vertical opaque white lace twists alternating with twists with intertwined pairs of four-ply bands, some with central vertical threads. The bell-shaped ribbed cover is formed of twists matching those on the bottle and has an applied finial composed of a colorless merese topped by a tiny inverted baluster and an opalescent white-striated molded berry prunt. Slight kick in the bottom with a small rough pontil mark; tiny pontil mark inside the cover.

Normal wear on the base of the bottle; no wear on the cover, which is cracked around the base of the finial.

Longwave fluorescence. Colorless glass: strong yellow-green. Opaque white twists: orange. *Shortwave fluorescence.* Colorless glass: purplish pink. Opaque white twists: purplish pink.

PROVENANCE: Otto Hopfinger, New York; [Blumka Gallery, New York].

EXHIBITED: New York 1983–84.

No. 68, *detail of cover*

No. 68

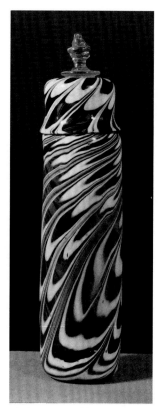

Figs. 68.1 and 68.2 (left and center left) Covered bottles. Rosenborg Castle, Copenhagen Fig. 68.3 (center right) Covered bottle. Formerly Rakow collection, New York. Photograph courtesty of the Corning Museum of Glass Fig. 68.4 (right) Covered bottle. Kunstgewerbemuseum, Staatliche Museen Preussischer Kulturbesitz, Berlin

Although at first glance the finial looks like translucent milky-white glass, it appears instead to have been made by twisting a gather of striped glass similar to that of the body. See also No. 56.

When King Frederick IV of Denmark visited Venice in 1708–9, he acquired several bottles shaped like this one. Those bottles, in *cristallo*, *vetro a reticello* (Fig. 68.1), and blue glass with combed white threading (Fig. 68.2), are still in Rosenborg Castle, Copenhagen.[1] Other bottles of this form are in the Kunstgewerbemuseum, Berlin (Fig. 68.4);[2] the Metropolitan Museum;[3] the Victoria and Albert Museum, London;[4] and the Corning Museum of Glass.[5] Two others were formerly in the collection of the late Dr. and Mrs. Leonard S. Rakow, New York (Fig. 68.3), and the Helfried Krug collection, Mülheim an der

Ruhr.[6] A *cristallo* bottle of similar form, without a cover, appears in a still life in the collection of the princes of Liechtenstein, Vaduz, that was painted by Gabriele Salci and is dated between 1710 and 1720.[7]

NOTES:
1. Rosenborg Castle, 22-437, 22-564a,b (Fig. 68.1), 22-67 (Fig. 68.2); Boesen 1960, nos. 10, 86, 43.
2. Kunstgewerbemuseum, K164a,b (Fig. 68.4), K166; Dreier 1989b, pp. 83–84, nos. 66, 67.
3. Metropolitan Museum, 91.1.1487, 91.1.1488 (both ex coll. Edward C. Moore).
4. Victoria and Albert Museum, 1823&A-1855; Savage [1975], p. 48, fig. 37.
5. Corning Museum of Glass, 63.3.4; *JGS* 6 (1964), p. 163, fig. 31; Weiss 1971, p. 110.
6. Klesse 1973, pp. 130, 131, no. 513.
7. Barovier Mentasti 1982, p. 138, fig. 129.

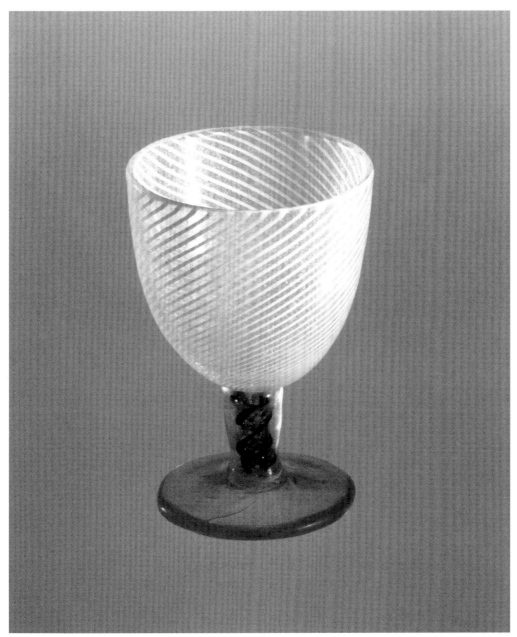

No. 69

Venice, late nineteenth century

69. Liqueur glass

1975.1.1152

H. 6.6 cm. Colorless (slightly gray), opaque white, copper-flecked (goldstone or aventurine), and transparent blue nonlead glass. Blown, *vetro a retorti*.

The small ovoid bowl incorporates spiral opaque white threads, and the short, straight stem contains intertwined blue and copper-colored goldstone or aventurine threads. The small foot is a colorless disk. Tiny rough pontil mark under the foot.[1]

Heavily crizzled.

Longwave fluorescence. Colorless glass: foggy gray, speckled. Opaque white threads: grayish white. *Shortwave fluorescence.* Colorless glass and opaque white threads: brilliant bluish white. Aventurine and blue glass: no observable fluorescence under either illumination.

PROVENANCE: Otto Hopfinger, New York; [Blumka Gallery, New York].

Fig. 69.1 Liqueur glass. Museo Vetrario, Murano

Avventurina (called aventurine or goldstone) glass is made by dissolving a copper salt in the batch. As the glass is heated, metallic copper begins to precipitate, forming tiny reflective crystals.

Avventurina glass first appeared in Venice in the late seventeenth century and became especially popular in the nineteenth.[2] Four glasses in the Museo Vetrario, Murano (see Fig. 69.1), that are nearly identical to the Lehman glass have been dated to the late nineteenth century.[3] Although crizzling like that on this liqueur glass is more typical of glasses made in the late seventeenth and early eighteenth centuries (see No. 66), the fault does occur from time to time on glasses made in Europe in the last half of the nineteenth century.

NOTES:
1. A rectangular gold metallic paper label printed 9 in black and a circular white paper label typed 9. (both Robert Lehman collection) have been removed and are in the Robert Lehman Collection files.
2. See Zecchin 1987–89, vol. 1, pp. 76–81.
3. Museo Vetrario, cl. VI, n. 1548 (Fig. 69.1; Murano 1983, pp. 46–47, no. 113), cl. VI, n. 5525, cl. VI, n. 6425, cl. VI, n. 7284.

Façon de Venise, northern Europe, possibly the Netherlands, seventeenth century

70. Wineglass

1975.1.1148
H. 19.4 cm. Colorless (slightly gray) and transparent turquoise blue nonlead glass. Blown, pattern molded, trailed, pincered, milled.

The tall, ovoid bowl has a flared rim; two trailed, milled blue threads encircle its lower half and at the base is a trailed and pincered colorless fringe. The short stem is composed of a flared disk above a waisted section and a hollow inverted baluster knop with eighteen ribs that flares at the base, where it meets the round, sloping foot. Small rough pontil mark under the foot. Painted in white under the foot: [ ]*1*[ ] (unidentified).[1]

Lightly crizzled; normal wear.

Longwave fluorescence. Strong yellow-green. *Shortwave fluorescence*. Apparently gray, but the surface fluoresces a strong mottled yellowish due to accumulated dirt and lint on the crizzled surface.

PROVENANCE: Otto Hopfinger, New York; [Blumka Gallery, New York].

The trailed fringe that decorates the base of the bowl of this wineglass was pincered with a tool that had at least six parallel grooves on each face. The crizzling suggests that this is a northern European, rather than Venetian, product.

NOTE:
1. A rectangular gold metallic paper label printed *31* in black and a circular white paper label typed *31*. (both Robert Lehman collection) have been removed and are in the Robert Lehman Collection files.

No. 70

Façon de Venise, northern Europe, or Venice, seventeenth century

71. Wineglass (pastiche)

1975.1.1144

H. 19.8 cm. Colorless (the bowl slightly tan, the stem and foot gray) nonlead glass. Blown, pattern molded, trailed.

A trailed slender thread encircles the conical bowl above the vertical ribbing (twelve ribs) that covers its lower half. The bowl is open at the base to two hollow, rounded conical knops spanned by two trailed and pincered wings with projecting tails. The bowl is cemented onto the stem, which is composed of a flared disk, a small rounded disk knop, and a slender hollow inverted baluster flared into a disk that is cemented to and penetrates a thin, circular foot.[1]

Longwave fluorescence. Bowl: light yellow-green. Stem: stronger yellow-green. Foot: stronger yellow-green. *Shortwave fluorescence*. Bowl: greenish gray. Stem: greenish gray. Foot: silvery gray.

PROVENANCE: Otto Hopfinger, New York; [Blumka Gallery, New York].

EXHIBITED: New York 1983–84.

The bowl, stem, and foot of this married glass were taken from three different glasses and cemented together. The bowl is crizzled. The foot rim has been trimmed and was possibly made from a window roundel.

The most impressive part of this composite glass is the bowl. In form, it has no recorded parallels. Indeed, it is amazing that this fragment survived otherwise undamaged, given the fragility of the trailed "wings" at the base.

A number of tall, slender inverted baluster or "cigar" stems like this one have been discovered in excavations of early seventeenth-century English sites and attributed to the glassworks Sir Robert Mansell established in Broad Street in the City of London in 1617. Mansell monopo-

Fig. 71.1 Wineglass (fragment). Museum of London. Reproduced from Robert J. Charleston, *English Glass and the Glass Used in England* (London: George Allen and Unwin, 1984), pl. 15a

Fig. 71.2 Tazza. The Metropolitan Museum of Art, New York, Gift of James Jackson Jarves, 1881 (81.8.143)

No. 71

lized English production of both "ordinary" and "cristall" glass, using new furnaces that burned coal rather than wood, from 1615 until Parliament canceled his patent shortly before 1642.[2] More than fifty glasses with "cigar" stems dated to the early seventeenth century that were excavated at the site of what might have been a glass and pottery shop in Gracechurch Street, London, are in the Museum of London (see Fig. 71.1).[3]

Stems of this form were also made in Venice and elsewhere in Europe. Examples in the Metropolitan Museum

Fig. 71.3 Jacopo Chimenti da Empoli, *Still Life* (detail). Private collection. Reproduced from Detlef Heikamp, *Studien zur mediceischen Glaskunst* (Florence: Kunsthistorisches Institut in Florenz, 1986), fig. 31

(Fig. 71.2);[4] the Museum für Kunsthandwerk, Frankfurt am Main;[5] and the Victoria and Albert Museum, London,[6] have been attributed to Venice and dated to the late sixteenth or early seventeenth century. A drinking glass with a tazza-shaped bowl and a tall inverted baluster stem is depicted in a still life (Fig. 71.3) by Jacopo Chimenti da Empoli (1551–1640).[7]

NOTES:

1. A rectangular gold metallic paper label printed 34 in black and a circular white paper label typed 34. (both Robert Lehman collection) have been removed and are in the Robert Lehman Collection files.
2. See Charleston 1980b, pp. 83–84, 89–92.
3. Oswald and Phillips 1949, pp. 31, 32, fig. 5; Haynes 1959, fig. 53c; Charleston 1978, pp. 285–87, fig. 1; Charleston 1980b, pp. 90, 93, fig. 32; Charleston 1984, pl. 15a.
4. Metropolitan Museum, 81.8.143 (ex coll. James Jackson Jarves).
5. Ohm 1973, p. 69, no. 132.
6. Honey 1946, pl. 26D. For other glasses with stems of this type, see Nesbitt 1871, pp. 83–85, nos. 434, 435, 442, 443, figs. 102, 103, 109, 110; Lorenzetti 1931, pl. 9; Lorenzetti [1953], pl. 9; Mariacher 1963, pp. 72, 73, 83; Mariacher [1970]b, p. 29, fig. 29.
7. Private collection; Heikamp 1986, p. 53, fig. 31.

Venice, seventeenth century

72. Cruet

1975.1.1171

H. 13.3 cm. Colorless (slightly grayish tan) and transparent turquoise blue nonlead glass. Blown, pattern molded, trailed, pincered.

The hourglass-shaped body is decorated with twelve vertical ribs and a trailed colorless rigaree collar. Pincered colorless trailing embellishes the applied blue scroll handle, which is hollow. The applied colorless S-shaped spout has twelve vertical ribs. A merese separates the body from the trumpet-shaped foot. Rough pontil mark under the foot.[1]

The tip of the spout broken cleanly (in manufacture); curved crack in the body above the lower attachment of the handle; normal wear on the foot rim.

Longwave fluorescence. Colorless glass: strong yellow-green. Blue glass: faint dark blue-green. *Shortwave fluorescence.* Colorless glass: tan. Blue glass: faint dark blue-green.

PROVENANCE: Otto Hopfinger, New York; [Blumka Gallery, New York].

The slightly grayish tan tint of the colorless glass relates this cruet to similar cruets – in the Uměleckoprůmyslové Muzeum, Prague (Fig. 72.1);[2] the Museo Vetrario, Murano;[3] and the Rijksmuseum, Amsterdam – that have been attributed to Venice and dated to the seventeenth

No. 72

Fig. 72.1 Cruet. Uměleckoprůmyslové Muzeum, Prague

century. Examples of the same form in opalescent white glass, colored glass with combed decoration, or *vetro a retorti* are in the British Museum, London;[4] the Museo del Settecento Veneziano, Ca'Rezzonico, Venice;[5] the Musée National de la Renaissance, Château d'Écouen (two examples); the Kunstmuseum Düsseldorf;[6] the Uměleckoprůmyslové Muzeum;[7] and the Museo Vetrario.[8] Cruets of this type were also made in the late nineteenth century in Venice, typically of noticeably amber- or amethyst-tinted glass. See also No. 73.

NOTES:

1. The following labels have been removed and are in the Robert Lehman Collection files: Unidentified: rectangular white paper label with a serrated edge and a printed blue meander border with *377* written in black ink. Robert Lehman collection: rectangular gold metallic paper label printed *16* in black; circular white paper label typed *16*.
2. Uměleckoprůmyslové Muzeum, 1299; Prague 1973, no. 157, fig. 36.
3. Museo Vetrario, cl. VI, n. 1169; Mariacher 1959a, p. 59; Mariacher 1963, p. 85; Venice 1982, p. 143, no. 204.
4. British Museum, s.765 (ex coll. Felix Slade); Nesbitt 1871, p. 129; Tait 1979, pp. 108, 109, no. 176.
5. Ex coll. Gatti Casazza; Venice 1982, pp. 150, 151, no. 225.
6. Kunstmuseum, 17674; Heinemeyer 1966, p. 83, no. 240.
7. Ex coll. Adalbert von Lanna; Hetteš 1960, p. 44, no. 64.
8. Museo Vetrario, cl. VI, n. 66; Venice 1982, p. 148, no. 219.

Venice (probably Salviati), late nineteenth century

73. Cruet and stopper

1975.1.1146a,b

H. with stopper 23.5 cm. Transparent topaz-tinted and dark amethyst nonlead glass. Blown, pattern molded, trailed, applied and impressed parts.

The cruet has a pointed ovoid body, a tall waisted neck with a trailed amethyst rigaree collar, and a flared trefoil rim decorated with two trailed amethyst threads. Encircling the upper part of the body are two trailed amethyst threads flanking four applied amethyst wads alternating with four applied oval pads stamped with faces in relief, two on either side, one at the base of the applied ribbed (fourteen ribs) S-shaped spout with a trailed amethyst ring on its tip, and one at the base of the applied ribbed (twelve ribs) scroll handle, which has another

applied amethyst face at its top and trailed amethyst fins pincered in an overall waffle pattern along its outer edge. The lower part of the body is covered with molded spiked gadrooning (eight ribs) and is set onto a short stem with a merese above a short true baluster and a capstan. The circular foot has a trailed amethyst rim. The hollow ovoid stopper is topped with a ribbed (sixteen ribs) flattened ball finial mounted on a capstan, with a tiny amethyst disk and ball finial at the top. One small rough pontil mark under the foot and another at the bottom end of the stopper.[1]

Two cracks in the body adjacent to the upper terminal of the handle; the projection above the applied mask at the top of the handle broken off and missing; the stopper chipped.

No. 73

No. 73, *detail of base of handle*

Fig. 73.1 Cruet. Museo Vetrario, Murano

Fig. 73.2 Stefano Zanetti, drawing of a cruet. Reproduced from *Vincenzo Zanetti e la Murano dell'ottocento* (Murano: Museo Vetrario, [1983]), fig. 169

Fig. 73.3 Salviati Dr. Antonio, catalogue (late 1800s), no. 203. Collection of Paolo Zancopé, Venice. Reproduced from Giovanni Sarpellon et al., *Salviati, il suo vetro e i suoi uomini, 1859–1987* (Venice: Stamperia di Venezia, 1989)

Longwave fluorescence. Topaz glass: weak yellow-green. Amethyst glass: weak yellow-green. *Shortwave fluorescence.* Topaz glass: faint greenish tan. Amethyst glass: opaque bluish tan.

PROVENANCE: Otto Hopfinger, New York; [Blumka Gallery, New York].

This cruet is a reproduction of a seventeenth-century glass. The model was probably a cruet with nearly identical decoration (though with its spout broken off) in the Museo Vetrario, Murano (Fig. 73.1).[2] Stefano Zanetti (1850–1917) of Murano sketched a cruet of almost the same design (Fig. 73.2).[3] And a drawing of a slightly simpler version with a more pear-shaped body (Fig. 73.3) appears in a catalogue issued by Antonio Salviati's Venetian glasshouse (see No. 34) in the last quarter of the nineteenth century.[4] A Salviati copy much like the Lehman cruet, also of topaz-tinted glass but with bright blue rather than amethyst trailings, is in the Musée du Verre, Liège. Reproductions of this form were also made in the 1880s in Germany at the Rheinische Glashütten-Actien-Gesellschaft in Ehrenfeld bei Köln,[5] and perhaps in other European glassmaking centers as well.

That the Lehman cruet is furnished with a stopper is unusual. Neither the Zanetti nor the Salviati drawing shows a stopper, and no stopper exists either for the original in the Museo Vetrario (Fig. 73.1) or for any of the other seventeenth-century cruets of similar form and with similar decoration that survive in the Kunstsammlungen der Veste Coburg;[6] the Museo Vetrario;[7] the Kunstmuseum Düsseldorf;[8] the British Museum, London;[9] the Musée d'Art et d'Histoire, Geneva;[10] and the Österreichisches Museum für Angewandte Kunst, Vienna.[11] Two examples without stoppers that Rückert has dated to the sixteenth century are in the Bayerisches Nationalmuseum, Munich.[12]

NOTES:

1. The following labels have been removed and are in the Robert Lehman Collection files: Unidentified: fragmentary paper label with printed border of white dots on blue and an illegible inscription; rectangular white paper label typed *174* (the *4* no longer legible) and *82.* written in black ink (while the cruet was in Robert Lehman's possession). Robert Lehman collection: rectangular gold metallic paper label printed *82* in black.
2. Barovier Mentasti 1982, p. 116, fig. 102 (right).
3. Murano 1983–84, pp. 100, 101, fig. 169.
4. Sarpellon et al. 1989, no. 203.
5. Schäfke 1979, pp. 162–63, no. 358 (in opalescent white glass).
6. Kunstsammlungen der Veste Coburg, HA387.
7. Museo Vetrario, cl. VI, n. 1170; Mariacher 1959b, p. 9, fig. 4; Mariacher 1960, pl. 72; Mariacher 1961, pl. 57; Schack 1976, p. 226, fig. 99; Barovier Mentasti 1982, p. 116, fig. 102 (left); Venice 1982, p. 144, no. 207.
8. Kunstmuseum, 13390; Heinemeyer 1966, p. 83, no. 239.
9. British Museum, S.513 (ex coll. Felix Slade); Nesbitt 1871, p. 95, no. 513, fig. 146.
10. Musée d'Art et d'Histoire, MF4088.
11. Schlosser 1951, pl. 26.
12. Bayerisches Nationalmuseum, G480, G481; Rückert 1982, p. 52, nos. 38, 39, pl. 9.

Façon de Venise, probably the Southern Netherlands or Germany, seventeenth century

74. Goblet

1975.1.1206

H. 28.1 cm. Colorless (yellowish), transparent turquoise blue, and opaque brick red, yellow, and white nonlead glass. Blown, trailed, pincered, *vetro a retorti*.

The large ovoid bowl is supported by a three-part stem. At the top is a short, colorless section with a flared top and a small basal ball knop. In the center is an elaborately coiled two-headed "dragon" with trailed and pincered blue jaws, combs, and fins, the combs and fins with an allover waffle pattern, and an inverted heart-shaped body formed of a continuous glass rod enclosing a loose spiral twist of two laminated red-and-white threads intertwined with floating yellow and white threads. At the bottom of the stem is another straight, colorless section with basal swelling. The large disk-shaped foot has an underfolded rim. Rough pontil mark under the foot.

Slight wear on the foot.

Fig. 74.1 Goblet. Museum für Angewandte Kunst, Cologne. Photograph: Rheinisches Bildarchiv, Cologne

Fig. 74.2 Goblet. Kunstmuseum Düsseldorf. Photograph: Walter Klein, Düsseldorf

Longwave fluorescence. Colorless glass: strong yellow-green. Blue glass: faint green. *Shortwave fluorescence*. Colorless glass: orange-tan. Blue glass: translucent dark green.

PROVENANCE: Otto Hopfinger, New York; [Blumka Gallery, New York].

EXHIBITED: New York 1991.

This goblet was produced at a furnace, not with a lamp. The dragon was formed in place: a colorless glass rod containing colored threads was attached to the small knop at the base of the short, colorless section at the top of the stem, where a large bulbous attachment is clearly visible. The rod was pulled and twisted into a thin pencil shape, then quickly manipulated into the contorted dragon form, undoubtedly in one maneuver and without reheating. The combs, jaws, and fins were formed by trailing bits of hot blue glass at the required points, then using pincers to shape them. Finally, the colorless lower section of the stem and foot were attached to the dragon.

The same technique was used to create the stems on Nos. 75 and 76, which have a similar colorless section with a basal ball knop at the top of the stem.

Wineglasses with fantastic "dragon" stems, or *vetri a serpenti*, were made in Murano beginning in the late sixteenth century. During the seventeenth century they continued to be produced in Venice and in northern European factories specializing in glass *à la façon de Venise*.[1] Furnace-made glasses with flat dragon stems like those on the Lehman goblets (see also Nos. 75 and 76) are usually attributed to the Southern Netherlands. As Charleston has noted, *verres à serpents* are mentioned in contracts the Bonhommes, who had glasshouses at Brussels, Liège, and elsewhere in the Southern Netherlands, made with their workers between 1667 and 1673, and in seventeenth-century documents from the Colinet glassworks at Barbançon. Between 1659 and 1663 some 8,000

No. 74

Fig. 74.3 Covered goblet. Schlossmuseum, Verwaltung der Staatlichen Schlösser und Gärten, Bad Homburg

Fig. 74.4 Rheinische Glashütten-Actien-Gesellschaft, Ehrenfeld bei Köln, catalogue (1881). Reproduced from Werner Schäfke, *Ehrenfelder Glas des Historismus* (Cologne: Walther König, 1979), p 65. Photograph courtesy of the Corning Museum of Glass

verres à serpents were sold in Brussels (as opposed to about 426,000 *verres ordinaires* and 43,000 *verres à la vénitienne*.)[2]

Furnace-made glasses with stems similar to that on No. 74 that have been attributed to the Southern Netherlands are in the Museum für Angewandte Kunst (four examples; see Fig. 74.1);[3] the Kunstmuseum Düsseldorf (Fig. 74.2);[4] the British Museum, London;[5] the James A. de Rothschild Collection at Waddesdon Manor (two examples);[6] the Fitzwilliam Museum, Cambridge;[7] the Corning Museum of Glass;[8] the Kunstsammlungen der Veste Coburg;[9] the Musées Royaux d'Art et d'Histoire, Brussels;[10] the Staatliche Kunstsammlungen Kassel (four examples);[11] the National Museums and Galleries on Merseyside, Liverpool;[12] the Kunstgewerbemuseum, Berlin;[13] the Royal Museum of Scotland, Edinburgh;[14] the

Toledo Museum of Art;[15] and the Musée du Verre, Liège.[16] Another was in the Fritz Biemann collection, Zurich,[17] and yet another was in the Helfried Krug collection, Mülheim an der Ruhr.[18]

Other similar dragon-stem glasses have been attributed to Germany. An impressive late sixteenth-century dragon-stem glass in the Schlossmuseum, Bad Homburg (Fig. 74.3), that bears a strong resemblance to No. 74 has been attributed to the glasshouse at Kassel, although the attribution is by no means certain.[19] A diamond-engraved goblet with a similar stem in the Metropolitan Museum is thought to have been made in Germany in the eighteenth century.[20] No glasses with flat dragon stems like these have been associated with Venice.

The discovery that a large number of lampworked dragon-stem glasses were made by C. H. F. Müller in

Hamburg in the late nineteenth century has prompted a wholesale review of these glasses during the last decade.[21] The lampworked glasses are now accepted as being nineteenth-century imitations of seventeenth-century glasses, but there is still no general agreement on how many or which of the furnace-worked specimens are of late date. The technique by which the stems were made provides one clue. On many, if not all, of the nineteenth-century glasses the dragon stems were formed separately and attached fully formed to the bowls and feet, rather than being formed in place as they were on the three Lehman glasses.

A variety of dragon-stem glasses were illustrated in the catalogues of the Rheinische Glashütten-Actien-Gesellschaft in Ehrenfeld bei Köln in the 1880s (see Fig. 74.4).[22] In keeping with typical nineteenth-century techniques, the stems were joined fully formed to the bowls of those goblets, and that the glass is too colorless and the workmanship too crisp also makes them relatively easy to spot.

NOTES:

1. See Tait 1979, p. 50, and Tait 1991, pp. 174–76.
2. Charleston 1977, p. 119, citing Chambon 1955, pp. 114, 320, and Pholien 1899, p. 81.
3. Museum für Angewandte Kunst, F4, F14, F16 (Fig. 74.1), F17; Cologne [1961], nos. 231, 233–35; Klesse 1963, pp. 108–9, nos. 217–20; Klesse and Reineking von Bock 1973, pp. 155–56, nos. 308–11.
4. Kunstmuseum, 1964-33A; Heinemeyer 1966, p. 91, no. 270.
5. British Museum, S.587 (ex coll. Felix Slade); Nesbitt 1871, p. 106, fig. 181; Vávra 1954, p. 101, fig. 90; London 1968b, p. 181, no. 254.
6. Rothschild Collection, W1/139/2, W1/140/1; Charleston 1977, pp. 119–23, nos. 26, 27.
7. Fitzwilliam Museum, C.139.1912; Cambridge 1978, p. 73, no. 164b.
8. Corning Museum of Glass, 50.3.56.
9. Kunstsammlungen der Veste Coburg, HA54.
10. Chambon 1955, p. 320, nos. 71, 72, pl. 23.
11. Dreier 1989b, p. 112, under no. 113.
12. National Museums and Galleries on Merseyside, 17.8.76.12; Gatty 1883, p. 45, no. 204; Liverpool 1979, p. 46, no. D16.
13. Kunstgewerbemuseum, 1971,115; Dreier 1989b, pp. 111–12, no. 113.
14. Royal Museum of Scotland, 1963.362; JGS 7 (1965), p. 125, fig. 23.
15. Toledo Museum of Art, 66.117 (ex coll. Étienne Leroy, Jacques Franchomme); JGS 9 (1967), pp. 138–39, fig. 34; Toledo Museum of Art 1969, pp. 54, 55.
16. Musée du Verre, Baar 600 (ex coll. Armand Baar); Venice 1982, pp. 160, 161, no. 241.
17. Sale, Adolf Weinmüller, Munich, 27 June 1962, lot 160; Klesse and Von Saldern 1978, p. 109, no. 46; Lucerne 1981, p. 161, no. 677; Biemann sale 1984, lot 60.
18. Klesse 1965, pp. 140–41, no. 96.
19. Schlossmuseum, R15; Schmidt 1912, p. 126, fig. 73; Schmidt 1922, p. 128, fig. 74; Dreier 1969, no. 11; Weiss 1971, p. 116, left.
20. Metropolitan Museum, 27.185.302 (ex coll. Jacques Mühsam); Schmidt 1914–26, vol. 2, no. 15, ill. p. 11.
21. See Ricke 1978.
22. See Schäfke 1979, pp. 64–67, 108–11, 174–75.

Façon de Venise, northern Europe, possibly the Southern Netherlands or Germany, probably late seventeenth century

75. Goblet

1975.1.1221
H. 27.9 cm. Bubbly colorless (very faint gray), opaque white, and transparent turquoise blue nonlead glass. Blown, trailed, pincered, *vetro a retorti*.

The short ovoid bowl is supported by a three-part stem. The short, colorless upper section has a flared top and a small basal ball knop. At the center is an elaborately coiled two-headed "dragon" with trailed and pincered colorless jaws, combs, and fins, the combs and fins with allover waffle pattern, and an inverted heart-shaped body formed of a continuous glass rod enclosing two floating spiral three-ply opaque white threads, with a straight, bobbin-knopped column of turquoise blue glass at its center. At the bottom of the stem is another straight, colorless section with a flattened ball knop at the base. The large disk-shaped foot has an underfolded rim. Small rough pontil mark under the foot.[1]

Slight wear on the foot rim.

Longwave fluorescence. Colorless glass: strong greenish. Blue glass: nothing. White threads: yellowish. *Shortwave fluorescence.* Colorless glass: creamy white, swirled. Blue glass: opaque yellowish. White threads: purple.

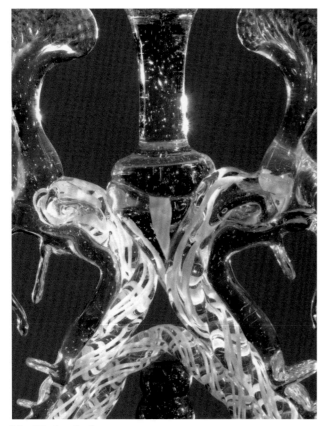

No. 75, *detail of stem*

Fig. 75.1 Goblet. British Museum, London. By courtesy of the Trustees of the British Museum

PROVENANCE: Otto Hopfinger, New York; [Blumka Gallery, New York].

EXHIBITED: New York 1979–80.

Like Nos. 74 and 76, this goblet was produced at a furnace, and the top section of the stem is the same on all three glasses. See No. 74 for a discussion of the technique used to create the dragons.

The form of this dragon stem, with its central bobbin-knopped column, is apparently unparalleled, although there is a seventeenth-century goblet in the British Museum, London, with a central column of four blue glass bulbs (Fig. 75.1).[2] The coiled dragon's body incorporating only opaque white twists, without other colors, and the pincered colorless trailings are also distinctly unusual and are found on only a few other glasses. The cover of the late sixteenth-century goblet in the Schlossmuseum, Bad Homburg (see Fig. 74.3), has a dragon ornament with colorless pincered trailing on a body formed of a rod containing only white threads, although the dragon in the stem has red and white twists.[3] On a goblet in the Metropolitan Museum that has been attributed to an eighteenth-century German glasshouse the twists in the dragon's body are white, but the pincered trailing is blue.[4]

See also the discussion under No. 74.

NOTES:

1. A rectangular gold metallic paper label printed *40* in black and a circular white paper label typed *40.* (both Robert Lehman collection) have been removed and are in the Robert Lehman Collection files. A four-digit number (*4271?*) once painted in red-orange under the foot has recently been removed.
2. British Muscum, 55,12-1,120 (ex coll. Ralph Bernal); Bernal sale 1855, pp. 235, 271, lot 2734; Bohn 1857, p. 329, no. 3315, ill. opposite p. 324; Tait 1979, pp. 85, 86, no. 136.
3. Schlossmuseum, R15; Schmidt 1912, p. 126, fig. 73; Schmidt 1922, p. 128, fig. 74; Dreier 1969, no. 11; Weiss 1971, p. 116, left.
4. Metropolitan Museum, 27.185.302 (ex coll. Jacques Mühsam); Schmidt 1914–26, vol. 2, no. 15, ill. p. 11.

No. 75

Façon de Venise, probably the Southern
Netherlands or Germany, probably seventeenth
century, possibly nineteenth century

76. Goblet

1975.1.1142

H. 30.2 cm. Colorless (slightly gray), transparent turquoise
blue, and opaque brick red, white, and yellow nonlead glass.
Blown, pattern molded, trailed, pincered, *vetro a retorti*.

The large ovoid bowl was patterned in a diamond-mesh mold
with fourteen vertical ribs at the top, each diamond with a
raised diamond-shaped boss in its center. The short, colorless
top section of the three-part stem has a flared top and a small
basal ball knop. At the center is an elaborately coiled two-
headed "dragon" with trailed and pincered blue jaws, combs,
and fins, the combs and fins with a raised pattern of parallel
horizontal ribs, and an inverted heart-shaped body formed of
a continuous glass rod enclosing two floating spiral twists of
four laminated colored threads (one set red, yellow, white, red;
the other white, red, white, yellow). At the bottom of the stem
is another straight, colorless section with basal swelling. The
slightly domed foot has an underfolded rim. Rough pontil
mark under the foot.[1]

Slight wear on the rim of the bowl; normal wear on the foot
rim.

Longwave fluorescence. Colorless glass: strong yellow-green.
Blue glass: light blue. *Shortwave fluorescence.* Colorless glass:
strong bluish white. Blue glass: dark blue.

PROVENANCE: A. de Frey, Paris; Otto Hopfinger, New York;
[Blumka Gallery, New York].

EXHIBITED: New York 1979–80.

The decoration on the bowl of this goblet appears at
first glance to be "nipt diamond waies," but the raised
bosses in the centers of the diamonds mean that the bowl
was formed in a diamond-pattern mold. Like Nos. 74
and 75, this goblet was worked at a furnace, and the top
section of the stem is the same on all three glasses. See
No. 74 for a discussion of the technique used to form
the dragons.

I know of no other dragon-stem glasses with bowls
molded in this pattern of diamonds enclosing raised
diamond-shaped bosses. The pattern was used on other
northern European and Venetian objects produced in the
sixteenth and seventeenth centuries, however, among them
glasses in the Uměleckoprůmyslové Muzeum, Prague
(Fig. 76.1);[2] the Metropolitan Museum;[3] the Zavičajni
Muzej, Belgrade;[4] the Kunstsammlungen zu Weimar (two
examples);[5] the Museo Poldi Pezzoli, Milan;[6] the Museum für Kunsthandwerk, Frankfurt am Main;[7] the
Österreichisches Museum für Angewandte Kunst, Vienna;[8]
the Kunstgewerbemuseum, Berlin;[9] and the British Mu-

seum, London (three examples).[10] A similar pattern appears on a glass excavated in Orléans[11] and on the knop
of a glass in the Germanisches Nationalmuseum, Nürnberg (see Fig. 45.1).[12]

The construction of this glass and the technique used
to form the dragon stem, though it seems rather stiff, are
consistent with a seventeenth-century date (see the discussion under No. 74). The strong bluish white shortwave fluorescence of the colorless glass does, however,
raise the slight suspicion that it may have been manufactured in the nineteenth century (see also No. 78).

NOTES:

1. According to a note in the Robert Lehman Collection files,
   a circular scalloped paper label annotated *199* (probably
   A. de Frey collection) was removed from the glass.
2. Uměleckoprůmyslové Muzeum, 30387/1948 (ex coll.
   Adalbert von Lanna, probably Émile Gavet, Eugen Miller
   von Aichholz); Gavet sale 1897, lot 594; Miller von
   Aichholz sale 1925, lot 59, pl. 59; Hetteš 1960, p. 35, no.
   21; Prague 1973, no. 137; Venice 1982, p. 116, no. 143.
3. Metropolitan Museum, 53.225.102 (ex coll. Julia A.
   Berwind).
4. Zavičajni Muzej, G43/1-9; Venice 1982, p. 140, no. 198.

Fig. 76.1 Goblet. Uměleckoprůmyslové Muzeum, Prague

No. 76

5. Kunstsammlungen zu Weimar, N603, N665; Hörning [1978], nos. 22, 23.

6. Museo Poldi Pezzoli, 1229; Roffia and Mariacher 1983, p. 183, no. 148, fig. 147.

7. Museum für Kunsthandwerk, 5446/5010; Ohm 1973, p. 69, no. 130.

8. Schlosser 1965, p. 151, fig. 124.

9. Kunstgewerbemuseum, K106; Dreier 1989b, p. 50, no. 19.

10. British Museum, S.740 (ex coll. Felix Slade; Nesbitt 1871, p. 127, no. 740; Tait 1979, p. 111, no. 182); 73,5-2,91 (ex coll. Felix Slade; Tait 1979, p. 124, no. 209). See also Nesbitt 1871, pp. 88, 89, no. 482, fig. 135; Vávra 1954, p. 104, fig. 98.

11. Barrera 1987, p. 346, no. 226, fig. 2.

12. Germanisches Nationalmuseum, G27; Schack 1976, p. 284, fig. 242A.

Façon de Venise, northern Europe, probably seventeenth century, possibly late nineteenth century

77. Wineglass

1975.1.1159

H. 13.8 cm. Colorless (slightly tan) and transparent bright blue-green bubbly nonlead glass. Blown, trailed, pincered.

The bell-shaped bowl has a flared rim and is open at the base to a series of three hollow ovoid bulges of descending size. The hollow, tubular stem has two applied blue-green B-shaped handles with trailed colorless fins pincered in an overall waffle pattern. A merese separates the stem from the circular foot, which has a plain rim. Rough pontil mark under the foot. Painted in white under the foot: *30* (unidentified).

Bloom in the base of the bowl (a manufacturing defect); no wear on the foot rim.

Longwave fluorescence. Colorless glass: strong yellow-green. Blue glass: transparent blue-green (probably no fluorescence).
Shortwave fluorescence. Colorless glass: strong bluish white. Blue glass: nothing.

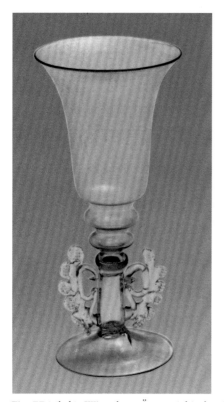

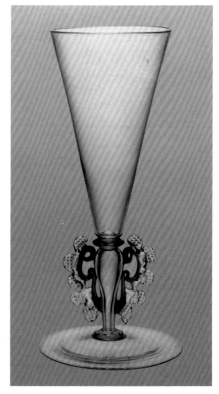

Fig. 77.1 (left) Wineglass. Österreichisches Museum für Angewandte Kunst, Vienna Fig. 77.2 (center) Wineglass. Museo Poldi Pezzoli, Milan Fig. 77.3 (right) Wineglass. Museum für Kunsthandwerk, Frankfurt am Main

No. 77

PROVENANCE: Otto Hopfinger, New York; [Blumka Gallery, New York].

EXHIBITED: New York 1979–80.

The bowl and handles of this glass resemble those of a seventeenth-century Venetian or *façon de Venise* glass in the Österreichisches Museum für Angewandte Kunst, Vienna (see Fig. 77.1);[1] another in the Museo Poldi Pezzoli, Milan (Fig. 77.2);[2] and two others, one formerly in the Max Strauss collection, Vienna, the present location of which is unknown.[3] The strong bluish white shortwave fluorescence, the weak form of the trailed handles, and the lack of wear on the Lehman wineglass, however, suggest that it might be a late nineteenth-century product. Two similar wineglasses made by Antonio Salviati (see

No. 34) in Venice before 1867 are in the Museum für Kunsthandwerk, Frankfurt am Main (see Fig. 77.3).[4] Another, with a ruby-colored bowl, is in the Bowes Museum, Barnard Castle, County Durham, England.[5]

See also No. 78, which has a similar bell-shaped, sectioned bowl but can definitely be dated to the late nineteenth century.

NOTES:
1. Bucher 1888, p. 72, no. 580, pl. 5.
2. Museo Poldi Pezzoli, 1330; Roffia and Mariacher 1983, p. 181, no. 125, fig. 124.
3. Strauss sale 1925, lot 229, ill.; Schrijver 1964, pl. 9d.
4. Museum für Kunsthandwerk, 67896/4962, 67902/4968; Ohm 1973, p. 80, nos. 163, 164.
5. Coutts 1992, p. 71.

Probably Venice, late nineteenth century

78. Goblet

1975.1.1211

H. 31.7 cm. Colorless (slightly gray) and turquoise blue nonlead glass. Blown, trailed, impressed, pincered.

The large bell-shaped bowl has a flared rim and is open at the base to three hollow ovoid bulges of descending size. Eight large blue molded berry prunts are applied to the side of the bowl. The stem has three thick, rounded mereses above a hollow dumbbell knop with two applied blue loop handles that curl at the lower terminals and have trailed colorless fins pincered in an overall waffle pattern. A merese separates the stem from the domed foot, which is decorated with a trailed blue chain near the plain rim. Small rough pontil mark under the foot. Painted in orange under the foot: *c.193.* (unidentified).[1]

Roughness on the inside of the bulges at the bottom of the bowl; almost no wear on the foot.

Longwave fluorescence. Colorless glass: strong yellow-green. Blue glass: light blue-green. *Shortwave fluorescence.* Colorless glass: strong bluish white. Blue glass: yellowish striations.

PROVENANCE: Princes of Liechtenstein, Vaduz and Vienna(?);[2] Otto Hopfinger, New York; [Blumka Gallery, New York].

Despite its resemblance to No. 77, the considerably poorer workmanship on this goblet marks it as a product of the late nineteenth century. The overall awkwardness of proportion, the odd use of heavy berry prunts on the bowl,

the weak form of the dumbbell stem and domed foot, the softness of the trailing style, the thickness of the mereses, and the lack of wear, as well as the brilliant bluish white shortwave fluorescence of the glass (see also No. 76), all point to a late date.[3] The goblet was undoubtedly made not to deceive but as a "historicizing" object.

Similar trailed blue chain decoration is sometimes found on seventeenth- and early eighteenth-century Venetian and *façon de Venise* glasses. Trailed blue chains decorate a tazza in the Robert Lehman Collection that has been attributed to the Southern Netherlands (No. 27), and another in the Hermitage, Saint Petersburg, that is attributed to Catalonia.[4] Examples of Venetian glasses with chain decoration are in the Corning Museum of Glass;[5] the Museo Vetrario, Murano;[6] and Rosenborg Castle, Copenhagen.[7] Another was in the Fritz Biemann collection, Zurich.[8] The chain pattern was also often used on late nineteenth-century Venetian glasses. It appears, for instance, on several drawings in a pattern book from the Fratelli Toso glasshouse in Venice that dates to about 1875.[9]

No. 78

NOTES:

1. The following labels have been removed and are in the Robert Lehman Collection files: Unidentified: torn oval white paper label with a scalloped edge and *171* written in faded blue ink; square white paper label with *333.* written in faded brown ink (only a small, illegible fragment remains). Robert Lehman collection: rectangular gold metallic paper label printed *73* in black; circular white paper label typed *73*.
2. A note in the Robert Lehman Collection files states that this goblet was once owned by the princes of Liechtenstein, but there is no documentation to support that provenance.
3. According to a note in the Robert Lehman Collection files, on 7 May 1964 Mariacher described this goblet as "possibly German; the unusual form and the raspberry prunts are indicative of that origin."
4. Mikhailova 1970, no. 28, pl. 8.
5. Corning Museum of Glass, 84.3.239 (ex coll. Rudolf von Strasser).
6. Reggio Calabria 1967, fig. [9].
7. Boesen 1960, no. 11.
8. Klesse and Von Saldern 1978, p. 112, no. 52; Biemann sale 1984, lot 67.
9. Barovier Mentasti 1982, p. 195, fig. 194.

Probably Venice, seventeenth century

79. Wineglass

1975.1.1141

H. 19.7 cm. Colorless (slightly tan) nonlead glass. Blown, pattern molded, trailed, pincered, wheel-engraved.

The straight-sided ovoid bowl is decorated with two wheel-engraved foliate wreaths, each enclosing a stag standing beside a bush on a grassy ground, the panels separated by two stylized flowers, one with large petals with feathered edges and highlighted with polished dots, the other roselike, with rounded petals and a crosshatched center. An angular merese separates the bowl from a tall, hollow, spirally ribbed (twelve ribs) stem with two elaborate trailed and pincered wings with projecting tails. The base of the stem flares into a disk above the thin, slightly conical foot. Tiny rough pontil mark under the foot. Painted in white under the foot: *J.153* (unidentified).[1]

Lightly crizzled; the top projections on the wings replaced, the top half of one wing broken and cemented to the stem, and the top loop of the other broken and cemented to the stem; small chip on the foot rim.

Longwave fluorescence. Bright yellowish. *Shortwave fluorescence.* Faint, creamy and whitish (the top projections on the wings).

PROVENANCE: Otto Hopfinger, New York; [Blumka Gallery, New York].

The number of glasses with elaborate wings like these, usually on knopped rather than straight stems, that survive is surprising considering their extreme fragility. Seventeenth-century Venetian glasses with comparable trailed wings are in the British Museum, London (Fig. 79.1);[2] the Franz Sichel collection, San Francisco;[3] the Museo Civico, Bologna;[4] the Museo e Gallerie Nazionali

Fig. 79.1 Goblet. British Museum, London. By courtesy of the Trustees of the British Museum

No. 79

No. 79, *detail of side of bowl*

No. 79, *detail of side of bowl*

No. 79, *detail of side of bowl*

No. 79, *detail of side of bowl*

Fig. 79.2 Wineglass. British Museum, London. By courtesy of the Trustees of the British Museum

Fig. 79.3 Rheinische Glashütten-Actien-Gesellschaft, Ehrenfeld bei Köln, catalogue (1886), no. 138. Reproduced from Werner Schäfke, *Ehrenfelder Glas des Historismus* (Cologne: W. König, 1979), p. 110. Photograph courtesy of the Corning Museum of Glass

di Capodimonte, Naples;[5] and the Kunstsammlungen zu Weimar.[6]

Wheel-engraved decoration is very rare on Venetian and Venetian-style glass, however, and the polished highlights on the flowers on the Lehman wineglass are particularly distinctive. The slightly tan cast to the metal of the Lehman glass also allies it with Venetian examples dated to the seventeenth century, rather than to *façon de Venise* glasses from northern Europe.

The closest parallel to the Lehman glass, a wineglass in the British Museum decorated with wheel engraving that is clearly by a different hand (Fig. 79.2), may be of a much later date.[7] A glass with a straight stem embellished with wings much like those on the Lehman glass was illustrated in the catalogue of the Rheinische Glashütten-Actien-Gesellschaft in Ehrenfeld bei Köln for 1886 (Fig. 79.3).[8]

NOTES:

1. A rectangular gold metallic paper label printed *33* in black and a circular white paper label typed *33.* (both Robert Lehman collection) have been removed and are in the Robert Lehman Collection files.

2. British Museum, s.455 (ex coll. Felix Slade); Nesbitt 1871, p. 86, fig. 119; Vávra 1954, p. 102, fig. 93; Tait 1979, pp. 56, 57, no. 60. For other examples formerly in the Slade collection, see Nesbitt 1871, pp. 81, 82, nos. 411, 421, 423, figs. 94, 99, 101.

3. San Francisco 1969, p. 27, no. 25.

4. Barovier Mentasti 1982, p. 84, fig. 70.

5. Omodeo [1970], p. 57, fig. 57.

6. Hörning [1978], no. 20.

7. British Museum, s.485 (ex coll. Felix Slade); Nesbitt 1871, p. 89, no. 485, fig. 138; Vávra 1954, p. 103, fig. 97; Zecchin 1957, p. 4. Tait agrees that this glass, which Slade must have acquired about 1860–70, is "not above suspicion" (telephone conversation with the author, 21 January 1991).

8. Schäfke 1979, pp. 110, 111.

Venice (possibly Salviati), late nineteenth to early twentieth century

80. Footed vase

1975.1.1143

H. 14.5 cm. Colorless, opaque turquoise blue, copper-flecked (goldstone or aventurine), and opalescent white nonlead glass. Blown, mold blown, trailed, *vetro a retorti*, gilt.

The ribbed (twelve ribs) shell-shaped bowl has a scalloped rim and is vertically striped with turquoise blue twisted tapes outlined with goldstone or aventurine threads, alternating with intertwined opaque white multispiral bands. The stem is a small colorless capstan above a hollow, vertically ribbed (fifteen ribs) section formed as three ball knops above an inverted baluster, with two elaborate trailed C-scroll handles with pincered wings and gold foil incorporated in the glass. The ribbed (twelve ribs) circular foot has twists matching those in the bowl. Tiny rough pontil mark under the foot.[1]

Top scroll missing on one handle; normal wear on the foot rim.

Longwave fluorescence. Colorless glass: strong yellow-green. Aventurine: orange. Opaque white: yellow-green. *Shortwave fluorescence.* All: strong bluish white.

PROVENANCE: Otto Hopfinger, New York; [Blumka Gallery, New York].

The bowl and foot were probably formed by the Pastorelli plate technique (see No. 64). As with No. 40, the glassmaker picked up bits of gold foil on the molten glass he used to form the handles, so that it looks as though gold dust has been scattered throughout the mass. This technique was unknown before the late nineteenth century.

A fanciful "pitcher" with a similar ribbed shell-shaped body and a pincered handle in the Museum Bellerive, Zurich (Fig. 80.1), is thought to have been made by Antonio Salviati (see No. 34) about 1885.[2]

NOTES:
1. The following labels have been removed: Unidentified: rectangular white paper label with a printed blue geometric border and [ ]6[ ] written on it (not in file). Robert Lehman collection: rectangular gold metallic paper label printed 38 in black (in the Robert Lehman Collection files).
2. Museum Bellerive, 1956-74; Billeter 1969, p. 106; Barovier Mentasti 1982, pp. 220, 221, fig. 223; Salviati [1880s], no. 129, pl. 13.

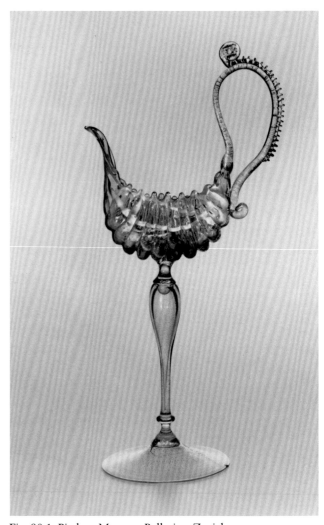

Fig. 80.1 Pitcher. Museum Bellerive, Zurich

No. 80

Venice, probably late seventeenth century

81. Dessert glass(?)

1975.1.1155

H. 15.2 cm. Opalescent bluish white nonlead glass. Blown, pattern molded, trailed.

The shallow, slightly flared bucket bowl is ribbed (twelve ribs) and has a wavy rim and a trailed rigaree collar at the base. A merese separates the bowl from a hollow spirally ribbed (fourteen ribs) stem formed of three ball knops above a slender inverted baluster that flares at the base. The circular foot has fourteen ribs. Small rough pontil mark under the foot. Painted in orange under the foot: *C.54* (or *L.54?*).[1]

No wear.

Longwave fluorescence. Yellowish. *Shortwave fluorescence.* Strong bluish white (striated on the interior).

PROVENANCE: Princes of Liechtenstein, Vaduz and Vienna(?);[2] Otto Hopfinger, New York; [Blumka Gallery, New York].

Stems related to that on this glass are found on several late seventeenth- and early eighteenth-century Venetian opalescent glasses. An example acquired by Frederick IV in Venice in 1708–9 is in Rosenborg Castle, Copenhagen (Fig. 81.1),[3] and another is in the British Museum, London (Fig. 81.2).[4] One of the few parallels for the form of the bowl is a colorless glass in the Victoria and Albert Museum, London, that has been dated to the early sev-

enteenth century and attributed to the Netherlands.[5] Opalescent glass objects were also made in Venice in the late nineteenth century, but none of this form have been documented. The fine workmanship on the Lehman glass points to an early date.

NOTES:

1. The following labels have been removed and are in the Robert Lehman Collection files: Unidentified: rectangular tan paper label with *C.54* written in faded brown ink; oval white paper label with a scalloped edge and *164.* written in light blue ink. Robert Lehman collection: rectangular gold metallic paper label printed *4* in black; circular white paper label typed *4*.
2. According to a note in the Robert Lehman Collection files, this glass once belonged to the princes of Liechtenstein, but that claim has not been documented.
3. Rosenborg Castle, 52; Boesen 1960, no. 77; Mariacher 1965a, p. 44; Barovier Mentasti 1982, p. 147, fig. 141.
4. British Museum, 55,12-1,125 (ex coll. Ralph Bernal); Bohn 1857, p. 289, no. 2794; Tait 1979, p. 108, no. 173.
5. Victoria and Albert Museum, C.229-1936 (ex coll. Wilfred Buckley); Buckley 1926, p. 41, pl. 20A; Buckley 1939, p. 252, no. 187, pl. 47; Honey 1946, p. 64, pl. 34C.

Fig. 81.1 Wineglass. Rosenborg Castle, Copenhagen

Fig. 81.2 Goblet. British Museum, London. By courtesy of the Trustees of the British Museum

No. 81

Probably Venice, probably late nineteenth century

82. Covered goblet

1975.1.1162a,b
H. with cover 42.8 cm. Opalescent bluish white nonlead glass.
Blown, pattern molded, trailed, pincered, applied parts.

The goblet's large ovoid bowl is molded in an allover diamond pattern (twelve diamonds in a row). The stem is composed of a merese above a hollow dumbbell knop with eight ribs; an ornate scrolled panel of spirally ribbed and twisted rods applied to which are a large pincered daisylike flower and six smaller stylized flowers, three at each side, and, on the back, two loop "handles" decorated with pincered trailing; a ribbed (eight ribs) section of two hollow ball knops and an inverted baluster with four applied loop handles, all with pincered trailing, two with a pincered waffle pattern; and, at the base, above the large disk foot, a coiled collar. The dome-shaped cover is diamond-molded to match the bowl, has a folded ledge and a cylindrical lip that fits inside the bowl, and is topped by an applied ribbed (twelve ribs) ball finial on a merese. Small rough pontil mark inside the bowl; rough pontil mark under the foot; rough pontil mark inside the cover (and also perhaps on the ball finial).

Petals missing on a flower at the left, the central flower, and the fringe at the right; one handle at the bottom of the stem broken off and cemented back; normal wear on the foot rim. The cover probably originally had an elaborate finial that is now missing.

Longwave fluorescence. Yellowish. *Shortwave fluorescence.* Strong bluish white.

PROVENANCE: A. de Frey, Paris; Otto Hopfinger, New York; [Blumka Gallery, New York].

EXHIBITED: New York 1979–80.

This is a difficult glass to classify. In form it is related to Bohemian glasses of the 1670s and 1680s, in particular the elaborate opalescent white glasses believed to have been made at the Buquoy factory at Nové Hrady (Gratzen), an example of which is in the museum of the Benedictine monastery at Kremsmünster, Austria (Fig. 82.1),[1] and the colorless floral-stemmed glasses attributed to the glasshouse at Borová (Mistelholz) that are preserved in the Uměleckoprůmyslové Muzeum, Prague (Fig. 82.2),[2] and the Universitätsmuseum für Kulturgeschichte, Marburg (Fig. 82.3).[3] The opalescent glass

No. 82, *detail of side of stem*

No. 82, *detail of back of stem*

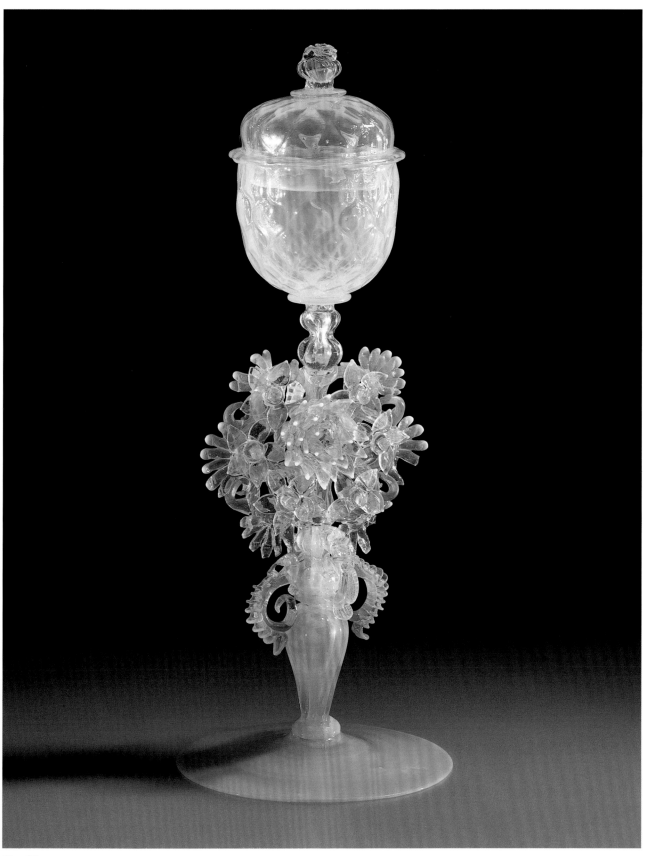

No. 82

Fig. 82.1 (left) Covered goblet. Museum of the Benedictine monastery, Kremsmünster, Austria. Photograph courtesy of the Corning Museum of Glass Fig. 82.2 (center) Covered goblet. Uměleckoprůmyslové Muzeum, Prague Fig. 82.3 (right) Goblet. Universitätsmuseum für Kulturgeschichte, Marburg. Reproduced from Hessisches Landesmuseum Darmstadt, *Deutsches Glas: Zweitausend Jahre Glasveredelung* (Darmstadt, 1935), pl. 58

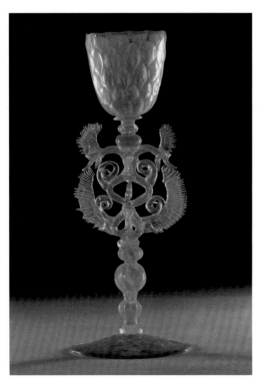 

Fig. 82.4 Goblet. British Museum, London. By courtesy of the Trustees of the British Museum

Fig. 82.5 Covered goblet. Corning Museum of Glass, Bequest of Jerome Strauss

made at the Buquoy factory is not as blue in color as that used in the Lehman goblet, however, and both the Buquoy and Borová glasses have a less finicky presence about them than does this goblet. The general heaviness of the mereses and knops on the Lehman glass are an even stronger indication of a later date.

Opalescent glass was popular in Venice at the turn of the eighteenth century and again in the late nineteenth century. The collection at Rosenborg Castle in Copenhagen includes a number of specimens that King Frederick IV of Denmark acquired when he visited Venice in 1708–9.[4] The closest parallels to the Lehman goblet are two opalescent bluish white goblets that were probably made in Venice in the last half of the nineteenth century, one in the British Museum, London (Fig. 82.4),[5] the other in the Corning Museum of Glass (Fig. 82.5).[6]

NOTES:
1. Drahotová 1981, p. 54, fig. 12.
2. Uměleckoprůmyslové Muzeum, 9832/1906 (ex coll. Adalbert von Lanna); ibid., p. 51, fig. 4 (left); Venice 1982, p. 161, no. 245. See also Drahotová 1981, p. 51, fig. 4 (right; Uměleckoprůmyslové Muzeum), and Venice 1982, pp. 161–63, nos. 244 (Uměleckoprůmyslové Muzeum, 2272/1887), 247 (unidentified collection).
3. Hessisches Landesmuseum 1935, p. 79, no. 489, pl. 58.
4. Boesen 1960, nos. 59–79.
5. British Museum, s.769 (ex coll. Buccleuch[?], Felix Slade); Nesbitt 1871, p. 130, no. 769, colorpl. 17,2; Waring n.d., pl. 3. Tait, too, regards this glass, which must have been acquired by Slade about 1860–70, as "not above suspicion" (telephone conversation with the author, 21 January 1991).
6. Corning Museum of Glass, 79.3.330 (ex coll. Jerome Strauss); Corning 1955, p. 43, no. 102; Corning 1958, p. 85, no. 85.

New York, Tiffany Studios, 1902–18

83. Vase

1975.1.1581
H. 38.3 cm. Transparent amber and green lead glass; cast and patinated bronze stem and foot. Blown, trailed, iridized.

The trumpet-shaped bowl is made of gold-iridescent amber-tinted glass; trailed on the exterior are transparent green and amber threads pulled into wavy, featherlike patterns and covered on the interior with iridescent gold. The cast bronze stem and foot have a red-speckled green patina. A baluster decorated with a raised scale pattern separates the cut, pointed petals at the top of the stem from the circular domed foot. Stamped under the foot: *TIFFANY STUDIOS / NEW YORK / 1043 / 26*, with *10452* scratched beneath. Under the foot, a circular white paper label with *94* written in black ink (probably Robert Lehman collection). Inscribed on top of the foot in Spencerian script: *MMB*.

Mint condition; normal wear.

Longwave fluorescence. Glass, inside: purple reflection. Glass, outside: green = black, gold = dark red reflection, amber = purple. Patinated bronze: mottled muddy bluish green. *Shortwave fluorescence.* Glass, inside: purple reflection. Glass, outside: green = black, gold = purple reflection, amber = purple reflection. Patinated bronze: purple reflection.

PROVENANCE: Not established.

Buried ancient glass occasionally develops a rainbow-hued iridescence on its surface (see Nos. 117–36). The surface of the glass decomposes into many thin layers that reflect and refract light, selectively producing colors through an optical effect called interference. In the late nineteenth and early twentieth centuries European and American glassmakers imitated this effect with chemicals. Not surprisingly, considering how many of his competitors would have liked him to be more specific, Louis Comfort Tiffany's comments on the process were more poetic than descriptive. He had produced iridescent glass, he said, "by a careful study of the natural decay of glass . . . and by reversing the action in such a way as to arrive at the effects without disintegration."[1] Frederick Carder of the Steuben factory in Corning, New York, who like Max Ritter von Spaun at the Johann Lötz Witwe factory in Klostermühle in southern Bohemia and several other glassmakers had successfully produced iridescent glass almost simultaneously with Tiffany, was more specific:

This glass depends entirely upon the property of certain glasses being able to keep in solution in an oxidized state salts of rare metals. This glass when made into articles and subjected to the reducing flame of either gas or oil becomes coated by reduction with a film of the metal, varying in intensity with the proper adjustment of flame. This development requires care on the part of the artist and when the reduced metallic film is sufficiently dense, it is sprayed with a solution of tin salt and then heated in an oxidizing flame. Iridescent colors will be produced, these varying in intensity and color values according to the heat treatment

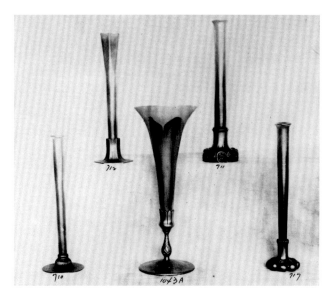

Fig. 83.1 Tiffany Studios, New York, page from a showroom catalogue (early 1900s). Photograph courtesy of Robert Koch

name was more often associated with art glass. His company began using the famous Favrile trademark (derived from *fabrile*, Old English for "handmade") in 1892, and in 1894 it was registered with the U.S. Patent Office. Favrile blown glass was marketed to the public starting in 1896.[6] Between 1902, when it was officially renamed Tiffany Studios, and 1918, when the war and changes in taste curtailed production, the company produced a wide array of glass and metal vases, lamps, desk accessories, candlesticks, and other household objects – some of them unique, some produced in quantity as, in Tiffany's words, "art for the people."[7]

The Lehman vase belongs to the latter category. The stamp under the foot, TIFFANY STUDIOS / NEW YORK, was in use between 1902 and 1918.[8] It identifies the vase as model number 1043, which is described in a 1906 Tiffany Studios price list (F.G. stands for Favrile Glass):

1043. TRUMPET VASES, F.G. Metal base, small..17.00
TRUMPET VASES, F.G. Metal base, large..20.00[9]

Number 1043A, priced at $35.00, also appears in one of the photographs (Fig. 83.1) in the loose-leaf catalogue used by Tiffany Studios salesmen.[10] Judging by the numerous surviving examples of this vase, one of which is in the Corning Museum of Glass, it must have been a popular item.[11]

Tiffany Studios fell on hard times when taste shifted from the languorous Art Nouveau to the angular Art Deco. A clearance sale of the entire stock of the company was held in 1920, the year after Tiffany retired from active participation. Although production continued at Tiffany Furnaces, now separately incorporated, until 1928, when Tiffany withdrew his financial support, there were few new designs. Tiffany Studios filed bankruptcy papers in 1932. Stock continued to be sold until 1938.[12]

it undergoes.... If iron chloride be sprayed on instead of tin salt, or after spraying with the iron chloride it is followed with the tin salt, a golden color is produced.[2]

The only "rare metal" mentioned in the Steuben records is silver.[3] Some have claimed that Tiffany used gold to achieve iridescence.[4]

Louis Comfort Tiffany (1848–1933), eldest son of Charles L. Tiffany, the founder of Tiffany and Company in New York, began his career as a painter and decorator. By the 1880s Louis C. Tiffany and Associated Artists, the partnership Tiffany had formed with Candace Wheeler and Samuel Colman in 1879, was one of the leading decorating firms in New York. Tiffany first experimented with glass to produce tiles, mosaics, and, especially, stained-glass windows in connection with his decorating business. The Tiffany Glass Company was incorporated in 1885 to "provide the manufacture of glass and other materials and the use and adaptation of the same to decorative and other artistic work of all kinds."[5] Tiffany began producing blown glass in 1892, the year the Tiffany Glass Company was reorganized as the Tiffany Glass and Decorating Company, and in late 1893 he established his own factory, Tiffany Furnaces, at Corona, Long Island. A foundry and metal shop were added in 1897.

Although the firm continued to execute commissions for stained-glass windows until 1938, by 1900 Tiffany's

NOTES:
1. Quoted in Koch 1971, p. 121.
2. Quoted in Gardner 1971, pp. 61, 63.
3. Ibid., p. 64.
4. See Koch 1971, p. 122.
5. Quoted in Koch 1982, p. 69.
6. See Koch 1971, pp. 17–19, 40, 84, and Koch 1982, pp. 118, 122–23, 126.
7. See Koch 1982, p. 65.
8. Koch 1971, pp. 92, 112–13, fig. 105.
9. Ibid., p. 179.
10. Ibid., p. 114, fig. 167; see also pp. 53, 187, fig. 53.
11. Corning Museum of Glass, 61.4.4.
12. Koch 1971, pp. 60–61, 112; Koch 1982, pp. 155–56.

No. 83

LAMPWORKED GLASS JEWELRY AND FIGURES

AND FIGURES

Sixteenth to Nineteenth Century

Lampworking

Lampworking, or flameworking, is the process of melting and manipulating rods and tubes of colored glass over a flame to form figures or objects. Today lampworking is often demonstrated at workshops, craft fairs, and even shopping malls by artisans who produce tiny, colorful animals, ships, fountains, and other elaborate confections. Lampworkers make lifelike human figures, animals, flowers, and fruit, which they sometimes encase in solid glass paperweights. The technique has also been used to produce botanically accurate models of plants, fruit, and sea life that serve as teaching aids. (The models by Leopold and Rudolph Blaschka in the Botanical Museum of Harvard University are perhaps the best known.) And lampworking has long been used to make glass eyes and complicated chemical apparatus.

The origin of lampworking is obscure. It probably grew out of metallurgy: a similar technique may have been used to create granulated gold jewelry as early as the third millennium B.C. in the eastern Mediterranean. Though still a matter of conjecture, it is possible that a combination of a glass furnace and lampworking was used to make the elaborate head-shaped beads from the same region that date from the fifth to the fourth century B.C. Some version of flameworking was almost certainly known before the third century A.D., when glass vessels were decorated with minute gilt glass threads formed into inscriptions and decorative patterns. A fragment of the base of a Roman footed vessel from the third to fourth century with an inscription formed of gilt glass threads that was probably flameworked is preserved in the Corning Museum of Glass (Fig. E).[1]

It is not known whether the art of flameworking or lampworking was practiced without interruption for the next thousand years or whether the technique was forgotten and rediscovered in Europe during the Renaissance. Lampworkers seem to have been practicing their craft in Europe by the mid-fifteenth century. In 1454 Olivier de la Marche described the presentation at a banquet at the Château de Lille of "a very beautiful fountain partly in glass and partly in lead of a very new aspect, for there were small trees made of glass with marvelous leaves and flowers; and in an empty space, as a clearing, surrounded by rocks there was a small St. Andrew standing erect with his cross in front of him."[2] Three ornamental pins in the Robert Lehman Collection (Nos. 84–86) may have been made in either Venice or Innsbruck in the late 1500s. A late sixteenth-century furnace-blown *Pokal* decorated with lampworked figures and scrolls on the cover and floral motifs on the sides of the foot and bowl, which contains a lampworked group representing the Crucifixion (Fig. F), is on view at Schloss Ambras, near Innsbruck (collection of the Kunsthistorisches Museum, Vienna).[3] The *Pokal* was likely made and decorated by Venetian craftsmen working at the Hofglashütte at Innsbruck.

By the seventeenth century, lampworkers, most of them Italian, were working not only in Italy and the Tyrol but in France, the Netherlands, and Germany.[4] Small human and animal figurines were perhaps the most popular products and were probably made by lampworkers everywhere the art was practiced. The Danish royal collection of glass at Rosenborg Castle in Copenhagen includes a group of two lampworked figurines depicting characters from the commedia dell'arte that King Frederick IV bought in 1670

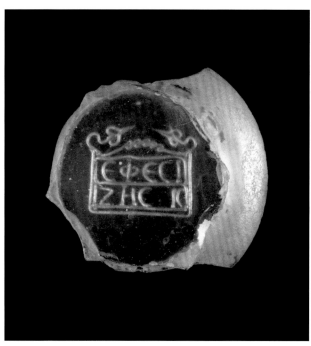

Fig. E. Base fragment from a footed vessel. Roman Empire, third to fourth century. Corning Museum of Glass

Fig. F. *Pokal* enclosing a lampworked group. Probably Hofglashütte, Innsbruck, late sixteenth century. Kunsthistorisches Museum, Vienna

artful, intricate figurines and groups made for a wealthy clientele and the nobility or the less skillfully executed figures that were probably sold as souvenirs, is attributed to workshops in Nevers, in the Loire Valley in central France. Indeed, the generic namé for these figures is *verre de Nevers*. Artisans from Altare, the glass-producing region in northern Italy, emigrated to Nevers in the late sixteenth century, after Ludovico Gonzaga, duke of Mantua, married Henrietta of Cleves, duchess of Nevers, in 1566. Glassmakers who specialized in lampworking, or *émailleurs*, as they were called, were active in Nevers by the early seventeenth century, if not before. The small glass animals the future Louis XIII is said to have played with as a child in 1605 were probably lampworked.[7] It is also recorded that in 1622 the city of Nevers presented the king with "a work in enamel representing the victory gained by His Majesty against the rebels of the so-called Reformed Religion in the Île de Ré."[8] A lampworked scent bottle in the Robert Lehman Collection (No. 87) may have been produced in the late seventeenth century by the Altarist immigrant Bernard Perrot, who worked at Nevers and later established his own glassworks at Orléans.[9]

Figures of so-called *verre de Nevers*, also called *verre filé*, were made in many places besides Nevers, however. Not only were there other glassworks – in France as well as in Venice, Germany, Spain, and England – where lampworked objects were produced in the eighteenth century, but the glassworks at Nevers itself supplied raw material in the form of tubes or rods of glass to *émailleurs* working in many parts of France. The factory's account books for 1752–55 and 1762–66 list clients in Nevers, Orléans, Saumur, Paris, Saint-Germain-en-Laye, L'Isle-Adam, and Clermont.[10] In fact, very few objects can be documented as products of Nevers workshops. Among them are two beautifully modeled lampworked groups in the Musée des Arts Décoratifs, Paris (see Fig. 88.2), that bear the name Haly, which also appears in the Nevers glassworks' records for the years 1753 and 1754.[11] Aside from the rare signed or documented pieces, the many individual figurines and tableaux that survive from the eighteenth century have yet to be assigned definitive attributions. Some religious tableaux have been attributed to convent workshops, but there is scant evidence to support such claims.[12]

Today, lampworkers shape figures and objects over a torch akin to a welding torch that burns compressed natural gas and oxygen. They use tubes and rods of borosilicate glass, which has a wide working temperature range (i.e., it does not suddenly become runny), or, less often,

from the Danish painter Karel van Mander, who lived in Italy in 1636–38. Three single figures so similar to the two in Copenhagen that they might have been made in the same workshop are in the Kunsthistorisches Museum in Vienna. The Vienna figures have been said to have come from the gallery in Ambras, the castle of Archduke Ferdinand of Tyrol near Innsbruck, but their provenance has not been documented.[5] The famous lampworked figurine of Henry IV (Fig. G; the horse the figure once rode has been stolen) long attributed to the Parisian Charles-François Hazard (1758–1812) may in fact be a product of the seventeenth century.[6]

In the seventeenth and eighteenth centuries lampworked figures – individual figurines or groups of figures assembled in tableaux depicting both secular and religious subjects – seem to have been produced in the greatest numbers in France. Most surviving work of this sort, whether the

Fig. G. Lampworked figure of Henry IV. Musée des Arts Décoratifs, Paris

"soft" or soda-lime glass, which has a narrower working range. Figures are typically built up of glass without additional internal strengthening.

Before the development of natural gas burners in the mid-nineteenth century, lampworkers used small lamps that burned oil, paraffin, or other flammable substances.[13] Jets of compressed air, generated by the artisan's own lung power or by treadle-powered bellows under the worktable, were directed at the flame through a glass tube to focus and increase its heat. *Glasschmelzkunst bey der Lampe*, published in 1769, includes a woodcut of a lampworker at his table, surrounded by examples of his craft (Fig. H). Diderot described the lampworkers' art in some detail in his *Encyclopédie* of 1759:

> The lamps filled and lit, and the bellows activated, if the enameler plans to make a human or animal figure that is solid and of some height, he begins by forming a small structure of brass wire; he gives this small structure the general shape of the limbs of the figure for which it will serve as a support. He takes the structure in one hand and a baguette of solid enamel in the other: he exposes this enamel to the lamp; and when it is sufficiently fused, he attaches it to his brass wire, on which he models it with the flame, his rounded and pointed pincers, his pointed iron, and the blade

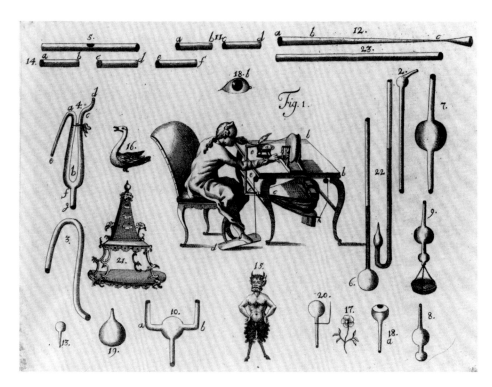

Fig. H. A German lampworker. Reproduced from [Diesing], *Die Glasschmelzkunst bey der Lampe* (1769). Photograph courtesy of the Corning Museum of Glass

233

Fig. I. A saint. France, probably Nevers, eighteenth century. Formerly Rakow collection, New York. Photograph courtesy of the Corning Museum of Glass

Fig. J. Portable wood shrine enclosing a grotto depicting the life of Christ. France, Nevers(?), early eighteenth century. Corning Museum of Glass

of his knife, as he deems appropriate; because the enamels he uses are extremely fragile, and handle like paste over the flame: he continues his work as he began, using enamels, glass, and colors as befits the work he has undertaken.

If the figure is not solid, but hollow, the brass structure is superfluous: the enameler uses only a hollow tube of enamel or glass, in the color he wants for the body of the figure; when he has heated this tube sufficiently at the lamp, he blows it; the pressure of the air carried the length of the cavity of the tube to its end, which is closed, distends the enamel and creates a bubble: the enameler, with the aid of the flame and his instruments, gives to this bubble the appropriate form; this could be, if he wishes, the body of a swan: when the body of the bird is formed, he elongates and contours the neck; he forms the beak and the tail; he then takes solid enamels of the proper color, with which he makes the eyes, he outlines the beak, he makes the wings and the feet, and the animal is finished.[14]

Close inspection of eighteenth-century French lampworked figures reveals that most if not all of them were built up on wire armatures like those Diderot describes. The armatures were probably incorporated to ensure structural integrity if the figures cracked (which most did). The wires also made it easier to attach figures to figural groupings. The frameworks of fairly heavy-gauge wire, in this case of iron, are visible on the radiographs that were taken of the individual figurines in the Robert Lehman Collection (Nos. 88–98). The radiographs also show that the figures were shaped from glass rods or tubes enclosing minute, threadlike copper wires that add further strength. The colored coatings that were trailed on and modeled into clothing and anatomical features were made of slender glass rods or tubes that also sometimes enclose thin copper wire.

Eight of the single lampworked figurines in the Robert Lehman Collection (Nos. 88–95) and the central figure on one of the tableaux (No. 98) may have been made in the same workshop. The elegant modeling of the facial features and clothing allies these figures with those that can be attributed with certainty to the Haly workshop in Nevers. The eight Lehman figures were all constructed using the same process of building up the bulk of the figurine with a waxy-looking colorless glass containing minute copper wire threads. The opaque white glass from which they were made fluoresces similarly under ultraviolet light. All these figurines have integral glass bases. The figurine of the Good Shepherd that is No. 98 is part of a tableau incorporating plants and small glass animals, but it can be assumed that Nos. 88–95 were made as independent works that were probably mounted on wooden stands and protected by clear glass domes. An eighteenth-century French figurine of a saint for which the original turned wooden stand and domed glass cover have survived was in the Rakow collection in New York until 1992 (Fig. I). Nos. 96 and 97 are also single figures with glass bases, but the condition of No. 97 precludes stylistic classification, and No. 96 is clearly the work of another hand. Both figures were constructed with wire armatures, but without the waxlike colorless glass used on Nos. 88–95 and 98.

Robert Lehman also acquired seven elaborate tableaux (Nos. 99–105) of lampworked glass figures and plants assembled on stands or in landscapes of papier-mâché or other composition material, with decorative details made of paper, fabric, glass chips, plaster, and shells glued in place. Nos. 99–104, all depicting biblical scenes, can be attributed to France, probably Nevers; No. 105, a cabriolet and driver, is undoubtedly from a different, possibly English, workshop. The human figures in these tableaux were not radiographed, but they too were most likely constructed on wire armatures. None of them have integral bases; most, perhaps all (it was not possible to view the undersides of many of them), are fastened down with wires that protrude from the glass. The small glass animals and plants that augment the compositions apparently have no wire infrastructure (or at least none was evident under close inspection).

Like others of these fragile groups that have survived from the eighteenth century, many of the tableaux in the Robert Lehman Collection have suffered considerable damage, loss of parts, and inept restorations. Figurines that came loose were often misplaced or reinserted in the wrong places in the composition, making interpretation of the scenes difficult. Most of these scenes must once have had wooden bases and glass covers; some of them may have been mounted in portable shrines like the one that encases a shell-encrusted grotto with scenes from the life of Christ that is now in the collection of the Corning Museum of Glass (Fig. J).[15]

NOTES:

1. Corning Museum of Glass, 66.1.31. I am indebted to David B. Whitehouse for pointing out this important type of Roman glass.
2. Quoted in Perrot 1956, p. 362.
3. Kunsthistorisches Museum, 26.242.
4. See Ricke 1978, pp. 58–62.
5. See Von Schlosser 1908, pp. 61, 64, fig. 48; Boesen 1960, pp. 13–18, 63–65.
6. Musée des Arts Décoratifs, 854U.C.; Perrot 1956, ill. p. 565; Barrelet 1960, pp. 306, 307–8, fig. 14. I thank Jean-Luc Olivié of the Musée for sharing his thoughts on this with me.
7. Perrot 1956, pp. 562–63; Clarke and Bourne 1988, p. 336.
8. Quoted in Barrelet 1960, p. 298: "un ouvrage d'émail représentant la victoire remportée par Sa Majesté contre les rebelles de la religion prétendue réformée en l'Île de Ré." See also Perrot 1956, pp. 563–64.
9. Clarke and Bourne 1988, p. 336.
10. Barrelet 1960, p. 302.
11. Musée des Arts Décoratifs, 38475A, B; ibid., pp. 303, 304, 306–7, figs. 11–13.
12. See ibid., p. 301.
13. See Ricke 1978, pp. 62, 69.
14. Diderot 1759, pp. 455–56: "Les lampes garnies & allumées, & le soufflet mis en action, si l'émailleur se propose de faire une figure d'homme ou d'animal, qui soit solide, & de quelque grandeur, il commence par former un petit

bâti de fil-d'archal; il donne à ce petit bâti la disposition générale des membres de la figure à laquelle il servira de soûtien. Il prend le bâti d'une main, & une baguette d'émail solide de l'autre: il expose cet émail à la lampe; & lorsqu'il est suffisamment en fusion, il l'attache à son fil-d'archal, sur lequel il le contourne par le moyen du feu, de ses pinces rondes & pointues, de ses fers pointus, & de ses lames de canif, tout comme il le juge à-propos; car les émaux qu'il employe sont extrèmement tendres, & se modelent au feu comme de la pâte: il continue son ouvrage comme il l'a commencé, employant & les émaux, & les verres, & les couleurs, comme il convient à l'ouvrage qu'il a entrepris.

"Si la figure n'est pas solide, mais qu'elle soit creuse, le bâti de fil-d'archal est superflu: l'émailleur se sert d'un tube d'émail ou de verre creux, de la couleur dont il veut le corps de sa figure; quand il a suffisamment chauffé ce tube à la lampe, il le souffle; l'haleine portée le long de la cavité du tube jusqu'à son extrémité qui s'est bouchée en se fondant, y est arrêtée, distend l'émail par l'effort qu'elle fait en tout sens, & le met en bouteille: l'émailleur, à l'aide du feu & de ses instrumens, fait prendre à cette bouteille la forme qu'il juge à-propos; ce sera, si l'on veut, le corps d'un cygne: lorsque le corps de l'oiseau est formé, il en allonge & contourne le cou; il forme le bec & la queue; il prend ensuite des émaux solides de la couleur convenable, avec lesquels il fait les yeux, il ourle le bec, il forme les ailes & les pattes, & l'animal est achevé."
15. Corning Museum of Glass, 58.3.218.

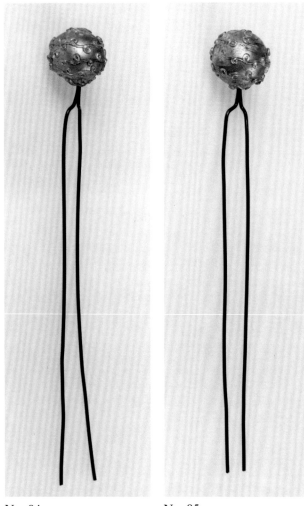

No. 84   No. 85

Probably Venice or Innsbruck (Hofglashütte), probably late sixteenth century

84. Ornamental pin

1975.1.1525

L. 11.7 cm., diam. of ball 1.5 cm. Colorless nonlead glass, copper(?) wire. Lampworked, trailed, gilt.

The solid glass ball, decorated with trailed and gilt colorless scrollwork applied over a layer of fused leaf gilding, is fused to two copper(?) wires (or one wire bent in half?).

The ball cracked; short segments of the trailing missing.

Longwave fluorescence. Glass: faint greenish. Gilding: dark red reflection. *Shortwave fluorescence.* Glass: strong bluish white. Gilding: dark purplish red reflection.

PROVENANCE: Not established.

EXHIBITED: Tokyo 1977, no. 102.

See No. 85.

236

Probably Venice or Innsbruck (Hofglashütte), probably late sixteenth century

85. Ornamental pin

1975.1.1527

L. 12.9 cm, diam. of ball 1.6 cm. Colorless nonlead glass, copper(?) wire. Lampworked, trailed, gilt.

The solid glass ball, decorated with trailed and gilt colorless scrollwork applied over a layer of fused leaf gilding, is fused to two copper(?) wires (or one wire bent in half?).

The ball broken in half but not cemented; short segments of the trailing missing.

Longwave fluorescence. Glass: faint greenish. Gilding: dark red reflection. *Shortwave fluorescence.* Glass: strong bluish white. Gilding: dark purplish red reflection.

PROVENANCE: Not established.

EXHIBITED: Tokyo 1977, no. 103.

The wires on Nos. 84 and 85 are a nonmagnetic material that may be copper or a copper alloy. The balls appear to have been wound directly on the wires, not preformed and stuck on.

Nos. 84 and 85, a pair of ornamental pins that may have been intended as either hairpins or hatpins, were probably made in imitation of contemporary gold filigree jewelry. They were most likely made in either Venice or Innsbruck, where we know that lampworked glass objects were being produced in the late sixteenth century (see Fig. F), but a definite attribution is not possible because so little sixteenth-century glass jewelry has survived to which they can be compared. The largest existing collection, now in the Kunsthistorisches Museum, Vienna, was made in the Hofglashütte at Innsbruck for Archduke Ferdinand of Tyrol (see No. 25).[1] There is nothing precisely like the Lehman pins in the Vienna collection, however, and all the lampworked glass beads on that jewelry appear to be hollow, rather than solid like these. See also No. 86.

NOTE:

1. See Boesen 1960, p. 64.

Probably Venice or Innsbruck (Hofglashütte),
probably late sixteenth century

86. Ornamental pin

1975.1.1526
L. 15.7 cm, diam. of larger ball 2.6 cm. Colorless and
transparent green and ruby red nonlead glass, copper(?) wire
and sheet metal. Lampworked, trailed, gilt.

The large colorless glass ball is hollow and is covered with
fused leaf gilding, over which five circuits of gilt colorless
scrollwork and, between the circuits, raised dots of red and
green glass have been applied. The copper(?) wire inserted
through a hole covered with a split copper(?) washer at either
end of the ball is curled decoratively at the top and at the
bottom is coiled into a spring with a pointed heavier copper(?)
wire pin attached to it. A tiny solid colorless glass bead, gilt
and decorated with a trailed colorless band and red and green
glass dots, dangles from a wire attached at the base of the
spring.

Short radial cracks around both openings in the larger ball;
short sections of the trailing missing; some colored dots
missing.

Longwave fluorescence. Colorless glass: faint greenish. Red
glass: dark red. Green glass: dark green. Gilding: dark red
reflection. *Shortwave fluorescence.* Colorless glass: strong
bluish white. Red glass: black. Green glass: black. Gilding:
dark purplish red reflection.

PROVENANCE: Not established.

The wires on No. 86, as on Nos. 84 and 85, are a nonmagnetic material that may be copper or a copper alloy.

The colorless glass balls on this pin and Nos. 84 and 85
were decorated with the same technique – scrollwork of
colorless glass trailed over a layer of fused leaf gilding –
and all three could well have been made in the same
workshop at about the same time. The larger glass ball
on this pin is hollow, not solid like the others, no doubt
because weight was a significant consideration with such
jewelry. The glass beads on the jewelry associated with
the Hofglashütte at Innsbruck (see No. 85) are apparently all hollow.

The ruby red dots on this pin appear to be made of
glass produced using gold, rather than copper, as a colorant. (Copper-ruby glass is orangish red.) Although gold-
ruby glass is widely believed to be a late seventeenth-
century invention, the German mineralogist Georgius
Agricola (Georg Bauer; 1494–1555) mentioned gold as
a colorant for producing ruby glass in his *De natura
fossilium* of 1546.[1] And Antonio Neri (see No. 32) gave
a detailed formula for producing imitation rubies using

No. 86

gold as the colorant in *L'arte vetraria*, first published in 1612. To produce "a transparent Red," Neri wrote,

> calcine Gold with Aqua-regis, many times, pouring the water upon it five or six times, then put this powder of Gold in earthen pots to calcine in the furnace till it become a red powder, which will be in many days, then this powder added in sufficient quantity, and by little and little, to fine Crystall glass which hath been often cast into water, will make the transparent red of a Rubie as by experience is found.[2]

When in 1679 Johann Kunckel (1630–1703), alchemist and chemist in the service of the elector of Brandenburg, translated the English edition of Neri's treatise into German in his *Ars vetraria experimentalis*, adding his own extensive notations, he declared Neri's recipe unworkable and claimed that he had perfected a formula for ruby glass, which he declined to give.[3] Later, in *Laboratorium chymicum* (first published in 1716), Kunckel gave Andreas Cassius of Hamburg credit for having developed a process using gold precipitated with tin, but said Cassius failed to realize the importance of

reheating the ruby glass after forming, a step that is also missing from Neri's formula.[4] Kunckel has often been credited with inventing gold-ruby glass at his glassworks at Potsdam, but it is more probable that he was merely the first to make gold-ruby glass vessels in quantity and of consistent quality.

NOTES:
1. Agricola (1546) 1955.
2. Neri 1612, book 7, chap. 129, pp. 108–9 (English translation by Christopher Merret, 1662): "Rosso trasparente. Si calcini l'oro, che venga in poluere rossa, & questa calcinatione si faccia con acqua regis più volte, ritornandola adossoli per cinque, o sei uolte, poi questa poluere d'oro, si metta in tegamino di terra a calcinare in fornello tanto che venga poluere rossa, che seguirà in più giorni allora questa poluere rossa di oro data sopra il vetro fuso, cioè in cristallo fine, che sia tragietato in acqua più uolte, fara allora detta poluere d'oro data a ragione, & a poco a poco, il vero rosso trasparente di Rubino, però si esperimenti per trouarlo."
3. Neri (Kunckel) 1679, p. 195 (comments on Neri 1612, book 7, chap. 129).
4. See Charleston 1977, pp. 31–32. For a concise discussion of the development of gold-ruby glass, see also Dreier 1989a, pp. 12–14.

Possibly France, Nevers or Orléans (possibly factory of Bernard Perrot), late seventeenth century

87. Scent bottle and stopper

1975.1.1561a,b

H. with stopper 6.2 cm, diam. 4.5 cm. Dark amethyst ("black"), opaque white, pink, dark and light blue, dark brown, yellow, and colorless glass; iron. Lampworked, trailed, gilt.

The base of the neck of the flattened, circular bottle is wrapped with a wavy ribbed band of gilt colorless glass, and the neck is lined with a threaded iron sleeve. Around the edge of the bottle is a row of dark amethyst glass bosses decorated with applied pink and white dots, with wavy ribbed bands of gilt colorless glass between each boss. In the center of each slightly convex side is a dark amethyst disk, on one side enclosing two white hands clasping a dark blue heart with a gilt coronet with white glass "pearls" above and two trailed white scrolls below, on the other side a white flower with six pointed, blue-veined petals encircled by a ring of florets formed of sets of clustered white dots. Framing each disk are two bands of finely ribbed waves of trailed and gilt colorless glass flanking a ring of large white glass balls with applied blue "eyes" separated by gilt colorless glass filaments. The stopper, built up on an iron core with an inset iron screw, is shaped like a male head, presumably representing a Turk, with a pink face with applied white eyes with dark brown pupils and outlines and applied pink lips, nose, and chin; a trailed dark amethyst mustache; applied

yellow earrings; and a dark amethyst pointed turban embellished with applied ball-shaped colorless "jewels."

The bottle cracked; several amethyst balls on the edge chipped and several applied dots missing; four areas around the white balls filled in with a dark resinous material. The head on the stopper cracked; one earring missing.

Longwave fluorescence. White glass: orange. Blue glass: faint bluish. Purple glass: black. Colorless glass: orange. Pink glass dots: pinkish orange. Pink glass face: pinkish orange. *Shortwave fluorescence.* White glass: strong bluish white. Blue glass: purplish blue. Purple glass: black. Colorless glass: black. Pink glass dots: faint pink. Pink glass face: strong bluish white.

PROVENANCE: Luigi Grassi, Florence (Grassi sale 1927, lot 449).

The metal sleeve on the bottle and the core and screw on the stopper are magnetic and slightly rusty; they are most likely either iron or an iron alloy. The screw on the stopper does not fit the threaded sleeve in the neck of the bottle, and the pink glass on the head and the pink dots

No. 87 *(enlarged)*

No. 87, *back of flask (enlarged)*

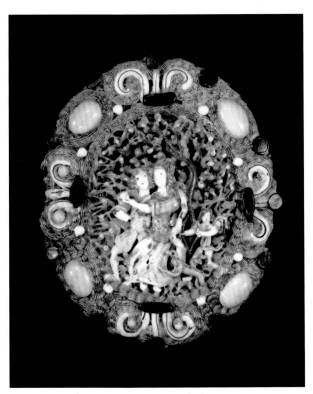

Fig. 87.1 Disk. Corning Museum of Glass

Fig. 87.2 Holy water font. Corning Museum of Glass

applied to the sides of the bottle fluoresce differently under shortwave ultraviolet illumination. Although it might be of the same date and origin, the stopper may therefore not have been made for this bottle.

The device of two hands clasping a heart suggests that this flask was a gift symbolizing devotion and affection. The use of what appears to be the decapitated head of a Turk as a stopper on a gift of friendship seems bizarre and may be a further indication that the flask and the stopper were not made for each other. Figures of Turks were sometimes used as decorative elements in Europe in the late seventeenth century, after the defeat of the invading Ottoman army at the gates of Vienna in 1683.

Both the bottle and the stopper may have been made in France in the workshop of the renowned Bernard Perrot (1619–1709), who was born Bernardo Perrotto in Altare and as a youth left Italy for France, where he worked first in Nevers and later established his own glasshouse in Orléans. Six-petaled blue and white flowers like this one appear among the motifs in the lavish baroque design in *millefiori* and lampworked glass that covers a tabletop that has been attributed to the Perrot workshop; the tabletop, which was discovered in 1975, is listed in an inventory taken during Louis XIV's reign among objects belonging to the French Crown before 1681.[1]

Wavy bands of finely ribbed gilt colorless glass like these also decorate a small lampworked disk in the Corning Museum of Glass (Fig. 87.1) that was probably made in Nevers and probably dates to the late seventeenth century.[2] And the figures on a small lampworked and assembled holy water font in the Corning Museum of Glass (Fig. 87.2) that has also been attributed to late seventeenth-century France have large applied eyes with dark outlines, perhaps meant to simulate kohl, like those on the face on the Lehman stopper.[3]

NOTES:
1. See Clarke and Bourne 1988, and also Tait 1991, pp. 14–16, figs. 7, 8. In 1975 the tabletop was in the collection of Sir Adrian Beecham, Clopton House, Stratford-on-Avon. It was offered for sale at Christie's, London, on 26 June 1975, lot 91, pl. 14 (see Herbert 1975, p. 373), and again at Sotheby's, London, on 24 November 1988 (see Morris 1989, pp. 388–90).
2. Corning Museum of Glass, 53.3.34; Corning Museum of Glass 1958 and 1974, p. 47.
3. Corning Museum of Glass, 58.3.215. Some of the lampworked figurines made in the late sixteenth century at the Hofglashütte at Innsbruck have outlined eyes (see Fig. F).

Probably France, Nevers (possibly Haly workshop), last half of the eighteenth century

88. Mercury

1975.1.1564
H. 15.8 cm. Opaque white, pink, tan, black, olive green, and waxlike colorless glass; copper and iron wire. Lampworked.

Mercury stands looking to his left, holding a caduceus in his raised right hand. He has white skin, tan hair, pink cheeks and lips, and black eyes and eyebrows, and his clothing – a fitted jacket with a peplum and elbow-length sleeves, a short skirt, a winged hat, and calf-length cuffed boots with wings at the heels – is white with pink trim. The figure is mounted on a convex base of finely trailed opaque olive green glass, with trailed white sides decorated with olive green swags and scattered pink florets. The undersides of the skirt and base are strengthened with coiled and radially trailed waxy-looking colorless glass enclosing threadlike copper wires.

The body of the figure covered with a network of brownish cracks; the caduceus, originally straight and vertical, broken and bent; the left arm, the back of the waist, the wings on the hat, the right hand, and the lower part of the caduceus painted white (indicating probable loss of glass and later repair).

Longwave fluorescence. Opaque white glass: brilliant orange. Pink glass: dark red. Green glass: mottled dark brown and green. Colorless glass: waxy tan and white. *Shortwave fluorescence.* Opaque white glass: mottled purplish pink. Pink glass: bluish white. Green glass: strong bright greenish. Colorless glass: waxy, opaque white. Tan glass: brownish tan.

PROVENANCE: Viva (Mrs. William) King, England (King sale 1958, lot 67, ill.).

LITERATURE: King 1939, p. 107, fig. 6.

This figurine of Mercury, its companion, Diana (No. 89), and Nos. 90–95 and 98 were all constructed in a similar way. The heavy internal lines in the radiographs are thick iron wires (on Nos. 90, 92, 94, and 95 the heavy wire projects from the base and was determined to be magnetic; the wire was analyzed on No. 98 and found to be iron). The iron wires are somewhat heavier on Nos. 88–90, the three largest figurines in the group. The iron armature was formed first and was probably tacked together with molten glass (as was done, for example, on

Nos. 88 and 89

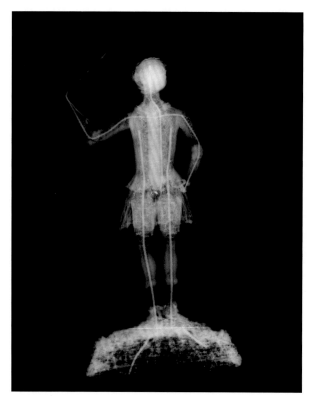

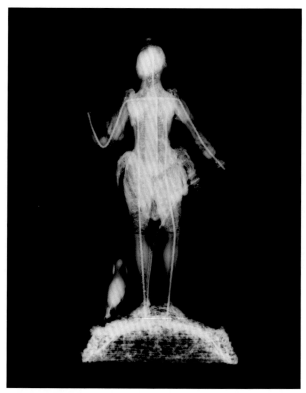

Fig. 88.1 Radiograph of No. 88

Fig. 89.1 Radiograph of No. 89

Fig. 88.2 Judgment of Paris. Musée des Arts Décoratifs, Paris.
Photograph: Laurent Sully Jaulmes

the cross on No. 91) or wrapped with fine copper wire. The heavy wires were then covered with molten glass that was produced by melting slender tubes of waxy-looking colorless glass that have minute, threadlike copper wires, probably meant to help strengthen the fragile figurine, running throughout their lengths. (The wires have a copper color where they are encased in glass and have corroded to a green color where the glass has broken and exposed them; the thin wire was analyzed on No. 98 and found to be copper.) The form of the figure was gradually built up using this glass, resulting in the jumble of wire evident in the radiographs. On Nos. 88 and 89 the copper wires are visible in the colorless glass, and their presence in the opaque white glass of the torsos (but not the legs or arms) is clearly shown in the radiographs (Figs. 88.1, 89.1). Finally, the colored outer coatings, also formed of slender glass tubes (sometimes also enclosing copper wires), were trailed on and modeled into clothing and anatomical features. A glass rod was used to hold the figure while it was being formed in the lamp; on Nos. 89 and 91 an opaque white scar left when the "pontil" was broken off can be seen on the underside of the base.

The exquisite depiction of the musculature, the delicate hands, and the very fine facial details distinguish these figures of Mercury and Diana, which were doubtless made as a pair. Six of the other lampworked statuettes in the Robert Lehman Collection (Nos. 90–95) were modeled with similar delicacy, perhaps in the same workshop. The ultraviolet fluorescence of the opaque white glass is nearly the same on Nos. 88–95, as well as on Nos. 97 and 98, which like the others have integral bases and were similarly constructed.

Although *verre de Nevers* has become the generic term for lampworked figurines like these, they were made elsewhere in France as well, and very few of them, either single statuettes or figures in tableaux, can be attributed to Neversian craftsmen with certainty. The workmanship on Nos. 88–95 and 98 allies them to three figural groups (all now in the Musée des Arts Décoratifs, Paris) made by one Haly, of the Saint-Sauveur quarter of Nevers, whose name appears (as Haly or Alis) in the account books of the Nevers glassworks for 1753 and 1754 among the *émailleurs*, or enamelers, as they were called, to whom the factory supplied raw material in the form of *pains*, *baguettes*, or *tubes* of glass in different colors.[1] One of those three groups, depicting Perseus and Andromeda, is signed *HALY* on the underside of the base; another, depicting the Judgment of Paris (Fig. 88.2), bears a pla-quette with Haly's name and the first three digits of a date, *177*.[2] The Musée des Arts Décoratifs has other lampworked figures made by the same technique with the same fine craftsmanship;[3] and still others are in the Musée Municipal de Nevers[4] and elsewhere.

NOTES:
1. Barrelet 1960, pp. 297, 302, 306, 310.
2. Musée des Arts Décoratifs, 38475A, B; Barrelet 1953, fig. 56; Barrelet 1960, pp. 303, 304, figs. 11, 12. The third group, representing Hercules and Omphale, is neither signed nor dated.
3. Bellanger 1988, p. 341.
4. Musée Municipal de Nevers, N.V.35; Bringuier 1982, p. 20, no. 22.

Probably France, Nevers (possibly Haly workshop), last half of the eighteenth century

89. Diana

1975.1.1563
H. 15.8 cm. Opaque white, pink, tan, black, brown, olive green, and waxlike colorless glass; copper and iron wire. Lampworked.

Diana stands with her right arm raised, her left hand holding a bow with a slack olive green string and its tip resting on the ground. Her cheeks and lips are pink, her eyes and eyebrows black, and she wears a pink flower in her tan hair; her nude body is partly draped in a white cloak with pink trim, and a quiver of arrows with opaque olive green feathers hangs at her side. Seated at her feet is a white dog with dark brown spots and black eyes, ears, and nose. The figures are mounted on a convex base of finely trailed olive green glass, with trailed white sides decorated with olive green swags and scattered pink florets. The underside of the base is strengthened with coiled and radially trailed waxy-looking colorless glass enclosing threadlike copper wires. Small opaque white glass "pontil" scar on the underside of the base.

The body covered with a network of brownish cracks; the right hand, the left hand and the area of cloak above it, and an area on the cloak at the back painted white (indicating probable loss of glass and later repair).

Longwave fluorescence. Opaque white glass: brilliant orange. Pink glass: dark red. Green glass: mottled dark brown and green. Colorless glass: waxy tan and white. *Shortwave fluorescence.* Opaque white glass: mottled purplish pink. Pink glass: bluish white. Green glass: strong bright greenish. Colorless glass: waxy, opaque white. Tan glass: brownish tan.

PROVENANCE: Viva (Mrs. William) King, England (King sale 1958, lot 67, ill.).

LITERATURE: King 1939, p. 107, fig. 6.

See No. 88.

Probably France, Nevers (possibly Haly workshop),
last half of the eighteenth century

90. Saint Francis de Sales

1975.1.1568

H. 25.6 cm. Opaque white, dark amethyst ("black"), pink,
brown, dark brown, black, yellow-orange, light blue, dark
blue-green, green, dark green, olive green, and waxlike colorless glass; copper and iron wire. Lampworked.

Saint Francis stands with his arms bent at the elbows, his
hands at his chest. His face and hands are opaque white, his
cheeks and mouth are pink, and his eyes, eyebrows, hair, and
beard are brown. He wears a black skullcap, a dark amethyst
cassock, a white lace-trimmed rochet, a dark amethyst mozzetta, and a green stole with yellow-orange trim and a yellow-
orange cross at each end. A yellow-orange cross is suspended
from his neck, and his pink slippers have yellow-orange crosses
on the toes. On the ground at his right is his black bishop's
miter, and behind him is a tree with a straight, knobby trunk
of brown glass and four straight brown limbs with olive green
foliage. The figure stands on a raised square pedestal of finely
trailed dark blue-green glass edged in opaque olive green and
decorated with opaque white and pink florets; on the front of
the pedestal is an opaque white oval plaque edged with light
blue trailing and inscribed in dark brown: *S*. *francois*. The
pedestal is mounted on a rectangular base with four projecting
ovoid feet formed of opaque white glass with trailed olive
green foliate decoration. The top surface of the base is covered
with finely trailed dark green "grass," the sides have white
panels outlined with olive green trailing and decorated with
scattered white and pink florets, and the underside is lined
with coiled and radially trailed waxy-looking colorless glass
enclosing threadlike copper wires. An iron wire projects from
the bottom.

The figure covered with a network of fine brownish cracks; the
tree trunk broken at the base and several limbs broken off and
missing; the left rear corner of the base and the left rear foot
rebuilt with composition (plaster?) and painted; a section of
applied florets missing from the front edge of the base and
other minor losses of trailing throughout. According to the
King sale catalogue of 1958, the figure once held a cross, now
missing, in his right hand.

Longwave fluorescence. Opaque white glass: brilliant orange.
Green glass: dark red. Dark amethyst glass: muddy green
(robe) and brown (cape). Brown glass: brownish purple reflec-
tion. Pink glass: dark red. Colorless glass: waxy tan and white.
Shortwave fluorescence. Opaque white glass: mottled pink.
Green glass: purplish reflection. Dark amethyst glass: bright
green (robe) and mottled greenish with dark spots (cape).
Brown glass: purplish reflection. Dark green glass: black.
Olive green glass: bright green. Pink glass: brilliant bluish
white. Colorless glass: brownish tan.

PROVENANCE: Viva (Mrs. William) King, England (King sale
1958, lot 84).

For a description of how the figure was made, see No. 88,
and see also the radiograph (Fig. 90.1). See also No. 96.

Saint Francis de Sales was born Francis Bonaventure at
the Château de Sales at Thorens in Savoy in 1567. At the
age of twenty-six, after studying at Annecy and the uni-
versities of Paris and Padua, he was ordained priest and
became provost of Geneva. A year later, in 1594, he was
sent on his first mission, to win back to the Church the
people of Chablais, on the south shore of the Lake of
Geneva, where armed conflicts and Protestantism had
considerably weakened its influence. Within four years
Francis had managed to restore much of the province to
Catholicism. In 1602 he became bishop of Geneva. He
and Saint Jane de Chantal, whom he met while preach-
ing in Dijon in 1604, founded the Order of the Visita-

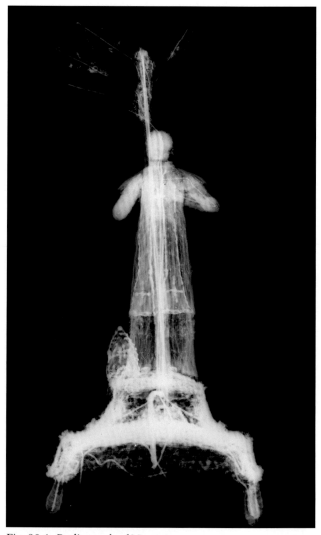

Fig. 90.1 Radiograph of No. 90

No. 90

tion in 1610. Saint Francis de Sales died at the convent of the Visitation in Lyons in 1622. In ceremonies at Saint Peter's in Rome he was beatified in 1662 and canonized in 1665. In 1877 he was declared a doctor of the Church, and he was later named patron saint of journalists by Pope Pius XI. His *Introduction to a Devout Life* and *The Love of God* are still widely read.[1]

Several related figures are in the collection of the Musée Municipal de Nevers.[2]

NOTES:
1. See Thurston and Attwater 1956, vol. 1, pp. 195–201.
2. Musée Municipal de Nevers, N.V.32, N.V.969.2.1, N.V.964.2.1; Bringuier 1982, pp. 17–20, nos. 11, 16, 23.

Probably France, Nevers (possibly Haly workshop), last half of the eighteenth century

91. A Carmelite

1975.1.1567
H. 7.6 cm. Opaque white, tan, black, brown, pink, olive green, and waxlike colorless glass; copper and iron wire. Lampworked.

The figure stands holding a cross in his extended right hand and pointing with the index finger of his left. He has a white face and hands, pink cheeks and lips, black eyes, brown eyebrows, and a brown tonsure. He wears a Carmelite habit – a tan tunic tied with a black belt, a tan scapular, and a white hooded cloak – and black shoes. The cross is formed of iron wire that has been tacked where the arms intersect with a blob of melted black glass. The figure stands on a convex circular base of finely trailed opaque olive green glass lined with coiled waxlike colorless glass enclosing thread-like copper wires. Opaque white "pontil" scar on the underside of the base.

A few fine cracks; the wire cross bent.

Longwave fluorescence. Opaque white glass: brilliant orange. Brown glass: purplish reflection. Pink glass: dark red. Tan glass: tan. Olive green glass: dark green. *Shortwave fluorescence.* Opaque white glass: pale pink. Brown glass: purplish reflection. Pink glass: bluish white. Tan glass: black. Olive green glass: faint greenish.

PROVENANCE: Viva (Mrs. William) King, England (King sale 1958, lot 80).

LITERATURE: Planchon 1913, pl. 7; King 1939, p. 109, fig. 4.

For a description of how the figure was constructed, see No. 88. Threadlike copper wires are visible in the opaque white glass of the cloak on the back of the figure, and the radiograph (Fig. 91.1) shows the internal iron wire framework and fine copper wires throughout. The opaque white scar on the base was left when the white glass rod used to hold the figure while it was being formed in the lamp was broken off.

This small figure probably represents a saint, but the lack of definite attributes makes naming him difficult. While the figure was in the collection of Viva King it was identified as Saint Dominic. The skillful modeling of the hands, the face with its applied eyelids, and the drapery of the habit, along with the way it was constructed and the fluorescence of the glass, relates this figurine to Nos. 88–90, 92–95, and 98, all of which could possibly have been made by the *émailleur* Haly of Nevers (see the discussion under No. 88).

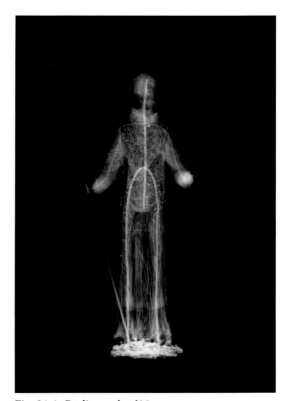

No. 91

Fig. 91.1 Radiograph of No. 91

Probably France, Nevers (possibly Haly workshop),
last half of the eighteenth century

92. A bishop

1975.1.1569
H. 7.6 cm. Opaque white, turquoise blue, pink, yellow, brown,
black, olive green, and waxlike colorless glass; copper and
iron wire. Lampworked.

The figure stands with his right hand raised in blessing, his left
holding a crosier. He has white skin, pink cheeks and lips,
black eyes and hair, and brown eyebrows. He wears an alb and
a speckled turquoise blue chasuble with yellow trim on the
orphrey and edges and a yellow cross on the back. The crosier
is formed of iron wire, with smaller gauge iron wire wrapped
in a spiral around its lower stem and the crook covered with
black glass. The figure stands on a convex circular base of
finely trailed opaque olive green glass. The underside of the
base is lined with coiled waxy-looking colorless glass enclosing threadlike copper wire. An iron wire projects from the
bottom.

A few minute cracks; mounted on a new plastic support.

Longwave fluorescence. Opaque white glass: brilliant orange.
Turquoise blue glass: tan. Pink glass: dark red. Black glass:
black. Yellow glass: dark red. Olive green glass: dark muddy
green. *Shortwave fluorescence.* Opaque white glass: pale pink.
Turquoise blue glass: dark purple. Pink glass: bluish white.
Black glass: black. Yellow glass: strong yellow-green. Olive
green glass: dark green.

PROVENANCE: Viva (Mrs. William) King, England (King sale
1958, lot 81).

LITERATURE: Planchon 1913, pl. 7; King 1939, p. 109, fig. 4.

For a description of how the figure was constructed, see
No. 88, and see also the radiograph (Fig. 92.1). The wire
that projects from the base is magnetic.

The way it was constructed, the delicate modeling, and
the fluorescence of the glass all indicate that this figure
may have been made in the same workshop as Nos.
88–91, 93–95, and 98. See the discussion under No. 88.

No. 92

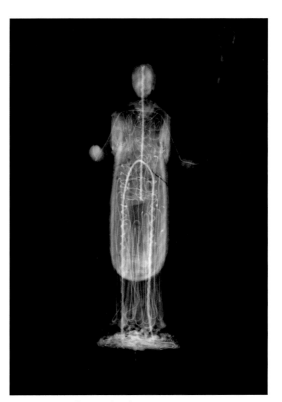

Fig. 92.1 Radiograph of No. 92

Probably France, Nevers (possibly Haly workshop), last half of the eighteenth century

93. A cleric

1975.1.1572
H. 7.6 cm. Opaque white, black, brown, pink, tan, green, and waxlike colorless glass; copper wire. Lampworked.

The figure stands with his right forearm raised and his left hand extended palm up at his side. He has white skin, pink cheeks, black eyes, brown eyebrows, and tan hair. He wears a black pleated cassock, a sleeveless surplice, a black cleric's collar with white trim, and black shoes. The figure is mounted on a now-fragmentary convex circular base of finely trailed green glass.

The right hand, which once held a biretta (now missing), restored; most of the glass base restored, filled in with composition material, and painted green.

Longwave fluorescence. Opaque white glass: brilliant orange. Black glass: black. Pink glass: dark red. Tan glass: waxy tan. Green glass: opaque gray (perhaps paint). *Shortwave fluorescence.* Opaque white glass: pale pink. Black glass: black. Pink glass: bluish white. Tan glass: bluish white.

PROVENANCE: Viva (Mrs. William) King, England (King sale 1958, lot 80).

LITERATURE: Planchon 1913, pl. 7; King 1939, p. 109, fig. 4.

For a description of how the figure was constructed, see No. 88, and see also the radiograph (Fig. 93.1).

This figurine's right hand still held a biretta when Viva King illustrated it in the article on *verre de Nevers* she wrote for *Apollo* in 1939. In the catalogue for the King sale in 1958 the figure is identified as a prelate. It can be grouped with Nos. 88–92, 94, 95, and 98, which may have been made in the Haly workshop in Nevers and which all show similarities in details of construction and modeling and in the fluorescence of the glass. See the discussion under No. 88.

No. 93

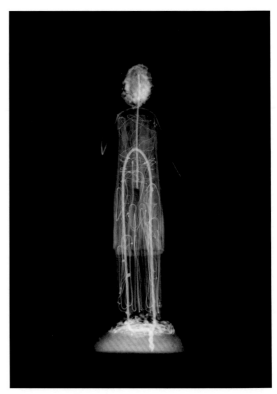

Fig. 93.1 Radiograph of No. 93

Probably France, Nevers (possibly Haly workshop), last half of the eighteenth century

94. Christ

1975.1.1565
H. 7.6 cm. Opaque white, brown, pink, blue, yellow, green, greenish brown, and waxlike colorless glass; copper and iron wire. Lampworked.

The barefoot figure stands with his right arm extended and his left arm bent at the elbow with his hand extended in front of him. He has white skin, pink lips and cheeks, long brown hair, and a greenish brown beard and eyebrows. He wears a white robe trimmed in blue at the neck and tied at the waist with a yellow cord. The figure stands on a convex circular base of finely trailed green glass lined with coiled waxlike colorless glass enclosing threadlike copper wire. An iron wire projects from the base.

The right arm broken and painted; mounted on a new plastic base.

Longwave fluorescence. Opaque white glass: brilliant orange. Brown glass: dark brown. Pink glass: dark red. Yellow glass: brown. Green glass: muddy green. *Shortwave fluorescence.* Opaque white glass: pale pink. Brown glass: black. Pink glass: bluish white. Yellow glass: tan. Green glass: dark green.

PROVENANCE: Viva (Mrs. William) King, England (King sale 1958, lot 81).

LITERATURE: Planchon 1913, pl. 7; King 1939, p. 109, fig. 4.

For a description of how the figure was constructed, see No. 88, and see also the radiograph (Fig. 94.1).

Its form and construction and the fluorescence of the glass relate this figure to Nos. 88–93, 95, and 98; see the discussion under No. 88. Similar figurines from a crèche are in a private collection.[1]

NOTE:
1. See Bellanger 1988, p. 342.

No. 94

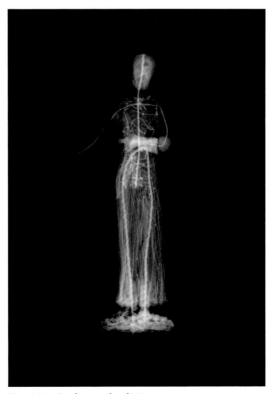

Fig. 94.1 Radiograph of No. 94

Probably France, Nevers (possibly Haly workshop),
last half of the eighteenth century

95. Saint John the Baptist(?)

1975.1.1566
H. 7.6 cm. Opaque white, blue, pink, brown, green, and
waxlike colorless glass; copper and iron wire. Lampworked.

The barefoot figure stands with his left arm raised and his right
arm bent across his chest. He has white skin and pink lips and
cheeks, and his hair, eyebrows, and beard are brown. He wears
a white robe tied at the waist with a pink cord and a blue cloak
that is draped over his left shoulder and wrapped around his
legs. The figure stands on a convex circular base of finely trailed
green glass lined with coiled waxlike colorless glass enclosing
threadlike copper wire. An iron wire projects from the base.

Mounted on a new plastic base.

Longwave fluorescence. Opaque white glass: brilliant orange.
Blue glass: dark purplish red. Pink glass: brilliant orange
(indistinguishable from white). Brown glass: dark brownish
purple. Yellow glass: dark red. Green glass: dark green.
Shortwave fluorescence. Opaque white glass: pale pink. Blue
glass: dark blue. Pink glass: bluish white. Brown glass: black.
Yellow glass: gray. Green glass: dark green.

PROVENANCE: Viva (Mrs. William) King, England (King sale
1958, lot 81).

LITERATURE: Planchon 1913, pl. 7; King 1939, p. 109, fig. 4.

For a description of how the figure was constructed, see
No. 88, and see also the radiograph (Fig. 95.1). The
opaque white glass was submitted to elemental analysis
by energy dispersive X-ray spectrometry (EDS) and was
shown to contain little or no lead; the glass was colored
and opacified with an antimony compound, possibly calcium antimonate.[1] See also Nos. 96 and 98.

This skillfully executed and detailed figurine, which was
identified as John the Baptist while it was in the King
collection but lacks definitive attributes, is part of the
group that includes Nos. 88–94, 98, and possibly No.
97. It was constructed like the others, and the glass
fluoresces similarly under ultraviolet light. See the discussion under No. 88.

NOTE:
1. EDS analyses by Mark T. Wypyski, Sherman Fairchild Center for Objects Conservation, The Metropolitan Museum
   of Art.

No. 95

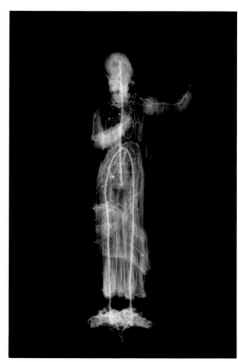

Fig. 95.1 Radiograph of No. 95

Probably France, Nevers, late eighteenth or early nineteenth century

96. A prelate

1975.1.1570
H. 8 cm. Transparent dark amethyst lead glass; pink, brown, black, and dark blue glass; copper wire. Lampworked.

The figure stands with his left arm extended at his side and his right arm across his chest. He has a pink face and hands and brown hair, eyes, and eyebrows. He wears a dark amethyst cassock, with a rosary tied at the waist, a black biretta, and black shoes. The figure is mounted on a convex circular base of trailed dark blue glass.

The neck and left arm broken and repaired.

Longwave fluorescence. Amethyst glass: dark red reflection. Pink glass (head, hands, lips): dark pink. Brown glass: brown. *Shortwave fluorescence.* Amethyst glass: purplish reflection. Pink glass: purplish white (head and hands) and dark red (lips). Brown glass: dark brown.

PROVENANCE: Viva (Mrs. William) King, England (King sale 1958, lot 68).

This figure proved to be much more radiopaque than Nos. 88–95, 97, and 98. The amethyst glass of the robe was submitted to surface analysis by energy dispersive X-ray spectrometry (EDS) and was shown to contain a large amount of lead. (The opaque white glass of Nos. 95 and 98 was also analyzed and was found to contain little or no lead.) The small amethyst glass shoes of the Good Shepherd in No. 98 also have a high lead content.[1] But the dark, nearly black amethyst glass used for the cassock and mozzetta of No. 90, the figurine of Saint Francis de Sales, shows little radiopacity, and it fluoresces differently from the purple glass of No. 96 under both longwave and shortwave ultraviolet light. When No. 96 was X-rayed again at higher settings, it was still largely radiopaque, but unfocused images of internal wires like those that support Nos. 88–95, 97, and 98 (see the discussion under No. 88) can be made out in the radiograph (Fig. 96.1). The figure's cassock is hollow, however, without the coils of waxlike colorless glass that were used to strengthen the undersides of the other figures. The shortwave fluorescence indicates that the pink glass of the lips may be different from that of the face and hands.

The relatively crude execution of the figural details, particularly the face and hands, sets this statuette apart from the group of more finely modeled lampworked figurines in the Robert Lehman Collection that may have been made in the Haly workshop in Nevers (see No. 88). That

No. 96

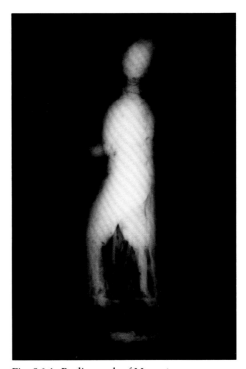

Fig. 96.1 Radiograph of No. 96

it was constructed somewhat differently from them also suggests that it was produced in a different workshop. A related figurine is in the Musée Municipal de Nevers.[2]

NOTES:
1. EDS analyses by Mark T. Wypyski, Sherman Fairchild Center for Objects Conservation, The Metropolitan Museum of Art.
2. Musée Municipal de Nevers, N.V.961.4.5; Bringuier 1982, p. 19, no. 19.

Probably France, Nevers, last half of the eighteenth century

97. An acolyte

1975.1.1571
H. 7.6 cm. Opaque white, black, pink, yellow, blue, and green glass; copper and iron wire. Lampworked.

The standing figure holds a banner with both hands. He wears a black cassock, a lace-trimmed white surplice, and what remains of a black biretta. The pink-edged white banner above his head bears a green crown of thorns on the front and a pink flaming heart pierced with arrows on the back; the iron wire cross supporting the banner has yellow ball terminals on its blue tip and arms.

The face and most of the biretta broken off (exposing the iron wire support of the banner); the base broken off and replaced with a new base of composition material painted green.

Longwave fluorescence. Opaque white glass: brilliant orange. Black glass: black. Yellow glass: dark red. Blue glass: black. Pink glass: dark gray (heart) and dark red (trim). Green glass: dark green. *Shortwave fluorescence.* Opaque white glass: pale pink. Black glass: black. Yellow glass: black. Blue glass: dark blue. Pink glass: black (heart) and bluish white (trim). Green glass: dark green.

PROVENANCE: Viva (Mrs. William) King, England (King sale 1958, lot 68).

For a description of how the figure was constructed, see No. 88.

Although the fragmentary condition of this figurine precludes relating it stylistically to Nos. 88–95 and 98, the radiograph (Fig. 97.1) reveals that it too is made of glass encasing thin wire and is supported by an armature of heavier gauge wire. The fluorescence of the glass is also similar to that of the others. See the discussion under No. 88.

No. 97

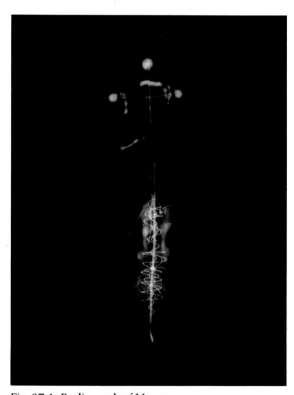

Fig. 97.1 Radiograph of No. 97

No. 98

Probably France, Nevers (possibly Haly workshop),
last half of the eighteenth century

98. The Good Shepherd

1975.1.1579

H. 24.9 cm, h. of shepherd figure 6.6 cm. Figures of lampworked glass (opaque white, pink, black, blue, green, waxlike colorless, and transparent amethyst), papier-mâché, wood, mirror plate, paper, composition material, paint, metal sequins, metal wire. Assembled.

The Good Shepherd, with a lamb on his shoulders, made of opaque white glass and supported by a column of opaque white glass, stands atop a conical papier-mâché hill covered with crushed green and colorless glass. He has black eyes and eyebrows; an applied white nose, mouth, and chin; and applied

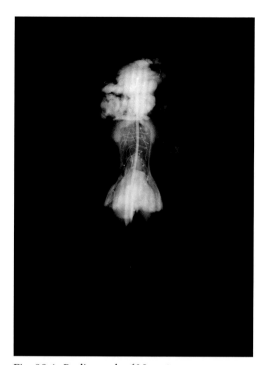

Fig. 98.1 Radiograph of No. 98

pink cheeks. He wears an opaque white waistcoat with three buttons and lined with coiled waxlike colorless glass, a blue hat with an amethyst brim decorated with colorless flowers and a green bow, white stockings, and amethyst shoes. The figure is mounted on a convex circular base of trailed green glass lined with coiled waxlike colorless glass enclosing thread-like copper wires. Behind him is a wire tree with a trunk wrapped in brown thread and green paper foliage and painted yellow composition pears, and beside him is a thread-wrapped wire standard holding a paper banner on which *pastor bonus* (good shepherd) is written in black ink. The hilltop is sprinkled with green paper grass and stylized painted paper flowers on wire stems, each with a colorful metal sequin. On the path that winds its way up the hill past caves and pools lined with pieces of mirror plate, a white sheepdog with black ears leads a flock of thirteen tiny white sheep. A pink-eyed white rabbit sits at the bottom of the hill. The composition is set in a round turned wood base that has been painted green and has a hole drilled in the center bottom. Written in white chalk on the underside of the base: *8.*

The shepherd figure broken from its glass base (held together by the internal wires) and the support behind it broken; the body cracked on the figure's right side, its right arm broken off, and its right leg broken and glued back together; part of the

bow on the hat missing; the rabbit's ears broken off, several sheep with broken legs, and the sheep now missing the paper labels with *R* written in black ink each once had affixed to its back; the composition leaning and dirty; the protective glass dome that apparently fit the turned wood base now missing.

Longwave fluorescence. Opaque white glass: brilliant orange (shepherd) and dark red (animals). Tan glass: tan. Blue glass: black. Green glass: faint green. Composition: strong white. Flowers: brilliant, electric orange. *Shortwave fluorescence.* Opaque white glass: strong bluish white (shepherd's body), pink (shepherd's face), and muddy white (animals). Tan glass: tan. Blue glass: strong bluish white. Composition: nothing. Flowers: nothing.

PROVENANCE: Viva (Mrs. William) King, England (King sale 1958, lot 88).

For a description of how the figure of the shepherd was constructed, see No. 88. Two samples of the wire armature that shows in the radiograph of the figure (Fig. 98.1) were analyzed by energy dispersive X-ray spectrometry (EDS): the thinner wire is copper, and the thicker wire is iron. The surfaces of the opaque white glass of the leg and the translucent amethyst glass of the shoes of the shepherd were also analysed by EDS. The amethyst glass was found to contain a large amount of lead, the opaque white glass very little. The white glass was found to contain antimony and may have been opacified with calcium antimonate.[1] See also Nos. 95 and 96, on which the glass was also analyzed.

Like Nos. 88–95, the figure of the shepherd, with its lampworked glass base, internal iron support strengthened by waxy colorless glass enclosing thin copper wire, and detailed modeling, may have been made in the Haly workshop in Nevers (see the discussion under No. 88). The pink shortwave fluorescence of the opaque white glass of the shepherd's face is also similar to that of the opaque white glass of the other figurines in the group. The white sheep, however, fluoresce dark red and muddy white.

NOTE:
1. EDS analyses by Mark T. Wypyski of the Sherman Fairchild Center for Objects Conservation, The Metropolitan Museum of Art.

No. 99

Probably France, Nevers, eighteenth century;
probably reassembled in the last half of the
nineteenth century

99. The Finding of Moses

1975.1.1580

H. 8.5 cm, w. 20 cm, d. 15 cm. Figures and plants of
lampworked glass (opaque white, pale pink, yellow, turquoise
blue, dark blue, bright blue, brown, dark red, green, black,
and tan), metal wire, composition material, glass mirror plate,
paint, string, coral. Assembled.

The infant Moses, a tiny white and yellow glass figure wrapped
with brown string, floats in a raft of brown string on the Nile,
a sheet of mirrored glass with an irregular green-painted

composition shoreline. Pharaoh's daughter, wearing a white
dress tied at the waist with a dark blue cord and with a
turquoise blue cape over one arm and a white veil covering her
brown hair, kneels at the river's edge between two fragmentary
stumps of green glass bushes, her arms raised in surprise. To
her left a maid, in a yellow dress, a bright blue tunic, and a
white kerchief, stands with clasped hands; like the other
figures, she has pale pink skin. Off to the right of Pharaoh's
daughter stands the baby's sister, a young woman with tan
hair wearing white shoes and a yellow cloak tied with a dark

blue cord over a bright green dress. A tiny green striped glass salamander lies in the grass at her feet, and to her right is a piece of coral. Two bearded men stand watching from the opposite shore: one, with both arms raised, has tan hair and wears a dark red robe, a yellow cape, and white shoes; the other wears an off-white turban with a bright green topknot, a dark red robe tied with a white sash, a yellow long-sleeved coat, and black shoes. The rectangular sheet of mirrored glass on which the scene is assembled is backed with red-orange paint.

The group dirty; the left foot missing from the figure of Pharaoh's daughter and the head broken off and cemented back on and the crack in the neck painted; the sister's left arm cracked at the wrist; the bushes broken. A stain on the mirror indicates that something is missing (perhaps a duck or swan). A loose glass rabbit stored with the group probably does not belong to it. According to the description in the catalogue of the King sale in 1958, the group once had a wooden base and a glass cover, both now missing.

Longwave fluorescence. Glass: same colors as in daylight. Composition: bright light green. *Shortwave fluorescence.* Opaque white glass: purplish white. Blue glass: dark blue. Green glass: muddy green. Yellow glass: creamy. Red-brown glass: dark brown. Composition: muddy green.

PROVENANCE: Viva (Mrs. William) King, England (King sale 1958, lot 60).

Although the figures in the tableaux (Nos. 99–105) were neither X-rayed nor removed from their bases to inspect their construction, they were most certainly made in the manner described in No. 88.

The story of the Finding of Moses is told in Exodus 2:1–10. This tableau and No. 100, depicting Susanna

and the Elders, were probably made by the same artisan. The two groups were constructed in a similar way with similar materials, and the lampworked figures all appear to have been made by the same hand. The workmanship on the figures is not as refined as that on most of the individual figurines in the Robert Lehman Collection (Nos. 88–95, 98). The fluorescence of the glass is also distinctly different from that of the individual figures.

The red backing on the mirror means that it was probably replaced and the group reassembled in the last half of the nineteenth century. Glass mirrors were being made in Venice in the late fourteenth century, but they were relatively rare until the mid-sixteenth century, when the Venetian mirrormakers organized themselves into a corporation and began selling their products throughout Europe. The Venetian method of making mirrors, by coating glass plate with an amalgam of tinfoil and mercury, was used by glassmakers in Italy and, later, elsewhere in Europe until the mid-nineteenth century. In 1835 the German chemist Justus von Liebig discovered a way of coating the glass surface with a thin layer of silver, and by about 1840 most mirrors were being made by this new method. To protect the delicate silver layer, the backs of Liebig-silvered mirrors were usually coated with red lead or paint. In the early twentieth century mirrors began to be backed with a coating of copper, rather than paint.[1]

NOTE:
1. See Singer et al. 1958, pp. 362–63, and Osborne 1985, pp. 570–72.

Probably France, Nevers, eighteenth century; probably reassembled in the last half of the nineteenth century

100. Susanna and the Elders

1975.1.1576
H. 8.5 cm, w. 19.7 cm, d. 15 cm. Figures and flowers of lampworked glass (opaque white, pink, dark blue, bright blue, brown, reddish brown, red, green, black, yellow, and tan), composition material, glass mirror plate, paint, coral, seashells. Assembled.

The nude figure of Susanna, wearing only an opaque white veil on her head, sits with both arms raised at the far left edge of a pond of mirrored glass with an irregular brown painted composition shoreline strewn with small pieces of coral and

seashells, a tiny lampworked glass forget-me-not, and stylized lampworked yellow flowers. Watching her are the two elders, one kneeling and wearing a bright green robe tied with a white sash, a white and dark blue turban, and black shoes, the other stooping and wearing a bright blue robe tied with a white sash, a white and reddish brown turban with a red jewel, and black shoes. All three figures have opaque pinkish white skin and brown hair and features. Two lampworked white swans and a yellow and green striped salamander are loose in the tableau. The underside of the rectangular mirror plate on which the scene is constructed is painted red-orange.

No. 100

The group dirty; the green-robed elder extensively cracked; a piece of coral loose; the two swans and a salamander stored with the group may not belong to it. According to the description in the catalogue of the King sale in 1958, the group once had a wooden base and a glass cover, both now missing.

Longwave fluorescence. Glass: same colors as in daylight (the green robe fluoresces a strong white in the cracks). Composition: strong greenish white in places. *Shortwave fluorescence.* Opaque white glass: purplish white. Pink glass: pinkish purple. Bright blue glass: turquoise blue. Dark blue glass: dark blue. Green glass: muddy green. Composition: muddy green in places.

PROVENANCE: Viva (Mrs. William) King, England (King sale 1958, lot 60, ill.).

Like its companion, No. 99, this group was probably reassembled and its mirror plate replaced in the last half of the nineteenth century. See the discussion under No. 99.

The story of the virtuous Susanna's triumph over evil, set in Babylon during the Exile, is from the Old Testament Apocrypha.

No. 101

Probably France, Nevers, eighteenth century

101. The Temptation of Saint Antony

1975.1.1577
H. 21 cm, w. 33.5 cm, d. 27.8 cm. Figures of lampworked glass (opaque and translucent white, brown, yellowish brown, black, yellow, blue, light blue, turquoise blue, amethyst, green, pink, gray, tan, and colorless), composition material (plaster?), glass mirror plate, wood, wire, shells, feathers, paper, paint. Assembled.

Saint Antony, a bearded old man with opaque white skin and translucent white hair, emerges from his cave in a rectangular brown painted composition landscape scattered with seashells and shrubs made of feathers. He is barefoot and wears a dark brown habit tied at the waist with a white cord, from which a white rosary is suspended, and a black cloak with a white *tau* on the shoulder. A yellow jug stands on the ground to his right, and to his left is a spring formed of two colorless glass rods

that feeds a mirror-glass pond ringed with stones. At the edge of the pond are a white bird, a turquoise blue and white bird, three white sheep, a black dog, a white ram with yellow horns, a white rabbit, a white billy goat with black horns, a gadrooned opaque white glass urn holding a white flower and green foliage, and what looks like a black tree stump. Two more birds, one white with red markings, the other blue, yellow, and pink, sit above the mouth of the cave, the white one near a wire pear tree with green paper foliage and red and yellow painted composition fruit. On a rock behind Saint Antony stands a figure, presumably the Devil, with an opaque brownish yellow body, a long, curved beak-shaped black nose, and a black horn, wearing a light blue and amethyst striped skirt and a blue strap across his chest, and holding a black pitchfork in his left hand. Gesticulating in the right foreground are two demons, one dark brown with female breasts, hairy legs, a pointed blue nose, dark green wing stubs, and a long, curved tail; the other opaque brownish yellow with a pointed animal-like face, black horns, blue wings, and a long tail wrapped around his waist. In the center foreground stands a demon with a white face with a pink nose and yellow cheeks, black horns, a dark brown torso and arms, brownish yellow legs, black wings, and a twisted tail. The demon in the left foreground has a black face and horns, pearl-like earrings, a dark brown body, variegated wings, and a brown tail with a yellow tip and holds a tubular, pink-tipped white object (a candle?) in each hand. At left center stands an opaque green figure with outstretched arms, hairy legs, a long beak, and black horns. Next are a demon with a gray skull and white teeth, a nude gray torso with pendant breasts, hairy black legs, and colorless wings; and one with a dark pink face and beak, black earrings, a dark brown torso with pendant breasts, hairy black legs, claw feet, and a curled tail. Behind them stands a white-skinned, pink-cheeked figure wearing pink earrings, a turquoise blue blouse with white trim and a pink bow at the neck, and an opaque yellow skirt and holding a brown glass mirror with a blue frame to admire an elaborate coiffure; the hair only partly conceals a pair of black horns, and the creature's black animal's paws can be seen beneath the hem of the skirt. At the back of the scene, to the left of the cave, are a demon with a blue body, a black face with a prominent beak, black hair and horns, a flared blue feather headdress, blue wings, and a bird's tail and a bearded demon disguised in a tan monk's habit, his small black horns visible beneath the cowl. A small opaque light blue flying demon is mounted on a wire at Saint Antony's right, and a tiny black glass figure with a ring for suspension on its head stands nearby. The composition is mounted on a rectangular wooden base with cut molded sides.

The group dirty; one of the Devil's horns missing and something missing from his belt; wing missing and left arm broken on dark brown female demon; one arm missing on opaque yellow demon; one wing broken and partly missing on brown and black demon; one hand broken and fingers missing on light green demon; wings broken and glued on female skeletal

demon; both arms broken, one cemented and painted, the other exposing wire, on dark brown demon; both arms and one wing missing on blue demon. The small black glass figure is undoubtedly a later addition to the scene and was perhaps originally made as a decorative charm for a necklace. Glass cover missing.

Longwave fluorescence. Brown glass (Saint Antony): dark brown. Pink glass face (Saint Antony): dark red. Opaque brownish yellow (demon at upper right): dark red. Yellow (jug): dark red. Composition: dark brown. *Shortwave fluorescence.* Opaque white glass (rabbit, ram, urn): brilliant bluish white. Pink glass faces: fainter bluish white. Remainder of glass: nothing.

PROVENANCE: Viva (Mrs. William) King, England (King sale 1958, lot 91).

Although the figures in the tableaux (Nos. 99–105) were neither X-rayed nor removed from their bases to inspect their construction, they were most certainly made in the manner described in No. 88.

Saint Antony the Abbot, also called Antony the Great, is said to have been born near Memphis, in Upper Egypt, in about 251. Before he was twenty years old, he distributed the wealth he had inherited to the poor and took up the life of a hermit. Although he attracted many disciples and organized a number of monastic communities, he spent most of his very long life alone. He died in 356 in his cave on Mount Kolzim, near the Red Sea.[1]

NOTE:

1. See Thurston and Attwater 1956, vol. 1, pp. 104–9.

Probably France, Nevers, eighteenth century

102. The Supper at Emmaus

1975.1.1573
H. 27 cm, w. 36 cm, d. 18 cm. Figures and flowers of lampworked glass (opaque white, pink, lavender, green, brown, purple, black, blue, light blue, and colorless), cardboard, paper, shells, glass mirror plate, glass chips, imitation leather (paper), cloth, paint, composition material, wire, fabric. Assembled.

On a raised platform at the center back of a trapezoidal cardboard box with a tapered top and sides and an open rectangular front, Christ and two disciples sit on square wooden stools with blue painted tops and black dots on the sides at a cardboard table with four wire legs. Christ, one arm raised in blessing, sits at the back of the table. He has pink cheeks, brown eyes and eyebrows, and a brown beard and hair, and he is barefoot and wears a pink robe and a blue cape. The disciple at the left, also barefoot, with both hands raised, has short,

curly brown hair and wears a purple robe and a black mantle. The disciple at the right, with a curly brown beard and hair and wearing a light blue robe and a black mantle, gestures toward Christ with one hand and clutches the other to his chest. The floor of the platform on which they sit is covered with paper painted in a red-and-black checkerboard pattern, and its front is covered with a piece of mirror plate. At either side of the platform are shell-encrusted stairs with painted dark green edges and red risers that lead down to a painted brown curving path. Below the platform is a rectangular glass mirror pond surrounded by decorative shrubs with paper foliage and painted composition fruit mounted on paper-wrapped wire stems, low flowering plants with lampworked pink and blue flowers, and raveled green fabric grass. Two servants stand at either side of the pond; the one at the left wears a white robe and blue-edged cloak, the one at the right, a white apron,

No. 102

a blue turban, green breeches, and white hose. The exterior of the box, covered with paper imitation leather, encases an inner frame of thick cardboard encrusted with multicolored glass chips and shells arranged on the sides in decorative roundels and across the front on pendant swags. The ceiling is painted variegated blue-green and brown; two rectangular glass mirrors framed with shells are affixed to each side, and on the back is another rectangular glass mirror (one edge of which is beveled) framed with shells and flanked by four hollow colorless glass columns stuffed with multicolored paper and set into stepped blue bases.[1]

The scene dirty; the cardboard torn, patched, warped, delaminating, and powdery; the paper imitation leather covering the outer surface patched with paper and cloth tape; dishes apparently missing from the table, where glue spots remain. The "glazed front" described in the catalogue of the King sale in 1958 now missing.

Longwave fluorescence. Opaque white glass: dark red. Pink glass: dark red. Green glass: dark red. Lavender glass: dark red. Black glass: black. Blue glass: black. Colorless glass (columns): gray. Mirrors: faint orange. Painted composition: dark green. *Shortwave fluorescence.* Opaque white glass: strong bluish white. Pink glass: faint bluish white. Green glass: faint greenish gray. Lavender glass: purplish white. Black glass: black. Blue glass: black. Colorless glass (columns): faint purple reflection (perhaps from the paper). Mirrors: purplish.

PROVENANCE: Viva (Mrs. William) King, England (King sale 1958, lot 93).

The scene depicts the story of the Supper at Emmaus, which is told in Luke 24:28–32.

NOTE:
1. A white rectangular paper tag printed *84* and attached to a string has been removed and is in the Robert Lehman Collection files.

No. 103

Probably France, Nevers, eighteenth century

103. The Life of Christ

1975.1.1578

H. 63.5 cm, w. 81.9 cm, d. 37.2 cm. Figures of lampworked glass (opaque white, turquoise blue, bright blue, light blue, green, yellow, orange, yellow-orange, brown, yellowish brown, dark brown, black, gray, gold aventurine, and colorless), mirror and glass plate (some reverse painted), wood, cardboard, paper, fabric, shells, glass bead, paint, wire, composition material, cork, metal. Assembled.

Thirteen scenes from the life of Christ are depicted on three levels in a trapezoidal cream-painted wooden box mounted within a larger wooden box. The inner box has a tapered top and sides and a rectangular front; its front edges are covered with printed paper borders, and its sides are encrusted with crumpled paper, shells, and a white granular substance to resemble the walls of a grotto. Scattered throughout the

tableau are paper plants, dried flowers, and seashells. The scenes represented are:

The Nativity (bottom tier left). Two brown glass camels with tan and green woven fabric saddle blankets and bearing red silk bundles stand in a deep, shell-encrusted tunnel, with two fragmentary flat glass panels, one reverse painted with a landscape with buildings, on the left wall. To the right is a cave, the walls and ceiling of which are covered with crumpled paper and encrusted with granular white bits, shells, and paper plants on wire stems. A white infant Jesus with brown hair lies on a white bed edged with yellow threading in the front of the cave. Mary, in a white robe with a black cord at the waist, a white veil, and a turquoise blue mantle, kneels to the left of the bed, and Joseph, in a light blue robe and gold mantle, kneels to the right. Standing behind the infant are a gold and gray ox with black horns and a brown donkey. A male figure wearing a blue

261

frock coat with white buttons, black breeches, white stockings, black shoes, and a green hat and carrying a brown glass osier basket on his back watches from the left front of the scene. A tiny brown stag and a brown dog stand in the foreground. In the back of the cave is a feeding trough below a rack of hay made of wood shavings.

The Flight into Egypt (bottom tier left center). Mary, wearing a white dress and a turquoise mantle and carrying the infant Jesus in her arms, rides on a brown donkey. Joseph walks at the left, wearing a light blue coat, a gold mantle, white stockings, black shoes, and a black hat. In the foreground is a white dog with black spots. Mounted on the left wall of the scene is a mirror panel, the back wall is covered with a flat glass panel reverse painted with an arched cave entrance flanked by rocks and trees, and the ceiling is covered with crumpled painted paper.

The Baptism of Christ (bottom tier right center). Christ, in a white loincloth, stands facing Saint John the Baptist, who holds a staff and wears a fringed brown cape draped over one shoulder. On the right wall is a rectangular piece of glass with a front- and reverse-painted scene of a mill, a waterwheel, and men fishing. A white dove hovers on a wire overhead, and another bird perches in a plant in the foreground.

Unidentified scene (bottom tier right). Christ, dressed in a white robe tied with a black cord at the waist and a turquoise mantle, stands at the right, gesturing to a man wearing a long black robe tied with a gold cord and a gold mantle and holding a pinkish object in his right hand. The right and back walls of the scene are covered with glass panels painted on the front and back with a landscape with buildings, and on the left wall is a mirror panel. In the background is an orchard of pear trees with wire bases and paper foliage and fruit, with two lampworked white glass birds sitting in one of the trees.

Jesus and the Woman of Samaria (middle tier left). A woman dressed in a green robe and a gold mantle stands by a lampworked white glass well with a wire frame and a black glass pulley but no bucket. The well stands in a room with an arched doorway, a mirror panel on its back wall, and its left wall covered with crumpled paper studded with granular white bits. The left wall, outside the arch, is covered with a glass panel painted on the front and back with a landscape with a mill and a waterwheel.

The Last Supper (middle tier left center). At the left side of a large room framed by a white balustrade and two Doric columns, with potted plants set along its front edge, eight male figures sit in two groups of four on benches with red silk cushions at a long table with turned bulbous legs and an X-shaped stretcher with a central finial. The table is covered with a lace cloth, and in its center is an oval tray holding a painted-composition fish, a dark brown glass jug, a conical glass decanter painted red, a tray of seven glass goblets, a faceted glass bead, a piece of cork (for bread), and a large tray filled with bits of crumpled tan paper. Gray paper plates, knives, and forks are scattered on the table in front of the figures, which are attached to the benches with long wires. The room has an orangish brown and white checkered floor, the ceiling is painted white, and the walls are covered with red silk, at the back above a paper dado painted to look like white marble with brown-veined marble insets and moldings. On the left wall is a mirror with a rounded top, on the right a miniature painting. Two more paintings hang on the back wall, on either side of a fireplace with a marbleized mantel and an overmantel with sconces, one with a candle, hung on a white frame enclosing a mirror below a painted landscape. Two painted paper fans or screens hang on the wall at the left of the overmantel, and the fireplace

is equipped with glass bellows and a metal shovel and tongs (but no andirons). Two caned chairs with cut cardboard legs and stretchers sit on either side of the fireplace and another sits against the right wall. On the chair to the right of the fireplace a painted-composition calico cat sits hissing at a white glass dog on the floor. On the right wall is a doorway with two paneled doors standing open to the garden that is the next scene. To the left of the doorway is a commode with double fielded-panel doors and two blue-trimmed gold aventurine glass candlesticks on top; to the right is a table holding an oval pan below a metal lavabo fastened to the wall.

Unidentified scene (middle tier right center). In a garden with C-scroll paths formed of bent wire and dark green fiber "pipe cleaners," a shepherd dressed in white, with a ruff and a brown hat, and carrying a brown openwork basket over one arm tends four white sheep and a black ram by a mirror-glass pond. Standing at the back of the scene is another male figure dressed in a blue jacket, yellow breeches, white stockings, and black shoes and playing a yellow pipe. In the foreground, facing into the scene, is a brown-haired figure wearing a yellow robe and a blue mantle. A white swan and several other birds, a yellow lion, a green striped snake, and a white rabbit are scattered in the garden. On the back wall is a mirror panel, and the ceiling is covered with crumpled paper and shells and sprinkled with a white granular substance.

Unidentified scene (middle tier right). In a landscape of glass birds perched in wire and paper pear trees, Christ, wearing a white robe and a turquoise mantle, sits at the right, facing a buxom woman wearing a fitted gold coat with a gray sash and a turquoise blue skirt and tending a white sheep and a black ram. On the right wall is a sheet of glass with a front- and reverse-painted scene of classical ruins, and on the back wall is a mirror panel. In the right foreground is an angel with a turquoise loincloth and gold wings, looking down on the scene in the bottom tier.

The Agony in the Garden (top tier left). Christ, in a white robe and turquoise mantle, kneels in the Garden of Gethsemane before an angel in a green loincloth who holds a yellow object in his left hand. The three disciples sleep in the foreground. On the left wall are a fragmentary reverse-painted glass panel and a large fragment of mirror panel; on the back wall is a glass panel reverse painted with a landscape.

Christ before Pilate (top tier left center). Christ, dressed in a white cape and loincloth and wearing the crown of thorns, his hands bound in front and his legs bleeding, stands at the top of a double staircase outside the door of Pontius Pilate's house, a white building with yellow vines painted over the doorway and around the two windows. Two mustached soldiers in spiked blue helmets, one with a green tunic and black boots, the other with a blue tunic and green boots, both carrying lances, stand behind Christ. Pilate stands beside him, dressed in a gold robe with an aventurine pattern and tied with a blue, black, and white striped sash; a turquoise cloak with an aventurine pattern, yellow trim, and a white collar; and a white and blue turban with aventurine trim. The interior of the house is mirrored, and the paved courtyard in the foreground is lined with potted plants.

The Road to Calvary(?) (top tier right center). Against a backdrop of a building reverse painted on a glass panel on the back wall of the scene, two soldiers dressed in blue, gold, and turquoise, with pointed helmets, and two other figures, one with a large hammer, the other wearing a brown tunic and a black hat topped by a green knob, surround Christ as he kneels on the ground. Christ wears a white robe and the crown of thorns.

The Crucifixion (top tier right center). The three crosses, with Christ with his crown of thorns in the center and the two thieves on either side, all three wearing white loincloths, stand against a mirrored background. Mary stands in the foreground, wearing a white dress and a turquoise mantle. Behind her stands a soldier in a pointed blue helmet. Two glass birds perch in the flowering trees at the back of the scene.

The Resurrection (top tier right). Christ, draped in a long, narrow white loincloth and with one arm raised in blessing, rises from an open sarcophagus lined with fabric. A guard in a green tunic and a blue helmet sits at the left, turning away and shielding his eyes. A black glass dog sits nearby. Another guard, in a blue tunic and a black helmet, lies asleep in the foreground. On the right wall are a mirror panel and a glass panel front and reverse painted with a landscape with buildings. The ceiling above the Resurrection is paper painted sky blue, with a gold and green glory in the center.

The grotto dirty; the stag and the dog in the Nativity probably recent additions; the figure of Christ missing from the Woman of Samaria scene; other figures and decorative details probably missing or incorrectly placed; the head of Jesus in the Resurrection repaired and painted. According to the catalogue of the King sale of 1958, the grotto had a glass front that is now missing; the outer wooden box is new (the outside of the inner box could not be examined).

Longwave fluorescence. Opaque white glass: brilliant orange. Bright blue glass: dark purplish blue. Light blue glass: dark purplish blue. Green glass: black. Yellow-orange glass: dark red. Brown glass: purplish red reflection. *Shortwave fluorescence.* Opaque white glass: strong bluish white. Bright blue glass: black. Light blue glass: light blue. Green glass: dark blue. Yellow-orange glass: faint yellow-green. Brown glass: mottled greenish.

PROVENANCE: Viva (Mrs. William) King, England (King sale 1958, lot 94).

Although the figures in the tableaux (Nos. 99–105) were neither X-rayed nor removed from their bases to inspect their construction, they were most certainly made in the manner described in No. 88.

A large diorama of the Nativity in the Kunstgewerbemuseum, Berlin, with lampworked figures similar to those in this tableau has been attributed to Nevers and dated to the first half of the eighteenth century.[1]

NOTE:
1. Kunstgewerbemuseum, 1971,88; Dreier 1991, p. 142, no. 161.

Probably France, Nevers, eighteenth century

104. The Crucifixion and the Entombment

1975.1.1575

H. 29.5 cm, w. 31.3 cm, d. 23 cm. Figures of lampworked glass (opaque white, black, red, yellow, brown, pink, green, light green, blue, bright blue, light blue, gold aventurine, and colorless), cardboard, papier-mâché, glass mirror plate, glass seed beads, shells, paper, ivory(?), wire, wood, cork, paint. Assembled.

The two scenes, with their papier-mâché walls, are mounted, one above the other, on a rectangular wooden base with applied black-painted moldings grooved to fit a glass cover. The upper scene depicts the Crucifixion, with the crucified Christ, made of a carved white material (ivory?), with red stains on his hands and feet, cemented to a wooden cross with a blank white paper tablet attached to its top. Saint John the Baptist, his left hand extended and his right hand on his heart, stands at Christ's left. Like all the glass figures (except the extraneous woman in the lower scene) he has opaque white skin, black eyes, brown hair, and pink cheeks. He wears a white mantle over a green robe with yellow trim at the neck and a yellow cord at the waist. The Virgin stands with outstretched arms at Christ's right, wearing a pale green mantle over a white robe with pink trim at the neck and a pink cord at the waist, her brown hair partly covered with a white veil. A woman with long curly brown hair (Mary Magdalene?), also in a white robe with pink trim at the neck and a pink cord at the waist but with a pale blue mantle, kneels behind the Virgin. A third woman (Mary or Salome?), wearing a white dress and a brown (painted) mantle and veil, her arms upraised, strides up the path toward the cross. Three figures with upraised arms kneeling behind John the Baptist might represent saints; all three have shaved tonsures and wear black robes tied with white cords, and two of them have yellow rosaries and crosses suspended from their belts. In the background is a bocage with trees made of paper and thread and seven colorful birds of lampworked glass. Scattered in the landscape are six stylized flowering plants formed of tiny glass seed beads strung on wires.

The lower scene depicts the Entombment, set in a shell-encrusted grotto. The dead Christ, lying on a bier, is attended by a female figure with long curly brown hair and upraised arms who wears a blue mantle over a white robe with pink trim at the neck and a pink cord at the waist. A much larger figure of a woman, mounted on a translucent light green glass base, stands at the right; she has translucent pinkish white flesh, a pink mouth, brown eyebrows, black eyes, and gold

No. 104

aventurine hair and is dressed in a sealing-wax red dress with a white collar and cuffs and a pale blue cord at the waist, a bright blue mantle, a white veil with yellow trim, and black shoes. At the back to the right is an oval mirror-glass pond, and there is another, round pond in the foreground. A white swan and another white bird sit on the water; another white bird sits amid the coral and seashells that edge the ponds.

From the back it can be seen that the crumpled paper used to make the grotto is printed with French text and that the corners of the scenes are reinforced with cylindrical bottle corks.[1]

The scene dirty; the out-of-scale ivory(?) figure of Christ a replacement; the arm of the cross replaced; a figure missing from the lower scene and the out-of-scale female figure added; several figures broken and repaired; several parts detached and reattached; glass cover missing.

Longwave fluorescence. White ivory(?) figure: strong white. Opaque white glass: dark red. One white bird: strong bluish white. Black glass: black. Green glass: faint blue. Pink glass: dark red. Yellow glass: faint yellowish. Composition: strong gray. *Shortwave fluorescence.* White ivory(?) figure: gray. Opaque white glass: gray. Black glass: black. Green glass: dark red. Pink glass: gray. Yellow glass: dark red. Blue glass: dark blue. Composition: faint gray.

PROVENANCE: Viva (Mrs. William) King, England (King sale 1958, lot 92).

Although the figures in the tableaux (Nos. 99–105) were neither X-rayed nor removed from their bases to inspect their construction, they were most certainly made in the manner described in No. 88.

The large female figure in the lower scene, which the catalogue of the King sale in 1958 called a Mourning Virgin, does not belong there. The scene may originally have had two female figures, representing Mary Magdalene and Mary the mother of Joseph and James, whom two of the Gospels (Matthew 27:58–61 and Mark 15:47) place at the sepulcher just after the Entombment.

NOTE:
1. A white rectangular paper tag printed 92 and attached to a string has been removed and is in the Robert Lehman Collection files.

Probably France, possibly England, mid-nineteenth century

105. Cabriolet with driver

1975.1.1574
H. 7.6 cm, w. 18.7 cm, d. 12.4 cm. Figure, horse, and cabriolet of lampworked glass (opaque white, yellow, yellow-orange, green, dark green, blue, light blue, dark blue, brown, dark brown, transparent amber, and colorless), composition material, iron wire, wood, fabric. Assembled.

The driver wears a dark blue tailcoat with white buttons, a yellow-orange stock, and white trousers. (An iron wire projecting from the top of his head presumably held a top hat.) He cracks a tapered and rippled iron wire whip with his left arm as he rides in an open cabriolet of opaque brown glass with yellow-orange decoration on the sides and back, white decoration on the flat front, and dark brown wheels mounted on an iron wire axle. The white horse harnessed to the upward-curving shafts of the carriage has a yellow-orange tail and a transparent

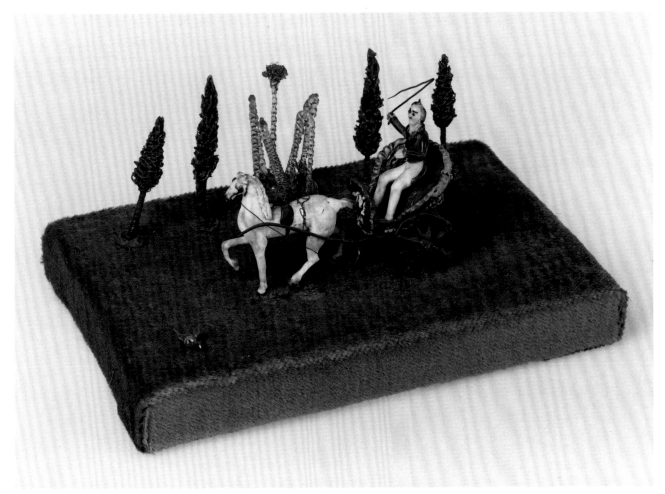

No. 105

amber bit. Behind the cart is a stylized fountain, a spiral of colorless glass with four arched sprays of spirally ribbed colorless glass around a froth-topped jet. On each side of the fountain are two cypress trees, with foliage formed of spun opaque green glass and darker green trunks, set into painted composition bases. A lampworked peacock of yellow and dark and light blue glass sits in the left foreground. The group is mounted on a rectangular wooden base covered with faded amber-colored velvet.

The wheels of the cabriolet (apparently meant to rotate freely on the wire axle), the bases of the trees, and the central jet of the fountain broken; the driver's top hat missing; the horse broken, repaired, and painted; the peacock broken and cemented back together; the velvet-covered base a replacement.

Longwave fluorescence. Opaque white glass: dark tan. Brown glass: dark brown. Blue glass: black. Yellow glass: yellowish white. Green glass: dark brown. Colorless glass: yellowish. *Shortwave fluorescence.* Opaque white glass: purplish white. Brown glass: dark brown. Blue glass: dark blue. Yellow glass: dark brown. Green glass: purplish black. Colorless glass: faint brownish orange.

PROVENANCE: Viva (Mrs. William) King, England (King sale 1958, lot 87).

The catalogue of the King sale in 1958 called this "an amusing group, perhaps by Lambourd." The attribution may have been Viva King's; in 1939 she wrote that "in 1845 one Lambourd was recommended by the 'Journal des Demoiselles' for 'the most terrible animals, the most pretty birds, the fruits of the earth, the sweet flowers executed in glass of a marvellous resemblance by means of a lamp. M. Lambourd melts the glass, turns it, pulls it out, rounds it and in five minutes his agile fingers have created two doves, an elegant hare and a rose.'"[1] I know of no documented work by Lambourd, however, unless either Mrs. King or the *Journal* got it wrong and meant René Lambourg (1780–1880), who as Barrelet put it "ends the line of great *émailleurs* and, more particularly, of Saumurian artisans, who probably executed a good number of works that have been attributed to Nevers." Barrelet illustrated a lampworked model of the cavalry school at Saumur that Lambourg made about 1820 and that is now in the Musée de Saumur.[2]

Whether our model was made by either Lambourd or Lambourg is impossible to tell. The carriage and the driver's clothing could be either French or English.

NOTES:
1. Quoted in King 1939, p. 110.
2. Barrelet 1960, pp. 308–10, fig. 19.

266

REVERSE PAINTING ON GLASS AND ROCK CRYSTAL

Sixteenth to Nineteenth Century

Reverse Painting on Glass and Rock Crystal

When an oil painting on canvas, wood, plaster, or metal is finished, the support essentially disappears, and the painting may even be (and occasionally is) removed from it. When an image is painted on the back of a transparent glass or polished rock crystal support and meant to be viewed through it, the substrate becomes an integral part of the painting. Reverse paintings have several other unique characteristics. The most obvious is that the paints seem to retain a wetness that most other types of older paintings lack. Also, although the bond between oil paints and glass is not very strong and the paintings are consequently very fragile, the paint seems to retain a freshness of color that does not fade over time and cannot be varnished (with consequent yellowing) or, with few exceptions, restored or repainted. When a reverse painting on glass survives in relatively undamaged condition, we see it in much the same way that the artist did when it was completed.

At least eighteen fundamentally different techniques of applying paint to glass to create a reverse painting have been identified.[1] The most primitive method is to paint the highlights first, then proceed backward to produce the complete image – the reverse of the approach of painting on a canvas. In a reverse-painted portrait this means that the pupil of an eye must be painted before the iris, and the iris before the white of the eye, and so on. Reverse paintings were frequently made by placing outline drawings or prints under the glass and tracing them, as was likely done on the twelve-lobed dish in the Robert Lehman Collection (No. 25). More complex works were created by working the colors so thinly they are translucent, and the layers of paint show through one another. The image could also be modeled by laying down the paint in varying thicknesses.

The technique of reverse painting on glass can be traced to the Roman era. Most of the surviving examples are vessels.[2] One of the most elaborate is the dish in the Corning Museum of Glass known as the Paris Plate, which has a depiction of the Judgment of Paris painted on its exterior (Fig. K). The Paris Plate, said to have been found in Syria just south of Damascus, has been dated to the third or fourth century A.D.[3] After the fall of Rome in the fifth century, reverse-painted glass objects seem not to have been made in Europe until about the twelfth cen-

tury, or at least none seem to have survived.[4] In the twelfth century small reverse-decorated glass or rock crystal panels began to be set into altars, tombs, pulpits, and religious paintings. There is little in the way of painted imagery in these works. The design was usually scratched out in a layer of gold leaf applied to the back of the panel, then sealed and protected with a contrasting layer of opaque pigment. Modeling could be accomplished only by hatching.

Fully developed reverse paintings on glass and rock crystal were being produced in northern and southern Europe by the beginning of the sixteenth century. Lombardy in northern Italy was one of the most important centers. Small reverse-painted panels incorporated in jewelry, particularly pendants like those in the Robert Lehman Collection (Nos. 107–11), displayed images of saints and biblical scenes in breathtaking, almost microscopic detail. Reverse-painted glass vessels were also made in both Venice and northern Europe in the sixteenth century (see Nos. 25, 26).

Fig. K. The Paris Plate. Roman Empire, third to fourth century, reputedly found in southern Syria. Corning Museum of Glass

269

In the early seventeenth century sophisticated reverse paintings were being produced in every country of Europe. As stained-glass panels for homes became less fashionable, many of the artists turned to reverse painting. One of the important centers was Switzerland, where three frames with reverse-painted glass friezes in the Robert Lehman Collection (Nos. 112–14) may have been made. The names of more than one hundred artists, more than twenty of them in Zurich alone, working in Switzerland in the early 1600s are known.[5] In addition to meeting local demands, the Swiss developed a brisk business exporting painted glass panels to Naples, where they were mounted in furniture.

The art of reverse painting reached its zenith in the eighteenth century. The medium was not especially adaptable to the cool, neoclassical style that was in vogue by the late 1700s. Reverse-gilt glass panels became popular at the end of the eighteenth century as mounts for frames and as decorative mats for drawings and prints. The most common (but inaccurate) term for reverse paintings on glass – *verre églomisé* – derives from the name of a late eighteenth-century Parisian art dealer, Jean Baptiste Glomy (d. 1786), who used the process for creating decorative mounts for prints.

Reverse painting on glass survived the eighteenth century as a folk art in practically every area of the world. Today artists occasionally toy with the technique, but few modern reverse-painted works have achieved significant artistic success.

NOTES:
1. See Ryser 1991, pp. 289–92.
2. Although they are often claimed to be reverse painted, the *fondi d'oro* (gold glasses) of Roman origin were not, in fact, created by that technique. Rather, they were most likely made by laying gold leaf on top of a glass disk, then scratching and stippling the decoration into the leaf. When the decoration was complete, molten glass was blown onto the disk, fusing with it and trapping and protecting the delicate gilt layer between the two sheets of glass. For examples of Roman gold glasses, see London 1968b, pp. 67–70; Corning (and other cities) 1987, pp. 276–86; Ryser 1991, pp. 34–35; Corning 1992, p. 11.
3. Corning Museum of Glass, 55.1.85 (ex coll. Ray Winfield Smith); Corning–London–Cologne 1987, pp. 260–61, 271, no. 149.
4. See Swarzenski 1940, pp. 55ff.
5. See Ryser 1992, p. 22.

Frame: probably Aachen (Reinhold Vasters), ca. 1870–90; reverse-painted panels: Italy, probably Lombardy, second half of the sixteenth century

106. Tabernacular house altar

1975.1.1558

H. 41 cm, w. 20.4 cm, d. 6 cm. Frame of ebony-veneered soft wood, rock crystal, agate, silver gilt; panels of cut and polished reverse-painted and reverse-gilt rock crystal. Assembled.

The tabernacle frame has a semicircular pediment, rock crystal columns with silver-gilt Corinthian capitals and bases, and turned rock crystal bun feet. A cast silver-gilt relief of God the Father in benediction fills the pediment, which is surmounted by an agate urn with silver-gilt mounts flanked by two pointed agate finials, and cast silver-gilt appliqués decorate the entablature, the columns, the wooden panel behind them, and the

predella. The columns flank an arched panel of thin, flat, polished rock crystal with a gilt frame set into an opening cut in the wood, and nine rectangular panels of rock crystal with reverse-gilt borders are set into recesses cut in the predella and the pedestals. The reverse-painted and reverse-gilt scene in the large arched panel represents the Adoration of the Shepherds; that in the horizontal panel in the center of the predella is of the Adoration of the Magi, and the four smaller, vertical plaques on either side depict, from left to right, the eucharistic host, chalice, and paten; the sudarium; Gabriel; the Virgin; a cloak and spears; and arma Christi. The back of the arched

No. 106

rock crystal panel is covered with thick silver paint or amalgam, gold leaf, and black paint. On the back of the frame, two gummed paper labels, one an oval tan label printed COLLECTION / 1893 / SPITZER in black; the other a rectangular tan label with cut corners, a printed border of two red lines, and C12047 / R.L. written in dark brown ink (Robert Lehman collection).

Severe separation of the paint from the crystal. On the frame, ebony veneer missing in several places; parts of the wooden molding missing from the sides; silver-gilt appliqué missing from the base of the left finial and from the top of the molding on the right side; urns missing from the projecting plinths at the sides and the plinths rounded off (the small sockets for the urns remain). The urns shown in the drawing (Fig. 106.1) were already missing by 1893, when the altar was illustrated in the

No. 106, *detail of center panel*

No. 106, *details of sides of column bases*

No. 106, *predella and column bases*

catalogue of the Spitzer sale. The plinths were not yet rounded off in the 1893 illustration; they are rounded off in the photograph that appears in the catalogue of the 1929 sale.

No fluorescence.

PROVENANCE: Frédéric Spitzer, Paris (Spitzer sale 1893, vol. 2, lot 2092, vol. 3, pl. 51; Spitzer sale 1929, lot 599, ill.).

LITERATURE: Molinier 1891, p. 64, no. 5; Hackenbroch 1986, pp. 253–54, fig. 185.

In most areas the colored pigments on the rock crystal panels appear to have been laid down first, before the gold leaf, which shows through scratches in the paint layers. The small rectangular crystal panels were cemented into recesses cut in the wood frame rather than being held in place with metal frames, as would have been typical in the sixteenth century.

The date of this house altar and several other pieces once owned by the dealer Frédéric Spitzer (1815–1890) was questioned in 1986, when Hackenbroch published a group of sketches from a large collection of goldsmiths' designs that the Victoria and Albert Museum in London acquired in 1919. Two of the drawings in the collection are signed by the German silversmith and goldsmith Reinhold Vasters (1827–1909), and several others bear notations in his handwriting.[1] From 1853 to about 1869 Vasters served as restorer at the Aachen cathedral treasury, where in the spirit of nineteenth-century historicism he not only restored but also replaced worn or damaged liturgical objects. Little is known about his career from the time he left the cathedral until he retired in 1895 except that he became more prosperous and that he amassed a large collection of decorative arts objects, but Hackenbroch has made a convincing if circumstantial case for a close and long-standing collaboration between him and Spitzer, who had a firm in Aachen from about 1855 to about 1868. It has become apparent that Spitzer, as Hackenbroch puts it, had "a proclivity for obscuring or inventing provenances, for combining old with old or old with new to complete, to beautify (in terms of contemporary taste), or simply to multiply objects."[2]

In the catalogue of the Spitzer collection published in 1891, Molinier describes this house altar as an Italian work of the sixteenth century. The catalogue of the 1929 Spitzer sale lists it as Italian, late sixteenth or early seventeenth century, and attributes the painting to the Florentine miniaturist Gianbattista Stefaneschi. The existence of a sketch of the altar (Fig. 106.1)[3] among the drawings

Fig. 106.1 Reinhold Vasters, *Design for a House Altar*. Victoria and Albert Museum, London. By courtesy of the Board of Trustees of the Victoria and Albert Museum

Fig. 106.2 Reverse-painted panel. Museo Civico d'Arte Antica, Turin. Photograph: Archivio Fotografico dei Musei Civici di Torino

in the Victoria and Albert Museum, however, leaves little doubt that though its style is early seventeenth century, the wooden framework was built in the nineteenth century, probably by Vasters or someone in his workshop, probably at Spitzer's request, to house a set of sixteenth-century reverse-painted panels. The unified program and the similarity of the style of the painting on the ten rock crystal panels suggest that they were scavenged from a single piece. The reverse painting of the Nativity on a small oval glass panel in the Museo Civico d'Arte Antica, Turin (Fig. 106.2), that Pettenati has called "Lombard(?), second half of the sixteenth century," may be by the same artist.[4]

NOTES:

1. See Hackenbroch 1986, p. 164, n. 3. The entire collection of drawings was apparently sold to the London dealer Murray Marks at the Vasters sale (Anton Creutzer, Aachen, 26–27 October 1909), then acquired at the Marks sale (Christie's, London, 5 July 1918, lot 17) by Lazare Lowenstein, who presented it to the Victoria and Albert Museum in 1919.
2. Hackenbroch 1986, p. 172.
3. Victoria and Albert Museum, E.2780-1919; ibid., fig. 186.
4. Museo Civico d'Arte Antica, V.O.206-3073/A (ex coll. Carlo and Federico Proglio); Pettenati 1978, p. 48, no. 70, fig. 78.

Italy, probably Lombardy, sixteenth century

107. Devotional pendant

1975.1.1519

H. 5.7 cm, w. 4.2 cm, d. .5 cm. Cut and polished, reverse-painted, reverse-gilt, and reverse-silvered rock crystal; gold wire; gold; enamel. Assembled.

The pendant is a flattened oval of rock crystal with its edge decorated with carved stylized foliage and a shallow oval recess cut in each face. Two convex oval rock crystal plaques held in place by narrow gold frames decorated with bead-and-reel molding are fitted into the recesses. On each plaque is a reverse-painted and reverse-gilt bust of a saint identified in Greek letters: Elias on one side; indecipherable on the other. Holes have been drilled through the pendant from top to bottom and from side to side and the openings covered with enameled gold foliate fittings. Two metal pins, one with loops on the ends, the other with balls, are threaded through the holes, and three sections of gold chain are attached to the loops at the top and on the mounts on the sides and to the lowermost of three large gold rings.

Slight separation of the paint from the crystal; a decorative pendant probably missing from the bottom loop.

No fluorescence.

PROVENANCE: Roman Abt, Lucerne (sale, Galerie Fischer, Lucerne, 18–19 August 1939, lot 269, pl. 16).

Fig. 107.1 Pendant. Museo Civico d'Arte Antica, Turin. Photograph: Archivio Fotografico dei Musei Civici di Torino

No. 107, *front (enlarged)*

No. 107, *back (enlarged)*

The backs of the reverse-painted panels could not be examined. The colored paints were probably applied first, the gold and silver leaf last.

This pendant was probably made in Lombardy, one of the principal centers for the production of reverse-painted devotional pendants in the sixteenth century. The painted and gilt decoration is typically more precise and more painterly on Lombard pendants than on those produced at the same time in Nürnberg and Spain.[1] Reverse paintings from Nürnberg tend to be more graphic, with a greater use of gold leaf to create images. A related carved rock crystal pendant in the Museo Civico d'Arte Antica, Turin, with reverse-painted inset plaques depicting Saint John the Baptist and (on the reverse) the Entombment

(Fig. 107.1), has been attributed to sixteenth-century Italy.[2] Another, similar pendant in the Wernher Collection, Luton Hoo, Bedfordshire, with a depiction of the Annunciation and a pearl-like ornament still suspended from the loop on the bottom, is said to have been made in Italy in the late sixteenth century.[3] Three other related pieces, attributed to Spain and dated to the sixteenth or seventeenth century, were formerly in the collection of José Lázaro and Paula Florido de Lázaro in Madrid.[4]

NOTES:
1. See Corning 1992, pp. 22, 45–47, 134–35.
2. Museo Civico d'Arte Antica, v.o.242; Viale 1948, pp. 153, 155, fig. 53; Pettenati 1978, pp. 49–50, no. 78, fig. 86.
3. Bradford 1953, ill. p. 40 (right).
4. Reinach et al. 1927, p. 395, no. 911.

Italy, late sixteenth century

108. Devotional pendant

1975.1.1511

H. 6.6 cm, w. 5.5 cm, d. 1.6 cm. Cut and polished, reverse-painted and reverse-gilt rock crystal; silver gilt. Assembled.

The pendant is a flattened oval composed of two convex rock crystal plaques held back to back in a silver-gilt frame edged with a twisted band. Applied to each side of the band are two loops flanking a knob in a silver-gilt foliate fitting, and two loops in silver-gilt foliate fittings are applied to the top and bottom (the larger top loop with a ring through it). The crystal plaques are reverse painted in transparent colors backed with gold leaf; one depicts Saint Peter, the other the Crucifixion with two female figures, presumably the Virgin and Mary Magdalene.

Slight separation of the paint from the crystal; a chain or pendants, or both, missing from the side and bottom loops.

No fluorescence.

PROVENANCE: Not established.

The backs of the reverse-painted panels could not be examined.

The style and technique of the painting on this pendant relate it to other Italian examples (see Nos. 107, 110, 111).

No. 108, *front (enlarged)*

No. 108, *back (enlarged)*

Italy or Spain, sixteenth century; the mount probably later

109. Devotional pendant

1975.1.1520
Diam. 3.3 cm. Cut and polished, reverse-painted, reverse-gilt, and reverse-silvered rock crystal; lampworked glass; gold. Assembled.

The pendant is a solid hemisphere of rock crystal mounted in a plain gold cup suspended from two gold chains, each with three tiny hollow lampworked glass pearls, that are attached at the bottom to loops at the sides of the cup and at the top to a ring. A gold pin topped by a floret is inserted in a hole drilled through the center of the crystal to hold it in the cup. The scene on the flat back of the rock crystal, executed in paint and gold and silver, depicts the Annunciation, with Mary praying under a canopy at the left, the angel Gabriel standing with his right arm raised at the right, and a large jug in the foreground.

Two lampworked pearls broken.

Longwave fluorescence. Rock crystal: nothing. Glass pearls: translucent milky white. *Shortwave fluorescence.* Rock crystal: nothing. Glass pearls: strong white.

PROVENANCE: Probably Keele Hall, Staffordshire;[1] Henry Oppenheimer, London (Oppenheimer sale 1936, lot 82). Acquired by Robert Lehman in 1936.

The back of the crystal could not be examined, but it appears that the gold leaf was applied first and the details scratched through it. Silver leaf was applied after the gold for the faces and hands. The transparent red and black layers were painted last.

The rock crystal is probably half of what was to be (or may once have been) a spherical bead that has been fitted

No. 109 *(enlarged)*

with a gold mount of later date. A rosary in the Museo Civico d'Arte Antica, Turin, that Pettenati has tentatively attributed to Italy or Spain and dated to the sixteenth century has thirteen such beads reverse painted with depictions of New Testament scenes and saints (Fig. 109.1).[2] Pettenati cites a similar rosary in the Louvre, Paris.[3]

NOTES:
1. The 1936 Oppenheimer sale catalogue attributed the pendant to sixteenth-century France and described it as "from the Keele Hall Collection." It has not been possible to confirm that provenance, however; the piece does not appear in the catalogues of the Keele Hall sales of 1902 and 1906 (Christie's, London, 7 July 1902 and 22 May 1906).
2. Museo Civico, v.0.97-2984; Pettenati 1978, p. 47, no. 69, fig. 77.
3. Louvre, Orf. 398 (ex coll. Rothschild, 1901).

Fig. 109.1 Rosary. Museo Civico d'Arte Antica, Turin. Photograph: Archivio Fotografico dei Musei Civici di Torino

Italy, late sixteenth century

110. Plaque

1975.1.1556
H. 5 cm. Rock crystal. Cut, polished, reverse painted, reverse gilt.

The plaque is a flat oval of rock crystal with both faces polished and the rim beveled. The reverse-painted and reverse-gilt scene on the back, framed by a border of red and gilt stylized flowers on a green ground between two gilt bands, depicts the Adoration of the Shepherds: the Christ Child lies in a woven basket in the foreground, Mary kneels at the left with Joseph behind her, and two shepherds kneel at the right. The painting is coated with a thick black tarlike substance. Attached to the back of the panel: a rectangular translucent tan paper label with a printed red linear border and *Verre églomisé* [ ] (the rest illegible) written in black ink; a smaller rectangular translucent tan paper label with a printed red linear border and *878* printed in black; a rectangular green paper label with no apparent inscription; a circular white paper label with *45* written in red ballpoint pen (the last possibly Robert Lehman collection, the others unidentified).[1]

Slight separation of the paint from the crystal; no evidence of repainting.

No fluorescence.

PROVENANCE: Not established.

See No. 111.

NOTE:

1. A rectangular tan paper label with rounded corners and *L.56.31.31* (a Metropolitan Museum loan number) written in pencil has been removed and is in the Robert Lehman Collection files.

No. 110 *(enlarged)*

Italy, late sixteenth century

111. Plaque

1975.1.1557
H. 5 cm. Rock crystal. Cut, polished, reverse painted, reverse gilt.

The plaque is a flat oval of rock crystal with both faces polished and the rim beveled. The reverse-painted and reverse-gilt scene on the back, framed by a border of red and gilt stylized flowers on a green ground between two gilt bands, depicts the Deposition, with the dead Christ in the foreground surrounded by the three Maries and a cross in the background bearing the crown of thorns and a plaque inscribed *I.N.R.I.* The painting is coated with a thick black tarlike substance. .

Paint loss in the center; no evidence of repainting; the rim chipped.

No fluorescence.

PROVENANCE: Not established.

On Nos. 110 and 111 the translucent colors were applied first, then scratched to produce the details, and finally backed with gold leaf. The borders were produced by painting the gold florets, then backing them with transparent red and green and translucent blue-gray colors.

Nos. 110 and 111 were probably originally mounted back to back in a metal frame to form a devotional pendant. The style of the painting and the techniques used to make them relate them to No. 108.

It is unusual to find transparent green on sixteenth-century reverse paintings, particularly if they are in relatively good condition. The green paint, made using oxidized copper, seems to react chemically with other colors and was used only rarely.[1] A related medallion is in the Bargello, Florence.[2]

NOTES:
1. Sibyll Kummer-Rothenhäusler of the Galerie für Glasmalerei, Zurich, pointed this out during a visit to the Metropolitan Museum and the Corning Museum of Glass in April 1989.
2. I wish to thank Sibyll Kummer-Rothenhäusler for drawing my attention to this unpublished example.

No. 111 *(enlarged)*

No. 112

Probably Italy or Switzerland, possibly Zurich
(Hans Jakob Sprüngli), early seventeenth century

112. Frame

1975.1.2169
33.3 x 29.6 cm. Wood, reverse-painted glass, silver wire.
Assembled.

The sight- and back-edge moldings of this cassetta frame are
highlighted with painted silver lines, whereas the thin applied
moldings set in the corners are inlaid with silver wire. The
glass frieze is reverse painted to simulate semiprecious stone
mosaic or *pietra dura*: the trapezoidal panels are gold-flecked
blue "lapis lazuli"; in the center of each is an amber oval
painted to resemble cat's-eye stone on a red and white marbled
arabesquelike ornament outlined with silver. On the back, a

circular white paper label with *192* written in black ink
(Robert Lehman collection).

Extensive separation of the paint from the glass; some losses of
paint; the left glass panel broken in three pieces.

No fluorescence.

PROVENANCE: Not established.

LITERATURE: Ryser 1991, pp. 130, 134, 330, fig. 148.

See No. 113.

No. 113

Probably Italy or Switzerland, possibly Zurich
(Hans Jakob Sprüngli), early seventeenth century

113. Frame

1975.1.2170
28 x 24.5 cm. Wood, reverse-painted glass, silver wire.
Assembled.

The sight- and back-edge moldings of this cassetta frame are
highlighted with painted silver lines, whereas the thin applied
moldings set in the corners are inlaid with silver wire. The
glass frieze is reverse painted to simulate semiprecious stone
mosaic or *pietra dura*: the trapezoidal panels are gold-flecked
blue "lapis lazuli"; in the center of each is an amber oval
painted to resemble cat's-eye stone on a red and white marbled
arabesquelike ornament outlined with silver. On the back, a

circular white paper label with *134* written in blue ballpoint
pen (Robert Lehman collection).

Extensive separation of the paint from the glass; the top glass
panel broken in seven pieces.

No fluorescence.

PROVENANCE: Not established.

As Ryser proposed in 1991, Nos. 112 and 113 may have
been made in Zurich by Hans Jakob Sprüngli (1559–
1637), who is known to have produced reverse-painted

281

decoration imitating stone for frames.[1] Sprüngli was but one of more than one hundred painters working on glass panels in the German-speaking areas of Switzerland around 1600. Among other products, they prepared *Kabinettscheiben*, or stained-glass panels to decorate the leaded glass windows of small rooms in homes. When *Kabinettscheiben* became less popular in the seventeenth century as windows became larger and interiors lighter, the stained-glass artists turned to producing framed reverse paintings on glass made to shimmer and glitter with the liberal use of gold leaf.

Sprüngli made stained-glass and reverse-painted panels and lavish silver- and gold-mounted table glass incorporating reverse-painted panels not only for Swiss families but also for wealthy clients in Prague, Nürnberg, Ulm,

and Mainz. When the Thirty Years' War reduced the demand for such luxurious objects, he and other artists in Switzerland began painting panels for furniture makers. Matching sets of small panels decorated with unified themes like the Caesars, Sibyls, or Fables were popular on cabinets of drawers. Frames for looking glasses or pictures were also ornamented with reverse-painted glass. Furniture makers in Naples, particularly, imported reverse-painted panels from several centers in Europe, including Zurich.[2]

NOTES:
1. See Ryser 1991, pp. 101–7, 130, 132.
2. See Corning 1992, pp. 22–25.

Glass panels probably painted in Italy or Switzerland, possibly Zurich (Hans Jakob Sprüngli), early to mid-seventeenth century; frame probably assembled in Italy, perhaps Rome, early twentieth century

114. Frame

1975.1.2297
87.3 x 78.4 cm. Poplar, ebonized pearwood, reverse-painted glass, gilt bronze, semiprecious stone. Assembled.

The rectangular frame, probably made to hold a looking glass, is formed of a half-lapped poplar backframe with applied ebonized pearwood moldings. The sight edge is oil gilt. Colored wood ripple moldings and stamped gilt-bronze moldings hold two friezes of reverse-painted glass panels painted to resemble stone mosaic or *pietra dura*. The outer frieze is made up of sixteen glass panels: three long sections, with curved ends, on each side and four heart-shaped corner pieces. The joints between the panels are covered with strips of gilt bronze stamped with scrollwork designs. The corner panels are painted red, green, white, orange, and gray to represent banded agate and are outlined with thin silver lines. In each of the panels flanking the corners an arabesquelike ornament outlined with silver encloses a striated "agate" oval, against a mottled blue and silver background meant to look like lapis lazuli. The center panels enclose red, white, and brown banded "agates" outlined with silver and flanked by "lapis lazuli" arabesques and small ovals of descending size representing cat's-eye stone. The eight smaller rectangular panels that make up the inner frieze, two on a side, are double glazed (each painted piece of glass is covered with a clear piece). The panels are reverse painted to resemble white-striated red marble; their centers are covered with gilt-bronze bosses stamped with children's heads. In the corners are octagonal table-cut glass "jewels," with separate anthemion collars, set into gilt-bronze mounts and backed with black and blue painted veining.

The gilt ripple moldings either new or repainted; the gilding inside the sight edge new; the upper right corner of the outer frieze broken and the lower left corner piece broken in several pieces; the glass strips of the inner frieze broken in several places, pieces of the outer colorless glazing missing, and the "jewel" at the upper left replaced with a faceted semiprecious stone; some paint separation.

No fluorescence.

PROVENANCE: [Mindak, Rome (May 1948, list 2, no. 50)].

The painting of the glass friezes in this frame is of the same quality as that of Nos. 112 and 113; all three frames are probably attributable to the same hand. Timothy Newbery has noted the existence of a related frame in the Galleria Colonna in Rome, framing the *Family Portrait of Alfonso III Gonzaga, Count of Novellara*.[1] Another similar frame was on the art market in London in 1989.[2]

NOTES:
1. Galleria Colonna, 104 (the frame Rome, ca. 1710). I am grateful to Timothy Newbery for sharing his notes on this frame with me.
2. Sale, Christie's, London, 23 November 1989, lot 130 (cover ill.).

No. 114

Probably Bohemia or Lower Austria, second half of the eighteenth century

115. Panel

1975.1.1555
H. 9.4 cm. Colorless nonlead glass. Cut, polished, reverse gilt, painted.

The panel is a flat oval of polished glass with a beveled rim. On the reverse, framed by a gadrooned border, is a depiction in gold leaf of a saint who may be Rosalia standing on and framed by clouds, with a crucifix and flowers in her left hand, a rosary in her right, and a radiance about her head.[1] The panel is backed with black and cream-colored paint.

The paint delaminated in some areas and flaking off slightly; no losses to the design.

Longwave fluorescence. Glass: greenish yellow. *Shortwave fluorescence.* Glass: nothing.

PROVENANCE: Not established.

The painting was produced by applying gold leaf to the back of the glass sheet, scratching in the details of the design, and then backing it with black and cream-colored paint.

The style of decoration on this panel is reminiscent of reverse-gilt panels by Johann Joseph Mildner (1765–1808) of Gutenbrunn, Lower Austria.[2] Mildner's panels usually decorate cylindrical, straight-sided tumblers, but he also occasionally produced framed, flat panels with scratched portraits in gold leaf backed with black or colored paint.

NOTES:
1. Sibyll Kummer-Rothenhäusler suggested that the saint might be Rosalia.
2. I am grateful to Frieder Ryser for pointing out this similarity; see also Ryser 1991, pp. 269–70. For a review of Mildner's works, see Prager 1983, and see also Pazaurek 1923, pp. 315–44; Pazaurek and Philippovich 1976, pp. 297–326; Baumgärtner 1981, pp. 104–6; Strasser and Spiegl 1989, pp. 128–30.

No. 115

No. 116

Europe, possibly France, about 1900

116. Monstrance

1975.1.2499

H. 36.8 cm, w. with shutters closed 15.5 cm. Carved, gessoed, and gilt wood; enameled glass; copper(?) wire. Assembled.

The elaborately carved, gessoed, and gilt wood frame has a circular opening surmounted by a carved "gothic" scrollwork finial and a carved, interlaced "gothic" scrollwork stem resting on a rectangular foot with molded sides. Attached with hinges to either side of the circular molding are two arc-shaped wings with inset semicircular transparent "cloisonné" enameled flat

glass panels. In the depiction of the Mocking of Christ in the right panel, Christ, wearing a white loincloth and a crown of thorns, with a painted gilt radiance above his head, stands in the foreground, before a crowd of figures in colorful dress. In the depiction of the Betrayal in the left panel, Judas, wearing a dark blue robe and holding a green money bag in his left hand, appears to be kissing Christ, who wears an amber-colored coat and a light blue robe; they are surrounded by a crowd of elders and soldiers, one of whom has fallen to the ground at their

285

feet. Attached under the foot: a rectangular white paper label printed *29* in black; a rectangular tan paper label with cut corners, outlined in red with reversed tan dots and *Mary / 27* written in dark brown ink; and attached to the back: a rectangular tan paper label with cut corners, outlined in red and *CI2053 / R.L.* written in dark brown ink (the first two unidentified, the third, Robert Lehman collection).

Some losses to the gesso and gilding; nail holes and the remains of glue indicate that something, probably a mirror, has been removed from the round panel, on which the wood has been painted dark brown.

Longwave fluorescence. Flat glass backing: slightly orange. Enamels, right panel: pink (hands and faces) = dark red, other colors = nothing (purple reflection). Enamels, left panel: white = cream-colored, pink (faces and hands) = faint tan. Gilt wood: dark reddish purple reflection (remains of glue in central opening fluoresce bluish white). *Shortwave fluorescence.* Flat glass backing: nothing (purple reflection). Enamels, right panel: white = gray (loincloth) and slightly pink (robe of a figure in the crowd), other colors = nothing (purple reflection). Enamels, left panel: all colors = various dark purple tints.

PROVENANCE: Not established.

The flat glass panels are decorated on one side with enamels in the cloisonné manner, with threadlike metal (copper?) wires creating the *cloisons,* or cells. Because the glass panels are transparent and are not backed, the scenes are translucent.

Enameling on metal using metal wires to separate the colors (cloisonné) is probably an early Near Eastern innovation. It was not until the late nineteenth century that cloisonné enamels were backed with glass. The technique was practiced in the Orient and Europe.

The cloisonné scenes on the wings may have been derived from as yet unidentified stained-glass windows. The form of the frame is very close to (and may have been copied from) that of a carved wood triptych formerly in

Fig. 116.1 Triptych. Present location unknown. Reproduced from Chevallier et Mannheim (Paris), *Catalogue des objets d'art et de haute curiosité, antiques, du Moyen-Age & de la Renaissance, composant l'importante et précieuse collection Spitzer* (sale catalogue, 17 April–16 June 1893), vol. 3, pl. 52

the Frédéric Spitzer collection, Paris (Fig. 116.1). The catalogue of the Spitzer sale of 1893 described the triptych as a "travail flamand (commencement du XVIᵉ siècle)."[1]

NOTE:

1. Spitzer sale 1893, vol. 2, lot 2126; vol. 3, pl. 52.

ROMAN AND ISLAMIC GLASS

First to Eleventh Century

Nos. 131, 132, 127 *(from left to right)*

Ancient Roman and Early Islamic Glass

In addition to forming the distinguished collection of later European glass catalogued in Nos. 1–116, Robert Lehman acquired twenty pieces of ancient Roman and early Islamic glass.

Most of these pieces represent well-known types to which specialized collectors would attach little value, and none of them can be considered outstanding. Laurence Kanter very kindly supplied me with the explanation of this apparent anomaly. Mr. Lehman, he explained, acquired these objects because he wanted to use them as "props" that helped him to display the jewels of his collection in the best possible manner.

Nevertheless, these objects are well worth cataloguing, for the sake not only of completeness but also of scholarship, and in order to make them available to those who have a particular interest in ancient glass.

Roman, probably first century

117. Bowl

1975.1.1595

H. 5.2 cm, diam. 11.8 cm. Transparent pale yellowish brown glass. Perhaps blown, the rim apparently finished by reheating.

See Isings form 1.[1] The bowl has a plain rim that is slightly everted and thickened. The wall curves downward and inward, and the plain base is slightly concave, with small rounded chips of glass fused to the underside, presumably by accident. No pontil mark.[2]

Incomplete: broken and repaired, with one small loss at the center of the base. Except for traces of pale pinkish brown enamel-like weathering, the surface is dull, pitted, and slightly iridescent; evidently cleaned.

PROVENANCE: Not established.

Although bowls of this type are usually cast, the thin wall and the hot-worked rim suggest that the Lehman example was formed by blowing.

NOTES:
1. Isings 1957, pp. 15–17.
2. The following unidentified labels have been removed and are in the Robert Lehman Collection files: circular white paper label with [JD]R / 22 written in black ink; circular white paper label with 89 written in black ink; rectangular white paper label with 47 written in pencil.

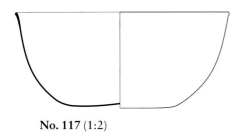

No. 117 (1:2)

No. 117

Roman, first century

118. Ribbed bowl

1975.1.1596

H. 3.9 cm, diam. 15.5 cm. Transparent pale bluish green glass with small spherical bubbles. Cast or poured as a disk, reheated and stamped with a circular mold to form the ribs, then slumped over a former mold to make a bowl; lathe-cut, ground, and polished.[1]

Isings form 3c. The shallow bowl has a plain rim, and its wall curves downward and inward to the plain, slightly concave base. Encircling the exterior is a band of sixty-four vertical ribs that vary in height from 10 to 30 mm, and in the center of the interior are three lathe-cut concentric grooves, the inner groove 2.5 mm wide and 10 mm in diameter.[2]

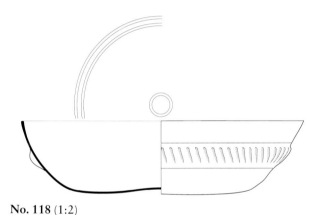

No. 118 (1:2)

Intact. Some silver and iridescent weathering; extensive pitting; evidently cleaned.

PROVENANCE: Not established.

This ribbed bowl is a common type that is well represented in public and private collections.[3] Isings listed examples datable to the first century from Colchester, Saintes, Nijmegen, and Vindonissa.[4] Other parallels have been found at Magdalensberg (Augustan-Claudian, or about 27 B.C.–A.D. 54)[5] and Herculaneum (before 79).[6]

NOTES:
1. For the technique, see Gudenrath in Tait 1991, p. 222.
2. The following unidentified labels have been removed and are in the Robert Lehman Collection files: oval beige paper label with a gray and black printed border and *JDR·16* printed in black; rectangular white paper label with *50* typed in black; circular white paper label with *85* written in black ink.
3. See, for example, Hamburg 1974, pp. 96–97, nos. 255, 257; Auth 1976, p. 194, nos. 301, 302; Constable-Maxwell sale 1979, lot 38; and Kofler-Truniger sale 1985, lot 152.
4. Isings 1957, pp. 20–21.
5. Czurda-Ruth 1979, pp. 26–34, nos. 294–316.
6. Scatozza Höricht 1986, pp. 30–31, no. 12.

No. 118

Roman, first century

119. Jar with two handles

1975.1.1582
H. 13.6 cm, diam. of rim 3.8 cm, diam. of shoulder 6.2 cm.
Transparent blue glass. Blown, tooled, the rim finished at the furnace, the handles applied.

Isings form 15a. The pear-shaped jar has a flanged rim that is folded outward, upward, and inward; a somewhat lopsided cylindrical neck; and a sloping shoulder with a rounded edge. The wall tapers and bends inward, outward, and inward at the bottom, forming a torus molding at the edge of the plain, slightly concave base. The two opposed ribbed handles were dropped on at the shoulder and drawn upward, outward, and inward, then attached to the top of the neck. No pontil mark.[1]

Incomplete: the upper part of one handle broken out and lost. The surface dull with patches of grayish brown to tan-colored weathering and some pitting and iridescence; presumably cleaned.

PROVENANCE: Not established.

Jars like this were first made in the Tiberian period (14–37). Their popularity reached its peak around the middle of the first century and declined sharply during the reign of Vespasian (69–79).[2] Many examples have survived.[3]

NOTES:
1. An unidentified circular white paper label with *90* written in black ink has been removed and is in the Robert Lehman Collection files. An oval beige paper label with a gray and black printed border and *JDR·61* printed in black and a rectangular white paper label with *54* typed in black (both unidentified) were once affixed to the underside.

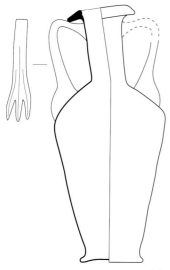

No. 119 (1:2)

No. 119

2. For an excellent discussion of the date, see Biaggio Simona 1991, vol. 1, pp. 212–13.
3. See, for example, Auth 1976, pp. 202–3, nos. 352 (deep blue), 353 (pale purple with deep blue handles); Constable-Maxwell sale 1979, lot 148 (deep blue); Matheson 1980, p. 24, no. 62 (pale blue); Oliver 1980, p. 51, no. 34 (pale green with opaque white handles); Barag 1985, p. 97, no. 133 (light purple with deep blue handles; from a Parthian cemetery at Warka, Iraq); Kofler-Truniger sale 1985, lot 121 (deep blue); Loudmer sale 1985, lot 155 (light green); and Corning (and other cities) 1987, p. 112, no. 45 (blue with colored flecks).

Roman, first to early second century

120. Bowl

1975.1.1594
H. 4.1 cm, diam. 8 cm. Transparent light purple glass. Blown, the rim finished at the furnace.

See Isings form 44a (bowl with a tubular rim but lacking the very thick base present on this example). The rim of the bowl is folded outward and downward, and its wall curves slightly outward, downward, and inward. The considerable thickening at the center of the disk-shaped base creates a dome in the floor and a small concavity on the underside. Pontil mark on the underside.[1]

Intact. Except for patches of grayish brown or grayish purple weathering, the surface dull, with areas of pitting and iridescence; evidently cleaned.

PROVENANCE: Not established.

Isings cited many examples of bowls like this from datable finds of the first century.[2] The date was confirmed by Czurda-Ruth, who noted that the type was well represented at Magdalensberg by about 20–30,[3] and by Scatozza Höricht, who recorded examples from Pompeii and Herculaneum that must be earlier than 79.[4] (Some of the bowls from Herculaneum were found in their original packing; that is, they were new in 79.) Biaggio Simona, reviewing the evidence from Ticino canton in Switzerland, reported the presence of such bowls there between the second quarter of the first century and the beginning of the second century.[5] Similar bowls were also made in red slip ware (*terra sigillata*); they are classified as Dragendorff form 37.[6]

NOTES:
1. The following unidentified labels have been removed and are in the Robert Lehman Collection files: circular white paper label with *JDR / 29* written in black ink; rectangular white paper label with *45* typed in black; circular white paper label with *86* written in black ink.
2. Isings 1957, pp. 59–60.
3. Czurda-Ruth 1979, p. 61.
4. Scatozza Höricht 1986, pp. 32–35.
5. Biaggio Simona 1991, pp. 83–85.
6. Dragendorff 1895, p. 154, pl. 3.

No. 120

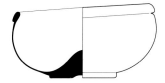

No. 120 (1:2)

Roman, mid-first to second century

121. Toilet bottle

1975.1.1592
H. 11.5 cm, diam. of rim 1.9 cm, diam. of body 2.6 cm.
Probably transparent green glass. Blown, the rim finished at
the furnace.

Isings form 28b. The bottle has an everted rim with a plain
rounded lip; a tall cylindrical neck with a slight constriction at
the bottom; a truncated conical body, the wall of which splays
outward and curves inward at the bottom; and a plain base. A
small scar centered on the underside may be a pontil mark.

Probably intact; possibly slight losses from the rim. Except for
traces of enamel-like dark brown weathering, the surface is
heavily pitted, with blue, deep green, and gold iridescence;
evidently cleaned.

PROVENANCE: Not established.

Isings published a long list of finds from datable contexts of which the earliest are Claudian-Neronian (between about 41 and 68) and the latest belong to the second
century.[1] Biaggio Simona has suggested that the type came
into use around 60–70 and was most popular in the late
first and very early second century.[2]

NOTES:
1. Isings 1957, pp. 42–43.
2. Biaggio Simona 1991, pp. 149–53. See also Matheson 1980,
   p. 62, no. 149, and Scatozza Höricht 1986, p. 61, no. 191.

No. 121

No. 121 (1:2)

Roman, late first to third century

122. Bottle

1975.1.1591
H. 14 cm, diam. of rim 1.7 cm, diam. of body 2 cm. Almost colorless glass with a yellowish green tint. Blown, the body tooled, the rim finished at the furnace.

Isings form 83. The bottle has an everted rim that is folded outward, upward, and inward and a long tubular neck, tapered slightly at the top and splayed at the bottom, that is two-thirds of the bottle's height. Four long vertical indentations decorate the vertical wall, which curves inward at the bottom to the narrow base. No pontil mark.

Intact. Part of the neck virtually unweathered, the rest of the surface with patches of dull brown enamel-like weathering (especially in the indentations) and iridescence; evidently cleaned.

PROVENANCE: Not established.

Isings noted indented bottles of this type from contexts dated from the late first to the third or fourth century.[1] Several other parallels, some of them with shorter necks, have been published.[2]

NOTES:
1. Isings 1957, p. 100.
2. See, for example, Harden 1936, p. 227, nos. 692–95; Fremersdorf 1958, p. 26, pls. 22–24; Vanderhoeven 1962, p. 57, no. 134; Goethert-Polaschek 1977, p. 122, nos. 667, 668, pl. 53; and Loudmer sale 1985, lots 305, 306.

No. 122

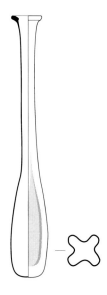

No. 122 (1:2)

Roman, perhaps second to fourth century

123. Jar

1975.1.1598
H. 6.8 cm, diam. of rim 3.9 cm, diam. of shoulder 5 cm.
Transparent blue glass. Blown (the body probably blown in a mold), the rim finished at the furnace.

See Isings form 102a. The cylindrical jar has an everted rim with a rounded lip; a very short cylindrical neck; and a sloping shoulder with a rounded edge. The vertical wall curves inward at the bottom to the plain base. Small pontil mark on the underside.[1]

Incomplete: approximately one-quarter of the rim broken out and lost. Patches of tan-colored enamel-like weathering with slight iridescence; elsewhere the surface is pitted; evidently cleaned.

PROVENANCE: Not established.

Stern discussed this very simple type of jar at length, noting examples that range in date from the first half of the second to the early fourth century.[2]

NOTES:
1. An unidentified square white paper label with *16* typed in black has been removed and is in the Robert Lehman Collection files.
2. Stern 1977, pp. 77–80, no. 21. See also Hayes 1975, pp. 66–67, 201, no. 200, pl. 15; Matheson 1980, pp. 82–83, nos. 221–23; and Loudmer sale 1985, p. 126, lots 328–31.

No. 123

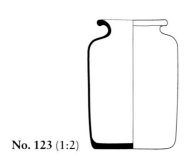

No. 123 (1:2)

Roman, perhaps third century

124. Jar

1975.1.1586

H. 10.8 cm, diam. of rim 3.2 cm, diam. of shoulder 4.8 cm. Almost colorless glass with a green or brown tint. Blown, the rim finished at the furnace.

The conical jar has an everted rim with a lip that is folded upward and inward; a short cylindrical neck that is splayed at the bottom; and a flat shoulder with a rounded edge. The tapered wall curves inward at the bottom to the rounded base. No pontil mark.

Intact. Most of the thick layer of weathering has been removed (especially on the outside), revealing a green and gold iridescent surface with extensive pitting.

PROVENANCE: Not established.

This jar was presumably made in the eastern Mediterranean. Three similar conical jars with rounded bottoms were found in mid-second- to mid-third-century tombs excavated at Homs in Syria in 1961.[1]

NOTE:

1. Abdul Hak 1965, figs. 8 (top row, fourth from left), 12 (second and third from left). See also Barag 1970, type 19-3; Stern 1977, pp. 80–82, no. 22B; and Loudmer sale 1985, lot 463.

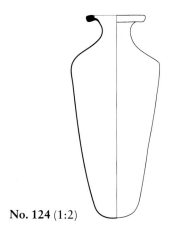

No. 124 (1:2)

No. 124

No. 125

Roman, third to fourth century

125. Jar

1975.1.1599
H. 9.1 cm, diam. of rim 8 cm, diam. of body 9.8 cm. Almost colorless glass with a yellowish green tint. Blown, the rim finished at the furnace.

See Isings form 104b. The spheroid jar has a plain, rounded, slightly thickened rim; a short, tapering neck; and a narrow shoulder with a rather uneven rounded edge. The wall curves outward, downward, and in at the bottom, and the base is plain, with a low kick. No pontil mark.

Incomplete: broken and repaired, with losses from the neck and shoulder. Partly covered with silver to brown weathering, much of which is missing; some iridescence and pitting.

PROVENANCE: Not established.

This jar represents one of the many variants of a common type. Isings cited numerous examples from dated finds, the earliest of which are attributed to the second half of the third century.[1] Hayes published two similar jars in the Royal Ontario Museum, Toronto, one as probably from the third century, the other as about late third or early fourth century.[2] The Lehman jar has a rounded, rather than flat-edged, rim, and its wall is unusually thin.

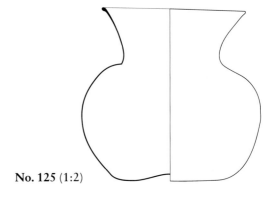

No. 125 (1:2)

NOTES:
1. Isings 1957, pp. 123–25.
2. Hayes 1975, pp. 68, 199, no. 211, pl. 13; pp. 120–21, 214, no. 474, pl. 28. Hayes cited as parallels Eisen 1927, vol. 2, fig. 255; Ruesch sale 1936, lot 248, pl. 60; and Abdul Hak 1965, fig. 9, center bottom.

Roman, about fourth century

126. Jar

1975.1.1600
H. 6.6 cm, diam. of rim 4.4 cm, diam. of body 6.5 cm.
Apparently almost colorless glass with a brown or yellowish tint. Blown, the body inflated in a dip mold, the rim finished at the furnace.

The jar has an everted rim that is folded upward, inward, and downward; a short cylindrical neck that is splayed at the bottom; and a spheroid body decorated with twenty-two mold-blown vertical ribs that are fairly prominent at the top and very faint at the bottom. The wall curves smoothly downward, outward, and inward at the bottom, and the base is plain. Low kick in the bottom with a pontil mark.[1]

Intact. The surface is partly covered with a thick layer of tan-colored enamel-like weathering; where that is missing, it is mottled and iridescent.

PROVENANCE: Not established.

Hayes proposed that a jar in the Royal Ontario Museum, Toronto, similar in shape to the Lehman jar but with a more flared rim and five round indentations rather than ribs on the body, was probably made in the third century.[2] Matheson dated an example with a plain shoulder and body in the Yale University Art Gallery to the fourth century.[3] Three other parallels with applied decoration were on the art market in Paris in 1985.[4]

No. 126

NOTES:

1. The following unidentified labels have been removed and are in the Robert Lehman Collection files: oval beige paper label with a gray and black printed border and *JDR·58* printed in black; rectangular white paper label with *51* typed in black; circular white paper label with *100* written in black ink.
2. Hayes 1975, pp. 79–80, 206, no. 291, pl. 20.
3. Matheson 1980, p. 114, no. 298.
4. Loudmer sale 1985, lots 549–51.

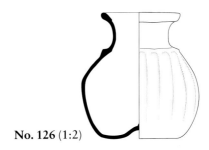

No. 126 (1:2)

Roman, late third to fifth century

127. Jar

1975.1.1589

H. 12.4 cm, diam. of rim 3.8 cm, diam. of body 7.6 cm.
Apparently colorless glass with a very pale green or yellowish
green tint. Blown, the rim finished at the furnace.

The biconical jar has an everted rim with a thickened lip and a
somewhat lopsided short cylindrical neck with a slight constriction at the bottom. The wall curves outward, downward,
and inward, and the base is plain, with a low kick. No pontil
mark.

Intact. The surface is partly covered with slightly iridescent
weathering, some of which (especially on the inside of the
mouth and the neck) retains a dark, enamel-like surface.
Elsewhere the surface is pitted.

PROVENANCE: Azeez Khayat, New York (Khayat sale 1928, lot
151[?]). Acquired by Robert Lehman in 1928.

Although this object bears a general likeness to flasks
made in the Syro-Palestinian region between the late third
and the fourth or fifth centuries,[1] I have found no close
parallel.

NOTE:
1. See Hayes 1975, pp. 81–82, 207, 208, nos. 300–322 (especially nos. 314–16), pls. 21, 22.

No. 127

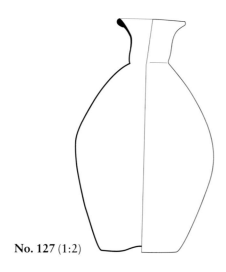

No. 127 (1:2)

Roman, third to fourth century

128. Dropper flask

1975.1.1590
H. 8.6 cm, diam. of rim 4.5 cm, diam. of body 5.7 cm. Almost
colorless glass with a pale green or yellow tint. Blown (the
body blown in a dip mold), tooled, the rim finished at the
furnace.

See Isings form 133 (without a diaphragm). The flask has an
everted rim with its lip folded upward and inward and a
somewhat lopsided cylindrical neck with a slight constriction
at the base and an inner diaphragm formed by folding. About
twenty to twenty-four faint, almost vertical ribs that slope
downward from right to left decorate the body, the wall of
which curves downward, outward, and inward at the bottom
to the plain base. Large dome-shaped kick in the bottom with
a pontil mark.[1]

Intact. Except for patches of iridescent silver to tan-colored
weathering, the surface is pitted, yellowish green, and iridescent; evidently cleaned.

PROVENANCE: Not established.

In an extensive discussion of these types of flasks, Stern
has noted that they seem to have been produced both in
the eastern Roman Empire and in northern Mesopotamia from the mid-third to the early fifth century. Roman
examples with diaphragms are common in Syria and eastern Palestine.[2] A flask from Syria with a diaphragm and
decorated with rows of pinched knobs on its body has
been dated from the late second to the mid-third century.[3]
See also Nos. 129 and 130.

NOTES:

1. A circular white paper label with 77 written in black ink
   and a square white paper label with 14 typed in black (both
   unidentified) have been removed and are in the Robert Lehman Collection files.
2. Stern 1977, pp. 95–100.
3. Hayes 1975, pp. 60–61, 198, no. 157, pl. 12. For other parallels, see Eisen 1927, vol. 1, p. 341, pl. 86; Stern 1977, pp.
   95–97, nos. 27A, B, pl. 9 (fourth to early fifth century);
   Oliver 1980, p. 120, no. 209 (third century); and Wolkenberg
   sale 1991, lot 44.

No. 128

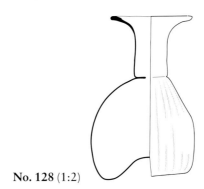

No. 128 (1:2)

Roman, probably third to fourth century

129. Dropper flask

1975.1.1584

H. 9.2 cm, diam. of rim 4.4 cm, diam. of body 6.6 cm. Almost colorless glass. Blown (the body blown in a dip mold), tooled, the rim finished at the furnace.

See Isings form 133 (without a diaphragm). The flask has a flattened, outsplayed rim that is folded upward and inward and a cylindrical neck with a slight bulge at the base and an inner diaphragm formed by folding. The spheroid body is decorated with about thirty very faint, almost vertical ribs that descend from right to left, and its wall curves outward, downward, and inward to the plain base. Conical kick in the bottom with a circular pontil mark.[1]

Intact. The surface covered partly with patches of buff to brown enamel-like weathering, partly with green to violet iridescence.

PROVENANCE: Azeez Khayat, New York (Khayat sale 1928, lot 247). Acquired by Robert Lehman in 1928.

See the discussion under No. 128.

NOTE:
1. A rectangular white paper tag attached to a string and with 247 printed in black on both sides has been removed and is in the Robert Lehman Collection files.

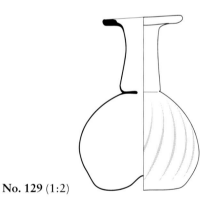

No. 129 (1:2)

No. 129

Roman, third to fourth century

130. Dropper flask

1975.1.1588

H. 9.6 cm, diam. of rim 5.2 cm, diam. of body 6.8 cm. Either colorless or transparent very pale green or very pale yellowish brown glass. Blown (the body blown in a dip mold), tooled, the rim finished at the furnace.

See Isings form 133 (without a diaphragm). The flask has a horizontal flanged rim, the edge of which is folded upward and inward and flattened, and a cylindrical neck that is slightly wider at the bottom than at the top and has a diaphragm formed by folding at the bottom. Faint mold-blown vertical ribs decorate the shoulder. The wall of the spheroid body curves outward, downward, and inward to the plain base. Dome-shaped kick in the bottom with a pontil mark.[1]

Incomplete: approximately two-thirds of the rim broken out and lost. The surface partly covered with brown, tan, or ocher weathering, partly pitted and iridescent.

PROVENANCE: Azeez Khayat, New York (Khayat sale 1928, lot 16). Acquired by Robert Lehman in 1928.

See the discussion under No. 128.

NOTE:
1. An unidentified round white paper label with 79 written in black ink has been removed and is in the Robert Lehman Collection files.

No. 130

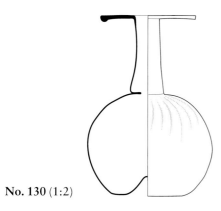

No. 130 (1:2)

No. 131

Roman, fourth century or later

131. Jar with sixteen handles

1975.1.1597

H. 6.9 cm, diam. of rim 8 cm, diam. of body 9.4 cm. Apparently very pale translucent green glass with translucent deep bluish green glass handles. Blown, tooled, the rim finished at the furnace, the trail and handles applied.

The jar has an everted rim with a lip that is folded upward and inward, a short cylindrical neck, and a slightly depressed shoulder with a rounded edge. A thin trail winds three times around the neck and shoulder. The sixteen almost identical handles were dropped onto the shoulder, pulled upward and inward, and then attached to the edge of the rim, with the excess glass pinched into vertical thumbrests. The wall curves downward and inward, and the base has a foot ring made by folding. Small kick in the bottom with a faint ring-shaped pontil mark.[1]

Incomplete: approximately one-third of the upper part of the wall broken out and repaired, with small losses. Patches of silver weathering and, where this is missing, some iridescence; cleaned.

PROVENANCE: Not established.

This jar is a common eastern Mediterranean type, many examples of which have been found.[2]

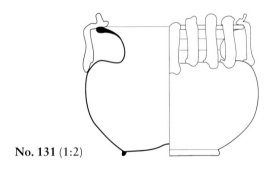

No. 131 (1:2)

NOTES:

1. The following unidentified labels have been removed and are in the Robert Lehman Collection files: oval beige paper label with a gray and black printed border and JDR·35 printed in black; rectangular white paper label with 48 typed in black; circular white paper label with 87 written in black ink.

2. See, for example, Eisen 1927, vol. 1, fig. 177, pls. 110, 111; Barag 1970, pls. 6, 7, 12, 13; Hamburg 1974, no. 97; Auth 1976, no. 177; Berlin 1976–77, no. 107; Matheson 1980, p. 119, no. 316 (with sixteen handles); Von Saldern 1980, p. 100, no. 96 (with twelve handles); and Kofler-Truniger sale 1985, lot 33 (with fifteen handles).

No. 132

Roman, fourth century

132. Ewer

1975.1.1585

H. 22 cm, diam. 13.5 cm. Transparent pale green glass, the handle perhaps somewhat darker. Blown, the rim finished at the furnace, the trails and handle applied.

Isings form 124. The roughly cylindrical ewer has an everted rim pinched to form a trefoil mouth; a narrow, decidedly lopsided cylindrical neck; and a sloping shoulder with a rounded edge. One trail decorates the outside of the rim, just below the lip; another encircles the base of the neck. The handle was dropped onto the bottom of the shoulder, drawn upward, inward, and downward, and then attached to the outside of the rim, with the excess glass pulled upward to form a small vertical thumbrest. The wall splays slightly and curves inward at the bottom to the plain base. Very low kick in the bottom with a large pontil mark.

Almost complete: approximately half the trail at the base of the neck broken out and lost. The exterior pitted,

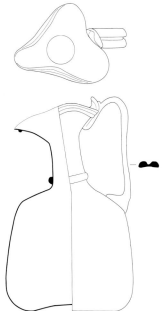

No. 132 (1:3)

305

accentuating the blowing spirals; patches of brownish silver weathering on the interior; evidently cleaned.

PROVENANCE: George D. Pratt, New York (Pratt sale 1937, lot 62, ill.). Acquired by Robert Lehman in 1937.

This is one of the numerous variants of Isings form 124. Hayes dated a similar ewer in the Royal Ontario Museum, Toronto, to the early to mid-fourth century.[1]

NOTE:

1. Hayes 1975, pp. 97–98, 209, no. 341, pl. 23. For other parallels, see Auth 1976, p. 208, no. 386; Matheson 1980, p. 107, no. 281; and Loudmer sale 1985, lot 363.

Byzantine, perhaps sixth to early seventh century(?)

133. Bracelet

1975.1.1601
Diam. 8.7 cm, w. 1.5 cm, d. .5 cm. Deep purple glass. Tooled.

The bracelet is a strip of glass that is flat in cross section and joined at the ends (the seam is clearly visible). It is decorated with five parallel horizontal ribs.

Intact. The exterior extensively weathered and pitted (most of the surface rough, with green iridescence); the interior dull, with patches of dark grayish purple weathering.

PROVENANCE: George D. Pratt, New York (Pratt sale 1937, lot 66).[1] Acquired by Robert Lehman in 1937.

This object belongs to type B4a of the pre-Islamic glass bracelets of Palestine, as defined by Spaer. Glass bracelets are notoriously difficult to date, but Spaer noted datable, or apparently datable, bracelets like this one, with horizontal ribbing and, usually, an undisguised seam, from a Byzantine tomb at Kafr Kama, Israel (registered as fifth century); from the Tyropoeon Valley, Jerusalem (sixth to early seventh century); and from Resafa in central Syria (also sixth to early seventh century).[2]

NOTES:

1. Lot 66 of the Pratt sale is described in the catalogue as "six iridescent Aquamarine Glass Bottles and Three Bracelets. Tall-necked narrow bottles with varying iridescence; pair of molded glass bracelets and a larger one with beautiful opal iridescence." According to the files, of the nine objects only this bracelet is in the Robert Lehman Collection at the Metropolitan.
2. Spaer 1988, p. 57.

No. 133

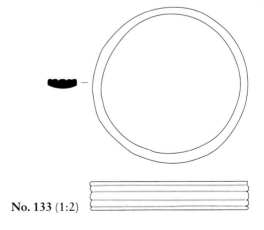

No. 133 (1:2)

Islamic, seventh to ninth century

134. Flask

1975.1.1587
H. 8.5 cm, diam. of rim 1.9 cm, diam. of body 6.6 cm.
Probably almost colorless glass with a green or yellowish tint.
Blown, the rim finished at the furnace, the decoration applied
and tooled.

The flask has a thickened rim, the outer surface of which is
beveled, and a short cylindrical neck. The wall of the globular
body curves outward, downward, and inward. The edge of the
sloping shoulder is decorated with a continuous horizontal
trail with transverse nicks, and around the body are five almost
identical rectangular appliqués with their corners pulled outward so that they look like schematic animal hides. The base
has a narrow foot ring made by folding. Pontil mark on the
underside. An oval beige paper label with a black and gray
printed border and JDR·52 printed in black is affixed to the
underside.

Incomplete: one area of the wall (with an appliqué) broken out
and mended, but with small losses. Patches of iridescent
silvery brown weathering with green to violet highlights.

PROVENANCE: Not established.

Appliqués shaped like the hides of animals occur on at
least three common types of early Islamic flasks: globular flasks with narrow necks,[1] globular flasks with wide,
flaring rims,[2] and ovoid flasks.[3] Kevorkian cited examples in a number of public and private collections,[4] including one in the Benaki Museum, Athens,[5] and two
formerly in the Andrew Constable-Maxwell collection.[6]
Kröger has attributed these objects to workshops in Syria
and dated them to the seventh to ninth century.[7]

No. 134

NOTES:
1. For example, Loudmer sale 1985, lots 552, 553.
2. Ibid., lots 549–51.
3. Ibid., lots 554, 555.
4. Kevorkian in ibid., pp. 226–27.
5. Clairmont 1977, pp. 78–79, no. 264 (with a useful bibli-
   ography).
6. Constable-Maxwell sale 1979, lots 346, 347.
7. Kröger 1984, pp. 145–46, no. 128.

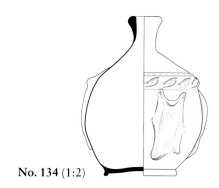

No. 134 (1:2)

Islamic, seventh to eleventh century

135. Jar

1975.1.1593
H. 5.8 cm, diam. of rim 3.3 cm, diam. of body 5.3 cm.
Probably almost colorless glass. Blown (the body blown in a dip mold), the rim finished at the furnace.

The spheroid jar has a plain rim, a cylindrical neck that tapers slightly toward the bottom, and a sloping shoulder. The wall curves outward, downward, and inward to the plain base and is decorated with twenty-four mold-blown vertical ribs that are prominent at the top, just below the shoulder, and faint where they end near the base. Small kick with a minute pontil mark centered on the underside.[1]

Intact. The surface partly covered with a thick film of mauve to green iridescent weathering.

PROVENANCE: Not established.

Spheroid jars with mold-blown ribs are not uncommon, but their origin and date are uncertain. Von Saldern, Auth, and Clairmont have attributed such jars to the early Islamic period.[2] Matheson, however, has suggested that a similar object with a mold-blown honeycomb pattern may date from the fifth or sixth century.[3] On balance, an early Islamic date appears probable. Kröger has dated an example in the Museum für Islamische Kunst, Berlin, to between the ninth and the eleventh century.[4]

No. 135

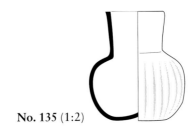

No. 135 (1:2)

NOTES:
1. The following unidentified labels have been removed and are in the Robert Lehman Collection files: oval beige paper label with a gray and black printed border and *JDR·45* printed in black; rectangular white paper label with *3* typed in black; circular white paper label with *78* written in black ink.
2. See Von Saldern 1974, p. 190, nos. 281, 282; Auth 1976, p. 232, nos. 537, 538; and Clairmont 1977, p. 62, no. 196.
3. Matheson 1980, p. 129, no. 348.
4. Kröger 1984, pp. 61–62, no. 56.

Islamic, ninth to eleventh century

136. Flask

1975.1.1583
H. 12 cm, diam. of rim 1.7 cm, diam. of shoulder 4.2 cm.
Almost colorless (brown tinged) and translucent purple glass.
Blown (the body blown in a dip mold), the rim finished at
the furnace, wheel-cut.

The plain, flat-edged rim and the top of the tapered neck
are of colorless glass; the lower part of the neck and the body
are translucent purple glass. A wheel-cut line encircles the
rounded, sloping shoulder, where there is a small opaque
turquoise blob, perhaps fortuitous. Eight mold-blown vertical
lines alternating with schematic vegetal scrolls decorate the
wall, which tapers and curves inward at the bottom to the
plain base. Pontil mark on the underside.[1]

Intact. The colorless glass dull with slightly iridescent grayish
silver weathering; the purple glass with patches of buff to
reddish purple enamel-like weathering; some pitting and
iridescence.

PROVENANCE: Not established.

Small flasks with mold-blown decoration were common
in the early Islamic period. Kröger published eight examples, all of which were first documented in Cairo.[2]
The partly unweathered condition of this object is consistent with the possibility that it, too, was found (and
perhaps made) in Egypt. Two Islamic copper or copper
alloy glassworkers' dip molds, one of which is decorated
with schematic vegetal ornament, are known.[3]

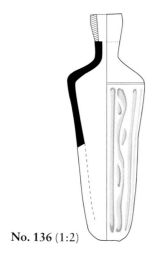

No. 136 (1:2)

No. 136

NOTES:
1. An unidentified round white paper label with *80* written in
   black ink has been removed and is in the Robert Lehman
   Collection files.
2. Kröger 1984, pp. 49–54, nos. 42–49.
3. Folsach and Whitehouse 1993.

APPENDIX

Appendix
Ultraviolet Fluorescence

When illuminated with ultraviolet light, most glasses emit light in the visible spectrum by a process called fluorescence. The intensity and color of the emitted light depends on the chemical composition of the glass, and especially on the metallic oxides in it. Ultraviolet fluorescence therefore provides a clue, though not a quantitative one, to the chemical composition of a glass. It has proved useful for examining and grouping glasses that may have been made in the same factory or region. I have examined the glass objects in the Robert Lehman Collection (except the Roman and Islamic glass catalogued in the last section of this volume) under ultraviolet light. It is my hope that these observations, like those of Rainer Rückert, whose 1982 catalogue of the glass in the Bayerisches Nationalmuseum in Munich includes notes on fluorescence, will become a stimulus for research by others.

To examine glass under ultraviolet light it is best to use two lamps: a shortwave lamp filtered to emit light at a peak wavelength of 254 nanometers and a longwave lamp filtered to a peak wavelength of 366 nanometers. There are many UV lamps available. Those used in this study were a Mineralight shortwave hand lamp (filtered to 254 nm), and a Blak-Ray longwave ultraviolet lamp (filtered to 366 nm).

It must be emphasized that describing UV fluorescence is highly subjective. No two people see or describe colors in exactly the same way. Nor can standard colors be used, as they cannot readily be viewed simultaneously with the fluorescence. Likewise, people cannot remember exact color tints, so switching between fluorescence and standard colors is not useful. I have found it best, therefore, to use fluorescence as a comparative test and to observe the specimens simultaneously. In addition, different UV lamps do not necessarily emit precisely the same spectra, and those spectra change gradually over time as the filters are bleached (solarized) and become less and less efficient through use. Using photometers to measure and record fluorescence spectra will ultimately provide objective standards.

I have listed specific longwave and shortwave fluorescences of the European glass in the Robert Lehman Collection in each catalogue entry. I attempted to keep the descriptors of the colors consistent throughout, and I have made direct comparisons between objects for which I found the fluorescences to be visually indistinguishable.

Nonlead colorless glasses decolorized with manganese tend to fluoresce brilliant yellow-green under longwave ultraviolet light and a faint creamy color under shortwave. Strongly colored glasses (such as blue) tend to have little or no observable fluorescence, although there are occasional exceptions (compare the UV fluorescence of No. 9 with that of No. 10, for example). I was able to draw other, less general conclusions from the fluorescences of the Lehman glass.

No. 24, for example, is a *Doppelscheuer*, or double cup, the date of which has been questioned on stylistic grounds. The cup and its cover emit longwave and shortwave fluorescences that are distinctly different from what one finds on "Venetian" glass unquestionably of early sixteenth-century date. The fact that the fluorescence of another of the five known related cups (and the accompanying cover "dated" nearly a century later) is identical to that of the Lehman cup and cover is strong confirmatory evidence for suspecting that both of these objects, and perhaps the three other parallels as well, are indeed copies of a lost, early *Doppelscheuer*.

The fluorescences of the three Lehman glasses with dragon stems (Nos. 74–76) also raise interesting questions. Although the three glasses seem to have been formed by the same technique, they fluoresce quite differently under ultraviolet light. The colorless glass of all three goblets fluoresces a strong greenish or yellowish green color under longwave ultraviolet illumination, but under shortwave UV the colorless glass on No. 74 fluoresces orange-tan, that of No. 75 shows marbled creamy white, and that of No. 76 is strong bluish white. The blue glass of No. 74 fluoresces faint green under longwave UV, translucent dark green under shortwave; that of No. 75 shows no longwave fluorescence and emits an opaque yellowish light under shortwave UV; and that of No. 76 fluoresces light blue and dark blue. Whether these glasses were made by a single glassmaker at different times, at different glasshouses during the same period, or two hundred years apart is not certain. What is certain, however, is that the three glass formulas must be different.

Separating lampworked figurines into distinct families is also very difficult. Comparisons of stylistic features and construction techniques show that fundamental differences do exist, and such comparisons may be all that is needed to identify the products of specific workshops, but UV fluorescence also helps to distinguish related groups. The large number of lampworked *verre de Nevers* figurines in the Robert Lehman Collection has made it possible to investigate the use of UV fluorescence to confirm the accuracy of groupings based on stylistic grounds and construction. Those groupings proved to be fairly consistent with the UV fluorescence of the opaque white glass used to make the figures.

The opaque white glass of Nos. 88–95 and 97, all of which appear on stylistic grounds to have been made in the same workshop, fluoresce brilliant orange under longwave UV and either mottled purplish pink or pale pink under shortwave. No. 96 has no white glass, but comparison of the fluorescence of other colors indicates that it does not fit into the group, the same conclusion that was reached on stylistic grounds. The white glass on the figures in Nos. 98 and 103 also fluoresces brilliant orange under longwave UV, but under shortwave UV it emits a strong bluish white. The figures in Nos. 99 and 100, which were probably made by the same hand, incorporate white glass that looks white under longwave UV as in daylight and purplish white under shortwave. Like No. 96, the figures in Nos. 101, 102, 104, and 105 cannot be grouped with any of the others.

Dwight P. Lanmon

CONCORDANCE
BIBLIOGRAPHY
INDEX

Concordance

Metropolitan Museum of Art Accession Numbers and Catalogue Numbers

accession no.	catalogue no.	accession no.	catalogue no.
1975.1.1141	79	1975.1.1175	38
.1142	76	.1176	9
.1143	80	.1177	15
.1144	71	.1178	16
.1145	47	.1179	66
.1146a,b	73	.1180	25
.1147	60	.1181	65
.1148	70	.1182	67
.1149	30	.1183	33
.1150	49	.1184	13
.1151	41	.1185	10
.1152	69	.1186	11
.1153	22	.1187	17
.1154a,b	24	.1188	14
.1155	81	.1189	7
.1156	43	.1190	6
.1157	45	.1191	8
.1158	44	.1192	26
.1159	77	.1193	52
.1160	42	.1194	1
.1161	2	.1195	27
.1162a,b	82	.1196	32
.1163	19	.1197	12
.1164	40	.1198	18
.1165	57	.1199	61
.1166a,b	68	.1200	34
.1167	4	.1201	50
.1168	46	.1202	23
.1169	56	.1203a,b	58
.1170	5	.1204	59
.1171	72	.1205	29
.1172	3	.1206	74
.1173	36	.1207	54
.1174	39	.1208	55

accession no.	catalogue no.	accession no.	catalogue no.
1975.1 .1209	20	1975.1 .1573	102
.1210	62	.1574	105
.1211	78	.1575	104
.1212a,b	63	.1576	100
.1213	31	.1577	101
.1214a,b	28	.1578	103
.1215a,b	51	.1579	98
.1216	53	.1580	99
.1217	64	.1581	83
.1218	21	.1582	119
.1219	48	.1583	136
.1220	37	.1584	129
.1221	75	.1585	132
.1511	108	.1586	124
.1519	107	.1587	134
.1520	109	.1588	130
.1525	84	.1589	127
.1526	86	.1590	128
.1527	85	.1591	122
.1555	115	.1592	121
.1556	110	.1593	135
.1557	111	.1594	120
.1558	106	.1595	117
.1561a,b	87	.1596	118
.1563	89	.1597	131
.1564	88	.1598	123
.1565	94	.1599	125
.1566	95	.1600	126
.1567	91	.1601	133
.1568	90	.1602	35
.1569	92	.2169	112
.1570	96	.2170	113
.1571	97	.2297	114
.1572	93	.2499	116

Bibliography

Abdul Hak, Sélim
 1965 "Contribution d'une découverte archéologique récente à l'étude de la verrerie syrienne à l'époque romaine." *Journal of Glass Studies* 7, pp. 26–34.

Agricola, Georgius
 1955 *De natura fossilium (Textbook of Mineralogy).* Translated by Mark C. Bondy and Jean A. Bondy. New York. First published in 1546 in Latin.

Amatller y Costa, Antoni
 1925 *Catàlech dels vidres que integren la colecció Amatller.* Introduction by Joseph Gudiol y Cunill [José Gudiol Ricart]. Barcelona.

Amsterdam
 1936 *Catalogus van de Tentoonstelling van Oude Kunst uit het bezit van den internationalen handel.* Exhibition, Rijksmuseum.
 1986 *Kunst voor de beeldenstorm: Noordnederlandse kunst, 1525–1580.* Exhibition, Rijksmuseum, 13 September–23 November. Vol. 1 of catalogue edited by W. Th. Kloek, W. Halsema-Kubes, and R. J. Baarsen; vol. 2 edited by J. P. Filedt Kok, W. Halsema-Kubes, and W. Th. Kloek. The Hague.

Auth, Susan H.
 1976 *Ancient Glass at the Newark Museum from the Eugene Schaefer Collection of Antiquities.* Newark.

Baar, Armand
 1938 "Verrerie des Flandres, fabrication anversoise." *Revue belge d'archéologie et d'histoire de l'art* 8, pp. 211–40.

Ballardini, Gaetano
 1933 *Corpus della maiolica italiana, I: Le maioliche datate fino al 1530. Bollettino d'arte,* pubblicazione annuale, no. 1. Rome.

Barag, Dan
 1970 "Glass Vessels of the Roman and Byzantine Periods in Palestine" (in Hebrew). Doctoral dissertation, Hebrew University, Jerusalem.
 1985 *Catalogue of Western Asiatic Glass in the British Museum.* Vol. 1. London and Jerusalem.

Barovier Mentasti, Rosa
 1974 "Roman Glassware in the Museum of Murano and the Muranese Revival of the Nineteenth Century," by Rosa Barovier. *Journal of Glass Studies* 16, pp. 111–19.
 1982 *Il vetro veneziano dal Medioeva al Novecento.* Milan.

Barovier Mentasti, Rosa, and Tullio Toninato
 1983 *Glass in Murano.* Venice.

Barrelet, James
 1953 *La verrerie en France de l'époque gallo-romaine à nos jours.* Paris.
 1960 "Le verre filé: A propos d'une crèche." *Cahiers de la céramique, du verre, et des arts du feu,* no. 20, pp. 294–310.

Barrera, Jorge
 1987 "La verrerie du XIVe au XVIe siècles recueillie à Orléans." *Annales du 10e Congrès de l'Association Internationale pour l'Histoire du Verre, Madrid–Segovie, 23–28 septembre 1985,* pp. 341–60. Amsterdam.

Basel
 1982 *10 Gläser, 10 Techniken.* Exhibition, Historisches Museum. Catalogue by Irmgard Peter-Müller.
 1988 *Venezianische Glaskunst aus Basler Privatbesitz.* Exhibition, Historisches Museum Basel, 2 September–27 November. Catalogue by Irmgard Peter-Müller.

Battie, David, and Simon Cottle
 1991 *Sotheby's Concise Encyclopedia of Glass.* London.

Bauer, Margrit
 1990 "Eine venezianische Scheuer aus der erste Hälfte des 16. Jhs." *Annales du 11e Congrès de l'Association Internationale pour l'Histoire du Verre, Bâle, 29 août–3 septembre 1988,* pp. 389–90. Amsterdam.

Baumgärtner, Sabine
 1977a *Gläser: Antike; Mittelalter; Neuere Zeit. Museum der Stadt Regensburg, Katalog der Glassammlung; Sammlung Brauser.* Karlsruhe.
 1977b *Sächsisches Glas: Die Glashütten und ihre Erzeugnisse.* Wiesbaden.
 1981 *Porträtgläser: Das gläserne Bildnis aus drei Jahrhunderten.* Munich.
 1987 *Glaskunst vom Mittelalter bis zum Klassizismus: Bremer Landesmuseum/Focke-Museum Bestandskatalog.* Hefte des Focke-Museums, no. 76. Bremen.

Bellanger, Jacqueline
 1988 *Verre, d'usage et de prestige: France, 1500–1800.* Paris.

Bénard, Jacques, and Bernard Dragesco
 1989 *Bernard Perrot et les verreries royales du Duché d'Orléans, 1662–1754.* Orléans.

Bergmann, Joseph, Ritter von
 1858 *Medaillen auf berühmte und ausgezeichnete Männer des oesterreichischen Kaiserstaates, vom XVI. bis zum XIX. Jahrhundert.* Vienna.

Berlin
 1965 *Ars Vitraria: 3000 Jahre Glas.* Exhibition, Kunst-

gewerbemuseum Schloss Köpenick. Catalogue by Günter Schade.

1976–77   *Antike Gläser*. Exhibition, Antikenmuseum Berlin, November–February. Catalogue by Gertrud Platz-Horster, 1976.

1981a   *Venezianisches Glas 16. bis 18. Jahrhundert aus Museen der DDR*. Exhibition, Staatliche Museen zu Berlin, August–October. Catalogue by Angelika Wesenberg.

1981b   *Venezianisches Glas 19. bis 20. Jahrhundert aus dem Glasmuseum Murano/Venedig*. Exhibition, Staatliche Museen zu Berlin, August–October. Catalogue by Attilia Dorigato and Rosa Barovier Mentasti.

Bernal sale
1855   *Illustrated Catalogue of the Distinguished Collection of Works of Art and Vertù, from the Byzantine Period to That of Louis Seize, Collected by the Late Ralph Bernal, Esq.* Sale catalogue, Christie and Manson, London, 5 March–30 April.

Bernier, Rosamond
1962   "Le Musée de Mouton." *L'oeil*, no. 91–92 (July–August), pp. 24–37.

Bernt, Walther
[1951?]   *Altes Glas*. Munich.

Berryer, Anne-Marie
1957   *La verrerie ancienne aux Musées Royaux d'Art et d'Histoire*. Brussels.

Biaggio Simona, Simonetta
1991   *I vetri romani provenienti dalle terre dell'attuale Cantone Ticino*. 2 vols. Locarno.

Biemann sale
1984   *European Glass, the Property of Mr. and Mrs. Fritz Biemann*. Sale catalogue, Sotheby Parke Bernet and Co., London, 16 June.

Billeter, Erika, ed.
1969   *Glas aus der Sammlung des Kunstgewerbemuseums Zürich*. Zurich.

Boesen, Gudmund
1950   *Gamle Glas*. Copenhagen.
1960   *Venetianske Glas på Rosenborg/ I vetri veneziani del Castello di Rosenborg/ Venetian Glass at Rosenborg Castle*. Copenhagen.

Bohn, Henry G.
1857   *A Guide to the Knowledge of Pottery, Porcelain, and Other Objects of Vertu; Comprising an Illustrated Catalogue of the Bernal Collection of Works of Art with the Prices at Which They Were Sold by Auction, and the Names of the Present Possessors. To Which Are Added an Introductory Essay on Pottery and Porcelain, and an Engraved List of Marks and Monograms*. London.

Bologna
1959   *Iridescenze e colori di vetri antichi*. Exhibition, Museo Civico, 12–26 April. Catalogue by Rosanna Pincelli, C. Volpe, and G. Gualandi.

Bondy, Oscar
n.d.   "Description of Objects in the Bondy Collection." Blumka Gallery, New York. Typescript.

Bonn–Basel
1988   *Phönix aus Sand und Asche: Glas des Mittelalters*. Exhibition, Rheinisches Landesmuseum Bonn and Historisches Museum Basel. Catalogue by Erwin Baumgartner and Ingeborg Krueger. Munich.

du Boulay, Anthony
1990   "Porcelain for Palaces: An Exhibition Sponsored by Fujitsu and Organized by the Oriental Ceramic Society Jointly with the British Museum." *Arts of Asia* 20, no. 4 (July–August), pp. 112–20.

Bourgeois frères sale
1904   *Catalogue des objets d'art et de haute curiosité composant la collection Bourgeois frères*. Sale catalogue, H. Lempertz, Cologne, 19–27 October.

Bradford, Ernle D. S.
1953   *Four Centuries of European Jewellery*. London.

Braunová, Dagmar
1980   *Renesanční a barokní emailované sklo*. Plzeň.

Breck, Joseph, and Meyric R. Rogers
1929   *The Pierpont Morgan Wing: A Handbook*. 2d ed. New York: The Metropolitan Museum of Art.

Bremen, Walther
1964   *Die alten Glasgemälde und Hohlgläser der Sammlung Bremen in Krefeld: Katalog*. Bonner Jahrbücher, Beiheft 13. Cologne.

Bremen
1968   *Ausstellung der neuerworbenen Gläsersammlung Dr. Alexander Lehmann im Haus Riensberg des Focke-Museums*. Exhibition, Haus Riensberg, Focke-Museum. Catalogue by Alexander Lehmann.

Brescia
1987   *Vetri nelle civiche collezioni bresciane*. Exhibition, S. Maria in Solario, June–October. Catalogue by Giovanni Mariacher et al.

Bringuier, Bernadette
1982   *Émaux ou verres filés; dits de Nevers*. Nevers: Musée Municipal.

Brooklyn
1958   *An Exhibition of Engraved Glass of Western Europe*. Exhibition, Brooklyn Museum. Pamphlet by Jerome Strauss.

Brooks, John A.
1973   *Glass*. New York.

Bucher, [Adalbert] Bruno
1888   *Die Glassammlung des K. K. Oesterreich. Museums*. Vienna.

Buckley, Wilfred
1926   *European Glass: A Brief Outline of the History of Glass Making, with Notes on Various Methods of Glass Decoration, Illustrated by Examples in the*

Collection of the Author. Boston and New York.

1929   *Diamond Engraved Glasses of the Sixteenth Century, with Particular Reference to Five Attributed to Giacomo Verzelini.* London.

1932   "Six Italian Diamond Engraved Glasses." *Burlington Magazine* 61 (October), pp. 158–61.

1939   *The Art of Glass: Illustrated from the Wilfred Buckley Collection in the Victoria and Albert Museum, London.* Edited by Bertha Terrell Buckley. New York.

Cambridge

1978   *Glass at the Fitzwilliam Museum.* Exhibition, Fitzwilliam Museum. Catalogue by Mrs. B. K. Schnitzer et al.

Carbonnier, A. A.

1893   "Katalog von Gegenstanden der Glasindustrie und der Malerei auf Glas" [in the Museum of the Stieglitz Central School of Design]. Translation of Russian original, Saint Petersburg. Manuscript, Corning Museum of Glass Library.

Castellani sale

1884   *Catalogue des objets d'art, antiques, du Moyen-Âge et de la Renaissance, dépendant de la succession Alessandro Castellani.* Sale catalogue, Hoffmann and Mannheim, Palazzo Castellani, Rome, 17 March–10 April.

Causa Picone, Marina

1967   *Vetri a San Martino.* Naples.

Chambon, Raymond

1955   *L'histoire de la verrerie en Belgique du IIme siècle à nos jours.* Brussels.

Charleston, Robert J.

1952   "The Art of Glass in France – Part I." *Antiques* 61 (February), pp. 156–59.

1972   "Enamelling and Gilding on Glass." *Glass Circle* 1, pp. 18–32.

1977   "Glass." In *The James A. de Rothschild Collection at Waddesdon Manor.* [Vol. 8], *Glass and Stained Glass, Limoges and Other Painted Enamels,* pp. 11–280. Fribourg.

1978   "Some Aspects of 17th Century Glass Found in England." *Annales du 7e Congrès de l'Association pour l'Histoire du Verre, Berlin–Leipzig, 15–21 août 1977,* pp. 283–97. Liège.

1980a   *Masterpieces of Glass: A World History from the Corning Museum of Glass.* New York.

1980b   "Section 6: 16th to 17th Century English Glass." *Bulletin de l'Association Internationale pour l'Histoire du Verre,* no. 8 (1977–80), pp. 77–99.

1984   *English Glass and the Glass Used in England, Circa 400–1940.* London.

Churchill, Arthur, Ltd.

1951   *Glass Notes,* no. 11, December. London.

1953   *Glass Notes,* no. 13, December. London.

Cincinnati

1959   *The Lehman Collection, New York.* Exhibition, Cincinnati Art Museum, 8 May–5 July.

Clairmont, Christoph W.

1963   *The Excavations at Dura-Europos, Final Report.* Vol. 4, part 5, *The Glass Vessels.* New Haven.

1977   *Catalogue of Ancient and Islamic Glass.* Based on the notes of C. J. Lamm. Athens: Benake Museum.

Clarke, Timothy H.

1974   "Lattimo – a Group of Venetian Glass Enameled on an Opaque-White Ground." *Journal of Glass Studies* 16, pp. 22–56.

Clarke, Timothy H., and Jonathan Bourne

1988   "Louis XIV's Glass Table." *Apollo* 128, no. 321 (November), pp. 334–39, 379.

Cleveland

1956   *Venetian Tradition.* Exhibition, Cleveland Museum of Art. Catalogue introduction by Henry S. Francis.

Cleveland Museum of Art

1958   *The Handbook of the Cleveland Museum of Art.* Cleveland.

Cologne

1960   *Ausstellungskatalog Cimelien, Kunstgewerbemuseum der Stadt Köln.* Exhibition, Kunstgewerbemuseum.

[1961]   *2000 Jahre Glas.* Exhibition, Kunstgewerbemuseum.

Columbus

1983   *Three Hundred Years of Venetian Glass: Selections from the Museo Vetrario, Murano.* Exhibition, Columbus Museum of Art, 1 October–20 November. Catalogue introduction by Dwight Lanmon.

Comstock, Helen

1950   "The Connoisseur in America: Venetian Glass Cup" [in the Cleveland Museum of Art]. *Connoisseur* 126, no. 517 (August), p. 52.

1957   "The Connoisseur in America: Venetian Tazza with the Medici Arms [in the Corning Museum of Glass]." *Connoisseur* 140, no. 565 (December), pp. 205–6.

Constable-Maxwell sale

1979   *Catalogue of the Constable-Maxwell Collection of Ancient Glass: The Property of Mr. and Mrs. Andrew Constable-Maxwell, Including a Late Roman Glass Diatretum or Cage-Cup Circa 300 A.D.* Sale catalogue, Sotheby Parke Bernet and Co., London, 4–5 June.

Corning

1955   *Glass Drinking Vessels from the Collections of Jerome Strauss and the Ruth Bryan Strauss Memorial Foundation.* Exhibition, Corning Museum of Glass. Catalogue by Jerome Strauss.

1958   *Three Great Centuries of Venetian Glass.* Exhibition, Corning Museum of Glass. Catalogue by Paul Perrot.

1962   *A Decade of Glass Collecting: Selections from the Melvin Billups Collection.* Exhibition, Corning Museum of Glass. Catalogue by Paul Perrot.

1987   *Glass of the Caesars.* Exhibition, Corning Museum of Glass; British Museum, London; Römisch-Germanisches Museum, Cologne; Musei Capitolini,

Rome. Catalogue by Donald B. Harden, with Hansgerd Hellenkemper, Kenneth Painter, and David Whitehouse. Milan.

1992 *Reverse Paintings on Glass: The Ryser Collection.* Exhibition, Corning Museum of Glass, 25 April–18 October. Catalogue based on *Verzauberte Bilder*, by Frieder Ryser; edited and translated by Rudy Eswarin.

Corning Museum of Glass
1958 *Glass from the Corning Museum of Glass: A Guide to the Collections.* 2d ed. Corning.
1974 *Glass from the Corning Museum of Glass: A Guide to the Collections.* Rev. and enl. ed. Corning.
1987 *Annual Report of the Corning Museum of Glass.* Corning.

Coutts, Howard
1992 "Cosmopolitan Collectors." *Antique Collector* 63, no. 4 (April), pp. 68–73.

Czurda-Ruth, Barbara
1979 *Die römischen Gläser vom Magdalensberg.* Klagenfurt.

Davidson, Ruth
1958 "Special Events: Venetian Glass at Corning." *Antiques* 73, no. 6 (June), p. 570.

Deboni, Franco
1989 *I vetri Venini.* Turin.

Delft
1970 *Een Glasie van vrienschap, de glazen van de Collectie Guépin.* Exhibition, Stedelijk Museum-"Het Prinsenhof."

Denis, Hans
1976 *Vitrum: Geschichte und Geschichten um Glas.* Munich.

Dexel, Thomas
1974 *Trinkgefässe aus Glas in der Formsammlung der Stadt Braunschweig.* Arbeitsberichte aus dem Städtischen Museum Braunschweig, 26. Brunswick.
1977 *Gebrauchsglas: Gläser des Alltags vom Spätmittelalter bis zum beginnenden 20. Jahrhundert*, with the collaboration of Uwe Friedleben. Brunswick.
1978 *Trinkgefässe aus Glas in der Formsammlung der Stadt Braunschweig.* 2d ed. Brunswick.
1983 *Gebrauchsglas: Gläser des Alltags vom Spätmittelalter bis zum beginnenden 20. Jahrhundert*, with the collaboration of Uwe Friedleben. 2d ed. Munich.
1986 *Die Formen des Gebrauchsgeräts: Ein Typenkatalog der Gefässe aus Keramik, Metall, und Glas in Mitteleuropa.* Munich.

Dexel, Walter
1939 *Deutsches Handwerksgut: Eine Kultur- und Formgeschichte des Hausgeräts.* Berlin.
1943 *Holzgerät und Holzform: Über die Bedeutung der Holzformen für die deutsche Gerätkultur des Mittelalters und der Neuzeit.* Berlin-Dahlem.
1950 *Glas.* Veröffentlichung des Braunschweiger Instituts für Handwerkliche und Industrielle Formgebung, 2. Ravensburg.

1973 *Das Hausgerät Mitteleuropas: Wesen und Wandel der Formen in Zwei Jahrtausenden: Deutschland, Holland, Österreich, Schweiz.* 2d ed. Brunswick and Berlin. First edition published 1939 as *Deutsches Handwerksgut.*

Diderot, Denis
1759 *Encyclopédie, ou Dictionnaire raisonné des sciences, des arts, et des métiers, par une société de gens de lettres, mis en ordre et publié par M. Diderot.... 2d ed., with notes by Octavien Diodati. Vol. 5. Lucques.

[Diesing]
1769 *Die Glasschmelzkunst bey der Lampe....* Vienna. Initialed on title page: J. d. B.

Douglas, R. Langton
1946 *Piero di Cosimo.* Chicago.

Dragendorff, H.
1895 "Terra Sigillata: Ein Beitrag zur Geschichte der griechischen und römischen Keramik." *Bonner Jahrbücher* 96, pp. 18–155.

Drahotová, Olga
1980 "Schürerové a Preusslerové jako výrobci kobaltového skla." *Acta UPM* 15, ser. C: *Comentationes* 2, pp. 72–96. German summary, pp. 219–22.
1981 "Identifying Glass from the Buquoy Glass Factory at the Nové Hrady Estate (Gratzen) in the Seventeenth Century." *Journal of Glass Studies* 23, pp. 46–55.

Dreier, Franz-Adrian
1969 *Glaskunst in Hessen-Kassel.* Kassel, Germany.
1989a "Glass Imitating Rock Crystal and Precious Stones – 16th and 17th Century Wheel Engraving and Gold Ruby Glass." *Glass Circle* 6, pp. 8–19.
1989b *Venezianische Gläser und 'Façon de Venise.'* Kataloge des Kunstgewerbemuseums, 12. Berlin.

Dresden
1975 *Sächsisches Glas.* Exhibition, Staatliche Kunstsammlungen, May–October. Catalogue by Gisela Haase.

Düsseldorf
1968–69 *Meisterwerke der Glaskunst aus internationalem Privatbesitz zusammengestellt vom Kunstmuseum Düsseldorf.* Exhibition, Städtische Kunsthalle, 22 November–5 January. Catalogue by Axel von Saldern, 1968.

Düsseldorf–Oldenburg
1979–80 *Deutsches Steinzeug der Renaissance- und Barockzeit.* Exhibition, Hetjens-Museum/Deutsches Keramikmuseum, 23 September–25 November; Landesmuseum für Kunst und Kulturgeschichte, 1 January–17 February. Catalogue by Ekkart Klinge, 1979.

Egg, Erich
1962 *Die Glashütten zu Hall und Innsbruck im 16. Jahrhundert.* Tiroler Wirtschaftsstudien 15. Innsbruck.

Eisen, Gustavus A.
1927 *Glass, Its Origin, History, Chronology, Technic and Classification to the Sixteenth Century.* Assisted by Fahim Kouchakji. 2 vols. New York.

Emden sale
1908　*Sammlung Hermann Emden, Hamburg*. Part 1. Sale catalogue, Rudolph Lepke's Kunst-Auctions-Haus, Berlin, 3–7 November.

Engen, Luc, ed.
1989　*Le verre en Belgique des origines à nos jours*. [Antwerp]. Also published in Dutch.

Ennès, Pierre
1982　*La verrerie ancienne*. Rennes.

Erlande-Brandenburg, Alain
1987　*Musée National de la Renaissance, Château d'Écouen: Guide*. Paris.

Eumorfopoulos sale
1940　*The Eumorfopoulos Collection: Catalogue of the Collection of Persian Ceramics and Islamic Glass; Egyptian, Greek, and Roman Antiquities; Choice Medieval and Renaissance Works of Art, Etc., Formed by the Late George Eumorfopoulos, Esq.* Sale catalogue, Sotheby and Co., London, 5–6 June.

Evison, Vera I.
1955　"Anglo-Saxon Finds near Rainham, Essex, with a Study of Glass Drinking Horns." *Archaeologia* 96, pp. 159–95.
1975　"Germanic Glass Drinking Horns." *Journal of Glass Studies* 17, pp. 74–87.

von Falke, Otto
1930　"Gotisch oder Fatimidisch?" *Pantheon* 5 (March), pp. 120–29. English summary.

Figdor sale
1930　*Die Sammlung Dr. Albert Figdor, Wien*. Part I, vols. 1–2. Sale catalogue, Artaria, Glückselig G.M.B.H., Vienna, 11–13 June.

Fleming, John, and Hugh Honour
1977　*Dictionary of the Decorative Arts*. New York.

Folsach, Kjeld von, and David Whitehouse
1993　"Three Islamic Molds." *Journal of Glass Studies* 35. In press.

Foote, Helen S.
1950　"Venetian Glass Cup." *Cleveland Museum of Art Bulletin* 37 (February), pp. 26, 31.

Frankfurt am Main
1966–67　*Kunst und Kunsthandwerk, Ausstellung der Dauerleihgaben des Mitteldeutschen Kunstgewerbevereins e.V. im Museum für Kunsthandwerk Frankfurt am Main*. Exhibition, Karmeliterkloster, 22 November–8 January. Catalogue by P. W. Meister and Annaliese Ohm, 1966.
1974　*Neuerwerbungen, 1956–1974*. Exhibition, Museum für Kunsthandwerk.

Fremersdorf, Fritz
1958　*Römisches Buntglas in Köln*. Cologne.
1961　*Die Denkmäler des römischen Köln*. Vol. 6, *Römisches geformtes Glas in Köln*. Cologne.

de Frey sale
1933　*Catalogue des tableaux anciens, tableaux modernes, objets d'art de haute curiosité du XVIIIe siècle et d'Extrême-Orient composant la collection de Mr. de Frey*. Sale catalogue, Galerie Jean Charpentier, Paris, 12–14 June.

Friedleben sale
1990　*Europäisches Formglas 15.–19. Jahrhunderts, sowie Emailglas und Farbglas, Sammlung Uwe Friedleben*. Sale catalogue, Kunstauktionshaus Dr. Fritz Nagel, Stuttgart, 5 October.

Fritz, Johann Michael
1964　"La raccolta Bremen al Rheinisch Museum di Bonn." *Vetro e silicate*, no. 47 (September–October), pp. 19–24.

Frothingham, Alice Wilson
1941　*Hispanic Glass with Examples in the Collection of the Hispanic Society of America*. New York.
1956　*Barcelona Glass in Venetian Style*. New York.
1963　*Spanish Glass*. London.

Fuchs, Ludwig F.
1956　*Die Glaskunst im Wandel der Jahrtausende*. Darmstadt.

de Gaigneron, Axelle
1991　"Verres de Nevers." *Connaissance des arts*, no. 471 (May), pp. 74–81.

Galerie Fischer sale
1937　*Zinnsammlung V.... Waffen,... Glassammlung aus Englischem Besitz....* Sale catalogue, Galerie Fischer, Lucerne, 30–31 August.

Gardner, Paul Vickers
1971　*The Glass of Frederick Carder*. New York.
1979　*Glass*. New York.

Gardner sale
1990　*The Ava Gardner Collection*. Sale catalogue, Sotheby's, London, 21 November.

Garnier, Édouard
1891　"Verreries." In *La Collection Spitzer: Antiquité, Moyen Âge, Renaissance*, vol. 3, pp. 75–111. Paris.

Gasparetto, Astone
1958　*Il vetro di Murano dalle origini ad oggi*. Venice.
1960a　"La verrerie vénitienne; ce qu'elle a emprunté et ce qu'elle a donné." In *Annales du Ier Congrès International d'Étude Historique du Verre des "Journées Internationales du Verre," Liège, 20–24 août 1959*, pp. 119–30. Liège.
1960b　*Vetri di Murano, 1860–1960*. Verona.

Gateau, Jean-Charles
1974　*La verrerie*. Geneva.

Gatty, Charles T.
1883　*Catalogue of the Medieval and Later Antiquities Contained in the Mayer Museum*. Liverpool.

Gavet sale
1897　*Catalogue des objets d'art et de haute curiosité de la*

Renaissance, tableaux, tapisseries, composant la collection de M. Émile Gavet. Sale catalogue, Galerie Georges Petit, Paris, 31 May–9 June.

van Gelder, Hendrik E.
1955   *Glas en ceramiek, de kunsten van het vuur.* Utrecht.

van Gelder, Hendrik E., and Beatrice Jansen
1969   *Glas in Nederlandse musea.* Bussum and Antwerp.

Gerspach, Édouard
1885   *L'art de la verrerie.* Paris.

Glass Collections
1982   *Glass Collections in Museums in the United States and Canada.* Corning.

Goethert-Polaschek, Karin
1977   *Katalog der römischen Gläser des Rheinischen Landesmuseums Trier.* Mainz am Rhein.

González-Palacios, Alvar
1984   *Il tempio del gusto: Le arti decorative in Italia fra classicismo e barocco; Roma e il regno delle due Sicilie.* 2 vols. Milan.

Grassi sale
1927   *Italian Art: The Collection of Professor Luigi Grassi, Furniture, Textiles, Sculptures and Jewelry.* Sale catalogue, American Art Galleries, New York, 20–22 January.

Grubert, Halina
1984   "Mr. Higgins' Fine Art Museum." *Antique Collector* 55 (January), pp. 24–29.

Gudiol Ricart, José
1941   *Los vidrios catalanes.* Barcelona. First published in Catalan, 1936.

Gudiol Ricart, José, and P. M. de Artíñano
1935   *Vidrio; resumen de la historia del vidrio: Catálogo de la colección Alfonso Macaya.* Barcelona.

Haase, Gisela
1988   *Sächsisches Glas: Geschichte, Zentren, Dekorationen.* Munich.
1990   "Zur Bedeutung der Glashütten Heidelbach im Erzgebirge." *Annales du 11e Congrès de l'Association Internationale pour l'Histoire du Verre, Bâle, 29 août–3 septembre 1988,* pp. 373–87. Amsterdam.

Hackenbroch, Yvonne
1954   "A Limoges Enamel Hunting Horn." *Connoisseur* 133, no. 538 (June), pp. 249–51.
1979   *Renaissance Jewellery.* London and Munich.
1986   "Reinhold Vasters, Goldsmith." *Metropolitan Museum of Art Journal* 19–20 (1984–85), pp. 163–268.

The Hague
1957   *Glas door de eeuwen/Old Glass.* Exhibition, Gemeentemuseum. Catalogue signed E. A.
1972   *Glas Empire Biedermeier, 1800–1850.* Exhibition, Gemeentemuseum, 26 August–2 October.

Hamburg
1974   *Gläser der Antike: Sammlung Erwin Oppenländer.*

Exhibition, Museum für Kunst und Gewerbe. Catalogue by Axel von Saldern et al.

Harden, Donald B.
1936   *Roman Glass from Karanis Found by the University of Michigan Archaeological Expedition in Egypt, 1924–1929.* Ann Arbor.

Hartshorne, Albert
1897   *Old English Glasses: An Account of Glass Drinking Vessels in England, from Early Times to the End of the Eighteenth Century. . . .* London and New York.

Haudicquer de Blancourt, Jean, 1699. *See* Neri, Antonio, 1699.

Hayes, John W.
1975   *Roman and Pre-Roman Glass in the Royal Ontario Museum: A Catalogue.* Toronto.

Haynes, Edward Barrington
1948   *Glass Through the Ages.* Harmondsworth.
1959   *Glass Through the Ages.* Rev. ed. Baltimore.

Hayward, Jane
1982   *Glass in the Collections of The Metropolitan Museum of Art.* New York.

Heikamp, Detlef
1986   *Studien zur mediceischen Glaskunst.* Florence.

Heinemeyer, Elfriede
1966   *Kataloge des Kunstmuseums Düsseldorf.* Vol. 1, *Glas.* Düsseldorf.

Hejdová, Dagmar
1981   "The Glasshouse at Rejdice in Northeastern Bohemia, Late Sixteenth–Early Seventeenth Centuries." *Journal of Glass Studies* 23, pp. 18–33.

Hejdová, Dagmar, and Olga Drahotová
1989   *České sklo.* Vol. 1. Prague.

Henkes, H. E., and H. M. Zijlstra-Zweens
1991   "Met wit email versierde beker- en kelkglazen uit ca. 1600." *Antiek* 26, no. 2 (August–September), pp. 60–68.

Herbert, John, ed.
1975   *Christie's Review of the Season, 1975.* London.

Hermelin, Carl F., and Elsebeth Welander
1980   *Glasboken.* Stockholm.

Hessisches Landesmuseum Darmstadt
1935   *Deutsches Glas: Zweitausende Jahre Glasveredelung.* Darmstadt.

Hetteš, Karel
1960   *Old Venetian Glass.* Translated by Ota Vojtísek. London. Also published in German.
1963   "Venetian Trends in Bohemian Glassmaking in the Sixteenth and Seventeenth Centuries." *Journal of Glass Studies* 5, pp. 38–53.

Hollister, Paul
1981   "'Flowers Wich Clothe the Meadows in Spring': The Rebirth of Millefiori, c. 1500." In *Annales du 8e Congrès International d'Étude Historique du Verre, London–Liverpool, 18–25 septembre 1979,* pp. 221–33. Liège.

d'Hondt, Pieter
[1893?]   *Venise: L'art de la verrerie; histoire et fabrication.*
Paris.

Honey, William B.
1946   *Glass; a Handbook for the Study of Glass Vessels of
All Periods and Countries and a Guide to the
Museum Collection.* London: Victoria and Albert
Museum.
1947   *Glass Table-ware.* London: Victoria and Albert
Museum.

Hörning, Jutta
[1978]   *Gläser vom XVI. bis XIX. Jahrhundert aus dem
Bestand der Kunstsammlungen zu Weimar.* Weimar.

Howell, A[lan] G[eorge] Ferrers
1913   *S. Bernardino of Siena.* London.

Hurst, Ruth
1968   "Rare Glass from the City of Liverpool Museum."
Liverpool Bulletin, Museums Number 14 (1967),
pp. 16–31.

Hutton, William
1963   "European Glass in the Museum Collection."
Museum News, Toledo Museum of Art, n.s. 6, no. 1
(Spring).

d'Huyvetter sale
1829   *Zeldzaamheden verzameld en uitgegeven door Joan.
d'Huyvetter....* Sale catalogue, P. F. de Goesin-
Verhaeghe, Ghent.

von Indermauer, Robert
1924   "Zweige der Madruzzi." *Heraldische Gesellschaft
"Adler"* (Vienna), n.s. 9, pp. 183–91.

Innsbruck
1959   *Alte und Neue Glaskunst.* Exhibition, Tiroler
Landesmuseum, March–May.

Isings, Clasina
1957   *Roman Glass from Dated Finds.* Groningen and
Djakarta.
1966   *Antiek Glas.* Amsterdam. Also published in German.

Jansen, Béatrice
1962   *Catalogus van Noord- en Zuidnederlands glas.* The
Hague: Gemeentemuseum.

Jantzen, Johannes
1960   *Deutsches Glas aus fünf Jahrhunderten.* Düsseldorf.

Jiřík, František X.
1934   *Kniha o skle* (Book of Glass). Prague. Also published
in English.

Joseph sale
1890   *Catalogue of the Renowned Collection of Objects
of Art and Decoration, of Mr. E. Joseph, of 158,
New Bond Street, Who Has Entirely Relinquished
Business: Third Portion.* Sale catalogue, Christie,
Manson and Woods, London, 10 June.

Kachalov, Nikolaï
1959   *Steklo.* Moscow.

Kämpfer, Fritz
1978   *Beakers, Tankards, Goblets.* Translated by Alisa
Jaffa. Leipzig. Originally published in German as
Becher, Humpen, Pokale, 1977.

Kämpfer, Fritz, and Klaus G. Beyer
1966   *Glass, a World History: The Story of 4000 Years of
Fine Glass-making.* Translated from the German
and revised by Edmund Launert. London.

Karlsruhe
1971   *Edles altes Glas: Die Sammlung Heinrich Heine,
Karlsruhe.* Exhibition, Badisches Landesmuseum,
5–31 October. Catalogue by Sabine Baumgärtner.

Khayat sale
1928   *Egyptian, Greek, Roman, and Persian Antiques
Collected by Azeez Khayat, Expert, in Egypt, Palestine, Syria, and Greece.* Sale catalogue, Anderson
Galleries, New York, 11–12 April.

King, Viva (Mrs. William)
1939   "Verre de Nevers." *Apollo* 30 (September), pp. 105–10.

King, William
1929   "Eine Gruppe emaillierter Venetianer Gläser im
Britischen Museum." *Pantheon* 4 (October),
pp. 473–75. English summary.

King sale
1958   *Catalogue of a Collection of English Drinking
Glasses, the Property of H. N. Hignett, Esq.; Rare
"Verre de Nevers" Figures and Groups, the Property
of Mrs. Viva King....* Sale catalogue, Sotheby and
Co., London, 17 October.

Klein, Dan, and Ward Lloyd, eds.
1989   *The History of Glass.* [2d ed.] New York. First
published in 1984.

Klesse, Brigitte
1963   *Kunstgewerbemuseum der Stadt Köln: Glas.* Kataloge,
vol. 1. Cologne.
1965   *Glassammlung Helfried Krug.* Part 1. Munich.
1973   *Glassammlung Helfried Krug.* Part 2. Bonn.

Klesse, Brigitte, and Hans Mayr
1987   *European Glass from 1500–1800: The Ernesto Wolf
Collection.* Translated by Perran Wood. Vienna.

Klesse, Brigitte, and Gisela Reineking von Bock
1973   *Kunstgewerbemuseum der Stadt Köln: Glas.* Kataloge,
vol. 1. 2d ed. Cologne.

Klesse, Brigitte, and Axel von Saldern
1978   *500 Jahre Glaskunst: Sammlung Biemann.* Zurich.

Kneschke, Ernst Heinrich
1852–54   *Deutsche Grafen-Häuser der Gegenwart in heral-
discher, historischer und genealogischer Beziehung.*
3 vols. Leipzig.

Koch, Robert
1971   *Louis C. Tiffany's Glass – Bronzes – Lamps: A
Complete Collector's Guide.* New York.
1982   *Louis C. Tiffany, Rebel in Glass.* 3d ed. New York.

Kofler-Truniger sale
1985   *Ancient Glass Formerly the Kofler-Truniger Collection: The Property of a Gentleman.* Sale catalogue,
Christie, Manson and Woods, London, 5–6 March.

Kohlhaussen, Heinrich
  1959   "Der Doppelmaserbecher auf der Veste Coburg und seine Verwandten." *Jahrbuch der Coburger Landesstiftung*, pp. 109–34.
  1960   "Der Doppelkopf: Seine Bedeutung für das deutsche Brauchtum des 13. bis 17. Jahrhunderts." *Zeitschrift für Kunstwissenschaft* 14, no. 1–2, pp. 24–56.

Kreisel, Heinrich, and Georg Himmelheber
  1981   *Die Kunst des deutschen Möbels: Möbel und Vertäfelungen des deutschen Sprachraums von den Anfängen bis zum Jugendstil.* Vol. 1, *Von den Anfängen bis zum Hochbarok.* 3d ed. Munich.

Kröger, Jens
  1984   *Berlin, Staatliche Museen Preussischer Kulturbesitz, Museum für Islamische Kunst: Glas.* Islamische Kunst: Loseblattkatalog unpublizierter Werke aus deutschen Museen, vol. 1. Mainz am Rhein.

Krug sale
  1981–83 *The Krug Collection of Glass.* Sale catalogues, Sotheby Parke Bernet, London: part 1 (7 July 1981), part 2 (7 December 1981), part 3 (15 November 1982), part 4 (14 March 1983).

Kubalska, Slawomira Ciepela
  1987   "Les verreries polonaises au XVIIe siècle." In *Annales du 10e Congrès de l'Association Internationale pour l'Histoire du Verre, Madrid–Segovie, 23–28 septembre 1985*, pp. 449–64. Amsterdam.

Kunckel von Löwenstern, Johann, 1679. *See* Neri, Antonio, 1679.

Kunstgewerbemuseum
  1937   *Verzeichnis der Erwerbungen, 1933–1935.* Berlin.

Labarte, [Charles] Jules
  1847   *Description des objets d'art qui composent la collection Debruge Duménil précédée d'une introduction historique.* Paris.

Laméris, Frides, and Kitty Laméris
  1991   *Venetiaans en façon de Venise glas, 1500–1700.* Amsterdam.

Lamm, Carl Johan
  1929–30 *Mittelalterliche Gläser und Steinschnittarbeiten aus dem Nahen Osten.* 2 vols. Forschungen zur islamischen Kunst, vol. 5. Berlin.

Lanmon, Dwight P.
  1978   *Glass from Six Centuries: Wadsworth Atheneum.* Hartford, Conn.

Lanna sale
  1911   *Sammlung des Freiherrn Adalbert von Lanna, Prag.* Part 2. Sale catalogue, Rudolph Lepke's Kunst-Auctions-Haus, Berlin, 21–28 March.

Lawrence (Kans.)–Chapel Hill–Wellesley
  1981–82 *The Engravings of Marcantonio Raimondi.* Exhibition, Spencer Museum of Art, University of Kansas, Lawrence, 16 November–3 January; Ackland Art Museum, University of North Carolina, Chapel Hill, 10 February–28 March; Wellesley College Art Museum, 15 April–15 June. Catalogue by Innis H. Shoemaker and Elizabeth Broun. Lawrence, 1981.

Lazarus, Peter
  [1973?] *The Cinzano Glass Diary, 1974.* London.
  1974   *Cinzano Glass Collection.* London.
  1978   *The Cinzano Glass Collection.* London.

L[ebeuf] de M[ontgermont] sale
  1891   *Catalogue des objets d'art composant la précieuse et importante collection de M. L. de M. . . .* Sale catalogue, Galerie Georges Petit, Paris, 25–30 May.

Lieb, Norbert
  1958   *Die Fugger und die Kunst im Zeitalter der Hohen Renaissance.* Munich.

Liège
  1958   *Trois millénaires d'art verrier à travers les collections publiques et privées de Belgique.* Exhibition, Musée Curtius et Palais des Congrès. Catalogue with introduction by Pierre Baar.

Lipp, Franz Carl
  1974   *Bemalte Gläser; volkstümliche Bildwelt auf altem Glas; Geschichte und Technik.* Munich.

Liverpool
  1979   *Historic Glass from Collections in North West England.* Exhibition, National Museums and Galleries on Merseyside, September.

Loewenthal, A.
  1934   "Les grands vases de cristal de roche et leur origine." *Gazette des Beaux-Arts*, ser. 6, 11, pp. 43–48.

Lohr am Main
  1984   *Glück und Glas: Zur Kulturgeschichte des Spessartglases.* Exhibition, Spessartmuseum. Catalogue edited by Claus Grimm. Munich.

London
  1930   *Exhibition of Italian Art, 1200–1900.* Exhibition, Royal Academy of Arts, 1 January–8 March. Catalogue, *A Commemorative Catalogue of the Exhibition of Italian Art . . .*, edited by Lord Balniel and Kenneth Clark, 1931.
  1968a   *English Glass.* Exhibition, Victoria and Albert Museum, 4 July–31 August. Catalogue by Robert J. Charleston.
  1968b   *Masterpieces of Glass.* Exhibition, British Museum. Catalogue by Donald Harden et al.
  1974   *Glass Through the Ages.* Exhibition, Allan Tillman (Antiques) Ltd., 12–22 June.
  1978   *English Glass.* Exhibition, Victoria and Albert Museum. Catalogue by Robert J. Charleston.

Lorenzetti, Giulio
  1931   *Vetri di Murano.* Rome.
  [1953] *Murano e l'arte del vetro soffiato: Guida del Museo Vetrario di Murano.* Venice.

Los Angeles–Chicago
  1970   *The Middle Ages: Treasures from the Cloisters and The Metropolitan Museum of Art.* Exhibition, Los Angeles County Museum of Art, 18 January–29 March; Art Institute of Chicago, 16 May–5 July.

Loudmer sale
  1985   *Verres antiques et de l'Islam.* Sale catalogue, Guy Loudmer, Paris, 3–4 June.

Lubin, Edward R., Inc.
[1959?] *Works of Art.* New York. Unpaged.
[1985] *European Works of Art: A Selection from the Gallery.* New York.

Lucerne
1981 *3000 Jahre Glaskunst: Von der Antike bis zum Jugendstil.* Exhibition, Kunstmuseum, 19 July–13 September.

McKean, Hugh F.
1980 *The "Lost" Treasures of Louis Comfort Tiffany.* New York.

McNab, Jessie
1960 "A Species of Creation." *Metropolitan Museum of Art Bulletin*, n.s. 19 (November), pp. 90–100.

Maedebach, Heino
1970 "Glas hinter Glas: Die Glas-Sammlung der Veste Coburg." *Artis* 22, no. 2 (February), pp. 14–20.

Maggi, Giovanni
1977 *Bichierografia.* Edited by Paola Barocchi. 4 vols. Facsimile of the 1604 ed. Florence.

Magne, Lucien
1913 *Décor du verre: Gobeleterie, mosaïque, vitrail.* Paris.

Mallè, Luigi, ed.
1971 *Vetri – vetrate – giade: Cristalli di rocca e pietre dure.* Turin.

Marandel, Patrice, et al.
1982 *Vetri, gioielli, smalti, tabacchiere.* Milan.

Marangoni, Guido, ed.
1927 *Enciclopedia delle moderne arti decorative italiane.* Vol. 3, *Le arti del fuoco: Ceramica – vetri – vetrate.* Milan.

Mariacher, Giovanni
1954 *L'arte del vetro.* Milan.
1959a *Vetri italiani del Cinquecento.* Milan.
1959b *I vetri della raccolta Fortuny al Museo di Murano.* Venice.
1960 *Le raccolte vetrarie del Museo Civico di Trieste.* Venice.
1961 *Italian Blown Glass, from Ancient Rome to Venice.* Translated by Michael Bullock and Johanna Capra. New York. First published in 1960 as *Il vetro soffiato da Roma antica a Venezia.*
1962 *Ambienti italiani del Cinquecento.* Milan.
1963 *Vetri italiani del Rinascimento.* Milan.
1964 *Il vetro europeo dal XV al XX secolo.* Novara.
1965a "Vetri del Museo Civico di Brescia." *Vetro e silicati*, no. 51 (May–June), pp. 18–21.
1965b *Vetri italiani del Seicento e del Settecento.* Milan.
[1966] *L'arte del vetro: Dall'antichità al Rinascimento.* Milan.
1967 *I vetri di Murano.* Milan and Rome. Text in Italian, French, English, and German.
[1970]a *Glass from Antiquity to the Renaissance.* Translated by Michael Cunningham. London. First published in 1966 as *L'arte del vetro.*
[1970]b *Il Museo Vetrario di Murano.* Milan.

1971 *Vetri della collezione Vito Manca.* Perugia.
[1976?] *Vetri graffiti veneziani del '500.* Venice.

Mariacher, Giovanni, and Marina Causa Picone
1972 *Vetri meravigliosi.* [2d ed.] Milan. First published as two separate works: *L'arte di vetro: Dall'antichità al Rinascimento*, by Giovanni Mariacher, 1966; and *L'arte di vetro, dal Rinascimento ai nostri giorni*, by Marina Causa Picone, 1967.

Mathesius, Johann
1927 *Die Predig[sic] von dem Glassmachen. Bergpostilla, oder Sarepta*, sermon 15. Munich. First published in 1562.

Matheson, Susan B.
1980 *Ancient Glass in the Yale University Art Gallery.* New Haven.

Merret, Christopher, 1662. *See* Neri, Antonio, 1662.

Meyer, Laure
1992 "Londres au Moyen Âge: Des objets de verre." *Archéologia*, no. 275 (January), pp. 64–66.

Mianni, Mariapia, Daniele Resini, and Francesca Lamon
1984 *L'arte dei maestri vetrai di Murano.* Treviso.

Mikhailova, Olga E.
1970 *Ispanskoe steklo v sobranii Ermitazha/Spanish Glass in the Hermitage.* Leningrad.

Miller von Aichholz sale
1925 *Versteigerung einer hervorragenden Sammlung (Zum Teil aus dem vormaligen Besitz Eugen Miller von Aichholz, Wien): Venetianische Gläser der Renaissance, frühe italienische Majoliken, Kunstgewerbe, Antiken, Miniaturen u. Gemälde.* Sale catalogue, C. J. Wawra and Albert Werner, Vienna, 26 November and following days.

Molinier, Émile
1891 "Les peintures sous verre." In *La Collection Spitzer: Antiquité, Moyen Âge, Renaissance*, vol. 3, pp. 53–73. Paris.
1898 Ed. *Collection Charles Mannheim: Objets d'art.* Paris.

Morgan sale
1944 *Furniture and Objects of Art . . . Property of the Estate of the Late J. P. Morgan . . . .* Part 2. Sale catalogue, Parke-Bernet Galleries, New York, 22–25 March.

Morin-Jean, Alexis Joseph
1913 *La verrerie en Gaule sous l'Empire Romain; essai de morphologie et de chronologie.* Paris.

Morris, Susan
1989 "French Furniture." In *Sotheby's: Art at Auction, 1988–89*, pp. 388–97. London.

Mosel, Christel
1957 *Die Glas-Sammlung.* Bildkataloge, vol. 2. Hannover: Kestner-Museums.
1979 *Glas: Mittelalter – Biedermeier.* Rev. ed. Sammlungskataloge, vol. 1. Hannover: Kestner-Museums. First published in 1957 as *Die Glas-Sammlung.*

Murano
1977 *Vetri di Murano del '900.* Exhibition, Museo Vetrario, August–October. Catalogue by Rosa Barovier Mentasti. Venice.
1978 *Vetri di Murano del '800.* Exhibition, Museo Vetrario. Catalogue by Rosa Barovier Mentasti. Venice.
1981 *Vetri di Murano del '700.* Exhibition, Museo Vetrario, July–October. Catalogue by Attilia Dorigato. Venice.
1983 *Murano: Il vetro a tavola ieri e oggi.* Exhibition, Museo Vetrario, July. Catalogue by Attilia Dorigato. Venice.
1983–84 *Vincenzo Zanetti, e la Murano dell'Ottocento.* Exhibition, Museo Vetrario, December–May. Catalogue by Rosa Barovier Mentasti et al. [1983].

Museo Correr
1909 *Guida illustrata del Museo Correr di Venezia.* Venice.

Museum für Kunsthandwerk
1956 *Erwerbungen, 1949–1956,* edited by Hermann Jedding. Frankfurt am Main.

Neri, Antonio
1612 *L'arte vetraria distinta in libri sette del r. p. Antonio Neri Fiorentino: Ne quali si scoprono, effetti maravigliosi & insegnano segreti bellissimi, del vetro nel fuoco & altre cose curiose....* Florence.
1662 *The Art of Glass; Wherein Are Shown the Wayes to Make and Colour Glass, Pastes, Enamels, Lakes, and Other Curiosities.* Translated from the Italian and annotated by Christopher Merret. London.
1679 *Johannis Kunckelii Ars vitraria experimentalis; oder, Vollkommene Glasmacher-Kunst, lehrende, als in einem aus unbetrüglicher Erfahrung herfliessendem Commentario, über die von dergleichen Arbeit beschriebenen sieben Bücher P. Anthonii Neri, und denen darüber gethanen gelehrten Anmerckungen Christophori Merretti....* Translated from Merret's English version and annotation of *L'arte vetraria* and further annotated by Johann Kunckel von Löwenstern. 2 vols. in 1. Amsterdam and Danzig.
1699 *Art of Glass: Shewing How to Make All Sorts of Glass, Crystal, and Enamel....* London. English translation of Jean Haudicquer de Blancourt, *De l'art de la verrerie.* Paris, 1697. Though published as an entirely original work, this is Haudicquer de Blancourt's translation and annotation of the Latin version of 1668 of Neri-Merret.
1980 *L'arte vetraria.* Edited by Rosa Barovier Mentasti. Facsimile of 1612 ed. Milan.

Nesbitt, Alexander
1871 *Catalogue of the Collection of Glass Formed by Felix Slade, Esq. F.S.A., with Notes on the History of Glass Making.* London.
1878 *A Descriptive Catalogue of the Glass Vessels in the South Kensington Museum.* London.

Netzer, Susanne
1986 *Kunstsammlungen der Veste Coburg: Die Glassammlung.* Grosse Kunstführer, vol. 137. Munich.

New York
1975 *The Secular Spirit: Life and Art at the End of the Middle Ages.* Exhibition, The Metropolitan Museum of Art, 26 March–3 June. Catalogue by Timothy Husband, Jane Hayward, et al.
1979–80 *Seventeenth Century Dutch and Flemish Drawings from the Robert Lehman Collection.* Exhibition, The Metropolitan Museum of Art, 24 October–27 January.
1983–84 *Fifteenth–Eighteenth Century Italian Drawings from the Robert Lehman Collection.* Exhibition, The Metropolitan Museum of Art, 13 December–3 June.
1984 *Renaissance Furniture from the Robert Lehman Collection.* Exhibition, The Metropolitan Museum of Art, 11 July–November.
1985 *Early German Drawings in The Metropolitan Museum of Art (1400–1600).* Exhibition, The Metropolitan Museum of Art, 13 February–21 April.
1991 *Dutch and Flemish Paintings and Drawings, 1525–1925.* Exhibition, The Metropolitan Museum of Art, 9 May–4 August.

Nikolenko, Lada
1966 *Francesco Ubertini, Called Il Bacchiacca.* Locust Valley, N.Y.

Oberhuber, Konrad, ed.
1978 *The Illustrated Bartsch.* Vol. 26, *The Works of Marcantonio Raimondi and of His School.* New York.

Ohm, Annaliese
1973 *Europäisches und aussereuropäisches Glas.* Frankfurt am Main: Museum für Kunsthandwerk.
1975 *Europäisches und Aussereuropäisches Glas, C. und M. Pfoh-Stiftung.* Frankfurt am Main.

Oliver, Andrew, Jr.
1980 *Ancient Glass in the Carnegie Museum of Natural History, Pittsburgh.* Compiled by S. M. Bergman. Pittsburgh.

Omodeo, Anna
[1970] *Bottiglie e bicchieri nel costume italiano.* [Milan.]

Oppenheimer sale
1936 *Catalogue of the Highly Important Collection of Italian Majolica and Bronzes, Jewels, Enamels, Ivories, Sculpture, and Works of Art Formed by the Late Henry Oppenheimer....* Sale catalogue, Christie, Manson and Woods, London, 15–17 July.

Osborne, Harold, ed.
1985 *The Oxford Companion to the Decorative Arts.* Reprint ed., with corrections. Oxford.

Oswald, Adrian, and Howard Phillips
1949 "A Restoration Glass Hoard from Gracechurch St., London." *Connoisseur* 124 (September), pp. 30–36.

von Parpart (Albert) sale
1884 *Kunst-Sammlung des verstorbenen Herrn Albert von Parpart auf Schloss Hünegg am Thuner See.* Sale catalogue, J. M. Heberle, Cologne, 20–25 October.

von Parpart (F.) sale
1912   *Kunstsammlungen F. von Parpart.* Sale catalogue, Rudolph Lepke's Kunst-Auctions-Haus, Berlin, 18–22 March.

Pazaurek, Gustav E.
1923   *Gläser der Empire- und Biedermeierzeit.* Leipzig.

Pazaurek, Gustav E., and Eugen von Philippovich
1976   *Gläser der Empire- und Biedermeierzeit.* 2d ed. Braunschweig.

Pellatt, Apsley
1849   *Curiosities of Glass Making; with Details of the Processes and Productions of Ancient and Modern Ornamental Glass Manufacture.* London.

Pelliot, Marianne
1930   "Verres gravés au diamant." *Gazette des Beaux-Arts,* ser. 6, 3 (May), pp. 302–27. English summary.

Périn, Patrick
1972   "Deux verreries exceptionnelles provenant de la nécropole mérovingienne de Mézières: La corne à boire de la tombe no. 74 et la coupe à décor chrétien de la tombe no. 89." *Journal of Glass Studies* 14, pp. 67–76.

Perrot, Paul N.
1956   "Verre de Nevers." *Antiques* 70, no. 6 (December), pp. 562–65.
1968   "The Magic of Glass." *Apollo* 88 (December), pp. 430–39.

Perth, C., and R. Coleman-Smith
1975   *Excavations in Medieval Southampton.* Vol. 2, *The Finds.* Leicester.

Pettenati, Silvana
1978   *I vetri dorati graffiti e i vetri dipinti.* Turin: Museo Civico.

Philippe, Joseph
1973   "Au Musée du Verre de Liège: La Collection Armand Baar." *Plaisir de France* 40, no. 411 (July–August), pp. 26–33.

Pholien, Florent
1899   *La verrerie et ses artistes au pays de Liège.* Liège.

Planchon, Mathieu
1913   *Notes sur le verre filé.* Bourges.

Polak, Ada
1975   *Glass: Its Makers and Its Public.* London.

Pope-Hennessy, John
1970   *Raphael.* Wrightsman Lectures, vol. 4. New York.

Prager, Wolfgang
1983   "Mildner fecit à Gutenbrunn." *Weltkunst* 53, no. 21 (1 November), pp. 2933–37.

Prague
1966–67   *Renesanční umělecké řemeslo ze sbírek Uměleckoprůmyslového Muzea v Praze.* Exhibition, Letohrádek Belvedere, October–March. Catalogue by Libuše Urešová, 1966.

1973   *Benátské sklo/ Vetro veneziano/ Venetian Glass.* Exhibition, Uměleckoprůmyslové Muzeum. Catalogue in Czech and English by Karel Hetteš.

Pratt sale
1937   *Paintings by Lawrence and Gainsborough.... Ancient Glass, Egyptian and Other Antiquities, Bronze Sculptures and Medals, Etchings and Drawings, Property of the Estate of the Late George D. Pratt... Together with Property Belonging to Mrs. George D. Pratt.* Sale catalogue, Anderson Galleries, New York, 15 January.

Rackham, Bernard
1929   "An Early Diamond-Engraved Glass at South Kensington." *Burlington Magazine* 54 (February), pp. 68–73.
1977   *Victoria and Albert Museum: Catalogue of Italian Maiolica.* 2 vols. 2d ed. London. First published 1940.

Rademacher, Franz
1933   *Die deutschen Gläser des Mittelalters.* Berlin.
1963   *Die deutschen Gläser des Mittelalters.* 2d ed. Berlin.

Rasmussen, Jörg
1989   *Italian Majolica.* Vol. 10 of *The Robert Lehman Collection.* New York: The Metropolitan Museum of Art.

Read, Charles Hercules
1899   *The Waddesdon Bequest: The Collection of Jewels, Plate, and Other Works of Art, Bequeathed to the British Museum by Baron Ferdinand Rothschild....* London.
1927   *The Waddesdon Bequest: Jewels, Plate and Other Works of Art, Bequeathed by Baron Ferdinand Rothschild.* Revised by A. B. Tonnochy. 2d ed. London.

Read, Herbert
1926   "The Eumorfopoulos Collection: Western Objects, I." *Apollo* 3, no. 16 (April), pp. 187–92.

Reggio Calabria
1967   *Forme e colori del vetro in Italia attraverso il tempo.* Exhibition, Museo Nazionale di Reggio Calabria, June–August. Catalogue by Titti Carta.

Reinach, Salomon, et al.
1927   *La colección Lázaro de Madrid.* Vol. 2. Madrid.

Revi, Albert Christian
1967   *Nineteenth Century Glass: Its Genesis and Development.* Rev. ed. New York.

Ricke, Helmut
1978   "Lampengeblasenes Glas des Historismus, die Hamburger Werkstatt C. H. F. Müller." *Journal of Glass Studies* 20, pp. 45–99. English summary, pp. 68–69.
1980   *Kunstmuseum Düsseldorf: Ausgewählte Werke.* Vol. 5, *Glas.* Düsseldorf.

Rochester (N.Y.)
1981–82   *Eighteenth Century Venetian Drawings from the Robert Lehman Collection, The Metropolitan*

Museum of Art. Exhibition, Memorial Art Gallery, Rochester, 3 September–25 October; Herbert F. Johnson Museum of Art, Ithaca, 21 April–30 May; Vassar College Art Gallery, Poughkeepsie, 29 August–3 October; Skidmore College Art Gallery, Saratoga Springs, 18 November–12 December. Catalogue by George Szabo, 1982.

Rodriguez Garcia, Justina
1987   "La influencia del vidrio de Venecia en Cataluña." *Annales du 10e Congrès de l'Association Internationale pour l'Histoire du Verre, Madrid–Segovie, 23–28 septembre 1985*, pp. 421–32. Amsterdam.

Roffia, Elisabetta, and Giovanni Mariacher
1983   "Vetri." In *Museo Poldi Pezzoli*, vol. 3, *Ceramiche – vetri, mobili e arredi*, pp. 166–307. Milan.

Rossi, Filippo
1967   *Il Museo Horne a Firenze*. Milan.

Roth, Paul
1971   "Studien zum innerösterreichischen Glashüttenwesen im 16. Jahrhundert." *Blätter für Heimatkunde* 4, no. 4.

Rückert, Rainer
1982   *Die Glassammlung des Bayerischen Nationalmuseums München*. 2 vols. Kataloge des Bayerischen Nationalmuseums München, vol. 17. Munich.

Ruesch sale
1936   *Sammlung A. Ruesch, Zürich: Griechische, etruskische und römische Altertümer*. Sale catalogue, Galerie Fischer, Lucerne, 1–2 September.

Ryley, Beresford
1902   "Old Venetian Glass." *Connoisseur* 4 (December), pp. 267–71.

Ryser, Frieder
1991   *Verzauberte Bilder: Die Kunst der Malerei hinter Glas von der Antike bis zum 18. Jahrhundert*. Munich.

von Saldern, Axel
1965   *German Enameled Glass: The Edwin J. Beinecke Collection and Related Pieces*. Corning Museum of Glass Monographs, vol. 2. Corning.
1968   *Ancient Glass in the Museum of Fine Arts Boston*. Boston.
1972   "Spiral-Schlangenpokale à la Façon de Venise." *Jahrbuch der Hamburger Kunstsammlungen* 17, pp. 67–80.
1974   *Glassammlung Hentrich, Antike und Islam*. Kataloge, vol. 1, part 3. Düsseldorf: Kunstmuseum Düsseldorf.
1980   *Ancient and Byzantine Glass from Sardis*. Corning Museum of Glass Monograph 6. Cambridge, Mass.

Salviati
[1880s]   *Salviati e C.: Verreries artistiques, miroirs, lustres, service de table, bronzes, meubles, mosaïques monumentales*. Illustrated trade catalogue. Venice.

Sanctuary, C. T.
1957   "Some Early Glasses." *Apollo* 66 (August), pp. 14–17.

San Francisco
1969   *Glass Drinking Vessels from the Franz Sichel Collection*. Exhibition, California Palace of the Legion of Honor, 2 May–14 September. Essay by Jerome Strauss.

São Paulo
1957   *4000 anos de vidro*. Exhibition, Museu de Arte Moderna, September–December. Catalogue by [Ernesto Wolf].

Sarpellon, Giovanni
1990   *Miniature di vetro murrine, 1838–1924*. Venice.

Sarpellon, Giovanni, et al.
1989   *Salviati, il suo vetro e i suoi uomini, 1859–1987*. Venice.

Savage, George
1965   *Glass*. New York.
[1975]   *Glass of the World*. New York.

Scatozza Höricht, Lucia Amalia
1986   *I vetri romani di Ercolano*. Rome.

Schack, Clementine
1976   *Die Glaskunst*. Munich.

Schäfke, Werner
1979   *Ehrenfelder Glas des Historismus*. Cologne.

Scheil, Elfriede
1977   "Fayencen in der Malerei des Mittelalters." Doctoral dissertation, Ludwig-Maximilians-Universität, Munich.

Schiedlausky, Günther
1956   *Essen und Trinken: Tafelsitten bis zum Ausgang des Mittelalters*. Munich.

Schlosser, Ignaz
1929–30   "Die Gläsersammlung des oesterreichischen Museums für Kunst und Industrie, Wien." *Glastechnische Berichte* 7, pp. 323–27.
1937   "Some Diamond-Engraved Glasses from the Ruhmann Collection." *Burlington Magazine* 70 (May), pp. 246–51.
1951   *Venezianer Gläser*. Vienna: Österreichisches Museum für Angewandte Kunst.
1965   *Das alte Glas*. 2d ed. Brunswick.

von Schlosser, Julius
1908   *Die Kunst- und Wunderkammern der Spätrenaissance: Ein Beitrag zur Geschichte des Sammelwesens*. Leipzig.

Schmidt, Robert
1911   "Die venezianischen Emailgläser des XV. und XVI. Jahrhunderts." *Jahrbuch der Königlich Preuszischen Kunstsammlungen* 32, pp. 249–86.
1912   *Das Glas*. Berlin: Kunstgewerbemuseum.
1914   *Brandenburgische Gläser*. Berlin.
1914–26   *Die Gläser der Sammlung Mühsam: Beschreibender Katalog mit kunstgeschichtlichen Einführungen*. 2 vols. Berlin.
1922   *Das Glas*. 2d ed. Berlin: Kunstgewerbemuseum.
1927   *Europäisches Glas: Die Sammlung Wilfred Buckley*. Berlin.

1931   "Die Glassammlung Neuburg." Typescript. Ann Arbor: University Microfilms.

Schrijver, Elka
1964   *Glass and Crystal.* Vol. 1, *From Earliest Times to 1850.* New York. English translation of *Glas en Kristal*, Bussum, 1961.
1980   *Glas en Kristal.* Haarlem.

Schwarz sale
1916   *Katalog der Sammlung Philipp Schwarz, Stuttgart: Alte Gläser in künstlerischer Veredlung.* Sale catalogue, Galerie Helbing, Munich, 25 October.

Seilern sale
1982   *English and Continental Glass the Property of the Estate of the Late Count Antoine Seilern and from Various Sources.* Sale catalogue, Christie, Manson and Woods, London, 26 May.

Seillière sale
1890   *Catalogue des objets d'art de haute curiosité et de riche ameublement provenant de l'importante collection de feu M. le Baron Achille Seillière au Château de Mello.* Sale catalogue, Chevallier et Mannheim, Galerie Georges Petit, Paris, 5–10 May.

Shelkovnikov, Bebut A.
1962   *Khudozhestvennoe steklo/Artistic Glass* (in Russian, with English translation of captions). Leningrad.

Singer, Charles, et al.
1958   *A History of Technology.* Vol. 4, *The Industrial Revolution, c1750 to c1850.* Oxford.

Singleton, Esther
1925   "Spanish Glass: Rare and Decorative Products of Old Provinces." *Antiquarian* 4 (February), pp. 5–8.

Smith sale
1968   *Catalogue of an Important Collection of Glass; the Property of the Late Walter F. Smith, Jnr. of Trenton, New Jersey. Fourth Portion: Continental Glass....* Sale catalogue, Sotheby and Co., London, 8 July.

Snouck Hurgronje sale
1931   *Collection Snouck Hurgronje de la Haye: Verrerie du XVe au XVIIIe siècles.* Sale catalogue, Mensing en Fils (Frederik Müller en Cie), Amsterdam, 8 July.

Somzée sale
1904   *Catalogue des monuments d'art antique ... composant les collections de Somzée.* Part 3, *Objets d'art anciens....* Sale catalogue, J. Fievez, Brussels [24 May–11 June].

Spaer, Maud
1988   "The Pre-Islamic Glass Bracelets of Palestine." *Journal of Glass Studies* 30, pp. 51–61.

Spiegl, Walter
1980   *Glas des Historismus: Kunst- und Gebrauchsgläser des 19. Jahrhunderts.* Brunswick.

Spitzer sale
1893   *Catalogue des objets d'art et de haute curiosité, antiques, du Moyen-Âge & de la Renaissance, composant l'importante et précieuse collection Spitzer.*

Vols. 2, 3. Sale catalogue, Chevallier et Mannheim, Paris, 17 April–16 June.
1929   *Medieval and Renaissance Art, Paintings, Sculpture, Armour, and a Few Pieces of 18th Century Furniture from the Frédéric Spitzer Collection, Sold By Order of His Heirs, Mme. la Baronne Coche de la Ferte & Mme. Augustin Rey de Villette, Paris.* Sale catalogue, Anderson Galleries, New York, 9–12 January.

Spitzner sale
1918   *Gläser ehemals im Besitz des Dr. Spitzner, Dresden.* Sale catalogue, Galerie Helbing, Munich, 16 May.

Stern, E. M.
1977   *Ancient Glass at the Fondation Custodia (Collection Frits Lugt), Paris.* Groningen.

Strasser, Rudolf von, and Walter Spiegl
1989   *Dekoriertes Glas; Renaissance bis Biedermeier, Meister und Werkstätten: Katalog raisonné der Sammlung Rudolf von Strasser.* Munich.

Strauss sale
1920   *Kunstschätze der Sammlung Dr. Max Strauss in Wien.* Sale catalogue, Glückselig und Wärndorfer, Vienna.
1925   *Nachlass Dr. Max Strauss, Wien: Venezianisches Glas, Keramik, Bronzen, Silber, etc.* Sale catalogue, Glückselig G.M.B.H., Vienna, 2–4 November.

Strohmer, Erich V.
1947   *Prunkgefässe aus Bergkristall.* Vienna.

Swarzenski, Georg
1940   "The Localization of Medieval Verre Eglomisé in the Walters Collection." *Journal of the Walters Art Gallery* 3, pp. 55–68.

Szabo, George
1975   *The Robert Lehman Collection: A Guide.* New York.
1983   *Masterpieces of Italian Drawing in the Robert Lehman Collection, The Metropolitan Museum of Art.* New York.

Taddei, Guido
1954   *L'arte del vetro in Firenze, e nel suo dominio.* Florence.

Tait, Hugh
1967   "Glass with Chequered Spiral-Trail Decoration: A Group Made in the Southern Netherlands in the Sixteenth and Seventeenth Centuries." *Journal of Glass Studies* 9, pp. 94–112.
1979   *The Golden Age of Venetian Glass.* London.
1981   *The Waddesdon Bequest: The Legacy of Baron Ferdinand Rothschild to the British Museum.* London.
1991   Ed. *Glass: 5,000 Years.* New York.

Taylor sale
1912   *Catalogue of the Renowned Collection of Works of Art Chiefly of the Mediaeval and Renaissance Times ... Formed by the Late John Edward Taylor.* Sale catalogue, Christie, Manson and Woods, London, 1–4, 9, 10 July.

Thewalt sale
1903   *Katalog der reichhaltigen, nachgelassenen Kunst-Sammlung des Herrn Karl Thewalt in Köln.* Sale catalogue, Lempertz' Buchhandlung und Antiquariat, Cologne, 4–14 November.

Thorpe, W. A.
1930   "A Newly Discovered Verzelini Glass." *Burlington Magazine* 56 (May), pp. 256–57.

Thurston, Herbert, and Donald Attwater
1956   *Butler's Lives of the Saints.* 4 vols. New York.

Tillman, Allan, (Antiques) Ltd.
1973   *Summer Catalog.* London.

Tokyo
1977   *Renaissance Decorative Arts from the Robert Lehman Collection of The Metropolitan Museum of Art, New York.* Exhibition, National Museum of Western Art, 3 November–15 December. Catalogue by George Szabo.

Toledo Museum of Art
1969   *Art in Glass: A Guide to the Glass Collections.* Toledo, Ohio.

Turin
1982–83   *Dagli ori antichi agli anni Venti: Le collezioni di Riccardo Gualino.* Exhibition, Palazzo Madama, Galleria Sabauda, December–March. Catalogue edited by Giovanna Castagnoli. Milan, 1982.

Vanderhoeven, Michel
1962   *De Romeinse glasverzameling in het Provinciaal Gallo-Romeins Museum: Het Romeins glas uit Tongeren van de Koninklijke Musea voor Kunst en Geschiedenis.* Tongeren.

Vávra, Jaroslav R.
1954   *Five Thousand Years of Glass-Making: The History of Glass.* Translated by I. R. Gottheiner. Prague. Also published in German as *Das Glas und die Jahrtausende,* 1954.

Vecht sale
1938   *Catalogue of a Fine Collection of Rare Gothic, Early Renaissance and Later European Glass, the Property of an Amateur, a Well-known Collector....* Sale catalogue, Sotheby and Co., London, 10 November.

Venice
1982   *Mille anni di arte del vetro a Venezia.* Exhibition, Palazzo Ducale, Museo Correr, 24 July–24 October. Catalogue by Rosa Barovier Mentasti et al.

Viale, Vittorio
1948   "I principali incrementi del Museo Civico d'Arte Antica." *Bollettino della Società Piemontese di Archeologia e di Belle Arti,* n.s. 2, pp. 113–78.

Victoria and Albert Museum
1963   *Fifty Masterpieces of Pottery, Porcelain, Glass Vessels, Stained Glass, Painted Enamels.* 2d ed. London.

Volk, Peter
1988   "Hinterglasmalerei der Renaissance, Kabinettstücke aus dem Bayerischen Nationalmuseum." *Kunst und Antiquitäten,* no. 2, pp. 52–63.

Wadsworth Atheneum
1958   *Handbook: Wadsworth Atheneum.* Hartford.

Walcher-Molthein, Alfred
1926   "Die deutschen Renaissancegläser auf der Burg Kreuzenstein." Parts 1, 2. *Belvedere* 9, pp. 37–47; 10, pp. 57–69.

Wallace Collection
1920   *Illustrated Catalogue of the Furniture, Marbles, Bronzes, Clocks, Candelabra, Majolica, Porcelain, Glass, ... and Objects of Art Generally, in the Wallace Collection.* 6th ed. (with additions and corrections). London.

Walters Art Gallery
n.d.   *The Walters Collection.* Baltimore.

Waring, John B., ed.
n.d.   *Examples of Ornamental Art in Glass and Enamel; Selected from the Collections of His Grace the Duke of Buccleuch....* London.

Washington, D.C.
1979–81   *Old Master Paintings from the Collection of Baron Thyssen-Bornemisza.* Exhibition, organized and circulated by International Exhibitions Foundation. Catalogue by Allen Rosenbaum, 1979.

Weihrich, Franz
1893   *Stammtafeln zur Geschichte des Hauses Österreich.* Habsburg.

Weiss, Gustav
1971   *The Book of Glass.* Translated by Janet Seligman. New York. First published in German, 1966.

Welander-Berggren, Elsebeth
1990   "Mer elegans än vardagsnytta." *Antik & Auktion,* no. 2 (February), pp. 49–53.

Winchester, Alice
1958   "Antiques" (Editorial). *Antiques* 73, no. 6 (June), frontis., p. 545.

Wolkenberg sale
1991   *The Alfred Wolkenberg Collection of Ancient Glass and Related Antiquities.* Sale catalogue, Christie, Manson and Woods, London, 9 July.

Zanetti, Vincenzo
1868   *L'arte vetraria alla esposizione industriale del Palazzo dei Dogi nell'anno 1868.* Venice.

Zecchin, Luigi
1951   *L'archivio annesso al Museo Vetrario di Murano.* Venice.
1957   *Appunti di storia vetraria muranese.* Venice.
1968   "Maria Barovier e le 'Rosette.'" *Journal of Glass Studies* 10, pp. 105–9. English summary.
1987–89   *Vetro e vetrai di Murano: Studi sulla storia del vetro.* 2 vols. Venice.

Zedinek, Hans
1927   "Die Glashütte zu Hall in Tirol." *Altes Kunsthandwerk* 1, no. 3, pp. 98–117.

Index